Religious Beliefs and Conscientious Exemptions in a Liberal State

Edited by
John Adenitire

·HART·
OXFORD · LONDON · NEW YORK · NEW DELHI · SYDNEY

HART PUBLISHING

Bloomsbury Publishing Plc

Kemp House, Chawley Park, Cumnor Hill, Oxford, OX2 9PH, UK

HART PUBLISHING, the Hart/Stag logo, BLOOMSBURY and the Diana logo are
trademarks of Bloomsbury Publishing Plc

First published in Great Britain 2019

A catalogue record for this book is available from the British Library.

Library of Congress Cataloging-in-Publication data

Names: Adenitire, John, editor.

Title: Religious beliefs and conscientious exemptions in a liberal state / edited by John Adenitire.

Description: Cambridge, United Kingdom ; New York, NY, USA : Hart Publishing, 2019. | "This volume is the
product of a conference held in June 2016 at the University of Cambridge. It was generously supported by the
Centre for Public Law (Faculty of Law, Cambridge) and by Fitzwilliam College, Cambridge."—
ECIP acknowledgements. | Includes bibliographical references and index.

Identifiers: LCCN 2018061353 (print) | LCCN 2019000536 (ebook) |
ISBN 9781509920945 (EPub) | ISBN 9781509920938 (hardback)

Subjects: LCSH: Liberty of conscience—English-speaking countries—Congresses. | Religious discrimination—
Law and legislation—English-speaking countries—Congresses. | BISAC: LAW / Discrimination.

Classification: LCC K3258.A6 (ebook) | LCC K3258.A6 R453 2019 (print) | DDC 342.08/52—dc23

LC record available at https://lccn.loc.gov/2018061353

ISBN: HB: 978-1-50992-093-8
        ePDF: 978-1-50992-095-2
        ePub: 978-1-50992-094-5

Typeset by Compuscript Ltd, Shannon
Printed and bound in Great Britain by CPI Group (UK) Ltd, Croydon CR0 4YY

To find out more about our authors and books visit www.hartpublishing.co.uk.
Here you will find extracts, author information, details of forthcoming events
and the option to sign up for our newsletters.

ACKNOWLEDGEMENTS

This volume is the product of a conference held in June 2016 at the University of Cambridge. It was generously supported by the Centre for Public Law (Faculty of Law, Cambridge) and by Fitzwilliam College, Cambridge. Sincere thanks are due to both institutions. Thanks are also due to those that presented and to the other participants of the conference. The editorial process of the volume began while in receipt of an AHRC-DTP Scholarship and was completed in the first few months of a lectureship at the Law School of the University of Birmingham. Thanks to both the AHRC and to Birmingham Law School for supporting the project. Infinite thanks to Raffael Fasel, Yalan Zhang, Joshua Neoh, Zoe Adams, Visa Kurki and Morgan Jones for their help and encouragement in pursuing this project. David Feldman, my doctoral supervisor, was a constant source of advice and endless support. Mark Elliott provided invaluable guidance during the conception stage of the book project. This volume is dedicated to Kasia Zielinska, who sacrificed so much for this.

John Adenitire

TABLE OF CONTENTS

PART C
COMPARATIVE QUESTIONS IN THE LAW
OF CONSCIENTIOUS EXEMPTIONS

PART D
CONCLUSION

NOTES ON THE CONTRIBUTORS

John Adenitire

John Adenitire is a PhD candidate in law at the University of Cambridge and a lecturer in Law at the University of Birmingham. His current research focuses on the right to exemption for religious and non-religious conscientious objectors from a wide variety of legal obligations (including anti-discrimination norms). More generally, his research and teaching interests lie in the fields of public law, legal theory, comparative public law, and law and religion. He has published in various journals including in *Public Law*, *Oxford Journal of Law and Religion*, *Modern Law Review* and *Jurisprudence*.

Paul Billingham

Paul Billingham is Associate Professor of Political Theory at the Department of Politics and International Relations, University of Oxford, and a Fellow of Magdalen College. His research focuses on debates within political liberalism and concerning the place of religion in public life. His work has been published in various journals in moral, political and legal philosophy, including *Politics, Philosophy & Economics*, *Journal of Moral Philosophy*, *Law and Philosophy* and the *Oxford Journal of Law and Religion*.

Gerald Chipeur QC

Gerald Chipeur QC is a Partner with Miller Thomson LLP in Canada. As a trial and appellate lawyer, Gerry has pleaded cases before administrative tribunals and every level of court in Canada, including over 20 matters before the Supreme Court of Canada. The legal issues Gerry has dealt with are diverse and include: charities, the Constitution, defamation, education, elections, the environment, ethics, First Nations, governance, health, human rights, media, municipalities, natural resources, professional duties and responsibility, privacy and public safety. His scholarship includes over 100 legal articles on these topics and others. He is frequently invited to appear as an expert witness before Senate and House of Commons committees studying legislative proposals.

Robert Clarke

Robert Clarke is a barrister, called to the bar of England and Wales, and serves as Director of European advocacy for ADF International at its international headquarters in Vienna, Austria. He specialises in religious freedom issues and cases before the European Court of Human Rights as well as leading advocacy efforts across Europe. During his time at ADF International, Clarke has been involved in more than 15 cases before the European Court of Human Rights including *Grimmark and Steen v Sweden*, which is challenging Sweden's refusal to recognise conscientious objection for medical professionals. Clarke is also the editor of a book, *The Conscience of Europe: Navigating Shifting Tides at the European Court of Human Rights* (Kairos, 2017).

John Corvino

John Corvino is Professor of Philosophy and the incoming Dean of the Irvin D Reid Honors College at Wayne State University in Detroit, Michigan, USA. He is the author of numerous articles, as well as three books from Oxford University Press: *Debating Same-Sex Marriage* (with Maggie Gallagher, 2012), *What's Wrong with Homosexuality?* (2013) and *Debating Religious Liberty and Discrimination* (with Ryan T Anderson and Sherif Girgis, 2017). He has lectured at over 250 campuses on sexuality, marriage and ethics. Read more at www.johncorvino.com.

Stella Coyle

Stella Coyle is a teaching fellow at the School of Law, Keele University. Stella holds degrees from University College London (LLB) and Keele University (LLM and PhD). Her PhD analysed the role of rights discourse in conflicts between religion and sexual orientation in equality law. Stella's areas of research are gender, sexuality and law, equality and human rights, law and religion, and criminal law.

Frank Cranmer

Frank Cranmer is Secretary of the Churches' Legislation Advisory Service. He is a Fellow of St Chad's College, Durham, and an honorary Research Fellow at the Centre for Law & Religion, Cardiff, where he teaches on the LLM in canon law. With Russell Sandberg and Celia Kenny he co-edited *The Confluence of Law and Religion* (2016), a *Festschrift* in honour of Norman Doe, and has recently published *Religion and Belief in United Kingdom Employment Law: An Introduction to the Case-Law* (2017).

Peter Jones

Peter Jones is Emeritus Professor of Political Philosophy at Newcastle University. Much of his work has focused on issues associated with the differences of belief, culture and value, including issues of toleration, recognition, freedom of expression, religious accommodation and discrimination law. He has also written on democracy, international justice and the nature of liberalism, and on different aspects of rights, including human rights, group rights and welfare rights. He is the author of *Essays on Toleration* (2018).

Ian Leigh

Ian Leigh is Professor of Law at Durham University. He has written extensively on many aspects of human rights and public law: domestic human rights protection, national security and intelligence accountability, local government law and politics, and religious freedom in particular. He is co-author of *Religious Freedom in the Liberal State*, 2nd edn (2013) (with Rex Ahdar). He is currently working on a three-year funded study 'Freedom of Conscience: Emerging Challenges and Future Prospects' as a British Academy Wolfson Research Professor.

Richard Moon

Richard Moon is Distinguished University Professor and Professor of Law at the University of Windsor, Canada. He is the author of *Putting Faith in Hate: When Religion is the Source or Target of Hate Speech* (2018), *Freedom of Conscience and Religion* (2014) and

The Constitutional Protection of Freedom of Expression (2000), editor of *Law and Religious Pluralism in Canada* (2008), co-editor of *Religion and the Exercise of Public Authority* (2016) and contributing editor to *Canadian Constitutional Law* (2006, 2010, 2016).

Mary Neal

Mary Neal is a senior lecturer in Law at the University of Strathclyde. She publishes and teaches in the fields of Healthcare Law and Bioethics. In 2014–15, she was Adviser to the Scottish Parliamentary Committee scrutinising the Assisted Suicide (Scotland) Bill, and she has provided evidence and advice to legislative bodies throughout the UK on the subjects of abortion and conscientious objection. She is a present member of the British Medical Association's Medical Ethics Committee. She is currently leading two funded projects: a British Academy/Leverhulme-funded project exploring conflicts between personal values and professional expectations in pharmacy practice, and a multi-disciplinary network of academics and healthcare professionals (the Accommodating Conscience Research Network), funded by the Royal Society of Edinburgh.

Yossi Nehushtan

Yossi Nehushtan is senior lecturer at the School of Law, Keele University, where he is also Postgraduate Research Director for Law, and the Co-Director of the MA in Human Rights, Globalisation and Justice. Yossi holds degrees from Striks Law School (LLB), the Hebrew University (LLM) and Oxford University (BCL, MPhil, DPhil). Yossi's areas of research are legal theory, political theory, public law, human rights law, and law and religion.

Lucy Vickers

Lucy Vickers is Professor of Law at Oxford Brookes University. Her main research area is the protection of human rights within the workplace and aspects of equality law. She has written extensively on issues relating to religious discrimination and age discrimination at work, including *Religious Freedom, Religious Discrimination and the Workplace*, 2nd edn (2016) and a report for the European Commission on Religion and Belief Discrimination in Employment – The EU Law (2007). She is the UK expert on non-discrimination for the European Equality Law Network.

1

Introduction

JOHN ADENITIRE

Liberal states, committed to individual freedom and neutrality between different conceptions of the good life, are facing a resurgence of claims for conscientious exemptions. Bakers and hoteliers want to be exempted from sexual orientation anti-discrimination norms because they believe serving same-sex couples would make them complicit in sexual immorality;[1] for-profit employers want to be exempted from the legal duty to provide their employees with contraception coverage to evade assisting what they see as a grave moral wrong;[2] employees want to be excused from the duty to wear uniforms so that they may wear religious garments at work.[3] These cases, and many others like them, test the resilience of the foundational commitments of liberalism in at least three ways.

First, how much should the commitment to individual freedom enable individuals to escape just legal requirements that bind all others? Surely, goes the argument, within the context of a reasonably just state, legal subjects ought to comply with all reasonably just laws which are mandatory for all. Granting conscientious exemptions seems to undermine one of the most obvious purposes of the law, which is to solve for all subjects the moral problems which gave rise to the initial need for legal regulation.[4] It seems self-defeating then that the law should recognise that its own solutions can be evaded by some individuals based on their own religious or moral views that the law has reached a wrong moral solution.

Second, how much can liberal states remain neutral towards different conceptions of the good, whether or not religious, which give rise to claims for conscientious exemptions? Judges, as paradigmatic representative of the state's impartiality, are put to test when confronted with beliefs which appear illiberal. Should it not make a difference to the resolution of a claim if the beliefs which motivate the demand for exemptions appear illiberal in their denial of equal economic and institutional opportunities to often persecuted minorities? For example, is the refusal of a Christian baker to bake a cake for a gay wedding not an illiberal act which should not be accommodated by a liberal state? Can the liberal state truly

---

[1] *Masterpiece Cakeshop, Ltd v Colorado Civil Rights Com'n* (2018) 584 U S ____ 1; Lee v Ashers Baking Company Ltd & Ors (Northern Ireland) [2018] UKSC 49; *Hall and another v Bull and another* [2013] UKSC 73.

[2] *Burwell v Hobby Lobby Stores, Inc* (2014) 134 SCt 2751.

[3] *Eweida v United Kingdom* [2013] IRLR 231; Case C-157/15 *Achbita v G4S Secure Solutions NV* [2017] 3 CMLR 21; Case C-188/15 *Bougnaoui v Micropole SA* [2017] 3 CMLR 22.

[4] J Finnis, *Natural Law and Natural Rights* (Oxford, Oxford University Press, 2011) 276, 277 (who argues that legal rules are those made by an effective authority for the common good of a community); S Shapiro, *Legality* (Cambridge, MA, Harvard University Press, 2013) 213 (who argues that the fundamental aim of legal activity is to remedy the moral deficiencies of the circumstances of legality through social planning).

hold steadfast to its neutrality when adjudicating such disputes? Is a decision either way not necessarily an endorsement of either typically conservative views which favour the baker or of progressive policies which favour the gay couple?

Finally, if the liberal state is to comply with Mill's injunction to exercise its legitimate political power only to prevent harm to others,[5] granting some conscientious exemptions would seem an abdication of that duty. For example, does the state not have a duty to protect schoolchildren whose parents and teachers believe they have a religious duty to administer corporal punishment? May it legitimately grant a conscientious exemption to the teachers and parents from the criminal prohibition of corporal punishment?[6] Furthermore, is Mill's Harm Principle even engaged by bakers and hoteliers turning away prospective gay customers? Should the offence and humiliation occasioned by being denied a commercial service even count as a form of harm for the purposes of the Harm Principle? If it counts as harm, then the state has a duty to prevent it. If it does not, the liberal state has no right to intervene, nor indeed seem to have a valid reason to withhold an exemption from the service-providers from complying with anti-discrimination norms.

It seems, then, that the apparently trivial cases about cakes and overnight stays at bed and breakfasts test the limits of liberalism itself. It is for this reason that this volume has brought together several scholars to confront the demanding questions raised by the practice of conscientious exemptions in a liberal state. These questions, and the answers provided to them by the contributors, are not necessarily grouped together thematically in this volume. Rather, they are grouped on the basis of the method used by the contributors to answer different but related questions. Consequently, legal theory takes the central stage in part A; doctrinal analysis focused on how courts should resolve legal claims for conscientious exemptions in part B; and comparative scholarship in part C. Part D, composed of a single essay, responds to several of the contributions in the volume while proposing a distinctively liberal framework for dealing with claims for conscientious exemptions. The rest of this introduction summarises the contributions of each part of the volume.

Part A: Theoretical Reflections on Conscientious Exemptions

Chapter 2. Is Religion Special? Exemptions, Conscience and the Culture Wars – John Corvino

John Corvino asks what makes religious beliefs special so that individuals can be exempt from complying with legal obligations which conflict with them. He first investigates three possibilities, which he rejects. First, a liberal state, without abandoning its inherent commitment to religious neutrality, cannot endorse the claim that religious beliefs are particularly binding because afterlife issues are at stake. While neutrality of the state is not undermined by accepting the alternative claim that some individuals feel strongly about not

---

[5] JS Mill, *On Liberty, Utilitarianism and Other Essays*, 2nd edn (M Philp and F Rosen eds, Oxford, Oxford University Press, 2015) 13.
[6] These questions were raised in the case of *R (on the application of Williamson) v Secretary of State for Education and Employment* [2005] UKHL 15.

complying with their religious beliefs, such feelings are not special in the sense that they can also be experienced by individuals towards certain non-religious beliefs. Second, he rejects the view that religious beliefs deserve special deference because religion is a distinctive human good. Corvino notes that religious beliefs can be both a force for good and a force for cementing fallible prejudices. Hence, the state cannot take the religiosity of a belief as a reason to grant an exemption without first investigating the consequences of acting on the belief. Finally, Corvino rejects the argument that religion is special because it is part of the category of meaning-giving beliefs and commitments which deserve particular protection. He analyses the arguments of several proponents for this view and finds them lacking, mainly on the ground that meaning-giving commitments do not only include religious or comparable moral beliefs.

Corvino then makes a positive case for granting religious exemptions: they are sometimes appropriate as a corrective for injustice suffered, especially by religious minorities whose needs and interests are often systematically discounted in law-making. He admits, however, that this means that religion is special but not unique as other factors, such as disability and sexual orientation, are the objects of intentional or unintentional unjust treatment in law. He concludes that, in general, religious claims deserve more scrutiny, and thus potentially more deference, than secular ones. However, to the extent that non-believers have their perspectives unjustly discounted, they too may have a valid, but rarer, claim to exemption.

Chapter 3. Conscientious Claims, Ill-Founded Belief and Religious Exemption – Peter Jones

Peter Jones' contribution interrogates an orthodoxy which is well-grounded in judicial practice and liberal political theory. The orthodoxy is that a court should not assess the correctness of a particular religious belief when considering whether the believer ought to be afforded an exemption from a law conflicting with his belief. Jones flirts with the thesis that a religious belief has less of a claim, and arguably no claim, to exemption if it is ill-founded, ie when a believer is mistaken in believing that his religion requires or forbids a certain conduct.

Jones does not find a principled reason for judges not taking into consideration the ill-foundedness of a belief. He rejects the argument grounded on the idea of respect for freedom of conscience mainly because he finds a dichotomy between religious conscience and non-religious conscience. Religious conscience, he argues, is paradigmatically grounded in sources external to the belief-holder such as sacred texts, religious teachings, the doctrines of an organised religion, the shared faith of a religious community, and so on. Unlike non-religious conscience, where the source of moral imperative is the belief-holder himself, a religious believer may be wrong as a matter of fact or interpretation as to what those external sources require. Jones is also quite sceptical about the claim that judges are not competent to enter into theological disputes which will be inevitably raised by the assessment of a religious belief's ill-foundedness. He argues that courts frequently have to deal with cases, such as complex financial or medical cases, to which an expertise is relevant that judges themselves do not have. As happens in those complex cases, judges can be guided by experts in assessing the sources of a particular religious belief and to conclude whether or not the beliefs of the claimant are ill-founded.

While this argument leads Jones to the conclusion that there are no principled arguments against judges assessing the ill-foundedness of a religious belief in the context of conscientious exemptions, he does find a pragmatic reason. He argues that the task could be very demanding in time and effort for judges. It could also be difficult to execute with confidence, given that religious faiths are so internally diverse and that religious belief is not subject to ordinary rules of evidence or even logic. Above all, it would frequently be difficult for a court to come up with decisions that escaped the sort of contention and controversy that it would not want to attract. So even though a particular religious belief would not warrant an exemption due to its ill-foundedness, these pragmatic considerations may militate in favour of granting the exemption even though it is not due in principle.

Chapter 4. Exemptions for Religious Groups and the Problem of Internal Dissent – Paul Billingham

Paul Billingham notices that standard liberal justifications for exemptions for religious groups appeal to the rights or interests of individuals. However, he also notices that standard liberal justifications face a significant problem – that religious groups invariably contain dissenters who object to the group's decisions, policies, or current exercise of an exemption. The standard liberal justifications do not make clear how these internal dissenters' individual interests are served by the group being granted exemptions. Billingham's chapter explores, and seeks to resolve, this problem. It first canvasses three standard liberal responses to the problem of internal dissenters – appealing to the religious groups' own decision-making procedures, to implied consent, and to exit rights. Allowing groups to enjoy exemptions in so far as they have decision-making procedures which can take adequate account of dissenters' interests would not justify exemptions for most religious groups. That is because the best liberal account would require groups to have in place a democratic procedure where internal dissenters' interests are given equal weight to other group members. However, given that it is rare for religious groups to be governed democratically – they are often governed hierarchically – this justification would only apply rarely.

The other two standard justifications are closely intertwined. The view that groups should enjoy exemptions because internal dissenters are held to have at least impliedly consented to the rules and doctrines of the group are also insufficient. This is because of the dissenters' explicit lack of consent to the group benefitting from an exemption, especially when the exemption would entail impunity for discriminatory treatment against the dissenters. While dissenters may be held to have impliedly accepted the rules and doctrines of the group in so far as they have freely chosen not to exit the group, the existence of a right to exit seems not to be a sufficient justification to the extent that being part of an established religious group is commonly an important interest to individuals and exiting a religious group often comes at a high personal price, even for dissenters.

Billingham then argues that liberal political theory nonetheless has the resources to justify exemptions for religious groups in the face of internal dissent, by highlighting the way in which dissenters' own interest in freedom of religion can be protected and promoted through religious group autonomy: respect for religious group autonomy protects the religious freedom even of dissenters, because that respect is what ensures that all individuals can unite around and practise particular religious conceptions. If the law sides with dissenters then the freedom to have a particular group with a particular religious conception will be liable to be overruled whenever there is internal dissent. Billingham uses this insight to strengthen the three standard justifications which he had found deficient.

Part B: How Should Courts Adjudicate Conscientious Exemptions?

Chapter 5. Conscience in the Image of Religion – Richard Moon

Richard Moon, by reference to the Canadian Charter's case law on freedom of conscience, asks whether non-religious beliefs should be given the same protection as religious beliefs in conscientious exemption cases. To answer this question he sets out his case for when exemptions are and are not warranted in the case of religious beliefs under the Charter's protection of freedom of religion. They are warranted, he argues, in order to avoid the marginalisation of religious groups from the wider society, especially when the conflicting laws support dominant cultural practices, some of which (such as holidays) may be religious in origin. They are not warranted when religious beliefs go beyond issues of personal ethics and instead address civic issues or are directly at odds with public policy (such as the permissibility of same-sex marriage). Such beliefs may be correctly viewed as a matter of political judgement and therefore be subject to the usual give and take of political decision-making.

Moon applies this framework to exemptions on the basis of non-religious beliefs and finds that it is not clear that there exists a compelling rationale for granting exemptions to non-religious believers. To the extent that non-religious beliefs touch on civic issues or public policy, they do not deserve special accommodations and should compete in the political process. Furthermore, he is sceptical that groups can be marginalised on the basis of a comprehensive non-religious world-view. Non-religious views on issues of personal ethics (such as vegetarianism and pacifism) may have therefore received accommodation from courts on the fragile rationale that such practices resemble and often directly stem from familiar religious ones.

Chapter 6. The Courts and Conscience Claims – Ian Leigh

By contrast to Moon, Ian Leigh argues that courts should embrace conscience claims both for normative and doctrinal reasons. He argues that the frequently voiced objections to conscience claims – that they involve special treatment of certain groups that somehow violates the rule of law or that claimants are privilege-seekers – rest on misunderstandings. He rejects the rule of law objection on the basis that equal treatment does not require uniformity of treatment, especially once it is accepted that conscience burdens some individuals in a way that it would be unjust not to recognise. Accordingly, in UK and European human rights law, there is a clear duty on courts when the right of freedom of conscience is engaged to make appropriate provision where the legislature has failed to do so.

Leigh also rejects the fear that by embracing conscience claims the courts would open the floodgates to anarchy. This argument, he goes on to say, underestimates the extent to which courts currently supervise the boundaries of conscience claims both by individuals and groups under exceptions and exemptions.

He then addresses the question of how to reconcile conscience with other societal interests and the rights and freedoms of others. He is sceptical that proportional balancing is the correct or best way to resolve all such potential conflicts. Indeed, he argues in favour of an unqualified right to freedom of conscience in some, but not all, situations. He acknowledges that even where conscience rights are qualified there may be more appropriate alternatives, involving more careful examination of whether either freedom of conscience or the ostensibly conflicting right is properly engaged. He finds, for example, that while certain service-providers correctly invoke a well-grounded human right (ie freedom of conscience) when they object to serving same-sex couples, the prospective clients do not do the same as there is no human right to non-discrimination by private service providers on the grounds of sexual orientation. Leigh concludes by conceding that there is likely to remain a smaller group of conscience claims – including those by healthcare professionals – where well-grounded rights conflict and proportional balancing is unavoidable and appropriate.

Chapter 7. The Difference between Illegitimate Conscience and Misguided Conscience: Equality Laws, Abortion Laws and Religious Symbols – Yossi Nehushtan and Stella Coyle

In their provocative contribution to the volume, Yossi Nehushtan and Stella Coyle seek to persuade courts to tackle the issue of conscientious exemptions through a perfectionist-liberal lens. This approach requires courts to evaluate the moral soundness and moral legitimacy of the conscience or the moral values that ground the conscientious objection. Consequently, the chapter offers a distinction between conscientious objections that, on the one hand, rely on unjustly intolerant, morally repugnant and illegitimate values and, on the other hand, objections that rely on misguided yet legitimate values. The authors argue that, all other things being equal, courts have strong reasons not to tolerate the former and weaker reasons not to tolerate the latter.

The chapter focuses first on cases of religious conscientious objection to equality laws, especially in the context of sexual orientation discrimination, as an example of conscientious objection that rely on illegitimate values. The authors forcefully argue that such discrimination should never be allowed in a perfectionist liberal state committed to autonomy and equality. They reject as Orwellian the counter-argument that refusing to exempt religious objectors to equality laws is itself discriminatory treatment on the basis of religion.

The chapter then uses the cases of wearing religious dress in the workplace and conscientious objection to performing human life-terminating treatment (eg abortions, certain contraception and euthanasia) as examples of conscientious objections that rely on misguided yet legitimate values. The authors are more sympathetic towards these types of objections but do not shy away from setting conditions which may translate in courts being less accommodating of these types of objections. They argue that in the case of religious dress and symbols, accommodations should be given from rules that restrict their display, only if anti-theist symbols (eg a shirt with 'There is no God') are equally allowed to be displayed or are equally prohibited. In the case of conscientious objection to performing human life-terminating treatment, they argue that exemptions should be granted from rules mandating the provision of these services only if doing so does not prevent full and easy access to these services which, from a liberal perfectionist point of view, should be viewed as morally permissible.

Chapter 8. Conscientious Objection, 'Proper Medical Treatment' and Professionalism: The Limits of Accommodation for Conscience in Healthcare – Mary Neal

Mary Neal starts her discussion where Nehushtan and Coyle ended theirs. She asks what limits should be set to conscientious exemptions in the medical context. To do this she queries what constitutes 'proper medical treatment' and identifies it as a spectrum within which there is a category where the properness of medical treatment can be regarded as 'liminal'. This category exists at the boundary of the spectrum of proper medical treatment due to the fact that the therapeutic benefit of treatment in this category is absent, uncertain, or contested. She argues that it is in relation to practices in this liminal category that conscientious exemptions ought to be granted. The paradigmatic instance of the liminal category is abortion. This is because, Neal argues, of the non-therapeutic reality of the overwhelming majority of abortions, at least in the UK (those provided on the ground of risk of physical or mental harm to the woman seeking the abortion), and because of the ongoing debate as to whether it constitute medical treatment at all.

It follows from Neal's account that the fact of performing a particular medical treatment would undermine the moral integrity of the medical professional is a necessary but insufficient condition for granting a conscientious exemption in the medical context. An additional requirement is that the particular medical treatment objected to falls within the liminal category. This ensures that conscientious objection to providing medical treatment contributes to the debate on medical professionalism and, in particular, to what treatment should count as proper within the profession.

Chapter 9. The Art of Living with Ourselves: What Does the Law Have to do with Conscience? – Gerald Chipeur QC and Robert Clarke

In their chapter Gerald Chipeur and Robert Clarke argue that freedom of conscience is both an individual and societal good, the enjoyment of which ought to be maximised through juridical means. Consequently, they advance a three-stage test for the juridical examination of conscience-based claims. The first is a threshold test which requires claimants to satisfy courts that their claims are sufficiently linked to a constraining moral framework, whether or not religious, as opposed to being based on mere preferences. The aim of this first stage is that frivolous objections can be quickly weeded out by courts without, however, permitting courts to question the truth or validity of the framework.

The second stage is divided into two parts. The first requires claimants to show that their objection is motivated, from a subjective point of view, by the moral framework. This should be a fairly easy test to satisfy. The second part of the second stage, conversely, imposes a very demanding obligation on the respondent, often the state, to justify refusing to grant an exemption only if doing so is absolutely necessary to pursue a legitimate interest. Under this stringent test, the state could not, for example, point to a generalised interest in combating discrimination in the context of conscientious objections to providing certain commercial services, eg baking a cake for same-sex couples.

The final stage is for the courts to evaluate whether there has been a robust attempt to accommodate the claimant in a way which does not unduly undermine the effects of the generally desirable legal rule being objected to. Consequently, Chipeur and Clarke engage in a thorough defence of the recognition of a duty of reasonable accommodation and argue against its detractors, by engaging closely with the sceptical arguments advanced by Lucy Vickers in chapter ten of the volume.

Part C: Comparative Questions in the Law of Conscientious Exemptions

Chapter 10. Conscientious Objections in Employment: Is a Duty of Reasonable Accommodation the Answer? – Lucy Vickers

Lucy Vickers considers how the law has dealt with requests for conscientious exemptions in the context of employment. She contrasts two models: the provisions of indirect discrimination law, as currently in use in UK law, and the duty of reasonable accommodation, which is currently adopted in US and Canadian law. She first provides a useful overview of how individuals may claim exemptions from employment law duties under the indirect discrimination framework before assessing the strengths and weaknesses of that framework. While the model is flexible and requires fact-sensitive decision-making, Vickers highlights that it may not protect individuals with beliefs which are not shared by others as indirect discrimination has been interpreted to protect against group disadvantage; it may not be apparent to the non-legally trained employee that the model affords them a right to seek exemptions; the fact that the model applies to protect individuals with different characteristics (eg sex or race) may undermine the protection for those other characteristics if the criteria currently used to justify refusing an exemption in the context belief discrimination, eg economic costs, are applied to justify indirect discrimination in other context where they may be inappropriate, eg sex or race indirect discrimination.

The chapter then considers whether the alternative framework of a duty of reasonable accommodation, which is sometimes suggested as a way to manage religious interests in the workplace, would be an effective mechanism for those seeking exemptions from workplace rules. After surveying the way that framework works in US and Canadian case law, Vickers concludes that the introduction of the duty of reasonable accommodation in UK law would not materially change the level of protection available for religion or belief in the workplace. While there might be some pragmatic and symbolic benefits to the use of that framework, those are likely to be counterbalanced by the fact that the indirect discrimination law route is now well-established and UK courts can draw on their long experience of protecting conscientious objectors under that framework.

Chapter 11. Who Should Give Effect to Conscientious Exemptions? The Case for Institutional Synergy – John Adenitire

This chapter tackles the problem of how to allocate to one or the other institution of government the responsibility of granting conscientious exemptions. It starts by advocating for a particular theory embedded in scepticism about the ability of individual institutions to deal properly with matters of rights. This shortcoming can be partially remedied if institutions work synergistically, each with their particular strengths, to compensate each other's weaknesses. This theory is then applied to the context of conscientious exemptions. To do so, the chapter identifies five salient characteristics of conscientious objections which give rise to specific institutional problems. It notes that claims of conscientious exemptions are potentially limitless in scope; granting conscientious exemptions may undermine the right of others or the public interest; they may raise issues which require particular expertise; they may require consideration of the sincerity of the objector; and conscientious exemptions may be required from obligations arising from a variety of legal sources.

The chapter analyses each of these features in light of their relevance for the allocation problem. Analysis of each helps to reach the conclusion that no one institution is able to cater adequately for the various issues raised by conscientious objections. Institutions may provide adequate solutions for some of those problems. Courts in determining the sincerity of claimants; the executive to help avoid some conflicts of rights; the legislature to provide clear, although contestable, statements of who is to be exempt through conscience clauses. Yet, if a holistic solution is to be found to the allocation problem, the best approach is to see institutions engaged in a synergetic effort to respond to the various complex problems raised by conscientious exemptions.

Chapter 12. Can Secular Non-Natural Persons be Said to Have a 'Conscience'? – Frank Cranmer

The contribution of Frank Cranmer confronts the issue as to whether a secular non-natural person such as a commercial company or limited liability partnership – as opposed to its individual directors, shareholders or partners – can be said to have a conscience. He analyses several cases, decided by the ECHR judicial institutions, UK courts and tribunals, and the US Supreme Court. His analysis shows that there has been a chronological shift towards a more benevolent acceptance that at least some commercial companies, to the extent that they are alter-egos of their owners, can possess religious sensibilities that should be accommodated by the law. Frank Cranmer is generally sympathetic towards this legal development; he would however caution extension to beyond small companies and business partnerships.

Part D: Conclusion

Chapter 13. Conscientious Exemptions in a Liberal State – John Adenitire

The concluding chapter, by engaging with the various contributions in the volume, sets forth a particular approach as to how a liberal state should deal with conscientious exemptions. This approach is called the Liberal Model of Conscientious Exemptions and has four propositions. The chapter defends the proposition that a liberal state should grant a general right to conscientious exemption. It sets out the nature of the general right and outlines why it is morally attractive. It then defends the second proposition which says that a liberal state should not pass judgement on the content of beliefs which give rise to a conscientious objection. The chapter takes particular issue with the approaches proposed in the volume by Jones, and by Nehushtan and Coyle, who seem to argue against this second proposition.

The chapter then defends the proposition that a liberal state should neither privilege nor disadvantage religious beliefs over non-religious ones when considering whether a conscientious exemption should be granted. The chapter takes issue with Corvino and with Moon, who seem to argue that religious exemptions should be somewhat privileged. Issue is also taken with Nehushtan whose anti-religious stance is well known in the literature, although slightly tempered in his contribution with Coyle in this volume. The chapter then defends the final proposition which says that exemptions should be granted to sincere objectors if doing so will not disproportionately affect the right of others or the public interest. The chapter concludes by directly confronting the issue of objections to sexual orientation anti-discrimination laws and argues that, in general, such exemptions should not be granted given the dignitary harms they may inflict on members of sexual minorities. Particular issue is taken with Leigh, and with Chipeur and Clarke, who appear to argue in favour of exemptions from sexual orientation anti-discrimination laws.

PART A

Theoretical Reflections on Conscientious Exemptions

2

Is Religion Special? Exemptions, Conscience and the Culture Wars

JOHN CORVINO*

I. Introduction

Some public accommodations laws[1] prohibit sexual orientation discrimination. Some wedding providers – bakers, florists, photographers and so on – have religious objections to same-sex weddings. They have therefore sought religious exemptions to these laws (and often oppose them more generally, as unduly interfering with business-owners' freedoms).

Against the history of religious liberty struggles, these 'gay wedding' controversies may seem frivolous: frosting and flowers versus, say, military conscription. However, not all classic cases involve life-or-death matters: consider controversies concerning religious garb or Sabbath observances. Moreover, if one believes that a decision affects one's hopes for eternal salvation, temporal life pales by comparison. Besides, the accusation of frivolousness cuts both ways. Just as one can tell the baker with religious scruples that 'It's only cake!', one can say the same to the customer, who can usually find a willing provider elsewhere.

The question I want to explore in this essay is that of what difference it should make whether the business owner's objection is specifically *religious*. I approach this question from the standpoint of political morality, not constitutional law, although some of what I say may be relevant to the latter. I proceed as follows: in this opening section, I clarify what it might mean to treat religion as special when contemplating exemptions. In those remaining, I consider four different broad rationales for treating religion as special: (1) that religion deserves special deference because religious obligations are especially binding on religious believers; (2) that it deserves special deference because religion is a distinctive good worth promoting; (3) that it deserves special deference alongside comparably deep secular commitments, because of the state's interest in such commitments; and (4) that it deserves special deference as a common site of discrimination. I conclude by returning briefly to the wedding controversies.

The question of whether religious objections deserve special deference may seem largely hypothetical with respect to those controversies: Fully secular moral objections to same-sex

---

* Some portions of this essay are adapted from J Corvino, R T Anderson, and S Girgis, *Debating Religious Liberty and Discrimination* (New York, OUP, 2017). I am indebted to John Adenitire, Joseph Dunne, Chad Hunter and Timothy Kirschenheiter for helpful comments on recent drafts of this essay.

[1] These are called anti-discrimination or equality legislation in the UK. In Canada they are commonly referred to as human rights laws.

marriage are rare. Yes, there are theorists who offer defences of 'traditional marriage' without appealing to religious premises, but objections 'on the ground' are nearly always religious. Nevertheless, the question matters insofar as the legal mechanisms for exemptions often require specifically religious reasons. Moreover, our response to the wedding controversies may have implications for other controversies where objections are less uniformly religious. Why treat a prisoner who wants to wear a beard for religious reasons any differently from one who is a non-believer, but wears one out of respect for family tradition? For that matter, why treat him differently from one who simply strongly dislikes shaving – not for medical reasons but because he experiences the practice as irksome, vain and unnatural? These questions are not, in the end, about beards, cakes and flowers, but about fairness – including fairness for non-religious citizens.

Note that I am not here exploring a question about what difference religious reasons make *to the religious believer*. Presumably, if one believes in a sovereign God who holds people eternally responsible for their earthly actions, one should weigh beliefs about God's commands quite heavily in deciding what to do. (Not all religious believers embrace this picture of divine justice, of course.) It is, rather, a question about what the rest of us should do in response. This is not to say that the religious believer's perspective is irrelevant: it is generally appropriate to take people's beliefs, feelings and reactions into account when interacting with them. Still, it is important to remember that what the believer should do and what the rest of us should do are separate questions, lest religious scruples function as a kind of get-out-of-the-law-free card, and lest we lose the distinction between respecting integrity and abetting bad reasons.

The question of how the rest of us should treat specifically religious reasons invites three broad categories of responses: (1) we should treat them with *less deference* than secular reasons; (2) we should treat them with *more deference* than secular reasons; and (3) we should treat them with the *same deference* as secular reasons. But this way of dividing things is also problematic. First, there is the crudeness of the notion of 'deference', which comprises many different possible postures and responses, not all of them commensurable. A fuller inquiry would need to specify in what respect deference was being given to, or withheld from, religion. Second, this taxonomy overlooks or obscures the fact that many theorists today wish to adopt a sort of middle ground between (2) and (3), grouping religious reasons with secular reasons of comparable weight, and then treating all of those with more deference (in some sense) than those outside the group.[2] The weighty category is often identified with reasons of conscience or something along those lines, the idea being that there are some things that the agent believes that they simply *must* do or refrain from doing.

This 'middle ground' move itself obscures some important points. As others have observed, not all religious practices involve duties of conscience.[3] Cécile Laborde, for instance, has argued that much of religion includes 'habitual, collective, "embodied practices" of religious devotion' that are not, strictly speaking, duties.[4] Wearing a cross or a Star

---

[2] Jocelyn Maclure identifies his own position explicitly as a 'middle' one and puts himself alongside Christopher Eisgruber, Lawrence Sager, Ronald Dworkin and Martha Nussbaum. See J Maclure, 'Conscience, Religion, and Exemptions: An Egalitarian View' in K Vallier and M Weber (eds), *Religious Exemptions* (New York, OUP, 2018) 10.

[3] I'm indebted to Joseph Dunne for helpful discussions on this point.

[4] C Laborde, 'Protecting Religion in a Secular Age' in WF Sullivan, ES Hurd, S Mahmood, and PG Danchin (eds) *Politics of Religious Freedom* (Chicago, University of Chicago Press, 2015) 274–75.

of David is surely a religious practice, but one that believers typically see as optional; the category of religion includes such practices; whereas the category of conscience does not (or at least, not obviously). Jocelyn Maclure and Charles Taylor have attempted to split the difference by referring to 'meaning-giving beliefs and commitments' – a category that is in some ways broader than religion, but perhaps overly so: it would seem to include a fitness fanatic's commitment to daily workouts or a chess champion's single-minded devotion to the game. (I'll say more about this problem further on.) It is also in some ways narrower than religion, given that a good deal of religious practice is perfunctory and thus not clearly 'meaning-giving'. If we were to map religion, matters of conscience, and 'meaning-giving beliefs and commitments' we would end up with three overlapping circles, with none being a full subset of any other.

Another point obscured by the 'middle ground' strategy is that there is an important difference between versions that perform an addition and those that perform a substitution: that is, whether they give more deference to the new category *plus* religion or the new category *instead of* religion. If the latter, they are not giving more deference to religion per se; they are giving it more deference only insofar as it fulfils some other criterion. For example, Maclure and Taylor's approach seems to give religious beliefs and practices more deference only when they are also 'meaning-giving'; the meaning-givingness is doing the relevant work. As already noted, however, much religious practice is quite perfunctory.

One might object here that the half-heartedly religious are far less likely than the devout to seek exemptions. That's certainly true in the wedding cases, where refusing service has material costs for the business-owner. However, it is not true in cases where exemptions have independent benefits. Consider, for example, exemptions from certain taxes or insurance requirements, as in the *Hobby Lobby* case.[5] Or consider exemptions from wartime conscription, and imagine two college students: the first, whom we'll call Mr Pacifist, has long been devoted to the cause of non-violence. Although only 20, he has participated in anti-war organisations for many years. At his university he is president of Students Against War. He is not religious. The second, Mr Mission, is nominally religious, although not especially devout: he mainly attends church and related activities because that's what his neighbours do. But Mr Mission learns that his church's youth group has a missionary programme that sends members overseas for a year, and it piques his interest: Living in a remote country sounds fun. Suppose the nation goes to war and tries to conscript both students. Should Mr Mission be favoured for an exemption simply because he has a religious reason, ie the year-long mission? In a regime that requires religious reasons for conscientious objection – such as the United States prior to *Seeger* and *Welsh* – Mr Mission would have avenues for exemption that Mr Pacifist would not.[6] By contrast, in a regime that countenances exemptions only for 'meaning-giving beliefs and commitments', Mr Pacifist would be eligible, but probably not Mr Mission. Finally, in a regime protecting religion plus 'meaning-giving beliefs and commitments', both would be eligible. The 'middle ground' is often ambiguous between these options.

For these reasons, it is important to stay focused on the question of whether religion per se deserves special deference, including a path to exemptions. I believe that it does,

---

[5] *Burwell v Hobby Lobby Stores, Inc* 573 US __, 134 S Ct 2751 (2014).
[6] See *United States v Seeger* 380 US 163, 85 S Ct 850 (1964) and *Welsh v United States* 398 US 333, 90 S Ct 1792 (1970).

although I also believe – and will argue here – that the best reason for countenancing distinctively religious exemptions cuts against granting them in the wedding cases. Let us turn now to evaluating some reasons.

II. Religion as Particularly Binding

One possible rationale for privileging religion is that religious believers experience its dictates as especially binding. The idea is that religious conscience derives from an external authority, God, who creates the moral law and then holds people accountable, possibly for eternity. Believers thus experience such dictates as 'non-optional' or 'volitionally necessary' – they simply *must* comply. As Michael McConnell, perhaps the best-known defender of this position, puts it, 'no other freedom is a duty to a higher authority'.[7] His defence of this rationale is worth quoting at length:

> This rationale can most easily be accepted by those who accept the idea of a divine authority whose demands are, as Madison stated, 'precedent both in order of time and degree of obligation, to the claims of Civil Society'. This idea may be sufficient in a nation, such as the United States, where the vast majority of the people believe in the existence of a God. However, belief in the reality of a God is not necessary to the argument. An individual needs only to believe conditionally that if there is a God, this idea can be revealed only through the 'conviction and conscience' of the individual and not through the hand of the state. Most atheists and agnostics share that opinion. Indeed, sincere atheists and agnostics are often passionate in the conviction that the force of the state should not be brought to bear in support of any understanding of religious truth. Moreover, it is logically possible, indeed humane and praiseworthy, for those who do not believe in the existence of God, but who recognize that many of their fellow citizens do, to refrain from using the power of the state to create conflicts with what are perceived (even if incorrectly) as divine commands.[8]

McConnell's elaboration reveals several problems. First, he claims that 'belief in the reality of a God is not necessary to the argument'. If he is wrong about that, the argument begs the question in favour of a particular religious viewpoint: one that represents God as actively involved in the world, issuing and enforcing moral commands. As Andrew Koppelman puts it: 'Because the state must not declare religious truth, it cannot say, as McConnell does, that religion is privileged because it involves a duty to God'.[9] Without postulating such a God, however, McConnell's argument fares poorly. That it is 'logically possible' for atheists and agnostics to avoid creating moral conflicts for their religious fellow citizens tells us nothing; that it is 'humane and praiseworthy' is debatable, depending crucially on what it is that God is allegedly telling those citizens to do.

But the bigger problem is that McConnell's position is both over- and under-inclusive. Not all claims that people experience as morally binding are religious, and not all religious claims are experienced as morally binding. Not all faiths subscribe to belief in a personal God, much less one who enforces justice. Even religions that do posit such a God contain various

---

[7] MW McConnell, 'The Problem of Singling Out Religion' (2000) 50 *Depaul Law Review* 1, 5, 30.
[8] ibid.
[9] A Koppelman, 'Is It Fair to Give Religion Special Treatment' (2006) 3 *University of Illinois Law Review* 571, 592–93.

optional practices, such as whether to wear certain religious garb. Because courts rightly wish to avoid adjudicating 'the place of a particular belief in a religion or the plausibility of a religious claim',[10] they typically defer to believers' self-reporting.[11] But there is no reason to think that believers are more candid or sincere than non-believers in reporting whether they experience a claim as morally mandatory.

One can understand the 'It is particularly binding' answer to the 'Why privilege religion?' question in two distinct ways, and the difference is important. One version states that religious conscience claims are more binding than non-religious conscience claims, because the stakes are higher: They involve eternity. As I have just argued, the state cannot adopt this approach without abandoning religious neutrality. The other version states that religious conscience claims *are felt as* more binding than non-religious conscience claims, because (some) religious believers believe that the stakes are higher. I grant that the state may take citizens' beliefs into account when determining a law's effects. Deep religious beliefs may lead groups to disregard certain laws, and as Simon Căbulea May has argued, the state has some reason (though not necessarily an overriding one) to grant exemptions from laws whose application is futile.[12] (Needless to say, 'some reason' does not necessarily mean an overriding one.) But again, there is little reason to think that the religious/non-religious distinction does a good job of tracking the distinction between claims felt as volitionally necessary and those that are not. Many atheists and agnostics feel a deep commitment to moral principle, and many religious people are half-hearted in their devotion, readily concluding that 'God will understand' if earthly law requires what divine law forbids.

III. Religion as a Distinctive Good Worth Promoting

Koppelman notes that elsewhere McConnell offers a better argument for singling out religion (among other things) for special deference: It is a distinctive human good, one that is not reducible to other goods. Here's McConnell again:

> Religion is a special phenomenon, in part, because it plays such a wide variety of roles in human life: it is an institution, but it is more that; it is an ideology or worldview, but it is more than that; it is a set of personal loyalties and locus of community, akin to family ties, but it is more than that; it is an aspect of identity, but it is more than that; it provides answers to questions of ultimate reality, and offers a connection to the transcendent; but it is more than that. Religion cannot be reduced to a subset of any larger category. In any particular context, religion may appear to be analogous to some other aspect of human activity – to another institution, worldview, personal loyalty, basis of personal identity, or answer to ultimate and transcendent questions. However, there is no other human phenomenon that combines all of these aspects; if there were such a concept, it would probably be viewed as a religion.[13]

Koppelman goes on to emphasise that although the state 'cannot regard religion as a superior source of moral obligation … it can say that religion is one of a plurality of goods'.[14]

---

[10] *Employment Div, Department of Human Resources of Oregon v Smith* 494 US 872, 110 S Ct 1595 (1990).
[11] For a contrasting position, see Peter Jones's contribution to this volume in chapter 3.
[12] SC May, 'Contempt, Futility, and Exclusion' in Vallier and Weber, *Religious Exemptions* (2018) 5.
[13] McConnell, 'Singling Out Religion' (2000) 42.
[14] Koppelman, 'Special Treatment' (2006) 593.

And that claim seems plausible. After all, religion engages the uniquely human capacity for grappling with basic questions about meaning and existence. It binds people together, often for charitable purposes which promote the general welfare. It provides a way to mark major life events, and it offers solace in times of grief and despair.

There is no doubt that religion does all of these things, and does them well. One could scarcely explain its pervasiveness and endurance otherwise. But there is also no doubt that it does great harm. The same fervour that makes some willing to die for their faith makes others willing to kill for it – witness, for example, the 9/11 attacks, Boko Haram suicide bombers, the Salem witch trials, the Crusades, and countless other examples. The flipside of religion's power at binding people together is that it can encourage groupthink; worse, it leads people to imagine that they have infallible backing for their all-too-fallible prejudices. University of Notre Dame philosopher Gary Gutting explains:

> The potential for intolerance lies in the logic of religions like Christianity and Islam that say their teaching derive[s] from a divine revelation. For them, the truth that God has revealed is the most important truth there is; therefore, denying or doubting this truth is extremely dangerous, both for nonbelievers, who lack this essential truth, and for believers, who may well be misled by the denials and doubts of nonbelievers.[15]

Some have taken religion's dependence on revealed truth as an argument for giving it less deference than other beliefs and practices. In his provocative book *Why Tolerate Religion?* Brian Leiter observes that one defining characteristic of religion is that it includes at least some beliefs that are 'insulated from ordinary standards of evidence and rational justification'; he argues that this insulation is one reason to be wary of giving religion special deference.[16] McConnell has criticised Leiter for 'stack[ing] the deck by assuming that religious belief "always" is to some degree "false, or at least unwarranted".[17] Religious believers do not think they are "insulating" themselves from all the relevant "evidence"', McConnell writes. 'They think they are considering evidence of a different, nonmaterial sort, *in addition to* the evidence of science, history, and the senses.'[18]

McConnell's rejoinder misses the force of Leiter's concern. Even if one grants 'evidence of a different, non-material sort', such evidence is often private in a way that renders it useless for the purpose of resolving interpersonal disputes. Accordingly, the law avoids inquiring into the plausibility of religious claims: it acknowledges that they are generally accepted 'on faith'. Consider the case of Frances Quaring, an unusually strict interpreter of the biblical commandment against graven images: She read it to forbid any likeness of *anything* in God's creation. Quaring went to court to argue that she should be exempted from the requirement of having her photo on her driver's licence. As the court observed:

> She possesses no photographs of her wedding or family, does not own a television set, and refuses to allow decorations in her home that depict flowers, animals, or other creations in nature.

---

[15] G Gutting, 'How Religion Can Lead to Violence' *The New York Times* (1 August 2016).

[16] B Leiter, *Why Tolerate Religion?* (Princeton, Princeton University Press, 2013) 34.

[17] MW McConnell, 'Why Protect Religious Freedom?' (2013) 123 *Yale Law Journal* 770–810, 786. For a reply from Leiter, see Brian Leiter, 'Why Tolerate Religion, Again? A Reply to Michael McConnell' *SSRN Scholarly Paper* (Rochester, NY, Social Science Research Network, 8 May 2016) at papers.ssrn.com/sol3/papers.cfm?abstract_id=2777208.

[18] McConnell (n 7) 786.

When she purchases foodstuffs displaying pictures on their labels, she either removes the label or obliterates the picture with a black marking pen.[19]

Quaring acknowledged that her fellow Pentecostal Christians did not generally share her interpretation of the second commandment: she based it on her own personal reading of the Bible. Nevertheless, the US Supreme Court upheld her right to be issued the photo-free licence.

McConnell concedes that 'we might be justified in dismissing the idiosyncratic beliefs of small numbers of persons, especially when these people do not appear rational in other respects'. But he then pivots to a more general point, arguing that 'religious belief has been attested to by millions of seemingly intelligent and rational people over long periods of time, who report that they have experienced, in some way, transcendent reality'.[20]

Unfortunately for McConnell, debates about religious exemptions and accommodations arise not from generalities about 'transcendent reality', but from very specific and often idiosyncratic claims about what God requires. Their idiosyncratic nature is to be expected: As Douglas Laycock observes, religious believers frequently 'draw their morality from ancient books written in a radically different culture that lived with radically different technology and had a radically different understanding of the world'; they see themselves as obeying a 'God whose commands may be beyond human understanding'.[21]

It is precisely by being 'beyond human understanding' that religious beliefs are 'insulated from evidence' in Leiter's sense, and precisely that reason why many are wary of them. One not need go as far as Leiter, arguing that religious belief deserves less deference than secular belief, to have doubts about giving it more deference simply on the grounds that 'religion is one of a plurality of goods'. At the very least, the Koppelman/McConnell approach is unlikely to persuade those not already inclined to give religion special deference.

IV. 'Egalitarian' Views

As noted in the introduction, some theorists call for giving religion special deference while also joining it with similarly strong secular commitments. As I argued above, it is not clear whether such theorists belong in the 'more deference' or the 'same deference' camp, for they seem to treat religion as special only insofar as it also satisfies some other criterion, such as being 'meaning giving' or of reflecting higher-order desires and commitments. If this criterion can be met by fully secular pursuits – as these theorists acknowledge – then it appears that they are not giving religion special deference at all. On the other hand, the 'deference' taxonomy may be more misleading than illuminating. It is therefore worth looking at this approach more directly. In this section I will briefly consider two recent versions, one from Jocelyn Maclure (who has developed the approach alongside Charles Taylor) and one from Ryan T Anderson and Sherif Girgis, who adopt it in our point-counterpoint book *Debating Religious Liberty and Discrimination*.

---

[19] *Jensen v Quaring*, 472 US 478 (1985).
[20] McConnell, 'Religious Freedom?' (2013) 788–89.
[21] D Laycock, 'The Religious Exemption Debate' (2009) 11 *Rutgers Journal of Law and Religion* 139, 171.

Maclure's most recent statement appears in his paper 'Conscience, Religion, and Exemptions: An Egalitarian View'.[22] There he argues that 'there is something special about religion that warrants, under specific circumstances, reasonable accommodation measures', but he also grants that religion should be analogised with a certain category of secular commitments that he and Taylor have called 'meaning-giving beliefs and commitments'. He contends that both kinds of commitments deserve special deference (hence: 'egalitarian'). His argument is worth quoting at some length:

> Many wonder what, given the fact of reasonable moral pluralism, could justify granting a special status to religion. What can justify singling out religion in an age where religious life is one path among many? My argument is that there is a special category of interests that humans have that has more normative weight and that deserve special legal treatment. These interests have to do with the capacity to act in accordance with one's deepest and meaning-giving convictions. 'Meaning-giving beliefs and commitments' should be seen as special and be singled out, at least for normative purposes. Such beliefs and commitments should not be treated on a par with the kind of beliefs, values, attachments and preferences that agents have but that are not related in strong and significant way to their sense of self or to their conception of what is a life worth living. The beliefs, values and practices that I have in mind are those that are at the core of one's moral identity. 'Moral identity' is roughly defined as the mutable set of aims, values and commitments that give substance to our personal identity, guide our conduct, and provide us with moral orientation.[23]

Maclure's defence is perplexing. He sets out to answer the question of what could justify 'singling out religion in an age where religion is one path among many', and the reader expects him to do just that. Instead, he goes on to concede that there are, in fact, many paths to meaning, both religious and otherwise, that deserve special legal treatment. Far from 'singling out religion', Maclure replaces it with a different, though overlapping, category.

There is another worry. Maclure aims to protect the 'mutable set of aims, values and commitments that give substance to our personal identity, guide our conduct, and provide us with moral orientation'. Simon Căbulea May among others has observed that the aims, values and commitments that fit this description go well beyond religion and even conscience. He gives the example of a young chess player, Chester, who seeks to avoid two years of mandatory military service so that he can pursue his dream of becoming a chess grandmaster: 'Already one of the best chess players in the country, Chester cannot afford to lose two years of play at his age if he is to stay competitive with other leading players around the world and have any chance of becoming world champion'.[24] Like his conscientious-objector friends, Chester feels his commitment intensely; indeed, May stipulates that he is far less likely to waver in his ambition than his friends are to waver in their moral commitment and that his 'ambition to be world champion is no less central to his self-conception than their moral principles are to theirs'.[25] Yet Chester does not feel *morally* obligated to be a chess champion, much less divinely commanded.

---

[22] J Maclure, 'Conscience, Religion, and Exemptions' in Vallier and Weber (n 2).

[23] ibid 11.

[24] SC May, 'Exemptions for Conscience' in Cécile Laborde and Aurelia Bardon (eds), *Religion in Liberal Political Philosophy* (New York, OUP, 2017) 191, 196.

[25] ibid 198.

Would Maclure protect Chester's meaning-giving commitments? He writes:

In practice, there is of course a grey zone between meaning-giving beliefs and commitments and more mundane interests, but I assume that there are also clear cases of both categories: caring for a close one who is gravely ill is radically more important than watching a show or a sport game for most of us. Contrarily to what some philosophers think, that outliers can be found or conjured up in an alternate possible world is not a good reason to oppose conscience-based accommodations and, in doing so, to reduce the scope of a basic right such as freedom of conscience and religion. [Here Maclure footnotes May.[26]] One of my assumptions is that fanciful cases imagined by philosophers do not make good theories in normative ethics.[27]

As a response to May, this passage is unhelpfully dismissive. Yes, there are clear cases and grey zones, but May's example of Chester is hardly fanciful: The actual world is full of people whose intense commitment to their sport, craft, career or vocation gives substance to their identity, conflicts with other interests – including at times, legal obligations – and has nothing to do with either religion or conscience, traditionally understood. If we stretch the category of religious exemptions to include 'meaning-giving beliefs and commitments', as Maclure advocates, should we include Chester? If not, why not? While I appreciate Maclure's egalitarian impulses, he has left unanswered the question of why his approach, far from giving special protection to religion, merely replaces it with something more nebulous.

Another recent 'egalitarian' approach comes from Ryan T Anderson and Sherif Girgis, in our point-counterpoint book *Debating Religious Liberty and Discrimination*.[28] Their account deserves attention in part because it aims explicitly to answer the question of why legal systems ought to shield 'moral and religious commitments more than commitments to becoming a master chef or a chess master, to making art or making the Olympics'.[29] Their basic argument is as follows: the primary role of the state is 'to empower and not encumber people's pursuit of basic goods', which they define as 'the most basic ways in which people can be well, or flourish … ways of being and acting that it makes sense for us to want for their own sake'.[30] Among these goods are certain forms of integration, or integrity, including 'harmony … within the self, and … between the self and the transcendent'.[31] Anderson and Girgis capture these two forms of harmony under the broad heading of 'moral and religious integrity'. You pursue such integrity by 'trying to harmonize your choices, actions, and expressions with your moral convictions: your best judgments about what morality requires', and 'with whatever transcendent source of meaning and value there might be'.[32]

Laws that substantially pressure people to violate their perceived moral and religious obligations deserve heightened scrutiny, they argue, because 'the underlying goods [moral and religious integrity] are especially fragile'.[33] They are fragile because one cannot

---

[26] He actually footnotes 'Chapter 4, this volume' which is May's 'Contempt, Utility, and Exemption' paper. But it seems he intended to footnote May's 'Exemptions for Conscience' paper, which was the paper May delivered at the Religious Exemptions conference on which the Vallier and Weber *Religious Exemptions* anthology – 'this volume' – was based.

[27] Maclure, 'Conscience, Religion' in Vallier and Weber (n 2) 12.

[28] J Corvino, R T Anderson and S Girgis, *Debating Religious Liberty and Discrimination* (New York, OUP, 2017).

[29] ibid 132.

[30] ibid 125.

[31] ibid 125.

[32] ibid 125, 126.

[33] ibid 134.

compensate for deficiencies in them by meeting some other obligation at some other time. Anderson and Girgis illustrate: 'If the law pressures someone into flouting her Muslim obligations, she can't make up for that – and escape deficiency in religion – by fulfilling a Mennonite duty instead.'[34] The same is true, on their view, for moral obligations derived from non-religious sources. They conclude that the law should make moral and religious obligations costly only if doing so meets strict scrutiny; that is, if applying the law is the least restrictive means to achieving a compelling governmental interest. Otherwise, the law amounts to a 'fine' on moral and religious integrity, thus violating the state's responsibility to empower, not encumber, basic goods.

There is much to unpack here; I will focus my remarks on the aspects most relevant to the discussion at hand. The main question I will consider is how Anderson and Girgis aim to meet the challenge of Chester, whose commitment to becoming a chess champion, although neither moral nor religious in nature, makes conscription especially costly for him. Their response depends on what I will call their 'no substitutions' point – the idea that moral and religious obligations do not allow for exceptions. They write:

> To respect … [moral or religious] integrity, the state needs to let you obey the specific convic-
> tions you already have. To respect … self-determination, it simply needs to let you choose and
> pursue some projects – not necessarily the ones you already have or most prefer. After all, if you're
> barred from pursuing one project, you can adopt another, live out that new one, and your self-
> determination doesn't take much of a hit. You need only a respectable range of options. But if
> you're pressured into flouting even one of your perceived *obligations*, you're stuck; your integrity is
> cracked. So integrity is more fragile than self-determination. That's why we should scrutinize legal
> burdens on conscience more exactly than legal burdens on other commitments or projects.[35]

This passage sounds plausible because much of what it says is true *in general*. However, it fails as a response to Chester. For Chester, becoming a chess champion is something he feels he simply must do, and conscription would wreck that goal. Telling him to do something else – such as organising bridge tournaments with his fellow soldiers – is no more helpful than telling the Muslim to substitute a Mennonite duty. Given his particular meaning-giving beliefs and commitments, Chester is stuck; there is no 'range of options' for him.

To put the point more generally, not all actions experienced as volitionally necessary are moral or religious in nature. What's more, not all religious actions are volitionally necessary: as already noted, much religion takes the form of optional ritual practice. (One could make a similar point about moral duties, which are sometimes 'imperfect' duties.) Even some of the best-known exemption and accommodation cases involve non-mandatory actions: consider *Employment Division v Smith*.[36] In that case, Alfred Smith and Galen Black had ingested peyote, an illegal, hallucinogenic, plant-based drug, as part of Native American religious rituals. After testing positive for the drug, they subsequently lost their jobs and were denied unemployment benefits by the state of Oregon. Although the US Supreme Court upheld Oregon's refusal, the pair garnered considerable national sympathy: Oregon changed its laws to allow ritual use of peyote, and the case eventually led to the passage of the federal Religious Freedom Restoration Act, which stipulated that even neutral laws

---

[34] ibid 135–36.
[35] ibid 134–35.
[36] *Employment Div, Dept of Human Resources of Ore v Smith*, 494 US 872 (1990).

should not interfere with religious exercise unless applying the law to the individual is the least restrictive means for promoting a compelling governmental interest. Yet as Andrew Koppelman has observed, neither claimant felt conscience-bound to use peyote: 'Al Smith was motivated primarily by interest in exploring his Native American racial identity, and Galen Black was merely curious about the Church'.[37] Insofar as it depends on the 'no substitutions' point, Anderson and Girgis's argument would offer little reason to exempt Smith and Black, much less one that distinguishes them from Chester.

There is a more general problem with Anderson and Girgis's argument. Anderson and Girgis treat integrity as a purely formal notion, consisting in harmony between belief and action *regardless of the content of the beliefs*. They write, 'Living by your best judgments about the right and the good – even when those judgments are mistaken – inherently makes you better off, *in one respect*, than ignoring or flouting them. The self, like the body, is wounded by division. For both, harmony is health'.[38]

This formal understanding of integrity produces counterintuitive results. It means, for example, that Hitler could have as much integrity as Gandhi – maybe more, if he was more successful at bending the world to his will. As Lynne McFall has argued, purely formal approaches to integrity rob us of the ability to explain what's funny about the following sentence: 'John was a man of uncommon integrity. He let nothing – not friendship, not justice, not truth – stand in the way of his amassment of wealth'.[39]

The problem can be made clearer by way of a real-world example. Consider Louisiana Justice of the Peace Keith Bardwell. In 2009, it came to light that Bardwell refused to officiate at interracial weddings.[40] Bardwell claimed, and probably sincerely believed, that he was not a racist: 'I have piles and piles of black friends', he told reporters. 'They come to my home, I marry them, they use my bathroom. I treat them just like everyone else'. But he personally morally objected to interracial marriages and therefore refused to perform interracial weddings. Instead, he politely referred the couples to his colleagues.

Notice that in these refusals, Bardwell was harmonising his 'choices, actions and expressions with [his] moral convictions'. He had integrity, as Girgis and Anderson define it. Yet his convictions were bad ones, and everyone (including him) would have been better off had he failed to execute them. It is therefore not clear that integrity – in the purely formal sense of harmony – is a basic good. And if it is not a basic good, then it is a fortiori not a basic good that the state must empower.

One might here distinguish two different ways of understanding the notion of a 'basic good', both of which appear in Anderson and Girgis's discussion. If we understand basic goods as 'ways of being and acting that it makes sense for us to want for their own sake', then formal integrity is clearly a basic good: it always makes sense to want to align one's actions with one's beliefs. But if we understand basic goods as 'the most basic ways in which people can be well, or flourish', in line with Anderson and Girgis's examples of 'health, knowledge, play, aesthetic delight, and skillful performances of various sorts', then the goodness

---

[37] Koppelman (n 9) 586.

[38] Corvino et al, *Debating* (2017) 126.

[39] L McFall, 'Integrity' (1987) 98 *Ethics* 989, 9.

[40] See The Associated Press, 'Interracial couple denied marriage license in Tangipahoa Parish' *Nola.com* (New Orleans, 16 October 2009) at www.nola.com/crime/index.ssf/2009/10/interracial_couple_denied_marr.html.

of mere formal integrity seems more dubious, especially from a third-party perspective.[41] For consider the following three scenarios:

(1) Bardwell wants to turn away interracial couples, and successfully does.
(2) Bardwell wants to turn away interracial couples, but is thwarted from doing so.
(3) Bardwell does not want to turn away interracial couples (and doesn't).

According to Anderson and Girgis's approach, Bardwell has less integrity in (2) than in (1) and (3), which are equal with respect to integrity; in other words, the Bardwell who is thwarted has less integrity than the one who succeeds. But surely, he is flourishing at least as well in (2) as he is in (1) – arguably more so, insofar as the disequilibrium between his convictions and the legal constraints he confronts might eventually lead him to better convictions.

Anderson and Girgis's answer to this problem is to argue that although Bardwell is better off in one respect in (1) than in (2) – he has more (formal) integrity – he may be worse off in other respects: namely, that he's giving effect to racist policy. Hence the italicised phrase in the passage already quoted: 'Living by your best judgments about the right and the good – even when those judgments are mistaken – inherently makes you better off, *in one respect*, than ignoring or flouting them'. So let us grant for the sake of argument that there is *some* sense in which Bardwell is better off when he is permitted to turn away interracial couples: he has more formal integrity than the Bardwell who is thwarted from doing so.

The question that remains is what difference all of this should make to the law, and the answer is: not much. For the value of protecting the merely formal integrity of the individual will nearly always be outweighed by the value of promoting the common good. That is the aim of just laws, including those that prevent Bardwell from discriminating racially. Why subject such laws to higher scrutiny simply because they burden his formal integrity – which is nothing more than a fancy way of saying that *they prevent him from doing what he really wants to do*?

The point bears emphasis: By invoking a purely formal notion of integrity, Anderson and Girgis's argument for protecting integrity boils down to an argument for letting people do what they want to do. They focus on moral and religious *obligations*, in which case, their argument boils down to an argument for letting people do what they believe they morally and religiously *must* do. Because the state is responsible for protecting the basic good of integrity, they argue, it should subject to higher scrutiny any law that makes it more difficult for people to fulfil their perceived obligations. But as I have argued, it is not clear that there is such a basic good (as Anderson and Girgis define it), and even if there is, it is not clear that the state has any extra responsibility for protecting it beyond its more general duty to protect liberty. If religion (or religion plus conscience) is special, we need to know why.

There is an ordinary sense of integrity according to which it makes sense for the state to want to promote, or at least to avoid undermining, moral and religious integrity: in general, people who do what they believe is right, rather than what is expedient, make better citizens: more generous, more honest, more other-directed. But, first, that 'in general' depends on certain values in the background; it does not work for a purely formal notion of integrity. Second, it is not clear how exemptions help integrity in this sense: They simply provide

---

[41] Corvino et al (n 28) 125.

integrity on the cheap. They do not do anything to build more moral citizens; they just make it easier for people to do what they really want to do. Anderson and Girgis hold that 'applying laws to you that would penalize you for living with integrity should trigger heightened scrutiny; our presumption should be to exempt you'.[42] That strikes me as exactly backwards: The presumption should be to enforce the law consistently, for the sake of the common good; exemptions for particular individuals bear the burden of proof.

Anderson and Girgis are certainly right that laws that impinge upon religious practice or moral conviction may be felt as particularly burdensome. But that is not, or not merely, because those cases permit 'no substitutions' – some do, some do not, and besides, there are other cases (such as Chester's) that share this feature. It is because, among other reasons, moral and religious convictions touch the core of people's identity; as Maclure puts it, they are 'related in a strong and significant way to their sense of self'.[43]

Of course, some laws are unjust. Some are unjust because they unfairly directly target particular moral and religious beliefs and practices; think, for example, of laws that prohibit the wearing of certain religious garb or that require religious tests for office. Even then, however, it would be odd to describe the laws as a direct attack on integrity (in Anderson and Girgis's formal sense); after all, the laws are not seeking disharmony for disharmony's sake. The direct pressure, in these cases, is not on integrity, but on the particular belief or practice.

More commonly, the burden on religious belief and practice is indirect, resulting from an unfair discounting of certain groups' needs and interests. Consider the landmark US case of *Sherbert*. Adell Sherbert was a Seventh-day Adventist who left her job after her employer switched from a five- to a six-day work week, thus requiring her to work on Saturday, her Sabbath.[44] South Carolina subsequently denied her unemployment benefits on the grounds that she was unavailable for Saturday work. But the US Supreme Court ruled in her favour, holding that South Carolina's denial 'forces her to choose between following the precepts of her religion and forfeiting benefits, on the one hand, and abandoning one of the precepts of her religion in order to accept work, on the other hand. Governmental imposition of such a choice puts the same kind of burden upon the free exercise of religion as would a fine imposed against appellant for her Saturday worship'.[45]

The Court's analogy to a 'fine' is overstated. Sherbert was free to do what she liked with her days; she simply could not collect an unemployment check while unavailable for Saturday work. More important, had Sherbert's unavailability for work been due to a non-religious reason – even a very important one – the Court would not have mandated benefits. As Justice Potter Stewart points out in a separate opinion, 'South Carolina would deny unemployment benefits for a mother unavailable for work on Saturdays because she was unable to get a babysitter … This is not, in short, a scheme which operates so as to discriminate against religion as such'.[46]

There is, however, a better argument for compensating Sherbert, one that the majority opinion mentions only in passing. South Carolina law also decreed that 'no employee

[42] ibid 136.
[43] Maclure (n 22) 11.
[44] *Sherbert v Verner* (1963) 374 US 398.
[45] ibid 404.
[46] ibid 416.

should be required to work on Sunday' as a condition of receiving unemployment benefits.[47] The law thus unfairly favoured Sunday worshippers over Saturday worshippers. In other words, *Sherbert* reached the right result for the wrong reason.[48] The problem with South Carolina employment law was not that it burdened religion: it did, although it also *favoured* religion, by elevating religious reasons over others when determining unemployment benefits. The problem was that it unjustly privileged Sunday worship over Saturday worship. That's not religious liberty; it's majority religious privilege.

By acknowledging secular meaning-giving beliefs and commitments, egalitarian approaches such as Maclure's or Anderson and Girgis's provide some check against one form of religious privilege; that is an appealing feature of egalitarianism. But they fail to explain sufficiently why either those commitments or their religious counterparts merit exemptions from laws *that are otherwise just*. To his credit, Maclure makes the point about justice explicit:

> [T]he 'meaning-giving' character of a commitment is a necessary but not sufficient condition for justifying legal accommodations. The law, norm, or rule from which one wants to be exempted also needs to be unfair. In most cases of warranted accommodation measures, a *prima facie* neutral norm distributes opportunities in an uneven way or proves to be disproportionately burdensome for the members of a minority group. Statutory holidays generally coincide with the religious holidays of the majority, dress codes that prescribe a uniform or prohibit head covers burden those for whom wearing religious garment[s] is not seen as optional, the absence of a vegetarian option in environments where people are fully or partially captive (prisons, hospitals, schools, airplanes) burdens vegetarians disproportionally, etc. It is in such situations of 'adverse effect' or 'indirect discrimination' that accommodation measures are required by justice.[49]

This proviso is important, but it also takes us further away from making 'religion' the key category: now, it seems that it is the injustice of the legal burden that is doing the heavy lifting. Indeed, it is not clear why 'meaning-giving beliefs and commitments' (or 'moral and religious integrity', to take Anderson and Girgis's formulation) are necessary in this argument at all: The fact that a law unjustly burdens some citizens is reason enough to try to accommodate those citizens, regardless of the form the burden takes.

V. Religion as a Site of Discrimination

The good news is that Maclure's proviso about injustice also points the way toward a better argument for singling out religion. (For the moment, we will need to put his egalitarian ambitions aside.) As a practical matter, it is unworkable to have a rule which countenances exemptions whenever a law is 'unfair'. The category is too broad, and the unfairness would be difficult to address politically for the very same reason that it occurred in the first place: Minorities' needs and interests have likely been systematically discounted. It is better to identify categories that are typical sites of unjust discrimination and then require heightened scrutiny with respect to those categories. Religion is one such category.

---

[47] ibid 406.
[48] Professors Ira Lupu and Robert Tuttle have made a similar point. See IC Lupu and RW Tuttle, *Secular Government, Religious People* (Michigan, Erdmans, 2014) 191–92.
[49] Maclure (n 22) 13.

According to this approach, religious exemptions function as a corrective for mistreatment. Sometimes this mistreatment is blatant, but often it is unintentional. As Martha Nussbaum observes, 'Laws in democracies are made by the majority … Majority thinking is usually not malevolent, but it is often obtuse, oblivious to the burden [its] rules impose on religious minorities'.[50]

Here I am reminded of how my university requires that professors make reasonable accommodations for students who miss exams for religious reasons. At first I feared that this policy would pose an administrative nightmare: I work at a large, diverse institution, and I often teach large classes; my students observe a plethora of holidays. On the other hand, even though I teach at a state university, my Christian students never have to take an exam on Christmas Day. The reason is that official holidays are chosen by the majority, and the majority observes Christmas: a Christian holiday (with elements borrowed from a pagan holiday) which has now become a secular holiday due to Christianity's dominance. Our university schedule thus places a burden on minority faiths that it does not place on Christians. Realising that, I came to see the accommodations policy as a reasonable way to restore fairness.

The point is that majority-made policy often squeezes minorities in ways that even well-meaning people can miss. In my view, the best reason for contemplating specifically religious exemptions is that they serve as an antidote to this tendency.

There are three important caveats, however. The first is that while religion is *special* in this regard, it is not *unique*. It is, rather, one among several factors that have been common grounds for (deliberate or unintentional) mistreatment. Disability is another good example – one where exemptions are also frequently justified. Indeed, we can now see how religious exemptions have something important in common with the anti-discrimination laws at the heart of the current conflicts: Both give greater scrutiny to factors that are common sites of injustice. The second caveat is that greater scrutiny need not always result in an exemption. Whether it does depends not only whether the rule disadvantages certain citizens, but also on what other values are at stake – including the needs and interests of third parties and the importance of legal consistency.

The final caveat – perhaps the most important – is that exemptions should not remove burdens from some minorities only to place burdens on other, possibly even more disfavoured, minorities. Otherwise, we undermine the strongest reason for contemplating exemptions in the first place. Indeed, exemptions to anti-discrimination laws are controversial in large part because they purchase inclusion for one group at the expense of exclusion of another.

How does my preferred approach compare with the hybrid views of the last section? I agree with Maclure, Anderson and Girgis that when laws and policies substantially raise the cost of practicing religion, they deserve greater scrutiny. But that is not because religion is 'meaning-giving' in ways that many secular pursuits are not (Maclure) or because the state has some special responsibility for allowing people to harmonise their actions with their religious convictions (Anderson and Girgis). It is because religion is a site of an unfortunate human tendency, which Anderson and Girgis helpfully describe as the temptation to 'create

---

[50] M Nussbaum, *Liberty of Conscience: In Defense of America's Tradition of Religious Equality* (New York, Basic Books, 2010) 116.

stable in-groups and out-groups; define a clan and prefer it to others in systematically unjust ways'.[51] (Note that I also disagree with Anderson and Girgis on more specific questions related to whether greater scrutiny in the wedding-provider cases should result in exemptions, although discussion of those differences would take me too far afield here.[52])

But what about their egalitarianism, which many find appealing? As a non-believer, I certainly appreciate the acknowledgement that secular citizens have deep and meaningful moral commitments. And one could even argue that, in a nation as religious as the United States, those commitments have at times been systematically discounted – or, alternatively, stretched beyond recognition so that they might fit a religious template. *Seeger* and *Welsh*, the famous conscientious objector cases, are good examples of this 'stretching'. Consider *Welsh* in particular: the petitioner explicitly denied that his objection to war was religious. But a plurality of the Court disregarded Welsh's self-understanding, holding that conscientious objection to war is 'religious' as long as it 'stems from the registrant's moral, ethical, or religious beliefs about what is right and wrong and these beliefs are held with the strength of traditional religious convictions'.[53] In other words, Welsh's beliefs qualified because they were sufficiently religious-*ish*.

So yes, non-believers have had their perspectives unjustly discounted. But they face this problem less commonly than believers do, for reasons to which we have already alluded. Here's Laycock again:

> Nonbelievers have many moral commitments, and they hold some of those commitments with religious intensity. But they do not hold many intense moral commitments that are at odds with the dominant morality reflected in government policy. Nonbelievers tend to have a modern sensibility. They do not draw their morality from ancient books written in a radically different culture that lived with radically different technology and had a radically different understanding of the world; they do not obey an omnipotent, omniscient God whose commands may be beyond human understanding. On the whole, nonbelievers take their morality from the same modern milieu that drives democratic decision making and government regulation. It is no accident that military service is the only prominent example where serious claims of nontheistic conscientious objection have been litigated.[54]

Laycock may be too quick in dismissing the likelihood of secular believers with strong commitments out of step with their fellow citizens: think of secular vegetarians struggling to find options in hospitals, prisons, airplanes and other confined environments; or of secular opponents of mandated vaccines, or jury duty, or institutions of government more generally. Laycock is correct, however, that these are likely to be less common than their religious counterparts. Moreover, there are pragmatic difficulties with extending the argument of this section to secular concerns: The whole point of enumerating categories of heightened scrutiny – whether in anti-discrimination law or in constitutional interpretation – is that legislators and judges are unlikely to see their own prejudices. 'Give heightened scrutiny to laws that unjustly overlook minorities' is not a workable legal rule; 'Give heightened scrutiny to laws that implicate race, religion, sexual orientation, and so on' is.

On the other hand, even if one opposes a general case for secular exemptions, one can still argue for them in more specific realms. Laycock explicitly mentions conscientious

---

[51] Corvino (n 28) 164.
[52] ibid esp 220–31.
[53] *Welsh v United States* 398 US 333, 340.
[54] Laycock, 'Debate' (2009) 170–71.

objection to military service, which is a special case on multiple counts: First, conscription requires a citizen to drop everything and take up arms. It is not like saying, 'If you want to open a business, then you must do such-and-such'. It is an absolute intrusion. Second, it involves life-or-death matters. Third, and most significantly: People are conscripted to fight, and pacifists by definition decline to fight; conscripting pacifists to fight undermines the very purpose of the law in question.

There are other cases where treating secular claims as similar to religious ones makes sense as a matter of administrative consistency. Recall our example of the non-religious prisoner who wished to wear a beard out of respect for family tradition, or even because he simply dislikes shaving. Once it is determined in the religious cases that short beards are no threat to prison safety, it seems at best silly and at worst unfair not to extend the permission more generally. Indeed, this has happened in some real-world cases. In *Holt v Hobbs* (2015), a Muslim prisoner in Arkansas won the right to wear a short beard.[55] Within a year, Arkansas allowed beards for all prisoners.[56]

VI. Conclusion

I conclude that, in general, religious claims deserve more scrutiny, and thus potentially more deference, than secular ones. But I also grant that there are a number of cases where exemptions are justified for secular claims. And I would reiterate that while religion is a familiar site of discrimination, it is not unique in that respect. Other factors provoke strife. Sexual orientation is among such factors.

Which brings us back to the wedding cake cases, which seem to pit a new minority against a longstanding one: opponents of same-sex marriage versus same-sex couples. While cultural power varies considerably with locale, and while the religious right's claims of being an oppressed minority are largely overblown, one cannot deny that support for same-sex marriage has risen dramatically in the last two decades and now enjoys a comfortable majority in the United States (64%, as of May 2017).[57] No doubt this shift is jarring, especially for those who remember when homosexuality was truly 'the love that dare not speak its name'. On one side we have couples enjoying newfound freedoms but carrying pain from earlier battles and fearing that progress is fragile. On the other side, we have traditional religious believers who see that 'progress' as deterioration, if not outright perversion, and who cannot understand why they are being ostracised as bigots for views that nearly everyone held just a few decades ago.

If we grant people in the second group exemptions from anti-discrimination laws designed to protect people in the first group, are we promoting tolerance or abetting intolerance? As we confront that question, we must keep in mind that it is not merely an abstract philosophical query; it demands political solutions that affect real people. These solutions have implications far beyond cakes and flowers: They concern citizens' sense of identity, dignity and security as they live their lives in the public sphere.

---

[55] *Holt v Hobbs*, 574 US ___, 135 S Ct 853 (2015).

[56] Sarah Whites-Koditschek, 'Arkansas Prisons Drop Beard Restrictions' (UA Little Rock Public Radio, 2016) at www.ualrpublicradio.org/post/arkansas-prisons-drop-beard-restrictions.

[57] Justin McCarthy, 'U.S. Support for Gay Marriage Edges to New High' (Gallup, 2017) at www.news.gallup.com/poll/210566/support-gay-marriage-edges-new-high.aspx.

3

Conscientious Claims, Ill-Founded Belief and Religious Exemption

PETER JONES[*]

I. Introduction

In the enduring controversy over religious exemptions, one matter seems reasonably settled. That is the matter of how courts should handle the religious beliefs of those who register a claim to exemption. Provided a court is satisfied that a claimant sincerely holds the belief he professes, it should take the belief at face value. In particular, it should not subject the belief to any test of merit, plausibility or reasonableness. That statement is subject to some qualification which I shall acknowledge in due course, but the general position is that a court should not vary the status or weight it gives a belief according to its estimate of the belief's merit or validity. Nor for judicial purposes should an individual's belief be subject to appraisal by a religious authority, including an authority that speaks on behalf of an organised religion of which the individual is a member.

Accordingly, when the question of exemption arises and the claimant's interest is weighed against various other sorts of consideration in deciding whether the claimant should receive an exemption all things considered, the weight the court accords the claimant's interest should not vary according to its estimate of the plausibility or reasonableness of the claimant's belief. As well as being generally accepted judicial practice, that position is pretty much an orthodoxy amongst liberal commentators on religious freedom in general and religious exemption in particular.

In this chapter, I want to question that orthodoxy. Perhaps I should say that I 'interrogate' it since I eventually acknowledge a justification for it. I do not call into question religious liberty in general. Rather, I take for granted that individuals have a right to embrace a religious faith, or none, as they themselves see fit and that others, including judges, are duty-bound to respect their use of that right. I question the immunity of religious belief from official appraisal only in a more limited way. We have a religious believer, B, who subscribes to faith X and who believes that his faith requires him to do y and to refrain from z. Suppose we have reason to doubt the correctness of B's belief; we reckon, with good reason, that he is mistaken in believing that X requires y or forbids z. His belief is 'ill-founded'. Should that affect the weight or the status we give to B's belief?

[*] I am very grateful to John Adenitire for his helpful comment and advice on earlier drafts of this chapter.

In some respects, it should not. Courts in applying Article 9 of the European Convention on Human Rights (ECHR) treat the freedom to hold a belief as absolute. If B's belief is ill-founded, that is a reason why he should not hold it, but does not diminish his right to do so. It also does not affect his right to manifest his belief by doing y or refraining from z. The ill-foundedness of B's belief becomes practically relevant when it impinges on and competes with the (legitimate) interests of others and, more particularly, when B seeks an exemption enabling him to engage in a practice manifesting his belief. B then presents his belief as a reason why he should not be subject to a law or rule with which others have to comply and very often as a reason why others should endure costs and inconvenience so that he can manifest his belief. To the extent that B's exemption would adversely affect the public or private interest of others, his belief ceases to be his business only and becomes the business of others too. That is reflected in the weighing process through which a decision should be made on whether someone should receive an exemption all things considered.

Why should that weighing process not take account of the well- or ill-foundedness of B's belief? If B's belief is ill-founded, he is not justified in holding it and, if he is not justified in holding it, how can his holding it justify his making positive demands upon others? At the very least and *ceteris paribus*, does not an ill-founded belief have a weaker claim to accommodation than a well-founded belief, and might its ill-foundedness jeopardise its claim to accommodation entirely?

These questions, of course, beg many others. One of the more obvious is how we are to determine whether B's belief is indeed well- or ill-founded. Even though we are to judge not the well-foundedness of B's religious faith (X) but only his belief about what his faith requires (y and not-z), that may still be a challenging task. But, prima facie, it is surprising that a belief's well- or ill-foundedness should make no difference to its bearer's claim to an exemption.

My examination of the questions raised by the issue of ill-foundedness unfolds as follows. In section II I give some real-life instances of belief-based practices that illustrate the general issue I have described. Section III says more to explicate the issue and sketches the current orthodoxy, with reference to Lord Nicholls' well-known remarks, that courts should refrain from subjecting religious beliefs to any sort of evaluation. Sections IV and V consider what might justify that abstinence. Section IV considers whether 'in principle' considerations, particularly the moral right to religious liberty, make it wrong to take account of the well- or ill-foundedness of a person's belief in considering his claim to an exemption. It finds that case not made. Section V turns to the more practical question of whether courts lack the knowledge and ability needed to arrive at a reliable assessment of a belief's well-foundedness. While not accepting the general view that their lack of competence is just obvious, I do find reason why judges should wish to avoid 'entanglement' with religious questions. Section VI considers, with reference to indirect discrimination law, whether we can circumvent the problem of entanglement by using a group test as a proxy test of well-foundedness. Section VII concludes.

II. Examples

In December 2013, an employee working on a cash register in the food section of Marks & Spencer refused to serve a customer, albeit politely, because his shopping included alcohol and she declared that, as a Muslim, she was forbidden to handle items containing alcohol. She asked the customer to join the queue for another register. In response to this incident a boycott was mooted by indignant customers of Marks & Spencer and the store quickly declared that it would no longer employ staff at its registers if they refused to handle alcohol. The issue had previously arisen in another supermarket chain, Sainsbury's, which had allowed its Muslim staff not to handle alcohol or pork. An objecting Muslim who was working at a cash register was allowed to summon another member of staff to put the offending item through the register in his or her stead. Once their indulgence attracted public comment, Sainsbury's took advice from Muslim authorities on whether Islam did indeed forbid the mere handling of alcohol or pork; having been advised that it did not, the supermarket changed its policy.

This is the sort of case in which we might question whether the objector's belief was soundly based and, if it was not, whether the employers either were, or should have been, duty-bound to accommodate it. As far as I know, a case concerning the handling of alcohol or pork by Muslims has not been tested in law in the UK. If Muslim objections were not accommodated and that, in turn, gave rise to a claim of indirect religious discrimination, I strongly suspect that an employer's requirement that its sales staff should be willing to handle all items sold by a shop would be deemed a 'proportionate means of achieving a legitimate aim' and so not indirectly discriminatory. But in that case the determining factor would be the proportionality test, whereas the issue I am raising concerns the merit of the belief with which that test competes and how its merit (or demerit) should affect the consideration it receives.

More recently, a dispute arose in Birmingham over a four-year old girl whose parents wished her to wear a hijab while attending a Catholic primary school, contrary to the school's uniform policy.[1] Birmingham City Council's equality chief, Waseem Zaffir, claimed (probably incorrectly) that the school's uniform code banning headwear, including Islamic headscarves, breached the Equality Act 2010. However, the case attracted attention not only as yet another clash between the claims of religion and a school's uniform policy but also because of the parents' zealotry in making a four-year-old girl wear a hijab, a zealotry which was widely deemed misplaced since Islam normally requires girls to cover their heads only when they reach puberty. This too was a case in which the questionable justification of a religious practice might be thought adversely to affect, if not to rule out altogether, its claim to accommodation.

That case, like the case of handling alcohol or pork, was not tested at law. A much older case that was and that provides a clear example of the issue I mean to raise concerned an employee of British Rail (BR) in the days of the closed shop when BR existed as a nationalised industry and required its employees to belong to a trade union.[2] Mr Saggers was a Jehovah's Witness who claimed that his religious beliefs forbade trade union membership. The Industrial Relations Act 1971, under which his case fell, had originally provided that employees could escape the closed shop requirement if they objected to trade union membership on 'conscientious' grounds. In 1974, the Act was amended so that the ground

---

[1] C Turner, 'Catholic School Prompts Uniform Row by Banning Muslim Girl from Wearing a Headscarf' (*The Telegraph*, 23 January 2017) at www.telegraph.co.uk/education/2017/01/23/catholic-school-prompts-uniform-row-banning-muslim-girl-wearing.

[2] *Saggers v British Railways Board* [1977] IRLR 266.

for exemption became 'religious belief' in particular rather than conscientious objection in general. Nothing in the doctrines of the Jehovah's Witness church proscribed membership of a trade union, as Mr Saggers himself acknowledged. For that reason, the industrial tribunal that heard his case decided that he did not qualify for exemption. On appeal, the Employment Appeal Tribunal (EAT) ruled that the industrial tribunal had applied the wrong test. Provided the industrial tribunal was satisfied that Mr Saggers himself sincerely believed that, for religious reasons, he should not join a trade union, he qualified for exemption. It mattered not that his belief was at odds with the official doctrines of the organised religion to which he subscribed.

The EAT remitted the case for rehearing by the industrial tribunal on the factual question of whether Mr Saggers' objection was really grounded in his religious belief. On remission, the industrial tribunal accepted the sincerity and genuineness of Mr Saggers' attitude that his objection to joining a trade union was based on his religious belief, but still held that, in fact, his objection was based upon more general grounds of conscience. Mr Saggers again appealed and the EAT again decided, by a majority, that the tribunal had erred in law.[3] Provided it was accepted (as it was by the tribunal) that Mr Saggers was sincere and genuine when he declared 'I do not think that a Christian can be a trade unionist', that sufficed to establish that his objection was 'due to religious belief'.[4]

Here I do not want to question whether the EAT was right in law. Rather, I want to ask whether it *should* have been right in law. Since Mr Saggers made his claim *as* a Jehovah's Witness and since we can reasonably suppose that his command of the doctrines of his church was inferior to that of the church itself, do we not have reason to doubt the well-foundedness of his belief? And, if we do, should that not make a difference to the legal status of his claim?

A more recent and better-known case, which raised similar questions about the subjective and objective dimensions of the religious belief protected by law, is the Canadian case of *Syndicat Northcrest v Amselem*.[5] The case concerned the Jewish festival of Succot, during which religiously observant Jews are to 'dwell' in a succah (a small enclosed temporary hut) for the nine days of the festival.[6] A number of practising Orthodox Jews who lived in co-owned luxury buildings in Montreal wanted to erect succot on the balconies of their units, contrary to the by-laws governing the building which prohibited decorations, alterations and constructions on balconies. The case turned partly on how the rights of the claimants to freedom of religion weighed against the rights of other co-owners and the steps taken by Syndicat Northcrest to accommodate the beliefs of the claimants, particularly its offer to provide a communal succah in the garden attached to the buildings. But it also turned on the nature of the religious belief whose freedom was protected by the rights enshrined in the Quebec Charter of Human Rights and Freedoms and it is upon that aspect of the case that I focus here. The specific point at issue was not whether the claimants were mandated by their faith to observe the festival of Succot; all parties accepted that they were. Rather it was whether their freedom of religion entitled each to construct

---

[3] *Saggers v British Railways Board* [1978] IRLR 436.
[4] ibid at 6.
[5] *Syndicat Northcrest v Amselem* [2004] 2 SCR 551, 2004 SCC 47.
[6] I put 'dwell' in scare quotes because, in view of the climate of Montreal, the extent to which practising Jews were required to live in a succah throughout the nine-day festival was limited; ibid at 113.

a private succah on his balcony rather than use the communal succah offered by the Syndicat (an offer approved by the Canadian Jewish Congress) or a succah at some other location.

The original trial judge ruled that, to be protected by the right to freedom of religion under the Quebec Charter, a claimant must prove that the practice at issue was required by the teachings of his or her religion. Sincere belief alone did not suffice.

> Freedom of religion can be relied on only if there is a connection between the right asserted by a person to practise his or her religion in a given way and what is considered mandatory pursuant to the religious teaching upon which the right is based. A sincere belief must be supported by the existence of a religious precept. ... the rite must have a rational, reasonable and direct connection with the teaching. How a believer performs his or her religious obligations cannot be grounded in a purely subjective personal understanding that bears no relation to the religious teaching as regards both the belief itself and how the belief is to be expressed (the rite).[7]

Having heard evidence that Judaism did not require Jews to erect their own succot and that there was no commandment governing where succot should be erected, the judge concluded that the by-laws governing the Syndicat's building did not prevent Jews from fulfilling their religious obligations and so did not infringe their freedom of religion.[8]

A majority of the Court of Appeal agreed.[9] A majority of the Canadian Supreme Court thought differently. They held that the lower courts' interpretation of freedom of religion was unduly restrictive. Speaking for the majority, Iacobucci J insisted that the freedom of religion protected by both the Quebec and the Canadian Charters was essentially 'personal' or 'subjective' and cited several judicial comments and decisions in support of that view.[10]

> In my opinion, these decisions and commentary should not be construed to imply that freedom of religion protects only those aspects of religious belief or conduct that are objectively recognized by religious experts as being obligatory tenets or precepts of a particular religion. Consequently, claimants seeking to invoke freedom of religion should not need to prove the objective validity of their beliefs in that their beliefs are objectively recognized as valid by other members of the same religion, nor is such an inquiry appropriate for courts to make.[11]

While a claimant had to show sincerity of belief, he or she did not need to show that the belief was 'valid'. To be protected by 'freedom of religion', the belief had to have 'a nexus with religion', but that nexus could be entirely subjective.[12] Accordingly the majority found that the Syndicat's rules, in preventing the appellants' constructing succot on their balconies, did interfere with their freedom of religion and went on to find no justification for that interference.

Three members of the Supreme Court dissented.[13] In a shared judgment, they rejected the majority's understanding of freedom of religion.

> [A] religion is a system of beliefs and practices based on certain religious precepts. A nexus between personal beliefs and the religion's precepts must therefore be established. ... Religious

---

[7] ibid quoted at 21.

[8] ibid at 22–24, 118.

[9] ibid at 28–30, 125.

[10] ibid at 40–42.

[11] ibid at 43.

[12] ibid at 56. For Iacobucci J's expansive comment on the 'intensely personal' nature of religious belief, see at 38–56, 67–69.

[13] A fourth judge also dissented but from the majority's view on justification, not from their interpretation of freedom of religion.

precepts constitute a body of objectively identifiable data that permit a distinction to be made between genuine religious beliefs and personal choices or practices that are unrelated to freedom of conscience. Connecting freedom of religion to precepts provides a basis for establishing objectively whether the fundamental right at issue has been violated.[14]

Thus, as well as establishing that the claimant's alleged belief was sincerely held, a court had also to be satisfied that it was genuinely connected to the religion that the claimant shared with others. That connection was subject to an 'objective test' and that was a test that, the dissenting minority concluded, the appellants' claim did not pass.[15]

The disputes evoked by *Amselem* provide a model instance of judges taking different positions on the question of whether claimants should be treated as self-authenticating authorities on the demands of their religion, or whether claims made in the name of a religion should be subject to scrutiny in respect of that religion. While the disputes formally concerned what Canadian law was, they also included judicial comment that clearly took sides on the issue of what the law ought to be.

Frequently, the subjective/objective issue relates not to whether a practice can plausibly claim a foundation in a particular faith but to the status the practice has with respect to that faith. One such issue is what should count as 'manifestation' of a belief for purposes of Article 9 of the ECHR and the protection it affords religion or belief. Strasbourg case law has distinguished an act or practice that 'manifests' a belief from one that is merely 'motivated' or 'influenced' by the belief. In *Arrowsmith*, the case in which the European Commission first made the distinction, the Commission decided that the claimant's activity of distributing leaflets exhorting British soldiers not serve in Northern Ireland, while it may have been motivated by the claimant's pacifism, was not a manifestation of her pacifism since the leaflets contained no statement of pacifism.[16] It was not therefore protected by Article 9(1). As that case made clear, the judgement of whether an act manifests, or is merely motivated by, a belief is an objective one. It is a judgement to be made by the court, not one to be outsourced to claimants and their sincere understanding of what their own beliefs demand of them.

Thus, for example, in *Williamson* the court held that use of corporal punishment was a manifestation of the belief of the Christian groups who were the claimants,[17] while in *Playfoot*, it decided that the claimant's act of wearing a 'purity ring' contrary to her school's uniform policy was not a manifestation of her Christian belief on sexual abstinence before marriage, even though it may have been motivated by her belief.[18] Let us return to the case of the Muslim supermarket workers who objected to handling alcohol or pork and suppose that their employer refused to accommodate their objections. The employees might have responded not by appealing to the law on indirect religious discrimination but by claiming that the employment laws which obliged them to comply with their employer's instructions on handling alcohol or pork had interfered with their human rights under Article 9 of the ECHR. In such an event, the judgment of a court might well have been that, while the employee's refusal to handle alcohol and pork was a belief-related preference, it did not

[14] ibid at 135.
[15] ibid at 135, 162.
[16] *Arrowsmith v UK* (1981) 3 EHRR 218.
[17] *R v Secretary of State for Education and Employment and others, ex parte Williamson* [2005] UKHL 15, at 30–35, 62–64, 78.
[18] *R (on the application of Playfoot) v Governing Body of Millais School* [2007] EWHC 1698, at 20–23.

manifest the belief that consuming alcohol or pork was *haram*; it was simply a preference motivated or influenced by that belief.[19] Similarly, had *Amselem* arisen as a case in European law, the dispute over the scope of the belief protected by law might have been recast as one concerning the distinction between manifestation and motivation.

Of course, the manifestation/motivation distinction retains a subjective element in that, in Strasbourg case law, it is the demands of the claimant's belief, not the orthodoxies of the religious faith with which he or she identifies, that are subject to assessment. Even so, that assessment involves a court's inquiring into the claimant's belief and reaching a judgment on its demands, a judgment that may well differ from the claimant's own conception of those demands. Use of the manifestation/motivation distinction has been criticised for that reason.[20] Moreover, a religious believer may find it harder to persuade a court that an act or practice manifests a belief if it is not so conceived by a significant number of others who subscribe to the same faith.

Suppose now that it is agreed on all sides that a practice does manifest a religious belief. A decision on an exemption requires that the claim of the believer be weighed against the other considerations with which it competes, such as how significantly the exemption would frustrate the aims of the law or rule from which the believer seeks exemption and how great are the costs and inconvenience the exemption would shift on to others. That weighing process requires us to assign a notional, if inevitably imprecise, weight to the believer's claim, which, in turn, requires attending to two considerations. First, how severely does the law or rule impinge upon the believer's faith? For example, other things being equal, a law or rule that frustrates an obligatory practice will be more severe in its effect than one that frustrates a practice that is only discretionary. Secondly, how directly does the law or rule frustrate the practice? If, for example, a law or rule effectively prohibits a practice, its adverse effect will be more direct than if it renders performance of the practice only more costly or inconvenient; if it does the latter, the less the cost or the inconvenience, the less direct will be the effect. Thus, the more severe and direct the effect, the weightier will be the believer's claim for an exemption.[21]

My interest here is in the criterion of severity. Some commentators insist that courts should refrain from investigating people's religious beliefs in an effort to assess how severely those beliefs are disadvantaged.[22] However, if there is to be a weighing process, it is hard to see how that can be avoided or why it should be deemed illegitimate. As Abner Green has observed, if people seek an exemption on religious grounds, they cannot reasonably

---

[19] In a case of this sort, a court may be more inclined to invoke the 'specific situation' rule: the employees freely chose to accept employment at the supermarket and they retained the option of resigning from it; for that reason their Article 9 rights had not been interfered with. Use of that rule has, however, recently been called into question: *Eweida and Ors v United Kingdom* (2013) 57 EHRR 8, at 83.

[20] R Ahdar and I Leigh, *Religious Freedom in the Liberal State*, 2nd edn (Oxford, Oxford University Press, 2013) 166–69; C Evans, *Freedom of Religion under the European Convention on Human Rights* (Oxford, Oxford University Press, 2001) 120–27. Russell Sandberg argues that, in determining whether a belief should receive protection, use of the manifestation/motivation filter, along with other sorts of filter, should be minimised and the focus should shift to the question of justification under Article 9(2); in R Sandberg, *Law and Religion* (Cambridge, Cambridge University Press, 2011) 83–87, 94, 98–99.

[21] I adopt the terms 'severe' and 'direct' from C Laborde, *Liberalism's Religion* (Cambridge, MA, Harvard University Press, 2017) 221–25.

[22] See, for example, the remarks of Iacobucci J in *Syndicat Northcrest v Amselem* [2004] 2 SCR 551, at 47–50, 67–68.

expect to veto any judicial entanglement with their religious beliefs.[23] Two distinctions that commonly arise both in judicial comment and in moral and political thinking on exemption are those between (i) obligatory and discretionary religious practices and between (ii) central or core practices and those that are more peripheral to a faith. Other things being equal, burdening a practice that is obligatory or central to a faith affects it more severely than burdening one that is discretionary or peripheral. Although these distinctions are eminently reasonable, they are not always easily deployed and they apply to some faiths more readily than to others. I pass over those difficulties. The relevance of the distinctions here is that they provide another occasion for the subjective/objective question: obligatory or discretionary, central or peripheral, according to whom?[24]

III. Ill-Foundedness and Judicial Agnosticism

The cases cited in the previous section exemplify the sorts of case in which we might think that the well- or ill-foundedness of an individual's belief should affect the weight or status that public decision-makers give to the belief. However, I should perhaps re-emphasise the limited context in which I mean to present that issue. The ill-foundedness of a belief does not affect the believer's right merely to hold or articulate his belief; nor is it relevant to every manifestation of his belief. Even if the belief that Islam forbids the mere handling of alcohol or pork is mistaken, Muslims who hold that belief should be free to manifest it by avoiding forms of employment or other activities which would involve their handling alcohol or pork. Even if Mr Saggers was mistaken in believing that his religion proscribed trade union membership, he should remain free to manifest his belief by avoiding forms of employment that would require him to join a trade union. The issue of a belief's well-foundedness becomes a practical issue only when an individual's freedom to manifest his belief competes with the (legitimate) interests of others.

We can think of a decision on a religious exemption as a two-stage process. At the first stage, we consider whether the claimant's belief-based practice should be a candidate for an exemption and, if it should, how strong its candidacy is. For example, a court's assessment of whether a claimant sincerely holds the belief he professes belongs to that first stage. If the court adjudges the claimant to be insincere, his claim falls at that hurdle. At the second stage, we take account of the considerations with which the claim for an exemption competes and consider whether the claimant should receive an exemption all things considered. The issue of well-foundedness belongs to the first part of that two-stage process. If a belief is

---

[23] AS Greene, 'Three Theories of Religious Equality … and of Exemptions' (2009) 87 *Texas Law Review* 962, 999–1000.

[24] For analysis and discussion of the distinctions, see P Billingham, 'How Should Claims for Religious Exemptions be Weighed?' (2017) 6 *Oxford Journal of Law and Religion* 1. Billingham argues for a subjective use of the distinctions: the relevant consideration should be how obligatory or how central a religious practice is to the individual claimant, not how it ranks within the official faith to which the claimant subscribes, although he allows that a court may draw on a practice's importance within an official faith for evidence of its being similarly important for an individual claimant; ibid, 9–13. For related discussions, see K Greenawalt, *Religion and the Constitution, Vol I: Free Exercise and Fairness* (Princeton, Princeton University Press, 2006) 202–14; Laborde, *Liberalism's Religion* (2017) 222–25; E Lim, 'Religious Exemptions in England' (2014) 3 *Oxford Journal of Law and Religion* 440, 449–57.

ill-founded, we might hold that it has no claim to be accommodated. Or, less severely, we might hold that it retains some claim to accommodation but one that is diminished by its ill-foundedness. If we allow an ill-founded claim to go forward to the second stage, it may of course be outweighed by competing considerations at that stage. But there is no reason to suppose that ill-founded beliefs, merely because they are ill-founded, are more likely than well-founded beliefs to be outweighed by stage two considerations. We cannot therefore rely on the second stage to do the dirty work for us. If a religious claim's ill-foundedness is a legitimate and relevant consideration, it is a consideration that we must confront and resolve at the first stage.

The question of well- or ill-foundedness should be distinguished from another sort of assessment: the screening of belief-based practices for moral acceptability. We might also adopt a stage one approach to that assessment. We may hold that a religious practice that involves, for example, injuring or killing children, or subjecting them to psychological trauma, should be ruled out of consideration at stage one simply because it is morally unac-ceptable. Alternatively, we might opt to keep that sort of issue out of the first stage and reposition it as a consideration that should come into play at stage two. My preference is to follow Cécile Laborde and locate the issue of moral acceptability at the first stage,[25] in part because we then more clearly distinguish between (a) belief-based practices that we exclude because they are morally unacceptable from (b) those that are intrinsically unobjection-able but which fail to qualify for accommodation simply because they are outweighed at stage two by the competing interests of others, public or private. My only concern here is to observe that, if we do locate the question of moral acceptability at stage one, we should not elide it with that of well- or ill-foundedness. It is no part of the thesis I mean to exam-ine that the practices spawned by ill-founded beliefs are morally objectionable and should count for less, or for nothing, because they are morally objectionable. In some cases ill-founded beliefs may be morally objectionable, but so too may be some beliefs that are theologically well-founded. We have no reason to suppose, optimistically, that the issue of well-foundedness is co-extensive with that of moral acceptability.

Article 9 of the ECHR does not make, but is consistent with, the two-stage distinction I have used above. Judges have sometimes commented on the issue of moral acceptability in a way that suggests a 'stage one' approach. Lord Nicholls, for example, in commenting in *Williamson* on the 'modest, objective requirements' a belief needs to satisfy to receive the protection of Article 9, observed: 'The belief must be consistent with basic standards of human dignity or integrity. Manifestation of a religious belief, for instance, which involved subjecting others to torture or inhuman punishment would not qualify for protection.'[26] Lord Nicholls made equally clear in a much-cited comment that what I have presented as the issue of well-foundedness should be no concern of a court.

> [E]mphatically, it is not for the court to embark on an inquiry into the asserted belief and judge its 'validity' by some objective standard such as the source material upon which the claimant founds

---

[25] Laborde (n 21) 207–09.

[26] *R v Secretary of State for Education and Employment and others, ex parte Williamson* [2005] UKHL 15, at 23. Understood according to a 'stage one' approach, beliefs that were morally unacceptable in ways that Lord Nicholls describes would not be protected by Article 9(1) from interference. Understood according to a 'stage two' approach, they would be protected by Article 9(1), but interference would be justified by considerations itemised in Article 9(2), especially 'protection of the rights and freedoms of others'.

his belief or the orthodox teaching of the religion in question or the extent to which the claimant's belief conforms to or differs from the views of others professing the same religion. Freedom of religion protects the subjective belief of an individual. … Each individual is at liberty to hold his own religious beliefs, however, irrational or inconsistent they may seem to some, however surprising.[27]

Lord Nicholls' words state a judicial orthodoxy that is widely shared, even if not without exception, in liberal democratic jurisdictions. He did go on to specify a number of 'threshold requirements' that a belief must satisfy if its manifestation is to be protected, one of which I cited above: the belief must be consistent with basic standards of human dignity or integrity. A belief had also to relate to more than trivial matters and to possess 'an adequate degree of seriousness and importance'.[28] It had to be belief 'on a fundamental problem'. The belief had to be 'coherent', a quality that may seem to open the door to the issue of well-foundedness. However, Lord Nicholls set the bar for coherence deliberately low: the belief had to be coherent 'in the sense of being intelligible and capable of being understood'; though 'too much should not be demanded in this regard' since belief in the supernatural 'is not always susceptible to lucid exposition or, still less, rational justification'.[29] Lord Nicholls' 'threshold requirements' therefore do little to qualify his general affirmation that courts should make no attempt to assess the 'validity' of the belief professed by a claimant.

IV. The Moral Right to Religious Freedom and the Relevance of Well-Foundedness

Why then should we be so diffident about claims people make in respect of their religious beliefs? Is this a matter of principle? Do we wrong someone if we find their beliefs ill-founded and allow that finding to influence the decision on whether they should receive an exemption? Or is it simply a matter of practicalities? Is it possible to assess the well-foundedness of someone's religious belief and, if it is, would an assessment be so fraught with difficulty that it is an exercise we should not undertake? Even if it is not wrong in principle to subject someone's belief to critical scrutiny, it may be prudent to handle religious claims *as if* such scrutiny were wrong. I consider principled objection in this section and practical objection in the next.

The most obvious 'in principle' argument in favour of allowing each individual to be the arbiter of what his religion or belief requires, appeals to freedom of religion or freedom of conscience. These freedoms, we might insist, are rightly comprehensive in scope. They properly encompass not merely the fundamentals of belief but every matter of detail as well. If B embraces faith X and goes on to assert that X requires y and abstinence from z, the religious liberty to which B has a right applies as much to his beliefs about y and z as it does to his belief in X. Thus, if we judge B's belief about y and z and find it wanting and then

---

[27] ibid at 22.
[28] The ECtHR had previously observed that the terms 'conviction' and 'belief' as they occurred in the ECHR denoted 'views that attain a certain level of cogency, seriousness, cohesion and importance'; *Campbell and Cosans v the UK* (1982) 4 EHRR 293, at 36.
[29] ibid at 23. For an argument that, even so, Lord Nicholls' criteria risk filtering out too much, see Ahdar and Leigh, *Religious Freedom* (2013) 154–55.

allow our judgement to weigh against B's claim to an exemption, we violate B's moral right to freedom of religion or, more generally, to freedom of conscience.[30]

What is it about religious practices that makes them candidates for exemption? The answer that I and many others find most compelling is that those practices are the subjects of normative imperatives. Religious practices are candidates for exemption if and because that they are 'ethically salient'.[31] But if ethical salience is the feature of religious practices that makes them *pro tanto* candidates for exemption, it follows that ethically salient non-religious practices can also be *pro tanto* candidates for exemption. We might then subsume freedom of religion, insofar as it pertains to exemptions, within freedom of conscience.

Subsuming religion under conscience is, however, hazardous in that the morality associated with 'conscience' is commonly subjective in ways that the morality encompassed by religious belief is not. I want to develop my response to the freedom of religion objection by commenting on that contrast between conscience and religious belief.

A morality focused on conscience is often subjective in two respects. First, for any particular individual, that individual's conscience is the well-spring and authoritative source of morality for that individual. The morality of conscience is 'subjective' in that the subject of that morality is also its source. Secondly, for any particular individual, right conduct consists in compliance with the dictates of his or her conscience. It could be that those dictates turn out to be the same for everyone, but then we shall be hard put to explain how it is that different individuals have different moral beliefs. The existence of moral disagreement frequently pushes thought on conscience in a different direction: the voice of conscience can speak differently to different individuals, but even so each individual should be governed by his or her own conscience. Thus right conduct for one individual will not always be identical with right conduct for another. The morality of conscience issues in a form of relativism. It is 'subjective' in that the morality governing people's conduct will vary, rightly, according to the subject of the morality.

If we think in those terms, it will always be wrong to sit in judgement on an individual's moral beliefs and find them wanting, since each individual will be, of necessity, the best authority on what is right for him or her. However, there is much that is implausible and unattractive about the subjectivism of conscience, even as a non-religious morality, and it is not easy to assimilate religious belief and its prescriptions to the model of conscientious subjectivism.

First, for most religious believers, their beliefs, including the moral dimensions of their beliefs, are not sourced entirely within themselves. Most commonly, their beliefs are grounded in external sources such as sacred texts, religious teachings, the doctrines of an

---

[30] It is fair to say, I think, that this 'subjectivism' is the prevalent position amongst contemporary moral and political philosophers. For examples, see P Billingham 'How Should Claims for Religious Exemptions be Weighed?' (2017); P Bou-Habib, 'A theory of religious accommodation' (2006) 23 *Journal of Applied Philosophy* 109; Laborde (n 21) 203–07, 222–25; J MacLure and C Taylor, *Secularism and Freedom of Conscience* (Cambridge, MA, Harvard University Press, 2011); M Nussbaum, *Liberty of Conscience: In Defense of America's Tradition of Religious Liberty* (New York, Basic Books, 2008). For a notable exception to the subjectivist orthodoxy, see A Eisenberg, 'What is Wrong with a Liberal Assessment of Religious Authenticity?' in GB Levey (ed), *Authenticity, Autonomy and Multiculturalism* (New York, Routledge, 2015) 145.

[31] Laborde (n 21) 197–203. See also P Jones, 'Liberty, Equality, and Accommodation' in T Modood and V Uberoi (eds), *Multiculturalism Rethought* (Edinburgh, Edinburgh University Press, 2015) 126; B Leiter, *Why Tolerate Religion?* (Princeton, Princeton University Press, 2013); MacLure and Taylor, *Secularism* (2011).

organised religion, the shared faith of a religious community, and so on. Individual inspiration can figure importantly in some faiths alongside shared external sources of belief, but for the most part the individuals who register legal claims with courts do so as 'ordinary believers' rather than as self-professed prophets or visionaries claiming direct inspiration from God.

Secondly, religious belief does not normally share in the subjective relativism that can be associated with the idea of conscience. It does not suppose there are different 'truths' for different individuals or that different moral imperatives rightly govern the conduct of different individuals. It usually takes its truth-claims seriously as truth-claims and its prescriptions seriously as prescriptions which are general in application. Again, that requires qualification. Not all faiths are, like Christianity and Islam, universalist in nature. The distinction between Jew and gentile is fundamental to Judaism, for instance, although Judaism still conceives its laws as objective givens. There are deep waters here which I shall not enter since I mean to observe only that, by and large, religious belief and its imperatives are conceived, neither by religions themselves nor by their individual adherents, as exercises in individual self-legislation. If courts are right not to subject claimants' religious beliefs to critical appraisal, the justification cannot be that correct religious belief for an individual consists only in what that individual supposes it to be. That cannot be the justification because it is at odds with the reality of religious belief as we know it. Moreover, if a court were to rely on that justification, it would take a stance on the nature of religious truth of precisely the sort that courts generally believe they should not.

Within established religions, there is manifestly scope for knowledge, expertise, informed judgement, interpretive acumen, and so on. Given the wealth of learning and scholarship to be found within the world's major religions, that point does not need labouring. By the same token, there is plenty of scope within established religions for ignorance, error, misconception, unwarranted inference, and the like. So we cannot dispose of the relevance of error or poor judgement simply by supposing that no religious judgement is or can be better than any other.

We should also notice what sort of 'judgement' is at stake here. Because it relates to religious practice and what believers believe they ought (not) to do, we might easily suppose that the relevant judgement must be a moral judgement. That, in turn, can bolster the sense that we should allow believers to comply with their beliefs for, to do otherwise, would be to compel them to violate their religious consciences or moral integrity. But the judgement at issue is not a first order moral judgement comparable to a decree of conscience. The matter to be judged is whether faith X requires or enjoins its adherents to do y or not to do z, and that is a judgement of fact or interpretation. Given that it is a judgement of that sort, it is not at all obvious why we should defer, routinely and equally, to the judgement of each individual. If we can assess the soundness of an individual's judgement, surely its soundness should matter. Indeed, it should matter to believers as conscientious adherents of their faith that they should be governed not by their own judgement, merely because it is their own, but by the best judgement.[32]

A possible riposte to this line of argument is that the badness of the bad of having to act contrary to one's beliefs, is independent of whether one's beliefs are well- or ill-founded.

---

[32] *cf* RJ Arneson, 'Against Freedom of Conscience' (2010) 47 *San Diego Law Review* 1015, 1036.

That may be true of the painful psychological experience or disagreeable mental condition one is caused to undergo as a consequence of being unfree or less free to comply with one's beliefs, but we should be reluctant to psychologise the bad of being made to act contrary to one's beliefs so that it becomes no more than a disutile mental state. However, the more decisive answer to the alleged irrelevance of a belief's well- or ill-founded character is readily apparent when we recall that the claim at issue here is the believer's claim to be accommodated by *others*. Even if it were true that, for the believer, the quality of her beliefs makes no difference to the badness of her inability to comply with them, it would not follow that the obligation of others to accommodate her beliefs should be similarly unaffected by their quality.

A second possible riposte is that we fail to treat believers with the respect to which they are entitled if we do other than take their beliefs at face value. Kantian thinking of that sort is frequently deployed on behalf of religious freedom but its force for the kind of case I am considering is questionable. Recall that the issue here is not whether someone should be free to hold or manifest a belief. It is whether they should be able to manifest a belief in circumstances where the manifestation requires an exemption. It is implausible to hold that the respect we owe believers must extend routinely to enduring the costs of their error.

Do we disrespect an individual in merely assessing that individual's judgement on what her faith requires? Obviously not. It is part of the religious liberty to which we are entitled that we should be free to assess the religious beliefs of anyone and everyone. But, if it is not disrespectful merely to assess, it may still be disrespectful to allow our assessment of an individual's belief to affect our treatment of that individual.

Even that is doubtful. Consider the parallel case of culture. Religion and culture are overlapping and interconnected. Often a religious claim can be re-presented as a cultural claim and accordingly the literature on exemptions flip-flops between the language of religion and that of culture. Kantian principles are also as commonly deployed in the context of cultural difference as they are in the context of religious difference. Yet the subjectivism so commonly invoked in relation to religion has little plausibility in the case of culture.

Suppose I claim a practice is a constituent of my culture. Whether it is indeed a part of my culture is a matter for objective assessment. If, for example, I register a claim of indirect racial discrimination because an employer's rule conflicts with a practice (eg a dress code) that is part of my ethnicity, a court has to establish whether the practice is indeed part of my ethnicity. That requires an objective judgement: is the practice a practice of an ethnic group of which I am a member? Ethnicities and cultures are of course internally diverse and not always easily defined, but that does not justify substituting the beliefs of the claimant for an objective judgement of what is the case. I cannot make a practice part of my culture merely by declaring it to be so. If, having investigated the matter, a court concludes that the practice does not belong to my ethnicity and for that reason dismisses my claim of indirect discrimination, it is hard to accept that the court's judgement constitutes an intolerable act of disrespect merely because it conflicts with and overrides my own claim about my culture. But, if that is true, it is hard to see why it should not be equally true in the case of religion. If a court were to make an objective judgement on whether my faith (eg my Roman Catholicism) requires that I should do *y* or not do *z* and reaches a conclusion different from mine and so dismisses my claim to exemption, why should that constitute an intolerable act of disrespect?

The sum of all this is that I am unpersuaded that, in laying claim to a religious exemption, people have a moral right that others should take at face value their own conception of what their faith demands. In principle, a court considering a claim to exemption would not behave wrongly (morally if not legally) if it assessed the well-foundedness of a religious claim and factored its assessment into the calculus of considerations that yielded its verdict.

V. Competence and Pragmatism

If it would not be wrong in principle for courts to assess the well-foundedness of an individual's belief, why else should they refrain from that assessment? Judges often protest that they are not 'competent' to evaluate religious beliefs, but what is the competence they lack?

The term 'competence' is ambiguous. In one sense, to have competence is to have authority or jurisdiction. A court has competence over those matters that fall within the limits of its jurisdiction; if it exceeds those limits, it acts ultra vires. In a second and more prosaic sense, competence means possessing the knowledge and ability required to deal adequately with a matter. A court may lack competence on religious questions simply in that it lacks the requisite knowledge and ability.

If we take competence in the first sense, my concern is not with how far courts have, or do not have, competence to deal with religious questions, which is a complex matter. Rather, my question is, insofar as courts should not have jurisdiction over religious matters, why should they not? The answer might be that that jurisdiction would be inconsistent with individuals' moral right to religious liberty, but I have already cast doubt on the force of that claim for the limited type of case that is my concern.

Why else then might courts be rightly denied competence, in the first sense, over religious beliefs? The obvious answer is because they lack competence in the second sense. Courts do frequently protest that they are not equipped to rule on theological matters. In remarks that seemed to suggest that even Lord Nicholls' threshold requirements were too demanding, Lord Walker declared that a court is 'not equipped to weigh the cogency, seriousness and coherence of theological doctrines'.[33]

I want to consider quite how it is that a court's lack of competence provides reason for its refraining from judging the well-foundedness of particular religious beliefs. However, I want first to set aside an answer that might seem to be yielded by liberal political theory.

John Rawls famously distinguished between public and non-public reason, a distinction that has been used widely in liberal political theory.[34] Public reason is the reason that the citizens of a society can share and which they and public officials should draw upon in deliberating on and making public decisions. Rawls supposes they will do so in a society that is plural, that is, a society whose citizens subscribe to different and conflicting 'comprehensive doctrines', religious, philosophical or moral. Reason grounded in a comprehensive doctrine he describes as 'non-public' reason. It is non-public because it can function as reason only for those individuals who subscribe to the relevant comprehensive doctrine. That is why it is a form of reason inappropriate to individuals in their public role as citizens and officials.

[33] *R v Secretary of State for Education and Employment and others, ex parte Williamson* [2005] UKHL 15, at 60.
[34] J Rawls, *Justice as Fairness: a Restatement* (Cambridge, MA, Harvard University Press, 2001) 89–94.

Citizens should justify the use of political power to one another by way of reasons they can share, which will not be reasons drawn from, for example, a religious faith possessed only by some.

Non-public reason is often said to be 'inaccessible' to those who do not subscribe to the comprehensive doctrine upon which it depends. However, the term 'inaccessible' is potentially misleading. A non-public reason is inaccessible to citizens who reject the associated comprehensive doctrine only in that it cannot function as a reason for them. It need not be inaccessible epistemically; it need not, that is, be unintelligible or beyond the individuals' comprehension simply because they do not subscribe to its associated comprehensive doctrine. We do not have to believe *in* a religious faith to be able to understand it and what it requires or permits of its adherents. There are copious instances of people who are experts on a religious faith to which they do not themselves subscribe and whose competence far exceeds that of the faith's 'ordinary' adherents. So Rawls's distinction between public and non-public reason is not obviously relevant here. If judges are not competent to rule on religious beliefs, it is not because those beliefs belong to a realm of non-public reason which, in most instances, judges will not themselves inhabit and which, for that reason, will lie beyond their comprehension.

The simple point remains that judges are equipped to staff courts because of their legal knowledge and judicial skill not because of their expertise in theology. Yet courts frequently have to deal with cases, such as complex financial or medical cases, to which an expertise is relevant that judges themselves do not have. They do not respond by simply washing their hands of such cases; rather, they call upon the advice of those who have the relevant expertise. So why should they not do so in religious cases? Of course, they frequently do.[35] That sometimes provokes the objection that, in relying upon experts, courts will privilege the views of elites over those of ordinary believers. But that complaint can be merely tautologous: if we want the best judgements, we must turn to those best qualified to make them, and the best qualified, simply in virtue of being so, will be an 'elite'.

That, however, is less than the full story. Those who complain about privileging elites often describe them as 'conservative'. They object to an elite not merely as a body of people distinguished by their expertise, but as one that is likely to be biased towards a particular version of the religion. If experts are drawn from an organised religion and are authorised to speak on behalf of the religion in its organised form, their expertise is especially likely to favour an established version of the religion. That has to be a concern. It is no part of my argument that courts should favour orthodoxy and discourage heresy. The cases with which I am concerned are not those in which some of a religion's adherents set out, deliberately and earnestly, to challenge their religion's orthodoxies, but cases in which 'ordinary punters' get things wrong, either because of innocent error or misplaced zealotry. But it may not always be easy to distinguish the error of the ordinary punter from the 'error' of the heretic.

---

[35] A good example is *Davender Kumar Ghai v Newcastle City Council* [2009] EWHC 978 (Admin). The case concerned Mr Ghai's wish, as a Hindu, to be cremated by open pyre; see at 21–45, 54–60. Having heard at length from two expert witnesses, Mr Justice Cranston commented, 'Notwithstanding all this, the starting point for me is the claimant's genuine belief, held in good faith, that he must be cremated on an open air pyre and the fact ... that this is a manifestation of his religious belief' (at 100). Later in the judgment he added, 'It is beside the point that typically Hindus in this country do not share that belief' (at 160).

There is another way in which the advice of experts must be less than decisive. My interest is in someone, B, who is an adherent of religious faith X and who believes that X requires him to do y or not do z. The issue is not whether he rightly subscribes to X but whether he rightly believes that X requires him to do y or to refrain from z. Given the nature of that question, a court would naturally turn to the organised version of religion X, supposing one exists, for an answer. But what matters about the question is whether B is justified in his belief about y or z, such that he has a *pro tanto* claim to exemption. The question therefore is not whether an organised religion deems B justified, but whether B *is* justified. If a court allowed itself to be governed by the view of an organised religion merely as the view of that organised religion, it would substitute one subjectivity for another. The view of an organised religion, or of anyone else, can be no more than evidence. Ultimately, the court itself would have to answer the question, *is* the believer justified?

It could not therefore avoid that directly religious question. Is it incapable of answering it? It is not obvious that it is. With sufficient time, effort and expert advice, it could come up with a defensible answer. The advice of experts is likely to be crucial, but judges are used to receiving the assistance of experts without sacrificing their independence of judgement. Of course, religious faiths are internally diverse so that no one view may be identifiable as the single correct view, but the judgement required of a court could easily be adjusted to accommodate that fact. All the court need establish in order to find in B's favour is that B has reasonable ground for believing that X requires y or not-z, not that X's requiring y or not-z is the only conclusion at which a well-informed adherent of X could arrive.

That said, a court still has reason to shun the task of assessing a belief's well-foundedness. The task could be very demanding in time and effort. It could also be difficult to execute with confidence, given that religious faiths are so internally diverse and that religious belief is not subject to ordinary rules of evidence or even logic. Due account would also have to be taken of heterodox as well as orthodox belief. Perhaps above all, it would frequently be difficult for a court to come up with decisions that escaped the sort of contention and controversy that it would not want to attract. So, even if the sorts of case I cited in section II are not entirely beyond the competence of a court to resolve, it may be reasonable that judges, or the society upon whose behalf they act, should take the view that, all things considered, the cake is not worth the candle.[36]

Ultimately therefore, we may conclude that there is reason for courts to abstain from assessing the well-foundedness of the religious beliefs that claimants present as warrants for exemptions, but that reason is to be found not amongst the glistening peaks of high moral principle but in the humble foothills of pragmatism and prudence.[37]

---

[36] David Golemboski argues in a similarly practical mode that, even if judges were epistemically capable of assessing religious beliefs, they should refrain from doing so (i) because their judgments would be likely to reflect cognitive and political biases, and (ii) because the controversial nature of their decisions would be liable to undermine public confidence in the judiciary. See D Golemboski, 'Judicial Evaluation of Religious Belief and the Accessibility Requirement in Public Reason' (2016) 35 *Law and Philosophy* 435, 451–55.

[37] Administrative ease does not always argue for conceiving religious belief subjectively rather than objectively. In *Saggers*, for example, British Railways Board suggested that, in deciding who should be exempt from obligatory trade union membership, 'simplification would be achieved if their review of the matter could be confined to an examination of the accepted creed of the body to which the employee belongs, so that they would have to do no more than consider whether the rejection of trade union membership was an integral part of that creed or not'; *Saggers* (n 3) at 10.

VI. A Group Test of Well-Foundedness?
The Case of Indirect Religious Discrimination

If courts are justifiably reluctant to assess the well- or ill-foundedness of people's religious beliefs, is there a more indirect device they might use which could act as a proxy test of well- or ill-foundedness? The most likely candidate is a form of group test: do most, or a significant number, of a faith's adherents subscribe to the belief at issue? If they do, that may serve as a rough indicator of the belief's well-foundedness; if they do not, we might set aside the belief as of questionable validity. That test may deliver rough justice, but perhaps rough justice is better than none.

Group tests figure in UK discrimination law and we might turn to that law for assistance. The Equality Act 2010 exempts organised religions from law prohibiting discrimination in employment on grounds of gender, sexual orientation, gender reassignment and marital status, but only insofar as that discrimination engages either the 'compliance principle' or the 'non-conflict principle'.[38] The compliance principle allows the discrimination insofar as it is necessary to comply with the religion's doctrines. The non-conflict principle allows the discrimination insofar as it is necessary to avoid conflict with 'the strongly held religious convictions of a significant number of the religion's followers'. The compliance principle is in harmony with the idea of well-foundedness. The non-conflict principle, by contrast, sets a group test but one designed to tap what we might describe as 'the living faith' of the religion's adherents. It might therefore model the sort of proxy test I have in mind.

Another group test that figures in discrimination law, and much more prominently, is that incorporated in the general definition of indirect discrimination. According to that definition, A (an employer or provider of goods or services) discriminates against B if A applies to B 'a provision, criterion or practice' (a PCP) that 'puts, or would put, persons with whom B shares the characteristic at a particular disadvantage when compared with persons with whom B does not share it' and which A cannot show to be 'a proportionate means of achieving a legitimate aim' (the PMLA test).[39] Thus, for B to have a prima facie claim to have suffered indirect religious discrimination, it is not enough that B himself is or would be disadvantaged by A's PCP; it has also to be the case that 'persons with whom B shares the characteristic [in this case, his religion or belief]' are or would be disadvantaged by it. That requirement is often described as a test of 'group disadvantage'.

Indirect discrimination law requires a form of exemption. If A's PCP disadvantages or would disadvantage B and those who share the relevant characteristic with B, and A's PCP does not pass the PMLA test, she is required not to apply the PCP to B. She is not required to abandon her PCP; she is required only to exempt B from it. Thus the group test incorporated in indirect discrimination law is a (partial) test of who is entitled to receive an exemption.

That exemption is of just the sort to which a belief's well- or ill-foundedness might be deemed relevant and for which a test of well- or ill-foundedness would be a desideratum.

---

[38] Equality Act 2010, Sch 9, Pt 1, para 2. 'Organisations relating to religion or belief' are also permitted to discriminate on grounds of sexual orientation in relation to their membership and some of their activities but, again, only insofar as that discrimination meets the compliance principle or the non-conflict principle; Sch 23, para 2.

[39] ibid Pt 2, ch 1, para 19.

No group test figures in direct discrimination law but well- or ill-foundedness is not normally relevant to direct discrimination. B may adhere to a manifestly ill-founded belief, but that does not justify A's discriminating directly against him in deciding whether she should employ or promote him (unless the belief was genuinely relevant to B's suitability for the post, in which case it would be relevant irrespective of whether it were well- or ill-founded). But the well- or ill-foundedness of B's belief is not similarly irrelevant to the justifiability of indirect discrimination. Suppose that A has to exempt B from her PCP in order to accommodate B's belief-based practice and incurs costs and inconvenience in so doing. If we discover that the belief upon which B's practice is based is ill-founded, that discovery would seem to undermine the case for imposing upon A the costs and inconvenience of accommodating B.

How far then might we look to a group test similar to that which figures in the definition of indirect discrimination to deal with the issue I have raised in this chapter? That test figures in the definition of indirect discrimination as it applies to all characteristics protected by the Equality Act 2010, not only to 'religion or belief'. Equivalent tests which figured in earlier discrimination legislation were also not limited to religious discrimination. Thus, the test was not put in place to deal with issues specific to religion or belief. Even so, we might ask how well a test of that sort serves the religious case.

An issue the test raises in the case of religion or belief is who constitutes the relevant group. Who are 'the persons with whom B shares the characteristic'? Are they, for example, those who share with B (i) the general faith to which he subscribes (eg Christianity or Islam), or (ii) the particular variant of that faith (eg Roman Catholicism or Sufiism), or (iii) the specific belief that is at issue in B's case (eg sabbatarianism or a belief relating to forms of dress)? The best-known UK discrimination case to have turned on that issue is *Eweida*.[40] Nadia Eweida was a Coptic Christian employed by British Airways (BA) who wanted to wear a silver cross visibly, contrary to BA's uniform policy. The issue that became central to her case was whether BA's PCP (its uniform policy) disadvantaged not only her but also persons with whom she shared her religion or belief. Those hearing her case deemed the relevant group to be Christians at large, which made it difficult for Eweida to claim convincingly that she had suffered indirect discrimination, since Christians in general did not share her belief that they should wear a cross visibly. Had the relevant group been defined more narrowly, the outcome could have been very different.[41] The relevant point illustrated by *Eweida* is that, if we use a group test as a proxy for well-foundedness, the result it yields could be merely an artefact of the particular group we have used.

That potential for arbitrariness is exacerbated by a further consideration. The definition of the group relevant to indirect discrimination can affect the burden of justification required to establish the proportionality of the PCP at issue. That possibility is illustrated by *Mba*. Celestina Mba was a Christian Sabbatarian who claimed indirect religious

---

[40] *Eweida v British Airways* [2008] UKEAT/0123/08/LA, [2010] EWCA Civ 80.

[41] There was also, however, a question of whether her strong desire to wear the cross was a manifestation of religious belief rather than only a belief-based preference; *Eweida v British Airways* [2008] UKEAT/0123/08/LA, at 35, 47–49. The ECtHR subsequently ruled that Eweida's wearing the cross was a manifestation of her religious belief, which was therefore protected by Art 9 of the ECHR; *Eweida* (n 19), at 89.

discrimination in respect of her employer's requirement that she should sometimes work on Sundays.[42] In reaching its judgment on her case, the EAT observed:

> [T]he weight to be given to the degree of interference with religious belief of a certain kind will inevitably differ depending upon the numbers of believers who will be affected by the particular PCP concerned. … To illustrate, if a PCP affected virtually every Christian to a given extent, it would have a greater discriminatory impact than if the same measure affected only a much smaller number of Christians to that extent. The greater the discriminatory impact on the group as a whole, the more that has objectively to be shown by the employer to demonstrate that the PCP is necessary, and proportionate.[43]

Thus a PCP that disadvantaged only Sabbatarians required less justification than one that disadvantaged Christians in general. But that inference was entirely an artefact of identifying Christianity rather than Christian Sabbatarianism as the 'religion or belief' that Mrs Mba shared with others and as definitive of the group that was the potential object of disadvantage. Hence, if we follow the model of discrimination law, the make-up of the group that we adopt for our group test can affect not only whether we find a claim to be well-founded but also how much the claim should count for if it is well-founded.

Aside from the issue of which group is the right group for a group test, the most pressing question is how well a group test is likely to perform as a proxy test of well- or ill-foundedness. The answer has to be, very imperfectly. A sizeable group of individuals may believe that a practice is required by their faith and yet still have poor reason for doing so. Perhaps more commonly, a practice may be limited to a small minority within a faith, but still have a plausible claim to be well-founded. Arguably that was true of Eweida's practice. As I noted above, the requirement that 'persons with whom B shares the characteristic' should be disadvantaged along with B himself is general to the characteristics protected by the Equality Act 2010 rather than particular to religion or belief. It aims to test the group-character of the disadvantage at issue. It is therefore little more than a happy accident if, in the case of religion or belief, it serves as a proxy test of a belief's well-foundedness.

In *Eweida* attention was drawn to the fact that visibly wearing a cross was not a *mandatory requirement* of Christianity; Eweida wore the cross as a personal expression of her faith, as she herself accepted.[44] In *Mba*, the Employment Tribunal observed that Mrs Mba's 'belief that Sunday should be a day of rest and worship upon which no paid employment was undertaken, whilst deeply held, is not a *core component* of the Christian faith'.[45] In neither case, however, was comment on that alleged feature of the claimant's practice intended to cast doubt on its doctrinal soundness; nor could any such doubt have been justifiably

---

[42] *Mba v The Mayor and Burgesses of the London Borough of Merton* [2012] UKEAT/0332/12/SM, [2013] EWCA Civ 1562.

[43] *Mba v The Mayor and Burgesses of the London Borough of Merton* [2012] UKEAT/0332/12/SM, at 46. The Court of Appeal took a more complex view of this issue; *Mba v The Mayor and Burgesses of the London Borough of Merton* [2013] EWCA Civ 1562 especially at 17–19, 30–42. The problem of taking account of 'discriminatory impact' arises from adopting a weighing or balancing approach to proportionality. Elsewhere I argue against use of that approach in indirect discrimination law and for a threshold version of the proportionality test; P Jones, 'Belief, Autonomy and Responsibility: the Case of Indirect Religious Discrimination' in GB Levey (ed), *Authenticity, Autonomy and Multiculturalism* (New York, Routledge, 2015) 66.

[44] *Eweida v British Airways* [2008] UKEAT/0123/08/LA, at 1, 15; [2010] EWCA Civ 80, at 8, 9, 34, 37.

[45] *Mba v The Mayor and Burgesses of the London Borough of Merton* [2013] EWCA Civ 1562, at 8 (my emphasis).

inferred from the practice's minority status. The practice's non-mandatory or non-core character was relevant simply as an indicator of the limited extent of group-disadvantage that could be ascribed to the employer's PCP.[46]

VII. Conclusion

It is highly unlikely therefore that a group test will serve as a satisfactory proxy for a test of well-foundedness. If we are to test for well-foundedness, we have to do so directly. I have argued that it is not in principle wrong to make a belief's well or ill-foundedness a consideration in assessing the believer's claim to exemption. A belief has less of a claim, and arguably no claim, to exemption if it is ill-founded. It would be strange if that were untrue. It would also be strange if a defender of the claims of religious belief protested that the issue could not arise because no religious belief could ever be more or less well-founded than any other. If there is reason to abstain from screening beliefs for their well-foundedness, it is neither moral nor epistemic but pragmatic in nature. That conclusion implies that religious belief will sometimes receive more than its due; beliefs will sometimes enjoy exemptions to which in principle their ill-foundedness gives them no right, but that will be a moral loophole that pragmatism requires us to tolerate.

---

[46] For *Eweida*, see [2008] UKEAT/0123/08/LA, at 14–16; [2010] EWCA Civ 80, at 28–29. For *Mba*, see [2012] UKEAT/0332/12/SM, at 42–49; [2013] EWCA Civ 1562, at 14–24, 30–33, 39. For further comment on these cases, see ch 10.

4

Exemptions for Religious Groups and the Problem of Internal Dissent

PAUL BILLINGHAM*

I. Introduction

Religious groups often seek a level of autonomy from state control. They desire an area in which they exercise self-governance, allowing them to structure their collective life according to their own religious and ethical precepts, without interference from the state. As Douglas Laycock puts it, 'a church autonomy claim is a claim to autonomous management of a religious organization's internal affairs'.[1]

This kind of religious group autonomy is manifested in various ways within liberal societies, including through groups being able to define their doctrines and beliefs, choose their members and leaders, set standards of conduct, and discipline those who violate those standards, all free from state interference. States are also hesitant to adjudicate property disputes that can only be resolved through judgements of religious doctrines, or to assess torts that would challenge the validity of religious rituals and practices. While the precise ways that these various issues are handled varies between different jurisdictions, all liberal democracies grant some level of religious group autonomy.

Several of these manifestations of religious group autonomy involve religious organisations being granted exemptions from various laws that might otherwise impinge on their freedom to control their internal structure. One common example is exemptions from laws governing employment relations – including prohibitions on (certain kinds of) discrimination in employment. In the UK, church ministers have traditionally been excluded from the ambit of various employment laws, either through being defined as 'office-holders' or due to a lack of intent to create a legally valid contract.[2] More recently, the Equality Act 2010 explicitly exempted 'organised religions' from elements of its non-discrimination requirements.[3] Fairly uncontroversially, these provisions permit churches to discriminate

---

* I owe thanks to John Adenitire for helpful comments on earlier drafts of this chapter.

[1] D Laycock, 'Church Autonomy Revisited' (2009) 7 *Georgetown Journal of Law and Public Policy* 253, 254.

[2] J Rivers, *The Law of Organized Religions: Between Establishment and Secularism* (Oxford, Oxford University Press, 2010) ch 4; PW Edge, 'Judicial Crafting of a Ministerial Exception: The UK Experience' (2015) 4 *Oxford Journal of Law and Religion* 244. Courts now examine the specific facts closely to determine legal intent. On this basis, they have found such intent in some recent cases, but not in others. See *New Testament Church of God v Stewart* [2007] EWCA Civ 1004; *President of the Methodist Conference v Preston* [2013] UKSC 29; *Sharpe v The Bishop of Worcester* [2015] EWCA Civ 399.

[3] Sch 9, paras 2–3.

on the basis of religion when choosing their leaders. But they also permit discrimination on other grounds, such as sex. Most prominently, the Catholic Church only permits men to be priests, and the same is true with regard to leaders within various Protestant denominations, as well as Orthodox Judaism and many branches of Islam.

The European Court of Human Rights (ECtHR) has also developed a doctrine of religious group autonomy, viewing it as 'at the very heart of the protection which Article 9 [of the European Convention of Human Rights] affords'.[4] This includes the freedom to select, discipline, and dismiss members and leaders based on their own standards, and even justifies certain infringements on individuals' other Convention rights – and thus exemptions from the requirements that would otherwise apply.[5]

In the USA, the 'ministerial exception', affirmed by the Supreme Court in 2012, gives churches even greater autonomy within their ministerial employment decisions, which are deemed to be outside the purview of secular law.[6] The Court stated that 'requiring a church to accept or retain an unwanted minister … interferes with the internal governance of the church, depriving the church of control over the selection of those who will personify its beliefs'.[7]

Some liberal theorists have argued against these various kinds of corporate religious exemptions,[8] including in relation to churches' employment decisions.[9] Most, however, endorse some form of religious group autonomy that would permit some such exemptions.[10] Some legal theorists focused on UK law have even argued that it ought to incorporate a narrow version of the US-style ministerial exception.[11]

---

[4] *Hasan and Chaush v Bulgaria* (2002) 34 EHRR 554, at 62.

[5] See I Leigh, 'Balancing Religious Autonomy and Other Human Rights under the European Convention' (2012) 1 *Oxford Journal of Law and Religion* 109; P Slotte and H Årsheim, 'The Ministerial Exception – Comparative Perspectives' (2015) 4 *Oxford Journal of Law and Religion* 171, 179–94.

[6] The question of who counts as a 'minister', and thus of the scope of the exception, is contested within the case law. See C Evans and A Hood, 'Religious Autonomy and Labour Law: A Comparison of the Jurisprudence of the United States and the European Court of Human Rights' (2012) 1 *Oxford Journal of Law and Religion* 81, 90–94.

[7] *Hosanna-Tabor Evangelical Lutheran Church and School vs. EEOC* 565 US_(2012), 3. See 15–20 for the Court's guidance on who counts as a minister.

[8] Throughout, I use the term 'corporate exemptions' to refer to exemptions granted to religious groups qua groups. My focus is primarily on churches, but similar arguments would apply to other religious associations, charities, and so on. My discussion is also relevant to religious corporations, but that case raises various further issues that I do not have space to consider, so I do not have them in mind here.

[9] eg, see LC Griffin, 'The Sins of *Hosanna-Tabor*' (2013) 88 *Indiana Law Journal* 981; S Conly, 'In Defense of the (Somewhat More) Invasive State' (2016) 6 *Philosophy & Public Issues (New Series)* 25, 35–6.

[10] The kind of religious group autonomy that is endorsed by most liberal theorists, and that is my focus in this chapter, should be distinguished from claims of 'sphere sovereignty' or 'freedom of the church' that have risen to prominence in recent US legal literature, under the banner of 'religious institutionalism'. For this kind of view, see RW Garnett, 'Do Churches Matter? Towards an Institutional Understanding of the Religion Clauses' (2008) 53 *Villanova Law Review* 273; RW Garnett, 'The Freedom of the Church: (Toward) An Exposition, Translation, and Defense' in M Schwartzman, C Flanders, and Z Robinson (eds), *The Rise of Corporate Religious Liberty* (New York, Oxford University Press, 2016). This view is trenchantly criticised in R Schragger and M Schwartzman, 'Against Religious Institutionalism' (2013) 99 *Virginia Law Review* 917. As they note (919 fn 7), proponents of religious group autonomy are not necessarily committed to the sovereignty of religious groups, the irreducibility of their moral status, or their distinctiveness compared to non-religious associations. This distinguishes the view from the stronger 'sphere sovereignty' account. For a response to Schragger and Schwartzman, defending the liberal credentials of the institutionalist view, see P Horwitz, 'Defending (Religious) Institutionalism' (2013) 99 *Virginia Law Review* 1049.

[11] eg Nicholas Hatzis, 'The Church–Clergy Relationship and Anti-Discrimination Law' (2013) 15 *Ecclesiastical Law Journal* 144; Edge 'Judicial Crafting of a Ministerial Exception' (2015).

The nature and scope of religious group autonomy has become increasingly controversial, however. In part, this is due to recent court decisions. The US Supreme Court has offered an expansive interpretation of the ministerial exception, and the ECtHR has permitted European states to side with church hierarchies in several recent employment disputes, even when other Convention rights were implicated.[12] More generally, the growing reach of state regulation has made conflicts with religious groups' claims to autonomy increasingly common, and thus raised new questions about that autonomy's proper scope.[13] These questions concern both the areas within which religious organisations should be granted exemptions and which organisations count as 'religious' in a way that makes them eligible for those exemptions.

The resolution of disputes over the scope of religious group autonomy depends upon its justification. Recent controversies have therefore led to a flurry of justifications being offered. *Liberal* justifications for group autonomy hold that the interests of individuals are its ultimate normative basis. Group autonomy is the conclusion of an argument that is grounded in individualistic normative premises.[14] Various liberal justifications have been offered in the literature. All such accounts face a significant problem, however, which is that religious groups always contain *dissenters* – individuals who are members of the group but disagree with its current policies, doctrines or structures. For example, these individuals might disagree with the group's current exercise of a corporate exemption. Or they might believe that they have been discriminated against in ways that ought to be legally redressed. Many of the cases that come to court involve (former) church employees who claim unfair dismissal, discrimination, or violation of some other right. If the focus is on the interests of individuals, then it is unclear how these internal dissenters' interests are promoted by the group being granted exemptions, or more generally enjoying an area of autonomy.[15]

This chapter explores this problem of internal dissenters, and ultimately seeks to defend corporate religious exemptions in the face of it, while remaining within the parameters of liberal theory. The chapter is structured as follows. First, I show in more detail why the presence of internal dissenters creates a problem for liberal justifications of corporate exemptions. I then consider three ways that liberal theorists might respond to the problem: appealing to religious groups' own decision-making procedures; to implied consent; and to exit rights. All of these arguments have some force, but none provide a fully satisfactory solution. Finally, I seek to develop my own solution, which builds on the insights contained in the various arguments we will encounter, but more directly confronts the problem by arguing that internal dissenters' *own* interest in freedom of religion can be promoted through religious groups enjoying a significant level of autonomy, including various corporate exemptions. My argument does not provide a full answer to questions regarding the scope of religious group autonomy, but it does offer some guidance. More importantly, it resolves a fundamental problem for liberal justifications of exemptions for religious groups.

---

[12] Including, most recently, *Fernández Martínez v Spain* (2015) 60 EHRR 3; *Travaš v Croatia* App no 75581/13 (ECtHR, 4 October 2016); *Károly Nagy v Hungary* App no 56665/09 (ECtHR Grand Chamber, 14 September 2017).

[13] For helpful discussion of the various reasons for the increased salience of this issue, see P Horwitz and N Tebbe, 'Religious Institutionalism – Why Now?' in Schwartzman et al, *Corporate Religious Liberty* (2016).

[14] This is in contrast to some 'religious institutionalist' views. See Schragger and Schwartzman, 'Religious Institutionalism' (2013).

[15] Griffin's objections to the ministerial exception in Griffin ('*Hosanna-Tabor*', 2013) centre on the harms that it permits to individuals.

II. Liberal Justifications and the Problem of Internal Dissent

Liberal justifications for corporate exemptions appeal to the interests of individuals, and claim that those interests are best served, in certain contexts, by religious institutions being granted significant autonomy to control their own membership, structure and ethos. Some of these arguments seek to justify exemptions by reference to *rights* held by individuals. Usually this involves appeal to rights of freedom of religion, freedom of association or some combination of the two. For example, Richard Schragger and Micah Schwartzman argue that 'individual rights of conscience do all of the conceptual and normative work'.[16] Thus, the ministerial exception 'is fully explainable as a defense of the freedom of conscience for individuals within the church'.[17] Lawrence Sager, meanwhile, argues that individuals have a 'right of close association' – a right to be free from governmental intrusion into close and personal relationships.[18] This includes the relationships among members of religious groups such as churches, and the relationships between individual members and their leaders. Religious groups should thus be permitted to discriminate in their decisions regarding membership and leadership. Imposing anti-discrimination legislation would violate individuals' rights of close association. Finally, Andrew Shorten argues that a combination of arguments appealing to individual rights to freedom of religion and of association give rise to religious institutions' (limited) right to direct their own affairs without interference.[19]

A different set of liberal arguments hold that religious institutions have distinctive rights qua institutions, which are ultimately grounded in individual *interests*, but are not simply aggregations of individual *rights*. For example, Mark Rosen argues that religious institutions aren't reducible to their members and are thus inadequately protected by an exclusive focus on individual rights. Some legitimate expressions of religious group autonomy cannot be plausibly construed as arising from individual conscience or associational rights.[20] Nonetheless, Rosen holds that the appropriate protections for groups do derive from individual interests, as modelled in Rawls's original position. He argues that the parties in the original position would endorse a 'Religious Institution Principle' that bars the state from imposing rules that the religious community deems incompatible with adherents' developing and fully exercising the religion's conception of the good.[21] Cécile Laborde, meanwhile, argues that religious groups can have two interests that justify certain corporate exemptions.[22] 'Coherence interests' concern the group's ability to live by its own standards, purposes and commitments by aligning its purpose, structure and ethos. They are interests in sustaining group integrity. 'Competence interests' concern the group's distinctive ability

---

[16] Schragger and Schwartzman (n 10) 921.

[17] ibid 975.

[18] L Sager, 'Why Churches (and, Possibly, the Tarpon Bay Women's Blue Water Fishing Club) Can Discriminate' in Schwartzman et al (n 10). For criticism, see C Laborde, *Liberalism's Religion* (Cambridge, MA, Harvard University Press, 2017) 59–61.

[19] A Shorten, 'Accommodating Religious Institutions: Freedom Versus Domination?' (2017) 17 *Ethnicities* 252.

[20] MD Rosen, 'Religious Institutions, Liberal States, and the Political Architecture of Overlapping Spheres' (2014) *University of Illinois Law Review* 737, 758–68, 782–84. Rosen criticises Schragger and Schwartzman, in particular. See also Rivers, *Between Establishment and Secularism* (2010) 318–22.

[21] Rosen, 'Religious Institutions' (2014) 768–84.

[22] Laborde, *Liberalism's Religion* (2017) 171–96. Importantly, for Laborde, it is not only religious groups that have these interests. What matters for Laborde is whether an association has the relevant interests, not whether it is a 'religious group'.

to interpret its own standards, purposes and commitments. An association can permissibly discriminate in its membership and leadership when this reflects its central doctrine and mission and/or when it has special competence to judge the relevant criteria for the office. These two salient group interests arise from individuals' exercise of their freedom of association in forming and sustaining the group, so groups' rights to exemptions are derived from the liberal value of freedom of association.

These arguments, and others like them, seek to justify some kind of religious group autonomy, including certain corporate exemptions. The strength and scope of the protections that they afford to religious groups, including the scope of the kinds of groups that merit exemptions, varies between the different arguments. For example, Sager's argument only extends to groups that can be plausibly viewed as enjoying 'close association', while Rosen's would include all institutions that a religion deems necessary for their adherents to flourish – which Rosen argues includes some educational institutions, and perhaps also some hospitals and even corporations.[23] The different arguments are also vulnerable to different objections.

There is one crucial problem that confronts all such liberal arguments, however: religious groups are rarely, if ever, homogeneous. They almost always contain some individuals who oppose the group's current policies, including those relating to the exercise of an exemption. For example, some Catholics believe that the Church should ordain female priests – as some other Christian dominations with formerly male-only priesthoods have done (most notably the vast majority of provinces with the Anglican Communion, including the Episcopal Church in the United States and the Church of England). There are also many examples of ministers, and other employees of religious organisations, accusing their employers of various kinds of discrimination, challenging a decision to fire them, or disputing restrictions placed upon them by their church.

Liberal justifications for corporate exemptions seem to falter in the presence of this kind of internal dissent, since it is unclear how the dissenters' interests are served, or their rights protected, by the religious institution enjoying the exemption.[24] For example, it is not obvious how a dissenter's close association rights are protected by her religious community being permitted to discriminate in ways that she considers objectionable. This is particularly evident in the case of Catholic women who want to be priests or individuals who believe they have been personally discriminated against. Similar comments apply to dissenters' rights to religious freedom. With regard to Rosen's Religious Institution Principle, the presence of internal dissent raises the question of what it means for 'the religious community' to deem some rule incompatible with the exercise of the religious conception of the good. When there is disagreement about precisely that issue, it is unclear whether Rosen's principle can prohibit the imposition of the state's favoured rule. Finally, internal dissenters reject some of the group's apparent commitments and doctrines, which makes it less clear that it

---

[23] Rosen (n 20) 775–77. For a more full-blooded defence of exemptions for various religious non-profit organisations, see TC Berg, 'Progressive Arguments for Religious Organizational Freedom: Reflections on the HHS Mandate' (2013) 21 *Journal of Contemporary Legal Issues* 279.

[24] N Perez, 'Why Tolerating Illiberal Groups Is Often Incoherent: On Internal Minorities, Liberty, 'Shared Understandings,' and Skepticism' (2010) 36 *Social Theory and Practice* 291 argues that internal dissent undermines many of the common liberal arguments for tolerating illiberal groups. My focus in this chapter is different from Perez's, but my arguments are relevant to his.

has a unified identity that could generate Laborde's exemption-justifying coherence and competence interests.

The ECtHR has explicitly stated that religious group autonomy must be protected even in the face of internal dissent.[25] I believe that this is correct. Religious groups should enjoy a significant degree of autonomy, including various corporate exemptions, even when they contain internal dissenters. But it is not clear how this view can be justified within existing liberal theories.

This is not a novel problem. Liberal theorists have long recognised that groups can both facilitate and restrict individual freedom.[26] There are three obvious responses to the problem of internal dissent that liberal defenders of corporate exemptions can offer. First, religious groups have their own procedures for handling internal disagreements, and should be free to follow those procedures. Second, even dissenters have given implied consent to the group's own determinations of the contested issues. Third, internal dissenters are free to leave the group and form or join another group whose beliefs better align with their own. All three of these responses contain important insights. But all three also have significant weaknesses, which prevent them from providing a complete answer to the problem of internal dissent. In the following three sections I will consider these responses in turn, in order to highlight both their strengths and limitations. While I argue that they are insufficient to solve the problem of internal dissenters, I do not mean to reject them completely; indeed, all three play a role within my own answer to the problem, which I present later in the chapter.

III. Internal Decision-Making

The first response is to hold that religious groups should be granted the freedom to resolve their internal disagreements in their own way, by following their own decision-making procedures when deciding on their policies. Indeed, for many this is precisely what religious group autonomy involves. This can be seen in the ECtHR's response to the issue of internal dissent: states 'should accept the right of [religious] communities to react, in accordance with their own rules and interests, to any dissent movements'.[27] National authorities must not act as arbiters between group authorities and dissident factions. US courts have similarly been clear that proper regard for religious group autonomy requires respect for decisions made by groups' own duly constituted authorities and decision-making procedures.[28] As the Supreme Court puts it, religious organisations' 'independence from secular control or manipulation' involves the 'power to decide for themselves, free from state interference, matters of church government as well as those of faith and doctrine'.[29] Internal dissenters should thus voice their complaints to religious authorities, and campaign for change

---

[25] See *Fernández Martínez* (n 12) at 128.
[26] For a helpful summary, see FM Gedicks, 'The Recurring Paradox of Groups in the Liberal State' (2010) *Utah Law Review* 47, 50–55.
[27] *Fernández Martínez* (n 12) at 128.
[28] CC Lund, 'Free Exercise Reconceived: The Logic and Limits of *Hosanna-Tabor*' (2014) 108 *Northwestern University Law Review* 1183, 1199.
[29] *Kedroff v St Nicholas Cathedral* 344 US 94 (1952) 116. The Court quoted this statement approvingly in *Hosanna-Tabor* (n 7) 11.

through the mechanisms provided by those procedures. Their success or failure at bringing about their desired reforms should depend on the operation of those procedures, rather than on state interference.

I think this position is largely correct, but it is not clear that the liberal accounts can justify it. Within the framework of the liberal justifications for exemptions, the argument for deferring to groups' own decisions only seems to have great force when those decisions are made using *democratic* procedures. The interests of individual group members will be adequately taken into account only if decisions are made democratically, so a concern for the interests of individuals will justify deference to the group's decisions only if democratic procedures are used.

This is clearest in Shorten's examination of groups' rights to institutional exemptions.[30] Shorten argues that while it is religious institutions who are granted the *legal* right to an exemption, the *moral* right attaches instead to the group of individuals on whose behalf the institution acts. The normative justification for the exemption comes from those individuals' interests in freedom of religion and association. The gap between the legal and moral right can be bridged only if decision-making agents within the institution have legitimate normative authority to exercise the exemption, and this is the case only if those agents are authorised by the group to act on its behalf. It seems, however, that for this kind of authorisation to occur the members of the group either must all share the same view of how the exemption ought to be exercised or must democratically authorise the decision-agent and/or their decisions.[31] The former condition obviously is not met in cases where there is internal dissent, so the latter condition – democratic decision-making – must be met if the exemption is to be justified.

Not all liberal justifications for corporate exemptions rely on as strict an account of authorisation as Shorten's. But his argument illustrates the more general point that it is not clear how deference to decisions made within non-democratic or hierarchical decision-making structures can protect the interests of ordinary group members, and especially the interests of those who disagree with the decisions that are made. This general point applies to all liberal accounts.

The reason that this is a problem, of course, is that many religious groups are internally hierarchical. While ordinary group members are free to express their opinions, there is often little, if any, formal deliberation about the group's rules and structures, and decisions are made without democratic decision-making procedures such as voting. Further, decisions are often made not by individual congregations, but by centralised denominational authorities. Of course, this is not true for all religious groups. In some Protestant denominations important decisions are made democratically by individual churches. Other denominations incorporate representatives of the laity into their formal decision-making structures. But many church polities are hierarchical, such that corporate exemptions would not be justified if it were a condition for such exemptions that decisions were made democratically. The same applies to other religious institutions such as seminaries and religious schools.[32]

---

[30] A Shorten, 'Are There Rights to Institutional Exemptions?' (2015) 46 *Journal of Social Philosophy* 242.

[31] This feature of Shorten's view is also noted by J Seglow, 'Religious Sovereignty and Group Exemptions' (2015) 44 *Netherlands Journal of Legal Philosophy* 231, 237 fn 12.

[32] And, indeed, to non-religious institutions, such as universities.

IV. Implied Consent

A natural response at this point is to appeal to some notion of 'implied consent'. Those who join religious organisations implicitly grant authority over religious matters to the institution and its internal procedures. Even if those procedures are not democratic, such that individual members cannot be said to have directly authorised every decision made by the institution, each member has given implied consent to the decision-making procedures that are in place and thus to the decisions made by the group's duly constituted authorities. In Michael Helfand's words, 'religious institutionalism amounts to a constitutionally protected contract of sorts'.[33] Helfand argues that religious group autonomy protects an agreement between the membership to have internal matters governed by religious law and doctrine. The US Supreme Court expressed this view in an important 1871 ruling:

> All who unite themselves to [a religious association] do so with an implied consent to this government, and are bound to submit to it. But it would be a vain consent and would lead to the total subversion of such religious bodies if anyone aggrieved by one of their decisions could appeal to the secular courts and have them reversed.[34]

The main problem with this argument is that in many cases it appears descriptively inaccurate. Many members of religious groups were inducted into those groups as children, and even those who join as adults rarely do so with full knowledge of all of the groups' doctrines, structures or decision-making procedures. It thus seems a stretch to hold that they have in some way consented to all of those things. And it is certainly implausible to view most individuals as giving consent to a fixed, monolithic set of beliefs, rules and hierarchies, since few religious groups are static or homogeneous in this way. The very problem of internal dissent arises precisely because religious communities are always sites of debate and contestation, in a way that makes it difficult to identify precisely what individuals can be said to have consented to. This is true even for groups' decision-making procedures and structures of authority; these matters are also often contested, and it is unclear that the majority of members can be said to have given consent to them simply through joining the group. These points are ably summarised by Jessie Hill, who has critiqued the implied consent argument at length: 'In fact, religious membership is probably best understood not as a form of consent to a particular set of precepts or a particular dispute-resolution mechanism, but rather as membership in a dynamic community, whose contours are constantly subject to contestation.'[35]

This point should not be overstated. Many religious groups are hierarchical, and known to be so. But even for those groups, it is not really clear that individuals have given (implied) consent to all of the group's structures or decisions merely by being members. Indeed, this is true even for ministers and employees; their choice to be employed by the group does not necessarily imply consent to all of its structures and decisions.

---

[33] MA Helfand, 'Religious Institutionalism, Implied Consent, and the Value of Voluntarism' (2015) 88 *Southern California Law Review* 539, 570.

[34] *Watson v Jones* 80 US 679 (1871), 729.

[35] BJ Hill, 'Change, Dissent, and the Problem of Consent in Religious Organizations' in Schwartzman et al (n 10) 426.

Implied consent theory's descriptive inaccuracies do not necessarily undermine the underlying normative claim, however. Even if membership in a religious group is not experienced or viewed by members as a form of consent, this does not mean that consent is not the correct normative concept to apply. There is a parallel here to the way liberal theorists treat conceptions of the good more generally. Within liberal political theory, an individual's conception of the good is seen as chosen by her, and she is viewed as having the capacity to revise or abandon that conception.[36] These claims are in one sense descriptively inaccurate. Many individuals experience their conception of the good as in some sense unchosen, and as a core component of their identity, such that abandoning that conception would fundamentally change who they are. They cannot (easily) stand back from, and reflectively revise, all of their ends in the way imagined within liberal theory. Even if all of this is true, however, it does not undermine the liberal theorist's claim that it is normatively appropriate to treat citizens *as if* their conception of the good is chosen, and to hold that their identity does not depend upon that conception, from the political perspective. This approach can lead to the correct political principles – for example, that changes in an individual's conception of the good do not affect her political rights and duties[37] – even if it is not an accurate reflection of most individuals' lived experience.

Something similar could be true for the implied consent argument in the context of religious group autonomy. Even if group members have not *actually* given consent in any meaningful sense, it might be correct to treat them as if they did, and to use the idea of consent as a guiding normative principle, because this best captures the normative situation.[38] But this can only be the case if there are *other reasons*, which do not depend on consent, to respect group autonomy, and in particular groups' own decision-making procedures, even in the face of internal dissent. Appeal to the normative idea of implied consent must be shorthand for an argument that establishes that this is the right way to view the normative situation. This being the case, however, the normative heavy lifting must be done by that underlying argument, not by implied consent itself.[39] And that means that the notion of implied consent cannot do independent work in response to the problem of internal dissent. We need some other argument for corporate exemptions in the face of internal dissent, before we can use implied consent as a label for this conclusion. But that other argument is exactly what we are searching for.

One might think that one form of consent can do independent work, however. Even if members of a religious group do not consent to all of its beliefs, rules and authority structures by *joining* the group, perhaps they give implied consent by *staying* in the group. This brings us to the third response to the problem of internal dissent: an appeal to exit rights.

---

[36] For example, see Rawls's explanation of the political conception of the person used within his political liberalism. J Rawls, *Political Liberalism*, expanded edn (New York, Columbia University Press, 2005) 29–35.

[37] ibid 30–31.

[38] Rawls makes this kind of argument about the authority of churches over their members. See J Rawls, *Justice as Fairness: A Restatement* (London, Harvard University Press, 2001) 93. For a fuller explication, see Schragger and Schwartzman (n 10) 958–62.

[39] This is explicitly recognised by at least one of the theorists to whom Hill attributes the implied consent argument. Lund writes that implied consent might be a useful label to capture the normative situation, but is not doing the real normative work. 'Implied consent is a fiction used to operationalize the constitutional right of churches to have control over their own decisions' (Lund, 'Free Exercise Reconceived' (2014) 1200). The actual argument for that right must be found elsewhere.

V. Exit Rights

A very common liberal response to dissenters within religious (and other) groups is to hold that they are free to leave the group, and to join or form another group whose beliefs or practices better fit with their own. The freedom to exit is the ultimate guarantee of each individual's freedom of religion and association. They are not forced to be members of a religious group, or to enjoy close association with people they disagree with. Even if the liberal state permits religious groups to govern themselves based on their own doctrines, including practising discrimination and imposing rules on members and employees, it will not allow any group to prevent individuals from leaving. Even the most ardent supporters of a strong form of religious group autonomy endorse this substantive limit upon it, due to its fundamental importance to protecting individual interests.[40]

As Christopher Lund puts this point:

> An important aspect of church autonomy is how every insider has the right to leave, the right to become an outsider. Maybe this is part of the church autonomy principle itself; maybe it describes the limits of church autonomy. But either way, church autonomy implies a constitutional right of exit from religious organizations.[41]

Lund explicitly links a lack of exit, in the presence of exit rights, to a form of consent: 'People can leave or stay. But so long as they choose to stay, they accept how the church handles its religious affairs'.[42] The normatively salient kind of implied consent is given by staying within the group. The ECtHR has also expressed this view: 'in the event of any doctrinal or organisational disagreement between a religious community and one of its members, the individual's freedom of religion is exercised by the option of freely leaving the community'.[43]

Exit rights are certainly an important part of a satisfactory answer to the problem of internal dissent.[44] But even this argument faces an important challenge, which is that it is not clear that freedom of exit is a sufficient protection for dissenting individuals' interests, in the light of the very arguments that justify religious group autonomy in the first place. Those arguments appeal to the great importance of religious institutions to individuals. An individual's interest in pursuing a (religious) conception of the good can rarely be satisfied alone, since much of religion is about corporate activity. Rex Ahdar and Ian Leigh, for example, appeal directly to the importance of the group for the individual to justify group autonomy: 'If an individual's religious life is dependent on the vitality of the group to which the individual belongs then if follows that the religious group must have some independent autonomy of its own'.[45] This thought is echoed by the ECtHR: 'Were the organisational

---

[40] Rosen (n 20) 787–98; Rivers (n 2) 336; R Ahdar and I Leigh, *Religious Freedom in the Liberal State*, 2nd edn (Oxford, Oxford University Press, 2013) 394.

[41] Lund (n 28) 1203.

[42] ibid 1194.

[43] *Fernández Martínez* (n 12) at 128. It is important to note that despite this strong statement, the ECtHR did consider Fernández Martínez's claim in detail, and sought to balance the infringement of his Art 8 rights against the Art 9 rights of the church. For discussion of this case, see Slotte and Årsheim, 'The Ministerial Exception' (2015) 186–93; I Leigh, 'Reversibility, Proportionality, and Conflicting Rights: *Fernández Martínez v Spain*' in S Smet and E Brems (eds), *When Human Rights Clash at the European Court of Human Rights: Conflict or Harmony?* (Oxford, Oxford University Press, 2017).

[44] I return to this point later – see text to n 60.

[45] Ahdar and Leigh, *Religious Freedom* (2013) 376.

life of the community not protected by Article 9 of the Convention, all other aspects of the individual's freedom of religion would become vulnerable'.[46]

Similarly, Rosen's justification for his Religious Institution Principle relies on the fact that parties in the original position would recognise the fundamental importance of religious institutions to many citizens' exercise of religion:

> For many people, the freedom to develop and fully exercise a conception of the good requires that they be able to live in accordance with their religious convictions, which in turn presupposes the existence of certain religious institutions. The political structure chosen under the original position accordingly would be one that afforded such religious institutions special protections.[47]

A notable feature of these arguments is that they rely on the particular importance to individuals of *existing* and well-established institutions. This is true, explicitly or implicitly, in many liberal accounts of religious group autonomy. Most religious individuals exercise their freedom of religion and association through membership in a pre-existing group, and their interests are invested in that particular community.

In the light of this, exiting a religious group into which one has been inducted and socialised comes at a high cost, and this cost is hardly mitigated by the ability to join or establish some new group. Of course, individuals do move between religious groups, and some establish new churches, denominations and other religious organisations. But for most religious individuals, their interests are intertwined with a *particular* existing group, and the value that this group gives is to a significant extent non-fungible.[48] Leaving would be costly to their interests. And this can be true for internal dissenters, just as much as for those who are in complete agreement with their group's doctrines and structures. Further, it might be especially true for ministers, and other employees. Their livelihood depends upon the group, and they are unlikely to be happy simply to find employment in some other denomination, given their likely theological and pastoral commitment to their current denomination.

The very premises concerning the relationship between individuals' interests and religious group autonomy that justify corporate exemptions seem to make the freedom of exit response to internal dissenters insufficient. Exit rights will certainly be a necessary feature of an adequate response, as I discuss below. But they cannot work alone.

VI. Justifying Deference to Religious Groups' Procedures

One response to my arguments thus far would be to conclude that religious groups should only be granted corporate exemptions when they are internally democratic. We have reason to respect such groups' decisions, since their decision-making procedures acknowledge and incorporate the interests of all group members, and the group can be said to have authorised the resulting decisions. When this is not the case, corporate exemptions should not be granted.

---

[46] *Hasan and Chaush* (n 4) at 62; *Fernández Martínez* (n 12) at 127.
[47] Rosen (n 20) 770–71.
[48] Hill, 'Change, Dissent' (2016) 426–27 makes a similar point. I should note, however, that I disagree with some of her claims and with the implications that she draws from the argument.

I think that this would be too restrictive, however. It would certainly be more restrictive than the present policies across Western liberal democracies, and than the positions defended by many theorists. One implication, for example, would be that the Catholic Church would no longer be permitted to have a male-only priesthood. While some theorists have defended this conclusion,[49] I think that the majority are right to hold, in line with current legal practice, that hierarchical religious groups should be eligible for exemptions. The question is whether this can be defended on liberal grounds, despite the presence of internal dissent, or whether one would need to look beyond the limits of liberal political theory in order to justify this position.

The key to providing a liberal justification is to argue that we have good reasons to defer to religious groups' own decision-making procedures on matters of their internal structure and policies, even when this involves decisions being made by a small group of elites within the group, and even when some members strongly disagree with those decisions. In other words, we need an argument that we have good reasons to defer to religious groups' means of reaching judgements, as well as to those judgements themselves. The question is what those reasons could be, if appeal to implied consent and exit rights are insufficient, as I have argued.

While some theorists seem to overlook this issue, and seem to premise their arguments on an unrealistic degree of internal homogeneity within religious groups, or to simply take groups' decisions as given, others have explicitly pointed in the right direction. For example, Rosen claims that his Religious Institution Principle should be interpreted as allowing groups' policies to be set by their leaders. He argues that 'what matters is the perspective of the religion's formal leaders, not its lay members. The principle presupposes the continued existence of necessary religious institutions, and religious institutions can survive only if the formal leaders' understandings of the institution's requirements are determinative'.[50]

This argument is unpersuasive, however. It is not clear why the survival of a religious institution would depend on the current leaders' perspectives being followed. Certainly, the institution would *change* if the leaders' judgements were not determinative. But this does not mean that it would cease to exist. Further, the changes might be in the interests of some group members, and particularly those of internal dissenters. Rosen seemingly fails to consider the perspective of these internal dissenters. Yet parties in the original position would take their interests into account, and it is thus not obvious that a principle chosen in the original position would grant group leaders the level of authority that Rosen suggests.

More promisingly, Laborde argues that religious groups have 'competence interests' that justify a level of judicial deference when it comes to decisions that involve interpreting the group's own standards and commitments.[51] Religious groups' decisions about their structures and policies are based on their theological beliefs and doctrines. The Catholic policy regarding the priesthood, for example, is based on an understanding of the role of the priest as representing Jesus and a doctrine of apostolic succession, both of which rule out female priests. Dissenters to that policy similarly base their opposition on theological arguments. The state is not in a position to adjudicate the merits of the relevant theological claims; it lacks competence. The religious group has an interest in making these judgements based

---

[49] eg Conly, 'Invasive State' (2016) 35–36.
[50] Rosen (n 20) 773. Rosen notes that this holds only if all members enjoy substantive freedom of exit.
[51] Laborde (n 18) 190–96.

on its own standards – an interest in deciding for itself what is required in order for it to pursue its purposes and commitments, and thus to serve its 'coherence interests'. The state, meanwhile, lacks the ability to assess those standards.

Courts have recognised these limits to their competence. The ECtHR has emphasised that states must not determine the legitimacy of religious beliefs or the means used to express them, including decisions regarding structure, employment, and so on.[52] It has thus refrained from taking sides in intra-religious disputes and from judging the substantive merits of the (religious) reasons underlying religious groups' decisions.[53] US courts have gone even further, holding that state interference in religious institutions' decisions about internal governance would amount to an establishment of religion.[54] In the context of the ministerial exception, the Supreme Court's ruling in *Hosanna-Tabor* states that 'According the state the power to determine which individuals will minister to the faithful also violates the Establishment Clause, which prohibits government involvement in such ecclesiastical decisions.'[55]

Once again, there is something importantly right about Laborde's argument. But it is still not clear that it is sufficient to justify deference to the religious institutions' own decision-making procedures in the presence of internal dissent. In particular, a critic could ask why the state should prioritise religious groups' competence interests in the face of complaints by internal dissenters who believe both that the group has got its religious judgements wrong and that they have been unjustly treated or discriminated against. Given the conflict of interest between the group authorities and dissenting individuals, it is not clear that the competence interest of the former are sufficient to justify a prohibition on the state from acting on behalf of the later.

So are further arguments available that explicitly defend group autonomy in the face of internal dissent? I think that there are, and will develop my own account in the next section. This account draws upon several of the arguments we have already encountered but includes crucial further elements that provide a stronger grounding for internally contested corporate exemptions.

VII. Group Autonomy in the Face of Internal Dissent

The key to solving the problem of internal dissent is to recognise that even dissenters can be exercising their religious freedom by being part of the group, and thus their religious freedom, as well as that of other group members, is protected by the state's non-interference. The religious freedom of all individuals, including the dissenters, is dependent on groups

---

[52] *Hasan and Chaush* (n 4) at 78; *Fernández Martínez* (n 12) at 128.

[53] Leigh, 'Balancing Religious Autonomy' (2012) 114–16; Evans and Hood, 'Religious Autonomy and Labour Law' (2012) 94–99.

[54] It is worth noting that there are important differences between the ECtHR and US courts with regard to their level of abstention from examining religious groups' decisions. See Evans and Hood (n 6). These differences are not directly relevant to my argument here, but I explore them in P Billingham, 'The Scope of Religious Group Autonomy: Varieties of Judicial Examination of Church Employment Decisions' (MANCEPT Workshop on Religion in Liberal Politics, University of Manchester, September 2018).

[55] *Hosanna-Tabor* (n 7) p 14. ('Also' because the court had just noted that the Free Exercise Clause would be violated.)

being given a certain level of autonomy. I take it that this is the idea that Ahdar and Leigh, Rosen, and the ECtHR are pointing toward, but it requires further explication if it is to justify their conclusions.

Internal dissenters believe that their religious group's current rules or structures are wrong, and want to see them changed. In the extreme cases that come to court, the dissenter believes that a particular decision made by the group was unjust or wrongfully discriminatory, and should be overturned by the state. In this sense, therefore, they believe that their interests are not adequately taken into account by the group, and that protection for those interests requires changes to the group's decisions or structures.

Nonetheless, respect for religious group autonomy protects the religious freedom even of these individuals, because that respect is what ensures that all individuals can unite around and practice particular religious conceptions. If the law sides with dissenters then this freedom will be liable to be overruled whenever there is internal dissent. Even if the individual's particular interest in (not) being treated in a certain way by the group seems to be ill-served by group autonomy in the specific case at hand, her broader interest in the freedom to form and pursue her own religious conception is protected. Everyone benefits from group autonomy, in this sense, even if some also bear costs.

Up to now I have presented the problem of internal dissent as a conflict of interests, with the group on one side and the dissenter on the other. The arguments for group autonomy that I have considered each try to show that the group's interest is overriding, or that the strength of the dissenter's interest should be given lesser weight – on account of her implied consent or exit rights, for example.[56] My central point in the previous sections was that these arguments do not seem to give adequate weight to the dissenter's interests.

My point here is that we can instead hold that *everyone* has interests on the side of group autonomy, even if dissenters might also have interests on the other side. We are not simply weighing the interests of the group against those of the individual; we are weighing the individual's own interest in religious freedom, along with that of the other members of the group, against her interest in a particular form of treatment in the specific case at hand. It is the fact that the dissenter also has interests on the group autonomy side of the equation that can justify granting that autonomy.

Lund argues that religious group autonomy protects everyone's freedom to practice their own understanding of the faith, because it prevents individuals from using the law to control others' religious choices. 'Dissenters do not get to control their churches through litigation,'[57] because this would involve them imposing their religious views through law. In cases implicating the ministerial exception, for example, the fired minister is in effect claiming a right to force the religious group to accept him as a minister – 'to practice religion with them, no matter what they want'.[58] 'Insiders should not be able to bring suits that impinge on a church's chosen religious beliefs or practices,'[59] because this would allow them to force their version of the faith on others.

The extra emphasis that needs to be added to Lund's argument here is that not allowing dissenters to shape the group via litigation protects the religious freedom even of those

---

[56] Ahdar and Leigh (n 40) 391–94, explicitly present the issue in this way.
[57] Lund (n 28) 1199.
[58] ibid.
[59] ibid 1215.

who are seeking to do the shaping. This is not only a case of protecting the group's religious freedom against the claims of dissenters; it also about protecting the religious freedom of the dissenters themselves. It protects their general interest in not being forced to practice their religion in ways that they reject or with people they do not wish to, and in not having others' understanding of the religion imposed upon them, since today's dissenters might well become tomorrow's defenders of orthodoxy. If dissenters can shape the group through litigation, then today's dissenters are at risk of having tomorrow's dissenters' version of the faith imposed upon them.

A critic might respond by arguing that the dissenters *are already* having others' understanding of the religion imposed upon them; in the particular case at hand, the group is enforcing a view that they reject. And this is true in a sense. But not in the same sense that would be involved in the state enforcing a particular understanding through law. The dissenter is forced by the group's internal decision-making procedures, along with their membership in the group. But this is different in kind to being forced through legal sanctions. The latter leaves the group with no choice but to comply with the view of the dissenter, since the state can enforce that view through financial and other penalties. Whereas the dissenter does continue to have other options, including both exercising her voice to seek to bring about change through the group's decision-making structures, and leaving the group.

This last comment brings us back to exit rights. I argued above that appeal to exit rights was not sufficient to justify legal deference to the group's internal decision-making. But the dissenter's freedom to leave the group and form or join a different one is still crucial, since it is the ultimate guarantee of their freedom from being forced to practice religion with people they do not want to. In order to be such a guarantee, exit rights must be substantive, or meaningful, and not merely formal.[60] As well as formal legal protections from being coercively constrained to remain in the group, adequate knowledge of other groups must be available, and individuals must have sufficient education and opportunities (including employment opportunities) to leave the group without facing great material loss.[61] If an employee of a religious organisation had no job prospects outside of the group then this would severely weaken the group's autonomy claims, and in some cases might even justify forcing the group to keep the employee against its wishes. More generally, ensuring substantive exit rights might at times involve a certain level of interference with religious groups, since it imposes informational and educational requirements that some might consider objectionable. This level of interference is necessary in order to guarantee the religious freedom of all, however.

Even substantive exit rights do not mean that leaving a religious group is easy. Indeed, it might still carry a great psychological cost, as I have already noted. Nonetheless, such rights are sufficient to ensure that dissenters are not forced to remain members of religious groups in the way that state intervention would force groups to change their policies. Further, as Jeff Spinner-Halev comments, 'liberalism does not ... have to make leaving one's community psychologically easy ... People in liberal societies are often confronted with all kinds of

---

[60] All defenders of religious group autonomy acknowledge this point, eg Rosen (n 20) 788–89; Ahdar and Leigh (n 40) 394. But there is scope for disagreement about exactly what it requires. My comments here are necessarily brief, leaving many questions of specifics unanswered.

[61] J Spinner-Halev, 'Liberalism and Religion: Against Congruence' (2008) 9 *Theoretical Inquiries in Law* 553, 568–71.

tragic choices, to which liberal theory has few answers'.[62] The requirement of liberalism is to ensure that everyone's freedom of religion is protected, and while this requires substantive exit rights, it does not require removing all psychological costs. This does not mean that those costs are irrelevant or can simply be ignored. As I argued above, they show that an appeal to exit rights cannot carry the full justificatory burden in an argument for religious group autonomy. Instead, my argument here is that the balance of interests involved in granting religious group autonomy, constrained by substantive exit rights, is justified overall, in the light of the fact that group autonomy protects the religious freedom of all individuals, including dissenters themselves.

We should also note here that many thousands of individuals in liberal democracies have left religious groups, joined alternative groups, and indeed started new groups and denominations. Exercising the option of exit is rarely easy or costless, but it is still something that many have done. Liberal democracies have proven to be fertile ground for a great diversity of religious groups, organisations and denominations to emerge. As well as the option of leaving the group, dissenters can also seek to change the group from within. Indeed, adequate protection for the interests of dissenters requires that religious groups have internal mechanisms through which individuals can express dissent and seek to convince others of their diverging views. Groups with no tolerance for dissenters thus have weaker autonomy claims. This does not mean that groups must be non-hierarchical or democratic, however. Even hierarchical groups almost always contain avenues for discussion and reform. Dissenters often exercise their religious freedom by acquiescing to policies that they object to, while at the same time campaigning for their reform, through both formal and informal channels.

Indeed, the fluid and dynamic nature of religious communities that Hill appeals to in her objections to implied consent as a grounding for religious group autonomy can actually provide further support for such autonomy. Hill argues that the pervasiveness of change and contestation within religious groups means that it is not always easy to identify with certainty their doctrinal beliefs or authority structures. It even 'may not always be possible to determine who is a dissenter and who represents the church itself'.[63] I think Hill somewhat exaggerates her point here. Nonetheless, her basic thought actually *supports* group autonomy by highlighting the fact that there is space for internal conflict and change within most religious groups. Hill claims that her arguments undermine religious group autonomy, because it is hard to appeal to the church's right 'to keep its beliefs pure against the influence of dissenters'[64] when it is difficult to say precisely who is 'the church'. But group autonomy was never about 'purity', or about protecting or reifying any particular policies or structures. It is about allowing disputes to be settled by the group itself, by whatever processes members collectively come to recognise as valid, free from state interference. The fluidity of groups' doctrines and structures actually bolsters the claim that all members, including dissenters (whether we can identify them or not), can have the exercise of their religious liberty protected by group autonomy. It thus supports the view, expressed by both the ECtHR and US Supreme Court, that states should not act as arbiters within internal disputes.

Hill's argument also points us back to Laborde's notion of 'competence interests'. Religious groups have an interest in working through the complexities that Hill highlights

---

[62] ibid 571–72.
[63] Hill (n 35) 431.
[64] ibid.

to form their policies and judgements based on their own understandings and processes, and the state lacks the competence to pass judgement on the results. Again, the religious freedom of all individuals, including internal dissenters, is protected by the state respecting religious groups' distinctive competence.

VIII. Internal Dissenters or Liberal Congruence?

Up to now I have assumed that the liberal concern is for 'internal dissenters' – individuals within religious groups who disagree with their policies or structures. The reply to this concern is that even internal dissenters can be exercising their religious freedom by being part of the group, and if the law regularly sides with the individual then it means there is no way to protect collective freedom to unite around religious conceptions, since this freedom will be overruled whenever there is internal dissent.

But perhaps the assumption that the concern is with *all* internal dissenters is mistaken. After all, internal dissenters are just as likely to be conservative as progressive. They can be individuals who believe that the group has strayed from traditional doctrine, and want to reassert old orthodoxies. For example, Reverend Paul Williamson brought a series of lawsuits in an attempt to prevent the ordination of women by the Church of England – including appealing to the ECtHR, claiming that his Article 9 right to freedom of religion had been violated.[65] According to Williamson, the ordination of women fundamentally changed the nature of the Church of England without his consent, required him to accept a policy that violates his religious conscience, and left him faced with constructive dismissal for not agreeing with the measure.

Liberals, or at least liberal egalitarians, are unlikely to have much sympathy for dissenters like Williamson. They would presumably deny that he has legitimate interests at stake in preventing female ordination, and hold that he is owed no compensation if he resigns from his post in protest. Perhaps this suggests that the liberal concern is not in fact for internal dissenters per se, but only for those individuals whose interests are set back by decisions that are incongruent with certain substantive liberal values, such as equality and non-discrimination. This would include women in the Catholic Church and those who are denied membership or employment within a religious group on discriminatory grounds. These individuals have their interests substantively neglected in a way that Williamson does not. Perhaps, therefore, the state should intervene on behalf of those individuals, and not grant corporate exemptions in those cases.

This kind of approach seems to be suggested by Jonathan Seglow, who argues that exemptions for religious groups might be permissible only if those in control of an association find their beliefs significantly burdened by a law, ordinary members of the group have in some sense consented to their control, *and* the proposed exemption will not set back the interests of ordinary members.[66] Seglow notes that this will not justify exemptions permitting discriminatory practices, since these will not be in members' interests. In other words, within Seglow's account, an independent judgement of what is in individuals' interests is

[65] *Williamson v UK* App no 27008/95 (ECtHR, 17 May 1995). His claim was dismissed as inadmissible.
[66] Seglow, 'Religious Sovereignty' (2015) 238.

what determines whether exemptions can be granted, rather than a concern with internal dissenters per se.

The upshot of this, however, is that the argument no longer concerns internal dissenters at all. Male-only priesthood would be ruled out even if no members of the group objected to it. The argument instead is simply about enforcing liberal egalitarian values upon religious groups who believe that they have religious or moral reasons to deviate from those values within their associational life. In effect, this approach holds that it is impermissible for individuals to form groups on the basis of non-liberal beliefs or practices. In other words, it endorses the 'logic of congruence',[67] according to which all civil society groups must be structured in accordance with the same values and principles that inform the liberal democratic state. Some advocates of religious group autonomy have expressed concern that the law might be heading in this direction.[68]

I do not have space to consider this view in detail. The key point for our purposes is that this argument is distinct from the internal dissenters objection, so cannot function as a direct reply to my argument for religious group autonomy in the face of internal dissent. Instead, it shifts the ground to a different debate. Further, many theorists have argued against the logic of congruence, arguing that individuals should be free to form groups whose internal rules and procedures do not replicate the principles that ought to govern the liberal democratic state.[69] While I cannot offer a full defence of this claim, I think that the arguments in favour of religious group autonomy and corporate exemptions apply even when the group's beliefs and practices run counter to liberal egalitarian ideals. Religious groups have rights to structure their affairs – including their decisions on membership and leadership – on the basis of their own beliefs and doctrines, even when this means discriminating in ways that would be impermissible for the state. These rights are grounded in the interests of individuals in freedom of religion and association – including the interests of those who are discriminated against by a particular group.

Indeed, if this argument for religious group autonomy is correct, then it suggests that groups' freedom to select their own members and leaders according to their own principles and procedures perhaps should not be seen as an exemption, but as itself being the rule. In the UK context, Rivers argues that the values at stake should be conceived not as an 'exception to a higher principle of non-discrimination', but as a question of whether there should be exceptions to the 'right of collective religious liberty'.[70] Lund makes a similar point in the US context, noting that the Supreme Court opinion in *Hosanna-Tabor* does not really conceive of the ministerial exception as an exemption: 'The Court does not ask whether churches should be exempt from employment discrimination laws. Instead, the Court asks whether churches have the right to choose their leaders. This is more than a

---

[67] This term comes from Nancy Rosenblum. For a recent articulation, see NL Rosenblum, 'Faith in America: Political Theory's Logic of Autonomy and Logic of Congruence' in A Wolfe and I Katznelson (eds), *Religion and Democracy in the United States: Danger or Opportunity?* (Princeton, Princeton University Press, 2010).

[68] eg Rivers (n 2) 146, 321, 333–34.

[69] For recent critique, see JT Levy, *Rationalism, Pluralism, and Freedom* (Oxford, Oxford University Press, 2015) 51–55; Ahdar and Leigh (n 40) 389–91. See also my 'Shaping Religion: The Limits of Transformative Liberalism' in J Seglow and A Shorten (eds), *Religion and Political Theory: Secularism, Freedom and the New Challenges of Religious Diversity* (Rowman & Littlefield International / ECPR Press, forthcoming 2019).

[70] Rivers (n 2) 136.

clever rhetorical flourish – it is a change in baseline'.[71] This is not to say that churches have complete jurisdictional authority, or enjoy a kind of 'sphere sovereignty' that prevents any kind of government regulation. The kind of religious group autonomy that I have discussed, and defended, falls short of 'sphere sovereignty'.[72] There are clear cases where a concern for the interests of individuals will mean penalising groups – such as when group members or leaders have been subject to sexual harassment or physical abuse,[73] or when groups have not adequately protected exit rights. My argument for religious group autonomy depends on balancing the interests of individuals, and this balancing leads to a robust but not absolute form of autonomy.

The precise kinds of government examination of, and intervention in, groups' decisions that are deemed (un)acceptable will depend on further details of the argument and of specific cases. I lack space to explore these detailed implications here, but believe that my account would justify many of the protections of religious group autonomy afforded in today's liberal democracies. I hope to have shown that such autonomy can be justified within liberal theory even in the face of internal dissent, through an appreciation of the way in which it protects the interests of all individuals, including dissenters themselves.

---

[71] Lund (n 28) 1192.

[72] See n 10 above. Many of the other theorists I have discussed, including Rosen, Rivers and Laborde, also explicitly distinguish their views from the 'sphere sovereignty' account.

[73] For discussion of such cases, see Lund (n 28) 1217–20; Laycock, 'Church Autonomy Revisited' (2009) 268–78.

How Should Courts Adjudicate Conscientious Exemptions?

5

Conscience in the Image of Religion

RICHARD MOON

I. Introduction

The term 'conscience' is used in two different ways in discussions about religious freedom. Sometimes it refers to a particular kind of accommodation claim. In *conscientious* objection cases (conscience claims), an individual asks to be exempted not from a law that *restricts* their religious (or other) practice, but instead from a law that *requires* them to perform an act that they regard as immoral (on religious or other grounds). In many of these cases the claimant asks to be excused from performing an act that is not itself immoral but that supports or facilitates (what they see as) the immoral action of others, and so makes them complicit in this immorality.[1]

More often, though, the term 'conscience' is contrasted with religion. Freedom of conscience, in contrast to freedom of religion, is concerned with the protection of fundamental beliefs or commitments that are not part of a religious or spiritual system. In this chapter, I will focus on the second use of the term and consider whether non-religious beliefs/practices should be given the same protection as religious beliefs/practices.[2] I will argue that while there may be a mix of practical and principled reasons for sometimes protecting religious practices from state restriction, these reasons do not apply clearly or directly to non-religious practices. Indeed, the protection of these practices may rest on nothing more than their formal resemblance to familiar religious practices and the understandable, but perhaps mistaken, assumption that if a particular religious practice is accommodated then so too should be the non-religious version of that practice.

---

[1] I have elsewhere argued that the significant issue in these conscientious objection cases is whether the religiously based objection should be viewed as a personal or communal spiritual practice that should be accommodated if this can be done without any noticeable harm to others. Or instead whether it should be viewed as political – as a position on the rights and interests of others in the community, or on the rightness of the law, that should be subject to the give-and-take of ordinary political decision-making. In many recent cases (such as those involving the refusal to provide goods and services for same-sex wedding receptions) the individuals seeking exemption from anti-discrimination laws have sought to convert a religious value or belief that was treated as a political position (opposition to the legal recognition of same-sex marriages), something that might influence public policy (but was rejected by policy-makers), into a private or personal religious practice/belief (a matter of personal religious conscience) that should be protected from politics. For a discussion see R Moon, 'Conscientious Objection in Canada: Pragmatic Accommodation and Principled Adjudication' (2018) 7 *Oxford Journal of Law and Religion* 274.

[2] In the remainder of this chapter, I will refer to either a practice or a belief and will avoid my preferred term, a 'belief/practice', which suggests both the idea of personal commitment (internal) and public manifestation (external).

If religious freedom is understood as a liberty that prohibits the state from coercing individuals in religious matters, then it is easily extended to non-religious practices. The state ought not to interfere with an individual's practices, religious or otherwise, unless this is necessary to protect the rights and interests of others or the general welfare. However, freedom of religion as a liberty has a broad scope but little weight. It precludes the state from compelling a religious practice and from restricting such a practice on the grounds that the practice is erroneous – the wrong way to worship God. It does not require the state to compromise its policies in order to accommodate the individual's religious practices. The state must have a public reason to restrict a religious practice, but any public reason may be sufficient. This was John Locke's position[3] and also the position taken by the US Supreme Court in the case of *Oregon v Smith*.[4] The Court in that case held that the 'free exercise clause' of the First Amendment did not require the state to exempt individuals engaged in a religious practice from an otherwise valid law. Justice Scalia thought that to exempt religious adherents from the ordinary law would be 'to make the professed doctrines of religious belief superior to the law of the land, and in effect to permit every citizen to become a law unto himself'.[5]

However, if religious freedom requires not just that the state refrain from compelling or restricting religious practices without public justification (individual liberty in religious matters), but also that the state remain neutral in religious matters, then it is less obvious that equivalent protection should be extended to the individual's non-religious practices. The requirement that the state remain neutral in religious matters precludes the state from supporting or preferring the practices of one religious system over another (or religious belief over atheism or vice versa) and from restricting religious practices unless there is good reason to do so (or put more positively, the state has a duty to make some accommodation for religious practices).[6]

The most common justification for the neutrality requirement, and more particularly the state's duty to accommodate religious practices, is that it serves to protect the individual's deeply held commitments or their decisional autonomy in important or fundamental matters.[7] But why should an individual's deeply held religious practices be insulated or excluded from politics? To bracket religion off from politics in this way is to treat it as a matter of (cultural) identity (similar to gender or race) rather than individual judgement.[8] The neutrality requirement is a form of equality right that rests on a recognition of the deep connection between the individual and his or her religious or cultural group and

[3] John Locke, *A Letter Concerning Toleration* (1685; repr New York: Irvington Publishers, 1979) 197 ff.

[4] *Oregon v Smith*, 494 US 872 (1990).

[5] *Reynolds v United States*, 98 US 145 at 167 (1879) quoted by Scalia J in *Oregon v Smith* (ibid) at 879. The US Congress responded to the *Oregon v Smith* decision, and its narrow reading of the free exercise clause, by enacting the *Religious Freedom Restoration Act of 1993*, which provides that the US government 'shall not substantially burden a person's exercise of religion, even if the burden results from a rule of general applicability,' unless 'it demonstrates that application of the burden to the person (1) is in furtherance of a compelling governmental interest; and (2) is the least restrictive means of furthering that compelling governmental interest': Pub L No 103–141, 107 Stat 1488, s 3(a) & (b) (1993). A number of US states have enacted similar laws.

[6] See R Moon, *Freedom of Conscience and Religion* (Toronto, Irwin Law, 2014).

[7] In Canada see *Syndicat Northcrest v Amselem*, 2004 SCC 47.

[8] I am not in this chapter advocating a particular approach to freedom of religion, but am simply arguing that the courts' approach to the freedom – specifically the requirement that the state remain neutral in matters of religion – rests on a particular conception of religion and requires a rethinking of the freedom's justification.

on a concern about the standing of such groups and their members in the larger society. The practices of a religious group are treated as part of the cultural identity of the group's members (described as deeply held or rooted) and excluded and insulated from politics, because experience has taught us that the restriction of these practices may contribute to the marginalisation of the group and the exclusion and alienation of its members from the larger society.

It is not obvious, though, that the regulation of 'deeply held' non-religious views raises similar equality concerns – about the status of identity groups within the larger community.

II. Freedom of Conscience and Religion

A. Freedom of Conscience

The term 'freedom of conscience' was once used interchangeably with 'freedom of religion' to refer to the individual's freedom to hold beliefs that were spiritual or moral in character. At this earlier time the moral beliefs of most individuals were rooted in a religious system. Freedom of conscience, though, is now viewed as an alternative to, or extension of, religious freedom. While freedom of religion protects fundamental religious practices, freedom of conscience extends protection to fundamental practices that are not part of a religious system – to deeply held secular practices. Together, then, freedom of conscience and freedom of religion protect the individual's most fundamental moral beliefs or commitments.

The problem of distinguishing religious practices from non-religious practices, which has bedevilled the US courts, was something that Canadian courts and commentators thought section 2(a) of the Charter of Rights had avoided by creating a single 'integrated' right to freedom of conscience and religion.[9] If freedom of conscience and religion protects all deeply held commitments or beliefs about right and truth, then the courts do not need to embark upon the difficult task of determining when a belief/practice is religious rather than 'secular'. Yet, despite the courts' formal definition of the scope of freedom of conscience and religion as encompassing both religious and non-religious beliefs and practices, religious beliefs and practices have been at the centre of the section 2(a) Charter jurisprudence. In their section 2(a) decisions, the courts seem to regard religious practices as special or as different from other, non-religious, practices. The test set out by the Supreme Court of Canada for determining whether a practice falls within the scope of section 2(a) asks whether the individual (sincerely) believes that the practice connects him or her to the divine. The test seems to be concerned exclusively with religious practices.[10] The courts' focus on religious practices has arisen in tandem with its adoption of a neutrality requirement – that precludes the state from either supporting particular (religious) practices or restricting such practices without significant reasons.

---

[9] Canadian Charter of Rights and Freedoms, Part 1 of the Constitution Act, 1982, being Schedule B to the Canada Act 1982 (UK), 1982, c 11 [Charter]. See *R v Big M Drug Mart* [1985] 1 SCR 295.

[10] In *Amselem,* (n 7) at para 46, the Supreme Court of Canada defined the scope of s 2(a) exclusively in religious terms: '[F]reedom of religion consists of the freedom to undertake practices and harbour beliefs, having a nexus with religion, in which an individual demonstrates he or she sincerely believes or is sincerely undertaking in order

While the Supreme Court of Canada in its earliest section 2(a) decisions said that free-dom of conscience and religion might be breached when the state restricts a deeply held non-religious practice, it is difficult to find cases in which section 2(a) has been success-fully used to protect such practices. The Canadian courts have only once required the state to accommodate a non-religious practice, and the circumstances of that case were exceptional.[11] In that case, a prison had refused to provide vegetarian meals to an inmate, who objected to eating meat on non-religious moral grounds, even though the prison was already providing vegetarian meals to inmates who did not eat meat for religious reasons. It is also worth noting that while the Canadian courts have said that the state must not support particular religious practices, such as the Lord's Prayer, they have not suggested that the state is similarly precluded from supporting (or compelling) non-religious prac-tices. In other words, while freedom of conscience may (in theory) protect the individual's freedom *to* conscience (freedom from interference with her fundamental practices), it does not protect his or her freedom *from* conscience (from the imposition of the deeply held non-religious practices of others).[12]

B. Religious Freedom: Liberty and Equality

The Canadian courts initially described section 2(a) of the Charter of Rights, freedom of conscience and religion, as the liberty to hold, and live in accordance with, spiritual or other fundamental beliefs without state interference.[13] Freedom of religion, understood as a liberty, precludes the state from compelling an individual to engage in a religious practice and from restricting their religious practice without a legitimate public reason. In later judg-ments, however, there has been a shift, in the courts' description of the interest protected by the freedom.[14] According to the courts, the freedom does not simply prohibit state

to connect with the divine or as a function of his or her spiritual faith, irrespective of whether a particular prac-tice or belief is required by official religious dogma or is in conformity with the position of religious officials.' At para 39, the Court offered a tentative definition of religion: 'While it is perhaps not possible to define religion precisely, some outer definition is useful since only beliefs, convictions and practices rooted in religion, as opposed to those that are secular, socially based or conscientiously held, are protected by the guarantee of freedom of religion. Defined broadly, religion typically involves a particular and comprehensive system of faith and worship. Religion also tends to involve the belief in a divine, superhuman or controlling power. In essence, religion is about freely and deeply held personal convictions or beliefs connected to an individual's spiritual faith and integrally linked to one's self-definition and spiritual fulfilment, the practices of which allow individuals to foster a connec-tion with the divine or with the subject or object of that spiritual faith.'

[11] *Maurice v Canada (Attorney General)* [2002] FCT 69.

[12] The leading case in which the courts held that the state could not support a particular religious practice is *Mouvement laique québécois v Saguenay (City)*, 2015 SCC 16 (a Christian prayer). The court also said that the state should not support or advocate atheism – the denial of the existence of God – or explicitly reject any or all forms of religious faith. Perhaps the ban on state support for religious belief/practice could sometimes be understood as protecting freedom of conscience. The complainants in many of the contemporary cases in which state support for religion has been challenged have been agnostics or atheists. Their complaint in these cases has not been that the state is supporting one religion over another, the religion of the majority over that of the minority, but rather that it is supporting religious belief/practice generally and sending a message of exclusion to citizens who are not religious, or imposing religion on them, or treating them unequally. Once again, though, the state is not precluded under s 2(a) from relying on non-religious practices when making law.

[13] *Big M Drug Mart* (n 9).

[14] R Moon, 'Liberty, Neutrality and Inclusion: Freedom of Religion under the Canadian Charter of Rights' (2003) 41 *Brandeis Law Review* 563.

coercion in matters of religion; it requires also that the state remain neutral in religious matters – that it treat religious traditions or communities in an equal or even-handed manner. The state must not support or prefer the religious practices of one group over those of another or religion over atheism and vice versa (religious contest should be excluded from politics) and it must not restrict the practices of a religious group, unless this is necessary to protect an important public interest (religion should be insulated from politics).[15] The requirement of state neutrality was explicitly affirmed in the unanimous judgment of the Supreme Court of Canada in *Mouvement Laique v Saguenay*: '[A] duty of religious neutrality on the state ... results from an evolving interpretation of freedom of conscience and religion.'[16] Freedom of religion, on this account, is a form of equality right – a right to equal treatment or equal respect by the state without discrimination based on religious belief/practice or association.

This separation of religion and politics (the requirement of state neutrality) rests on a conception of religion as a cultural identity. Religion orients the individual in the world, shapes their perception of the social and natural orders, and provides a moral framework for their actions. It ties the individual to a community of believers and is often the central or defining association in their life. The individual believer participates in a shared system of practices and values that may in some cases be described as 'a way of life'. If religious adherence or membership is central to the individual's sense of self and place in the world, then a judgment by the state that the practices of his or her group are less important or less true than those of another may be experienced by the individual (in the same way that they might experience disadvantage based on race or gender) as a denial of his or her equal worth and not simply as a rejection of their views and values. The centrality of religion in the life of the adherent also means that the social and economic exclusion or marginalisation of their religious group may negatively affect their sense of self and place in the community. Or, more positively, because it is a source of value and meaning for its members, it is important that space be preserved for a religious community and its practices or way of life.

The Canadian courts, though, have not required the state to remain neutral towards all elements of a religious belief system and have accepted that some beliefs may play a role in political decision-making or may be subject to legal regulation without any claim to accommodation. The problem is not, or not simply, that religious beliefs involve claims about what is true and right, which may be viewed as a matter of personal judgement or commitment (rather than cultural identity) and open to contest in the public sphere. The more fundamental difficulty with the requirement of state neutrality is that religious beliefs sometimes have public implications.[17] Religious belief systems sometimes say something about the way we should treat others and the kind of society we should work to create. Religious beliefs about civic issues such as homelessness, same-sex marriage and reproductive rights can neither be excluded nor insulated from political decision-making. On these issues, the state is not, and cannot be, neutral.[18] The courts then have applied the neutrality requirement

---

[15] Moon, Freedom of Conscience and Religion (n 6).

[16] *Saguenay* (n 12) at 71.

[17] R Moon, 'Freedom of Religion in the Canadian Court: The Limits of State Neutrality' (2012) 45 *UBC Law Journal* 497.

[18] The Supreme Court of Canada in *Chamberlain v Surrey District School No 36*, 2002 SCC 86 said that political decision-makers cannot be expected to leave their values at the door-step of the legislature.

selectively, sometimes treating religion as a cultural identity toward which the state should remain neutral (that should be insulated and excluded from political decision-making) and other times (when it addresses civic matters) as a contestable political or moral judgement by the individual that should be subject to the give-and-take of politics.

Behind the courts' uneven application of the neutrality requirement lies a complex conception of religious commitment in which religion is viewed as both a cultural identity and as an individual judgement or commitment to certain claims about truth and right. The courts have struggled to fit this complex conception of religious commitment into a constitutional framework that that relies on a distinction between personal choices or commitments that should be protected as a matter of individual liberty, and shared attributes or cultural practices that should sometimes be respected as a matter of equality. The constitutional framework, and perhaps more deeply our conception of rights and agency, imposes this distinction between judgement and identity on the complex experience of religious commitment.

How the courts view a particular belief/practice, as a spiritual practice or as a political belief or position, will depend on whether they see it as otherworldly in its orientation or instead as addressing civic concerns – the public interest. Where the line between the civic/public and spiritual/private elements of a religious belief system (between 'value' and 'practice') is drawn by the courts will reflect their views about the nature of human welfare and the proper scope of political action. The familiar claim that a religious belief/practice may play a role in political decision-making, (only) when there is a parallel secular argument (when the same or a similar position can be stated in non-religious terms), points to this distinction between spiritual and civic. When a religiously grounded value (such as support for the eradication of poverty or a ban on public nudity) has a secular analogue, it will be seen (by non-adherents) as addressing a public or civic concern – as intended to advance the public interest or prevent harm to others. When there is no parallel secular argument, those outside the religious group are bound to see the religiously grounded value as concerned simply with the spiritual (the honouring or worshiping of the divine). State action based on such a value will be seen as advancing or compelling a religious belief/practice.[19] In other words, a religiously motivated action will be viewed as a religious practice, if non-adherents cannot understand it as addressing human welfare.

The protection of religious freedom then requires the courts to draw a line between the spheres of spiritual and civic life, even if that line is contestable and often seems porous or adjustable. Religious freedom, as a constitutional right in a democratic political system, must be limited in what it protects to matters that can be viewed as private and outside the scope of politics – as personal to the members of the religious group or internal to the group.[20]

---

[19] Moon (n 6) 62.

[20] Sometimes the accommodation claim is made not by an individual, who is seeking exemption for a specific practice, but instead by a religious organisation or institution, which is seeking a degree of autonomy in the governance of its affairs – in the operation of its internal decision-making processes. In these institutional autonomy cases, the court must determine (1) whether the exemption from state law will impact the rights and interests of others (whether the group's application of its norms will negatively affect outsiders to the group) but also (2) whether the members of the group should be protected by state law from internal rules that are unfair and contrary to public policy. The courts have generally treated religious organisations as voluntary associations

III.　Religious Accommodation

When a religious belief directly addresses a civic issue, or is directly at odds with public policy, it will be viewed as a political judgement by the individual or group that falls within the sphere of civic action (the give-and-take of ordinary political decision-making), and outside the protection of section 2(a) of the Charter. If, as a democratic community, we have decided, for example, that gender discrimination or discrimination on grounds of sexual orientation are wrong and should be prohibited in the provision of market and government services, why should an exemption to these bans be made for an individual or group that holds a different view on religious grounds?[21] And, of course, why should those whom the law is intended to protect be denied that protection (eg from employment discrimination or from discrimination in access to civil marriage services) simply because someone believes that their religion requires them to act in a way that society has judged to be wrongful or harmful? An individual may be free to live their personal life in a way that does not respect the equality of the sexes or sexual orientation equality. Similarly, a religious group or organisation, such as the Roman Catholic Church, may be free to discriminate against women or gays and lesbians in its internal affairs.[22] However, an employer who believes, based on scripture, that women should not work outside the home, should not be exempted from the ban on gender discrimination in employment. And a civil marriage commissioner who believes that homosexuality is sinful and that the law should not recognise same-sex relationships ought not to be exempted from his or her obligation to perform civil marriage ceremonies for same-sex couples.

Religious practices that do not directly address civic issues may sometimes be impacted by state action that is intended to advance the public interest. When state law incidentally

---

(of individuals pursuing common ends) that should be free to operate as they choose. However, the state may sometimes decide to intervene in the affairs of a religious community characterised by hierarchy and insularity when the prevailing practices in that community are thought to be harmful to some of its members, even though the members have, in a least a formal sense, chosen to participate in those practices. The deep communal connections that are part of the value of religious life and commitment (a source of meaning and value for adherents) may also be the source of what the courts regard as harm – the lack of meaningful choice or opportunity open to the members of such communities or the oppression of vulnerable group members. In Canada see *Bruker v Marcovitz*, 2007 SCC 54.

[21] But, even in cases involving religious beliefs about gender (and in particular about interaction with members of the opposite sex), it may not always clear whether the religious belief/practice should be viewed as a political position or a spiritual practice. A much-publicised and highly controversial accommodation dispute arose a few years ago at York University in Toronto. A male student, doing an online course, informed the instructor that for religious reasons he could not participate in a required group project that involved meeting and interacting with female students. How one responded to the student's claim seemed to depend on whether one saw his refusal to meet with women students as simply a spiritual practice – like praying at certain times or refusing to eat pork – or instead as a position about gender equality – that women are a source of temptation or that women should not participate in university programmes. Those who saw it as a spiritual practice thought it should be accommodated, since accommodation would have no significant impact on others. Those who saw it as a moral/political position thought that no accommodation should be granted, even though accommodation would have only a minor or indirect impact on others in the course. For a discussion of the case see R Moon, 'Religious Accommodation and Its Limits: The York University Case' (2014) 23 *Constitutional Forum* 1.

[22] For example, s 18 of the Ontario *Human Rights Code* RSO 1990, Chapter H19 grants a form of exemption to 'a religious … institution or organization that is primarily engaged in serving the interests' of its members. If a religious association seeks only to regulate the affairs of its members then it will ordinarily be free to operate in accordance with its own spiritual rules or norms. But if the group's actions directly impact outsiders, then these actions will be subject to ordinary law (often anti-discrimination law).

restricts such a practice, the Canadian courts have said that the state has a duty to accommodate the practice, if this can be done without significant cost to public policy. The conflict between religion and law may be described as indirect (or incidental) when the religious practice conflicts not with the law's public purpose but rather with the way the law advances that purpose – with the means rather than the ends of the law.

For example, an individual, who is employed by the government, may seek an exemption from a job requirement that is inconsistent with her or his religious practice. A Sikh man who wears a turban or a Muslim woman who wears a hijab may seek an exemption from a police or military uniform requirement. A student or teacher may seek an exemption from the school board's term schedule if their religious practices require them to be absent at certain times during the term. The Canadian courts have held that reasonable exceptions should be made to uniform requirements or dress codes for individuals whose religious clothing is inconsistent with the code or uniform and that school boards should make reasonable accommodations for students and teachers whose religious holidays conflict with the schedule.[23] In such cases, the requested exemption is from a rule or standard that is based on, or takes account of, dominant cultural practices, including practices that are religious or, at least, have a religious origin.

There is no conflict in these cases between different understandings of public morality (concerning the rights and interests of community members) and so accommodation can generally occur without any significant impact on state policy or on the interests of others. The practice can be treated as personal to the individual, as a spiritual rather than a civic matter. But even in the case of an indirect conflict between law and religious practice, the accommodation of the practice – the adjustment of the law's means to avoid or limit interference – will often detract to some extent from the law's ability to advance a particular policy. The issue for the court, in such cases, is whether the state can pursue its objective as, or almost as, effectively in another way that does not interfere to the same extent with the religious practice.[24]

The Canadian courts, unlike their European counterparts, have generally treated religious practices related to dress and diet as personal to the individual or internal to the spiritual community (as spiritual practices towards which the state should be neutral) and outside the scope of political judgement or direct legal regulation. However, this distinction between a civil servant's personal religious expression and the performance of her public role or duty was erased in the ill-fated Quebec Charter of Values, which treated the wearing of religious dress or symbols, such as a hijab or turban, by a civil servant, as a political act – even a state act – that was incompatible with the requirement that the state remain neutral in matters of religion.[25]

---

[23] In *Commission scolaire régionale de Chambly v Bergevin*, [1994] 2 SCR 525, the Supreme Court of Canada held that a public school board must accommodate Jewish teachers by providing them with paid leave for Yom Kippur. The court noted that the holidays of the majority of teachers were already incorporated into the school calendar. See also *Multani v Commission scolaire Marguerite-Bourgeoys* (2006) 1 SCR 256.

[24] This is sometimes described as the 'minimal impairment' requirement for limits on rights and freedoms. See *R v Oakes* [1986] 1 SCR 103.

[25] For a discussion of the Quebec Charter of Values see J Maclure, 'The Meaning and Entailment of the Religious Neutrality of the State: The Case of Public Employees' in BL Berger and R Moon (eds), *Religion and the Exercise of Public Authority* (Oxford, Hart/Bloomsbury, 2016) and Moon (n 6) at 118–24. The wearing of a niqab is sometimes

Religious accommodation (creating an exception to the legal requirement) may rest on a variety of concerns. Charles Taylor and Jocelyn Maclure argue that accommodation may be necessary to prevent the 'moral harm' that occurs when individuals are required to act in a way that is inconsistent with their deepest moral convictions or commitments, both religious and non-religious.[26] It is not obvious, though, why 'deeply rooted' or 'deeply held' practices should be insulated from political action. In a democracy, the strongly or deeply-held views of citizens on civic issues shape public policy – with the consequence that the views of some citizens prevail over those of others. In any event, most of the accommodation claims that come before the courts involve (religious) rituals or practices (forms of collective worship or markers of cultural identity or group membership) rather than moral convictions. These practices may not even be binding on the individual and so are not easily described as 'deeply held', at least not in the way this term is ordinarily used.

The requirement that the state remain neutral in religious matters, means treating religious practices as aspects of the adherent's identity (as the equivalent of traits or characteristics rather than civic judgements or choices) that are bracketed off from politics – excluded and insulated from political decision-making. To understand the depth or significance of (religious) belief/practice to the individual, and to justify its exclusion and insulation from politics, we need to see it as collective or cultural in character. If the individual's religious beliefs or moral commitments are 'deeply held' or 'rooted', it is because they are part of (and grew out of) a shared religious tradition or group culture to which his or her identity (their world view and sense of place in the world) is tied.[27]

I am inclined to think that the justification for accommodation (and the treatment of religious practices as a matter of cultural identity) rests on a practical concern about the status of religious groups, and not on the principled protection of the liberty or integrity of individual conscience. Accommodation should be made to avoid the marginalisation of such groups within the larger community. Or more positively, accommodation should be made for the practices of different religious groups, because these groups are a source of identity and meaning for their members. If religious association is central to the individual adherent's sense of self and place in the world, then a judgement by the state that the practices of their group are false or less important than those of other groups, may be experienced by him or her as a denial of their equal worth. If the law prevents the members of some religious groups from fully participating in society, their identification or connection with the larger community may be negatively affected and this in turn may result in social conflict. The ties between religious group members, which may be intergenerational and comprehensive, also make the group particularly vulnerable to discrimination and marginalisation. Accommodation may seem particularly appropriate when the restrictive law supports dominant cultural practices, some of which (such as holidays) may be religious in origin.

---

limited when there is a public reason for the wearer to be identified. Experience suggests that the need for identification is often overstated and that other options are sometimes available that would not necessitate the removal of the niqab. In Canada see *R v NS* (2012) 3 SCR 726, which considered whether a witness in a criminal trial could wear a niqab while giving testimony.

[26] J Maclure and C Taylor, *Secularism and Freedom of Conscience* (Trans Jane Marie Todd) (Cambridge, MA, Harvard University Press, 2011).

[27] R Moon, 'Religious Commitment and Identity: *Syndicat Northcrest v. Amselem*' (2005) 29 *Supreme Court Law Review* 201, 216.

Accommodation in these cases, though, can never be more than minor. Judgements about the necessity and extent of accommodation for a particular religious practice do not depend on the balancing of competing religious and civic interests. A court has no way to attach value or weight to a religious belief/practice. From a secular or public perspective, a religious belief/practice has no necessary value; indeed, it is said that a court should take no position concerning its value – that the court should remain neutral on the question of religious truth. The belief/practice is significant, from a civic-secular perspective, because it matters 'deeply' to the group and its members or because it is part of their cultural identity. But there is no way to balance this value against the purpose or value of the restrictive law. The secular concern is not with the belief/practice itself but rather with its importance and meaning to the group's members and with the potential impact of its restriction on the position of the group in the larger society. Religious *freedom* does not protect a valued activity from state interference, but is instead a form of equality right that seeks to limit the exclusion or marginalisation of religious groups, by requiring the state to reasonably accommodate the group's religious practices (by treating these practices as the equivalent of group traits).[28]

In religious accommodation cases, an individual claimant must argue (before a secular court) that their practice should be accommodated not because it is true but rather because he or she *thinks* it is true or valuable, and so is important to their group.[29] For various, mostly practical, reasons, the courts are prepared to view religious practices as part of a rooted cultural identity (as the equivalent of a group characteristic) that should be accommodated, if the cost to public policy is minor. The issue in religious accommodation cases, then, is not the right or appropriate balance between competing religious and civic values but is instead whether space can be carved out from state law for the practices of a religious minority, without significantly compromising the public interest. To prevent the marginalisation or alienation of a minority religious group, the courts are willing to adjust, in minor ways, the line between the political sphere (of government action) and the private or communal sphere (of religious practice).

IV. The Scope of Freedom of Conscience

If the requirement that the state accommodate religious practices – that it treat religious practices as a matter of cultural identity that lies outside the scope of politics – is tied to the

---

[28] In this way religious freedom is different from rights, such as freedom of expression, which is protected because there is value in the activity of expression (its contribution to democracy, knowledge, individual agency). Limits on freedom of expression rest on public values or interests, such as preventing the spread of hatred, or protecting individual reputation. In deciding whether to uphold a limit on expression, the courts must make a judgment about the reasonable trade-off between these competing values or interests.

[29] While a religious group may think that its practices should be protected because they are true and that anything less than full accommodation (or even the repeal of the law) is wrong, the group must argue before the courts that its practices should be protected because it believes them to be true or because they are part of their culture – adopting a detached perspective. If the practice matters to the individual/group because it is true, it might be said that the courts, at least indirectly, are protecting spiritual truth, as it is understood by some in the community – by treating truth claims as group attributes. If religion or religious practice is valued or protected for reasons other than its truth, then that protection (or the refusal to give it) will sometimes be seen, by religious adherents, as trivialising their religion or their religious commitment.

role of these practices in the life of a religious group, then it is not clear when or whether the accommodation requirement should extend to an individual's non-religious practices. In the public imagination, the conscientious objector is someone, often a lone figure, who takes a moral or political stand against the dominant assumptions of the culture. She refuses to conform to the norms of the general community and holds to his or her own judgement about what is right or just. But in a democratic system some views or values will prevail over others. It cannot be enough, then, that the conscientious objector is committed as an individual to views or values that are inconsistent with state policy, however deep his or her commitment.

The courts, though, seem to accept (even if there is a dearth of case law) that a conscientiously held belief will fall within the scope of section 2(a) (freedom of conscience) and be treated as a matter of identity, or as a virtual trait, that should be reasonably accommodated, when it resembles a paradigmatic religious belief/practice – that is significant to the individual, specific in content, peremptory in force, and fundamental in the sense that it runs against the conventional practices of the general community.

The only reported cases in Canada in which freedom of conscience under section 2(a) was found to have been breached involved a refusal by the federal prison authorities to provide an inmate with vegetarian meals. In *Maurice v Canada (AG)*, an inmate had previously received vegetarian meals on religious grounds, as a member of the Hare Krishna community.[30] After he had disassociated himself from that community, he asked that he continue to receive vegetarian meals in the prison for moral rather than religious reasons. The prison authorities took the position that they were only obligated to provide vegetarian meals for religious reasons. A judge of the Federal Court of Canada, however, rejected this argument noting that section 2(a) protects both religious and non-religious beliefs and practices. In the judge's view, the prison could accommodate the inmate's vegetarianism without difficulty, particularly since it was already providing vegetarian meals to inmates on religious grounds.

Two factors may have been critical to the success of this claim, setting it apart from other (possible) claims to accommodation for non-religious practices. The first has to do with the character of the practice. The judgment provided little information about the inmate's commitment to vegetarianism; however, it appeared that the practice was basic for him and not derived from more general principles, the elaboration of which might have been the subject of debate and disagreement. The practice was both specific in content and peremptory in force and so looked much like a religious duty. The inmate's claim was helped by the similarity of his particular practice, vegetarianism, to a recognised religious practice and indeed by the fact that he had previously been provided with vegetarian meals on religious grounds. Second, the court may have been willing to protect a practice that in ordinary circumstances is simply a private or personal matter. Outside the prison context, vegetarianism is a practice in which the individual is free to engage and that has no obvious impact on the rights or interests of others. The state ordinarily has no direct involvement in the individual's dietary choices. Within the prison, however, all aspects of an inmate's life are controlled by the prison authorities. The inmate can do nothing without the support or co-operation of the state.

---

[30] *Maurice* (n 11). In *R v Chan* [2005] ABQB 615, a prisoner had a right to receive vegetarian meals for religious reasons.

A number of lower court decisions in Canada have considered conscience-based claims to exemption from paternalistic laws such as the requirement that car passengers wear seatbelts or that bicycle riders wear helmets.[31] In each of these cases, the claim for exemption was dismissed with few reasons given. In *R v Locke*, however, the provincial court judge, when rejecting the conscience claim, observed that 'Mr. Locke's belief that wearing a seatbelt may cause him more harm than good is not of the same order as the comprehensive value system protected by section 2(a)'.[32] Locke's opposition to the legislation was based not on a commitment to a different set of values (concerning personal safety or physical integrity) but instead on a different judgement about the safety consequences of (not) wearing a seatbelt. He believed that he would be safer if he did not wear a seatbelt. The legislature, though, had specifically addressed this question and, relying on empirical evidence, had determined that the safety of passengers will be better protected if they wear seatbelts.[33]

In most of the other lower court seatbelt cases, the individual's objection to the law seemed to be based on a libertarian view that the state has no right to regulate self-regarding behaviour. The opposition to the law in these cases, then, was based on a 'deeply held' moral/political view that is in tension with the state's justification for the law. The difficulty with the accommodation claim, though, is that it represents a direct challenge to the legitimacy of paternalistic laws and perhaps state authority more generally. The accommodation claim is based not on the value the claimant attaches to the particular practice (of not wearing a seatbelt) but instead on his or her views about the importance of liberty and autonomy and the legitimate scope of state power. Such a claim may be too political and too sweeping for the court to contemplate under section 2(a).[34]

---

[31] See, for example, *R v Dubbin*, 2009 BCPC 164; *R v Locke*, 2004 ABPC 152; and *R v Warman*, 2001 BCSC 1771.

[32] *Locke* (ibid) at 25.

[33] Similarly, s 2(a) claims for exemption from mandatory vaccinations, whether framed in religious or non-religious terms, should be rejected (even before taking account of the harm they may cause to others) if they rest on a belief about the health risks of the vaccinations. The obvious contrast is with the refusal of a blood transfusion by a Jehovah's Witness who is a minor (or an adult for her child) which rests on a fundamental (scripturally based) objection to receiving the blood of another person.

[34] The Canadian courts have considered and rejected the claim that the requirement that new citizens take an oath of allegiance to the Queen breaches the freedom of conscience of anti-monarchists: See *McAteer v Canada (Attorney General)*, 2014 ONCA 578. The principal argument in this case was that the oath was an unjustified instance of compelled speech contrary to s 2(b) of the Charter. In her concurring judgment *R v Morgentaler*, [1988] 1 SCR 30, Wilson J held that the Criminal Code ban on abortion breached section 7 of the Charter because it deprived a woman of her liberty and security of the person in a way that was not in accordance with principles of fundamental justice. To interfere with the decisions a woman makes concerning her body, and more particularly concerning reproduction, would be to deprive her of her liberty and security of the person. Furthermore, such a deprivation would interfere with her freedom of conscience, a principle of fundamental justice. According to Wilson J: '[T]he decision whether or not to terminate a pregnancy is essentially a moral decision, a matter of conscience. I do not think there is or can be any dispute about that. The question is: whose conscience? Is the conscience of the woman to be paramount or the conscience of the state? I believe, for the reasons I gave in discussing the right to liberty, that in a free and democratic society it must be the conscience of the individual' [175–76]. In Wilson J's decision, conscience refers to a sphere of autonomous judgement. The individual has the right to make decisions about deeply personal matters such as reproduction. This, I think, is different from the standard section 2(a) freedom of religion or freedom of conscience claim. The standard claim is not that the state should refrain from regulating a particular matter (that all persons should be exempted from legal regulation) but rather that those individuals, and only those individuals, who have a deep moral commitment that is inconsistent with the law should be exempted from its application. It may be that an exemption will be granted only if the (religious) practice is sufficiently 'private' (ie limited in its impact on the rights and freedoms of others), but that is not the same as defining a sphere of autonomous judgement that applies to all persons.

Freedom of conscience, like freedom of religion, may only protect practices that lie outside (or can be bracketed-off from) political contest and treated as part of a personal or communal set of practices. This must be what is meant when non-religious practices are described as 'profound' or 'fundamental': that they are part of a distinctive world view that runs contrary to conventional morality or mainstream practice. Even when the individual understands his or her objection to the law (and his or her claim to be exempted from the law's application) as a moral position, it may be viewed by others as personal or cultural rather than universal and political, because it is not derived from widely accepted moral principles. It seems to lie outside the scope of political contest or public reason. However, as a practical matter, it may be that such beliefs/practices are seldom sustained outside cultural or religious communities.

While it is easy enough to see vegetarianism, and other practices about diet, as a private or personal matter that lies outside politics, it is not as easy to view the objection to military service in this way, regardless of whether the objection is based on religious or non-religious moral grounds. Yet the courts and legislatures in many jurisdictions have been willing to accommodate these objections.[35]

The US Supreme Court, in its application of the religious exemption from compulsory military service in the *Universal Military Training and Service Act*,[36] has adopted an approach to freedom of conscience similar to that which is described above. The statutory exemption from military service, although confined to religious objections, has been interpreted by the court as encompassing objections to military service that are more often considered non-religious or conscience-based in character. The statute exempts from military service those who by reason of their 'religious training and belief' are 'conscientiously opposed to participation [in military service] in any form.'[37] In the statute, 'religious training and belief' is described as 'an individual's belief in a relation to a Supreme Being involving duties superior to those arising from any human relation, but [not including] essentially political, sociological, or philosophical views or a merely personal moral code.'[38] The US Supreme Court in *United States v Seeger* noted that the section used the expression 'Supreme Being' rather than God and decided that 'the test of belief "in a relation to a Supreme Being" is whether a given belief that is sincere and meaningful occupies a place in the life of its possessor parallel to that filled by the orthodox belief in God'.[39] It was not necessary, said the court, that the individual believe that God had forbidden her to participate in war but only that she believe that she was bound by a rule or command beyond her will not to participate in war in any circumstance. This reading of the exemption, said the court, 'embraces the ever-broadening understanding of the modern religious community'.[40]

---

[35] Conscientious objection to military service has been an issue in a number of recent European Court of Human Rights decisions involving Jehovah's Witnesses in Turkey and Armenia. See, for example, *Savda v Turkey* App no 42730/05 (ECtHR, 12 June 2012), in which it was held that the state had a duty under art 9 of the *Convention for the Protection of Human Rights and Fundamental Freedoms* [*European Convention on Human Rights*] to establish a system for determining whether an individual has a conscientious objection to military service.

[36] *Universal Military Training and Service Act*, 50 USC App § 456(j) (1958).

[37] ibid at § 6(j).

[38] ibid.

[39] *United States v Seeger*, 380 US 163 (1965) at 165–66. In that case, the Court found that the exemption did apply to Seeger, and several other applicants, who the Court accepted may have been 'bowing to "external commands" in virtually the same sense as is the objector who defers to the will of a supernatural power' [186].

[40] ibid at 180.

The court in *Seeger* sought to distinguish the religious objections to military service that fall within the scope of the exemption from those objections that are not exempted because they are part of the individual's personal moral code or based on 'political, sociological, or economic considerations'.[41] It is difficult, though, to make sense of the distinction between, on the one hand, a duty or obligation that fills the same role in the individual's life as a religious duty and, on the other hand, a personal moral commitment, since the latter, as a moral commitment, must be understood by the adherent as external to their will, binding upon them, and even universal in its application. It is unclear what work the modifier 'personal' does here – how it affects our understanding of the individual's moral commitment.[42]

The more substantial limitation identified by the court is that the objection to military service must not be based on economic, political or social factors. The obvious consequence of this limit is that an exemption will not be granted to an individual who objects to participation in a *particular* war for social, political, or economic reasons. Political judgements of this kind, said the court, have historically been reserved for the government. It appears, then, that the exemption from military service, as defined by the US Supreme Court, will only apply when an individual holds a profound belief that she must not go to war in any circumstances.[43] The individual's conscientious objection must be peremptory in the sense that it does not depend on the contextual application of more abstract principles about which there might be reasonable debate among citizens. Either one accepts that war is wrong (or that it is wrong to take a life, even in self-defence) or one does not accept this and believes that 'it all depends' or that 'it is a complicated matter'. A circumstantial objection may be rooted in either a secular or a religious morality; the Roman Catholic 'just war' doctrine is an example of the latter.

Because the individual's opposition to military service (in any circumstances) runs contrary to mainstream opinion or conventional morality her claim to an exemption from conscription may be viewed by the courts as a personal or communal belief/practice rather than a political position about the rights and interests of others that is subject to democratic contest and regulation. If the individual's objection to military service can be seen as an expression of religious commitment or personal conscience, rather than a political statement or civic act, then it may be accommodated, even though exemption from compulsory service will place a greater burden of public service on other members of the community – although it will not directly cause harm to them. Even if compulsory military service during wartime is seen as necessary to the security of the nation, it is an extraordinary intervention into the individual's life – requiring him to participate in war. In addition to this concern, there may also be a more pragmatic concern that conscription will result in acts of civil disobedience. In time of war, the risk of civil disobedience may be particularly destabilising.[44] The fear of instability may outweigh concerns that the burden of military service will be unevenly distributed. For these reasons, governments (and courts) have been prepared to treat an objection to military service as a matter of

---

[41] ibid at 173.

[42] Even if we could make sense of the idea of a personal moral commitment that was distinct from a morally binding commitment, it is not clear why the personal claim would be subject to legal regulation, while the more general – universal – claim would not.

[43] See also *Gillette v United States*, 401 US 437 (1971).

[44] Moon (n 6) 197.

personal conscience (that should be accommodated), rather than political opinion that should be open to democratic contest.

Part of the motivation for the US Supreme Court's broad reading of the conscientious objection exemption in the military service legislation (which by its terms seemed only to protect religious objections) may have been to ensure that a law that was intended to protect the 'free exercise' of religion did not at the same time breach the 'establishment clause' of the First Amendment, which precludes the state from favouring religion over non-religion. The argument, sometimes made, is that when the state exempts a religious practice from the application of ordinary law without also exempting a similar non-religious practice, it is preferring religion over non-religion, contrary to the establishment clause.[45] However, if religious accommodation is based not simply on the deep significance of (religious) practice to the individual, but also on the particular vulnerability of minority religious practices which may be overlooked in the legislative process and the risk that religious groups will be marginalised and their members alienated, then non-religious objections by an individual may not have the same claim to accommodation. When the state accommodates a religious practice, it is not preferring religious over non-religious practices. It is maintaining the separation of religion and politics – excluding and insulating religion from politics – for the reasons earlier described related to the value and standing of religious associations in the larger society.

V. Conclusion

Religious beliefs/practices are excluded and insulated from political contest not because they are intrinsically valuable but instead because they are aspects of a collective or cultural identity and markers of membership in the collective. Religious traditions or belief systems are a source of meaning and value for their adherents. Religious communities connect their members and locate them in the world. Community ties can sometimes be as deep and significant to the individual as his or her family relationships. This is what is meant when religious practices are described as deeply held or rooted – that they are a source and expression of identity. The separation of religion and politics – the exclusion and insulation of religion from politics – rests on the idea that religion is a matter of cultural identity rather than contestable political opinion and that the restriction of a religious group's practices, and more generally the marginalisation of the group, whether intended or not, can be damaging to individual members and undermining of social stability.

If the state's duty to accommodate religious practices is about the status of religious groups rather than the liberty of individuals (a matter of equality rather than liberty) then it may not extend to practices that are idiosyncratic and have no link to a religious or cultural group/tradition (noting here that cultural traditions invariably include spiritual beliefs and rituals). We can, of course, imagine several individuals, who share a particular belief (eg that consuming hallucinogenic drugs provides valuable insights), organising themselves around that belief. However, a group that is voluntarily formed around a particular issue does not

---

[45] This argument was made in *Gillette* (n 43).

play the same role in the life of the individual as a religious or cultural group that is characterised by a comprehensive world view, or form of life, that is transmitted through family and community. Such a group is not, in the same way, a source of identity or meaning for its members, and is not similarly vulnerable to discrimination and systemic exclusion.[46] The state's rejection or regulation of the practices/beliefs of such a group is simply that – the rejection of a particular position or perspective.

The requirement that the state should accommodate religious beliefs or practices (and sometimes compromises its policies) is most often justified as necessary to ensure that the individual's deepest values and commitments and more generally his autonomy in decision-making are respected. I have argued, however, that reasonable accommodation is better understood as a form of equality right that is based on the importance of community or group membership to the individual. Understood in this way, the accommodation requirement may not extend to an individual's deeply held non-religious practices, if they are not part of a shared belief system. The willingness of the courts to protect certain non-religious practices (to require their accommodation by the state) may rest simply on their formal similarity to familiar religious practices such as pacifism or vegetarianism – that are specific in content, peremptory in force and that diverge from mainstream practices. Yet, as a practical matter, practices of this kind are seldom sustained outside a religious or cultural community. It is not an accident then that the very few instances of non-religious, 'conscientious', practices that have been accommodated are similar in content and structure to familiar religious practices, and indeed may have arisen from these religious practices.

---

[46] JT Levy, *Rationalism, Pluralism & Freedom* (Oxford, OUP, 2015) reminds us that the distinction between voluntary associations and cultural groups is not always clear-cut.

6

The Courts and Conscience Claims

IAN LEIGH*

I. Introduction

In a memorable scene in Richard Attenborough's 1982 film *Gandhi*, Mahatma Gandhi appears before a colonial judge charged with an act of civil disobedience based on his conscientious violation of legislation enforcing the tax on a basic commodity – salt. Given the opportunity to ask for mitigation Gandhi, in a bid for martyrdom, argues that the judge's duty, faced with such deliberate and symbolic disobedience towards the colonial authority, is to impose the maximum permitted sentence. This is an account, exaggerated no doubt for dramatic effect, of events surrounding the Salt March of 1930. Nonetheless, the episode neatly illustrates the dilemma facing the courts when dealing with individuals motivated by conscience, or by what they claim is a higher duty. Should they ignore the motivation or should they treat it as somehow better (or worse) than that of others who have done the same acts for more prosaic reasons?

The whole question becomes much more complicated, of course, in legal systems in which human rights or constitutional protections apply. The conscience claim frequently takes the form of a challenge to the constitutionality or rights-compatibility of the law. If the courts recognise the claim they are not strictly exempting the conscience question so much as finding that the law in question is overbroad. Moreover, even aside from these broader ways in which conscience questions become constitutionalised there are other routes to legal recognition that figure in the contemporary treatment of conscience questions and which add further complexities. Parliament may have provided exceptions to statutory provisions to reflect conscience concerns or exemptions for the benefit of certain groups that hold these views. In such cases questions about the scope of the defences or protections may arise. Although this is a conventional question of statutory interpretation, naturally

* This work was undertaken with the assistance of the British Academy and the Wolfson Foundation under a British Academy Wolfson Professorship. I am grateful to John Adenitire for his helpful comments on an earlier draft. In places I have drawn on the following: I Leigh and A Hambler, 'Religious Symbols, Conscience and the Rights of Others' (2014) 3 *Oxford Journal of Law and Religion* 1, 2–24; I Leigh, 'Reversibility, Proportionality and Conflicting Rights: Fernández Martínez v Spain' in S Smet and E Brems (eds), When Human Rights Clash at the European Court of Human Rights: Conflict or Harmony? (Oxford, Oxford University Press, 2017) 218–41; I Leigh, 'Conceiving Religious Freedom in Terms of Obedience to Conscience' in I Benson and B Bussey (eds), *Religion, Liberty and the Jurisdictional Limits of Law* (Toronto, Ontario, LexisNexis, 2017); I Leigh, 'The Legal Recognition of Freedom of Conscience as Conscientious Objection: Familiar Problems and New Lessons' in R Ahdar (ed) *Research Handbook on Law Religion* (London, Edward Elgar, 2018).

there is an interplay with constitutional or human rights considerations affecting both the conscience claimant and, in some instances, the human rights of others.

Owing to recent clashes of rights in equality law (especially over sexual orientation and religion) much contemporary discussion has focused on role of the courts in balancing these rights. One of the aims of this chapter, however, is to contextualise and broaden discussion of the role of courts in handling conscience claims. In doing so the objective is to identify the range of judicial tasks and approaches that apply to handling these claims and, in the process, to correct an over-emphasis on balancing. I shall discuss two basic positions that the courts can take to treat conscience as legally irrelevant or as relevant, arguing that in appropriate circumstances the latter is not merely desirable but obligatory in human rights law. Three specific questions that arise from recognition are then tackled: the weight to be attributed to legislative silence or non-recognition, the limiting role of judicial supervision in setting the boundaries of conscience claims and, finally, problems of reconciling these claims with other societal interest and the rights and freedoms of others. It will be argued that where conscience claims are concerned (as distinct from freedom of religion and belief) there are difficulties in limiting such claims through the conventional means of proportionality balancing and that greater attention needs to be given to alternative judicial techniques.

First, however, it is helpful to set out the positive case for recognising freedom of conscience by way of addressing two commonly voiced objections.

II. Responding to Preliminary Objections

A common objection to the recognition of conscience claims in the form of exceptions to more general legal duties is that to do so would violate the rule of law and/or amount to unequal treatment of individuals or undue preference based on their beliefs. There is, however, a straightforward response to this position: a sound understanding of equality recognises that the criteria identifying which individuals or actions qualify for like treatment can easily take account of distinctions based on conscience. The formal conception of justice is to treat like cases alike *and* to treat different cases differently in proportion to their differences.[1] Once it is recognised that conscience imposes different burdens on some individuals in complying with legal rules there is no difficulty in recognising that justice requires them to be treated differently from other people who do not carry those burdens.

Although it is not the purpose of this chapter to engage in a comprehensive defence of this position, since the focus is on judicial treatment, it is nonetheless worth outlining two steps in the argument a little more fully. These are to elaborate on the nature of the rule of law and of conscience claims, respectively.

Firstly, it is a misunderstanding of the rule of law to equate it with identical treatment of all persons. The underlying question is whether it follows from acceptance of the universalist principle that law applies to all that it must therefore apply to all *in the same way*. For AV Dicey, whose work is forever associated with the rule of law, the second meaning

[1] Aristotle, *Nicomachaean Ethics*, trans by R. Crisp (New York, Cambridge University Press, 2000).

of the concept involves the 'equal subjection' of all to one law administered by the ordinary courts. What Dicey had in mind was that there should be no distinct system of administrative law, rather than the uniform application of the law to all individuals.[2] In a modern state the law differentiates in myriad ways between different individuals and groups, not only according to role but also on occasion according to characteristics such as age and sex. The core issue is not identical treatment of all but rather treating different cases differently proportionately. The limited legal recognition that differences in treatment based on religion can be appropriate on occasion gives effect to this principle. For example, in discrimination law through concepts of Genuine Occupational Requirements and justification in relation to indirect discrimination; even differential treatment based upon a person's religion may in some contexts be permissible.[3] As explained more fully below, the European Court of Human Rights has also recognised that a failure to treat religiously motivated lawbreakers differently to other people committing the same offence is itself discriminatory.[4] It is doubtful therefore if a requirement of identical treatment for all to the exclusion of difference based on conscience is a necessary implication of the rule of law.

A second objection is to characterise conscientious objection or refusal as privilege-seeking. This is arguably a mischaracterisation based on a failure to appreciate the nature of conscience claims and the historical basis of recognition. It arises, understandably, from a modern tendency to focus on personal autonomy as the basis for freedom of religion and to view freedom of conscience as a subsidiary or derivative aspect. In an historical analysis of conscientious objection, however, Jose de Sousa e Brito points out that freedom of conscience (rather than freedom of religion) was recognised in the constitutions of several American colonies, culminating in the adoption of the First Amendment to the US Constitution.[5]

It is important to understand that in historical perspective freedom of conscience was seen to be worthy of recognition because of the obligatory moral nature of conscience upon the individual and the consequent dilemma that non-recognition creates. James Madison, for example, regarded conscience as 'an imperious sovereign; its demands [were] experienced as imperatives, as "dictates"'.[6] In *Memorial and Remonstrance* Madison argues:

> The Religion then of every man must be left to the conviction and conscience of every man; and it is the right of every man to exercise it as these may dictate. This right is in its nature an unalienable right. It is unalienable because the opinions of men, depending only on the evidence contemplated by their own minds cannot follow the dictates of other men: It is unalienable also, because what is here a right towards men, is a duty towards the Creator. It is the duty of every man to render to the Creator such homage and such only as he believes to be acceptable to him.[7]

---

[2] J Jowell, 'The Rule of Law and its Underlying Values' in J Jowell and D Oliver, *The Changing Constitution* (Oxford, Oxford University Press, 2011) 13–15.

[3] Equality Act 2010, Sch 9, paras 2 and 3, discussed below.

[4] *Thlimmenos v Greece* (2000) 31 EHRR 411 (violation of Art 14 ECHR in the case of a convicted conscientious objector to military service who was thereby prevented from becoming an accountant).

[5] Jose de Sousa e Brito, 'Conscientious Objection' in T Lindholm, W Cole Durham Jr, B Tahzib-Lie, *Facilitating Freedom of Religion or Belief: A Deskbook* (Leiden, Brill | Nijhoff, 2004) 275.

[6] W Cole Durham Jr, 'Religious Liberty and the Call of Conscience' (1992) 42 *De Paul L Rev* 71, 85.

[7] 'Memorial and Remonstrance against Religious Assessments' (1785) in A Adams and C Emmerich, *A Nation Dedicated to Religious Liberty: The Constitutional Heritage of the Religion Clauses* (Philadelphia, University of Pennsylvania Press, 1990) 104.

Likewise, another writer summarises Roger Williams' position as:

> [T]he freedom to be captive to the Divine will, the freedom to be subject to a power other than Caesar's. Liberty of conscience protected the individual from the dilemma of having to choose between sovereigns, under temporal penalties for failure to heed one, but suffering eternal consequences for failure to obey the other.[8]

Robert George cites Newman's pithy summary: conscience has rights because it has duties. George distinguishes this understanding of conscience from a modern tendency to sometimes regard conscience as an outworking of autonomy (what he calls 'conscience as self-will'). He elaborates:

> The right to follow one's conscience and the obligation to respect conscience – especially in matters of faith, where the right of conscience takes the form of religious liberty of individuals and communities of faith – obtain not because people as autonomous agents should be free to do as they please; they obtain, and are stringent and are sometimes overriding because people have duties and the obligation to fulfil them. The duty to follow one's conscience is a duty to do things or refrain from doing things not because one wants to follow one's duty but even if one strongly does *not* want to follow it. The right of conscience is right to do what one judges oneself to be under an obligation to do, whether one welcomes the obligation or must overcome an aversion to fulfil it.[9]

People who assert that their consciences forbid them from complying with general legal rules are, then, making a claim firmly within this long historical tradition. An appeal to conscience is a claim by an individual to be bound by a higher authority that transcends and trumps legal obligation. In seeking relief from legal obligation, the person making the appeal is seeking to avert the moral harm that would follow from being compelled to act against their conscience.

This is especially important to understand in the face of criticism suggesting that these are somehow novel, spurious or contrived objections that go beyond the acceptable and agreed recognition given to religious freedom in a liberal state. As Javier Martínez-Torrón points out, however, this is not open season for 'any and every intellectual opinion inspired by personal views but the ensemble of supreme personal rules of conduct, rooted in religious or non-religious beliefs, which leave for the individual a compelling force higher than any other normative reference'.[10] State recognition allows the individual following their conscience to integrate their beliefs and their actions, so avoiding the need to partition the two.

III. The Dangers of Judicial Conscience-Blindness

As noted above, faced with claims of this kind in relation to general or neutral laws, one approach is for the court to disregard the conscience-based motivation of the actor.

---

[8] T Hall, 'Roger Williams and the Foundation of Religious Liberty' (1991) 71 *Boston UL Rev* 455, 514.

[9] R George, *Conscience and its Enemies: Confronting the Dogmas of Liberal Secularism* (Wilmington, ISI Books, 2013) 112.

[10] J Martínez-Torrón, 'Protecting Freedom of Conscience Beyond Prejudice' in Silvio Ferrari (ed), *Routledge Handbook of Law and Religion* (Oxford, Routledge, 2015) 192.

Treating conscience as legally irrelevant may seem an attractive option: in line with the understanding of the rule of law, criticised above, it has a veneer of equal treatment. Moreover, it corresponds with the dominant positivist model of law, which separates questions of legal validity from morality. In a criminal case, for example, a court may in its discretion consider the conscientious motivation of the party in mitigation or (in a civil case) when deciding upon remedies, but not to absolve her of legal responsibility in the first place. Such an approach also puts the onus firmly on the conscience-stricken person to choose whether to bear the cost of their beliefs, rather than requiring the state or some third party to accommodate them. In the history of civil disobedience, in particular, willingness to suffer has been taken as a mark of sincerity: either as a political lever in its own right or as an acknowledgement of the social contract.

Nonetheless, when the law disregards conscientious reasons for non-compliance, it reinforces a societal view of the conduct in question which squeezes the individual's perception into the category of 'private' beliefs or, depending on one's view, marginalises or trivialises them. At worst, disregarding conscience sets up a dissonance between permitted conduct and beliefs that means the individual must either in their own eyes deny their beliefs by acting contrary to them or face penalties in effect for following them.

Sometimes in a contemporary context, judges attempt to defend failure to legally recognise conscience by suggesting that it has been adequately accommodated because dissenters from the prevailing view are free simply to hold countercultural opinions or to teach them within their religious communities. Such judicial comments are no doubt meant to be consolatory – to avoid the appearance of wholesale winner and losers in the 'Culture Wars' – but they also embody a telling contradiction and reinforce the privatisation of conscience: finding that the beliefs in question are important enough to be acknowledged but not so important that they can be allowed to be acted upon. Whereas for the conscience-stricken individual the crisis they face is precisely over integrating their conduct and beliefs.

At other times the process is subtler and is a consequence of the hegemonic effect of legal categorisation of commonplace situations and transactions. For example, when discrimination law characterises behaviour as nothing more than the supply of goods and services it appears to follow unquestionably that *suppliers* should simply 'do their job' (provide a cake with a message of the customer's choice, for example) and disregard any other consideration, such as their personal beliefs.[11] Failure to provide services is accordingly constructed as discrimination against people of same-sex orientation.

Reductionism of this kind has been the dominant approach of UK courts and tribunals to recent direct religious discrimination claims involving matters of conscience. Thus, employees refusing for conscientious reasons to perform certain duties have been found to be no less favourably treated than any other employee who (for any other reason) fails to perform their contractual duties. The courts have on several occasions found that penalties an employee attributed to discrimination on grounds of their faith did not constitute direct discrimination, because the employer would have treated any employee who failed

---

[11] Even on this basis a marriage registrar might be treated differently since their performative speech or signature literally creates the marriage or civil partnership.

to perform their duties (for whatever reason) in the same way.[12] '[I]t cannot constitute direct discrimination to treat all employees in precisely the same way.'[13] Moreover, in direct discrimination cases where *defendants* claim that the apparently less favourable treatment they have given to a claimant is based on conscience, judges have applied an outcome-driven 'but-for' approach that treats motive or the defendant's own explanation of their conduct as beside the point.[14]

Reductionist approaches rest, however, on unarticulated assumptions about the nature of employment, the running of a business, or the conduct of a profession. By treating them as a mechanistic performance of functions or supply of services they adopt a particular perspective, calculated to exclude from consideration the ethical or moral perception of the employee or proprietor.[15] From a different perspective, however, employment cannot be reduced to mere performance of functions – what in an employment context Alvin Esau characterises as an 'instrumental' approach to work[16] – and is not a sphere sanitised from spiritual or moral concerns. Secularists are not required to accept such viewpoints, of course, but in good faith they could acknowledge that there are alternative ways of seeing familiar activities and that the decision to reduce them to specific legal categories is a choice of perspective and is not self-evident, value-free or even-handed.

The thrust of this section of the argument has been to criticise judicial exclusion of questions of conscience and to argue against conscience-blindness. Finally, it can be noted that there is human rights provenance for such an approach. In the next section the duty that arises under human rights law on occasions to make exceptions from general legal rules for conscience will be addressed. It can also be noted in relation to other Article 9 claims that *Eweida et al v UK*[17] confirms that that the domestic courts' earlier approach of simply disregarding conscientious motivation in discrimination law cannot stand. It does not follow that conscience arguments are automatically conclusive but UK courts will certainly be obliged in future to consider them, irrespective of the statutory wording.

The next section develops the argument that conscience questions are legally relevant. This is naturally the case when legislation provides for explicit recognition of conscience, as it does in limited cases. It can though be seen more clearly perhaps when legislation is silent on the recognition of conscience. In these circumstances it is clear that courts not only may but on occasion should take account of relevant questions of conscience.

---

[12] For example: *Macfarlane v Relate Avon Ltd* [2010] EWCA Civ 880, where a Christian relationships counsellor who was dismissed for refusing to give some forms of sexual counselling to same-sex couples was found not to have been treated less favourably on grounds of religion, but rather because of his unwillingness to provide counselling; *Azmi v Kirklees MBC* [2007] ICR 1154 in which a bilingual support worker at a school who was dismissed for insisting on wearing the niqab veil had not suffered directly discrimination on grounds of religion or belief, since she had failed to show that she had suffered less favourable treatment than others in circumstances which were materially the same. In both instances an indirect discrimination claim also failed.

[13] *London Borough of Islington v Ladele* [2009] IRLR 154, at 53.

[14] *Hall and another v Bull and another* [2013] UKSC 73. See also *R(E) v Governing Body of JFS* [2009] UKSC 15.

[15] As an example of this approach see R Wintemute, 'Accommodating Religious Beliefs: Harm, Clothing or Symbols, and Refusals to Serve Others' (2014) 77 *MLR* 223–53.

[16] A Esau, '"Islands of Exclusivity": Religious Organizations and Employment Discrimination' (2000) 33 *UBC L Rev* 719.

[17] *Eweida and Ors v United Kingdom* (2013) 57 EHRR 8.

IV. When Legislation is Silent

What weight should be attributed by the courts to the failure of the legislature to recognise a conscience claim? On occasion it is clear that the omission of conscience protection was a deliberate legislative choice, for instance where the possibility of exemption *was* directly considered by way of unsuccessful legislative amendments.[18] For example, following the introduction of civil partnerships for same-sex couples in the UK, an unsuccessful attempt was made in the House of Lords by Lady O'Cathain to include conscience provisions for marriage registrars.[19] Equally, part of the background to the so-called 'Gay Cake' appeal recently decided by the UK Supreme Court is the failure to provide exemptions from Northern Ireland sexual orientation discrimination regulations for religious ethos small businesses despite responses to the consultation on the regulations that urged ministers to do so.[20]

Where the legislature has considered and rejected such options, should this leave any room for a later appeal to conscience to the courts? The reason for the legislature not granting an exemption may be *because* recourse lies to the courts in any event to protect conscience and to balance it against other rights. But in any event, and without delving too deeply into the extensive literature about the contestable nature of rights, few commentators are prepared to give legislators exclusive or conclusive right to determine their meaning and scope in constitutional democracies. There appears to be no more reason to treat Parliament's refusal to recognise the right as binding the courts in this than in any other context. The short but compelling answer is that if there is no reason why unsuccessful political campaigners for changes such as assisted suicide or opposite-sex civil partnership, to take two recent examples,[21] should be barred from the courts following rebuff by the legislature, then why should conscience claimants?

A (slightly) longer short answer is that even when change follows a period of consultation, societal reflection and consensus-seeking contentious moral conflicts that have sometimes extended over decades cannot be settled in a democracy by stroke of the legislator's pen. Legislation does not oblige those with serious objections of conscience who are on the losing side of a parliamentary debate to henceforth regard themselves as estopped from claiming judicial protection from being bound to act contrary to their beliefs. Otherwise individual conscience would be subordinate to majority opinion.[22] Conversely, though, in the context of balancing between different rights by a domestic court or to the application of the margin of appreciation by the European Court of Human Rights then a degree of judicial deference may be due to the balance the legislator has struck between competing rights.

---

[18] For detailed discussion of debates about the inclusion of such clauses in relation to same-sex marriage legislation in several countries see R Ahdar, 'Solemnisation of same-sex marriage and religious freedom' (2014) *Ecc LJ* 283; B MacDougall, E Bonthuys, K Mck.Norrie and M van der Brink, 'Conscientious Objection to Creating Same-Sex Unions: An International Analysis' (2012) 1 *Canadian Journal of Human Rights* 127.

[19] HL Deb 13 July 2005, vol 684, col 1147.

[20] *Lee v Ashers Baking Company Ltd & Ors* (Northern Ireland) [2018] UKSC 49 (text at fn 78 ff).

[21] See respectively, *R (on the application of Conway) v Secretary of State for Justice* [2018] EWCA Civ 1431; *R (on the application of Steinfield and Keidan) v Secretary of State for International Development* [2018] UKSC 32.

[22] Here I disagree with the view of Richard Moon in his contribution to this volume but lack of space prevents full discussion. For an eloquent refutation see H Thoreau, *Walden and On the Duty to Civil Disobedience* (New York, Signet Classic, 1962) 242–43.

Unsurprisingly, then, in the recent Northern Ireland cake appeal counsel for Mr Lee and the Equality Commission, Robin Allen QC argued that because of the considered decision not to provide a conscientious exemption to suppliers of goods and services, the Supreme Court should be reluctant to find any limitations to the appellants' Convention rights to be disproportionate.[23]

Protection of freedom of conscience may on occasion require the courts to craft an exception even if the legislature or policy-makers have failed to provide one. This can be seen both from Convention jurisprudence and in its implementation by the domestic courts. In *Thlimennos v Greece* the applicant was prevented from becoming a chartered accountant because of a serious conviction, arising from his refusal to wear a military uniform during conscription to the armed services. The Greek government argued that this was a neutral and general provision and that the domestic authorities could not be expected to go behind the reasons for the conviction; in his case the refusal was based on his beliefs as a Jehovah's Witness. The European Court of Human Rights held, however, that the refusal to make an exception discriminated against the applicant on grounds of religion and belief contrary to Article 14: 'The right not to be discriminated against in the enjoyment of the rights guaranteed under the Convention is also violated when States without an objective and reasonable justification fail to treat differently persons who situations are significantly different'.[24] The Court found that the rule barring persons with a serious conviction from the accountancy profession could have a legitimate aim (preventing dishonesty or moral turpitude). However, this was not applicable in the case and, in any event, bearing in mind that the applicant had already served a prison sentence for the offence, the effect was disproportionate so that the criteria of objective and reasonable justification were not fulfilled.

A second clear instance at Convention level comes from *Bayatyan v Armenia*,[25] in which the European Court of Human Rights found that conscientious objections to military service falls within Article 9. The Armenian government had argued that, in the context of an active conflict with its neighbour Azerbaijan in which there was a national policy of compulsory male conscription, to provide for alternative service for conscientious objectors like the applicant (a Jehovah's Witness) would be to treat them in an unfairly favourable way. The Grand Chamber held, however, that the failure to provide for alternative military service interfered with the applicant's rights and was not necessary in a democratic society. In response to the government's argument it contended:

> [A] balance must be achieved which ensures the fair and proper treatment of people from minorities and avoids any abuse of a dominant position [citing Leyla Şahin, § 108]. Thus, respect on the part of the State towards the beliefs of a minority religious group like the applicant's by providing them with the opportunity to serve society as dictated by their conscience might, far from creating unjust inequalities or discrimination as claimed by the Government, rather ensure cohesive and stable pluralism and promote religious harmony and tolerance in society.[26]

---

[23] n 20 above.
[24] *Thlimennos v Greece* (2001) 31 EHRR 15, at 44. It is noteworthy that Greek law provided a procedure for conscientious objection (within three months of call-up) which the applicant had *not* used but the Court found this did not debar his claim arising from the conviction.
[25] *Bayatyan v Armenia* (2012) 54 EHRR 15.
[26] ibid at 126.

The same approach can be seen at a domestic level in *Adath Yisroel Burial Society*[27] where a coroner's 'cab rank' policy of dealing with deaths in strict chronological order and without reference to religious considerations was found to be unlawful. In the context of an average delay of 15 days from the date of death until release of the body, the coroner had formulated her policy so as to treat all families fairly, regardless of religion, and so to avoid having to defer some inquests because others had been prioritised for religious reasons. By choosing to disregard the needs of Orthodox Jewish and Muslim families that their relative's body be buried as soon as possible after death, however, the coroner had, the court found, acted unlawfully. She had fettered her discretion, acted irrationally, breached Articles 9 and 14 of the European Convention on Human Rights, and had discriminated indirectly contrary to the Equality Act 2010.[28]

It is the Divisional Court's treatment of Articles 9 and 14 that is of particular interest here. In relation to Article 9, Singh J pointed out that:

> [W]hat Article 9 requires is not that there should be any favouritism, whether in favour of religious belief in general or in favour of any particular religious faith, but that there should be a fair balance struck between the rights and interests of different people in society. The fundamental flaw in the present policy adopted by the Defendant is that it fails to strike any balance at all, let alone a fair balance.[29]

There could be a need to differentiate between cases according to individual circumstances based on religion: 'What on its face looks like a general policy which applies to everyone equally may in fact have an unequal impact on a minority. In other words, to treat everyone in the same way is not necessarily to treat them equally. Uniformity is not the same thing as equality'.[30] Under Article 14 equality required not only that like cases to be treated alike, but also that different cases be treated differently.[31]

It is also clear from the human rights jurisprudence that the mere existence of a limited conscience clause does not bar claims that fall outside their scope on which the legislation is silent. The clearest instance is perhaps the early Convention decision of *Young, James and Webster v United Kingdom* in which the Strasbourg court found that the then UK closed shop legislation (the Trade Unions and Labour Relations Act 1974, as amended) was contrary to the negative right of freedom of association, under Article 11, not to be compelled to join an association against one's will.[32] The impugned legislation contained a right of conscientious objection for those with genuine religious objections to joining a trade union. A further proviso for those with 'any reasonable grounds'[33] to being a member of a particular trade

---

[27] *R (on the application of Adath Yisroel Burial Society) v Senior Coroner for Inner North London* [2018] EWHC 969 (Admin).

[28] An argument that the coroner was in breach of the public sector equality duty under s 149 of the Equality Act was rejected.

[29] *Adath Yisroel Burial Society* (n 27) at 107.

[30] ibid at 111, citing *Jakóbski v Poland* (2012) 55 EHRR 8, in which the ECtHR found a violation of Art 9 because of the failure by the Polish prison authorities to take account of the applicant's religious dietary needs in providing food in prison.

[31] *Adath Yisroel Burial Society* (n 27) at 117.

[32] See also *Thlimennos v Greece* (n 24): the Greek law provided a procedure for conscientious objection (within three months of call-up) which the applicant had *not* used, but the Court found this did not debar his claim arising from the conviction.

[33] ie not limited to conscience grounds of any kind.

union contained in the 1974 Act was repealed by amendments in 1975, giving rise to the dilemma faced by the applicants since their employer, British Rail, had a closed shop agreement. Two of the applicants (Young and Webster) who objected on grounds of conscience to joining a trade union fell outside the scope of the revised provision since their objection was non-religious in character.[34] This did not prevent the Court from finding in their case that:

> The protection of personal opinion afforded by Articles 9 and 10 in the shape of freedom of thought, conscience and religion and of freedom of expression is also one of the purposes of freedom of association as guaranteed by Article 11. Accordingly, it strikes at the very substance of this Article to exert pressure, of the kind applied to the applicants, in order to compel someone to join an association contrary to his convictions.[35]

V. Judicial Supervision

In view of the case made so far for judicial recognition of conscience claims, this section seeks to argue that recognition need not lead to an anarchical situation in which conscience claimants can opt out of legal duties at will in the way critics sometimes claim. This is because the courts supervise these claims both by individuals and groups, and keep them within boundaries.

The point can first be demonstrated from the judicial treatment of the conscience provision against being required to 'participate' in an abortion (Abortion Act 1967, s 4(1)). At first sight, this appears to grant extremely broad protection from statutory or contractual compulsion subject only to the formality that the burden of proof lies on the claimant to establish their conscientious objection.[36] However, the courts have limited its application by interpretation of what 'participate' means. Thus, in *ex p Janaway*[37] it was held that a secretary asked to type a letter referring a patient for an abortion did not have the right to invoke the provision since she was not participating in the treatment. In *Greater Glasgow Health Board v Doogan and another* the UK Supreme Court faced a similar question in relation to whether two Roman Catholic midwives, who worked as labour-ward coordinators in the Glasgow Southern General Hospital and whose duties included supervising staff participating in abortions, could claim the protection of section 4.[38] The Supreme Court found in a preliminary ruling that 'participate' meant 'taking part in a hands-on capacity: actually performing the tasks involved in the course of treatment, rather than the ancillary, administrative, and managerial tasks which the appellants, as supervisors, were obliged to carry out'.[39]

With regard to groups, although the provisions in the Equality Act 2010 designed to protect the autonomy of religious groups are often described as exemptions, this is

---

[34] Mr James' objection was not based on conscience.

[35] *Young, James and Webster v UK* (1982) 4 EHRR 38, at 57. Having found a violation of Art 11, the ECtHR found, at 66, that it was not necessary to determine if Art 9 was violated.

[36] Abortion Act 1967, s 4(2).

[37] *R v Salford Health Authority, ex p Janaway* [1988] 2 WLR 442.

[38] *Greater Glasgow Health Board v Doogan & Anor* [2014] UKSC 68. The question of whether arrangements made by the Board in relation to respondents were compatible with Art 9 ECHR was referred to the tribunal hearing the case.

[39] ibid at 38.

misleading since they do not take the form of a straightforward exclusion. Only certain activities, bounded by qualifying tests, are excepted under the provisions. They are applicable to 'employment for purposes of an organised religion' and allow an employer to apply a requirement related to sex, marriage and sexual orientation in two circumstances.[40] These are to comply with the doctrines of the religion,[41] or to avoid conflicting with the strongly held religious convictions of a significant number of the religion's followers.[42]

The wording may appear wide, but the responsible minister was at pains to argue in Parliament that 'organised religion' was substantially narrower than a religious organisation and that the exception was intended to apply to a very small number of posts on a 'case by case' basis.[43] The courts have approached it in this light.[44]

This exception was considered in *Reaney*[45] in which an employment tribunal found that the refusal to employ a homosexual church-youth-worker notwithstanding his undertaking at interview to remain celibate constituted direct discrimination on grounds of sexual orientation. The Diocese's claim to invoke the organised religion exception failed because, in the tribunal's view, bearing in mind his undertaking, Reaney satisfied the conditions and the bishop was not acting reasonably in doubting Reaney's undertaking to remain celibate. The tribunal found that the exception applied to a youth worker post[46] and that the Church of England's doctrinal stance on homosexual celibacy was within its scope.[47] It held, however, that the final requirement of the exception was not met (that the person to whom that requirement is applied does not meet it or the employer is not satisfied in all the circumstances and it is reasonable for him not to be satisfied if that person meets it).[48]

Subsequent decisions have shown that the courts probe whether the objection is clearly based on doctrine, as the recent decision on whether denial by an Anglican bishop of an Extra-Parochial Ministry Licence to a clergyman who had married his same-sex partner amounted to discrimination on grounds of sexual orientation demonstrates.[49] Without the licence the plaintiff was unable to work as a hospital chaplain, where the duties included conducting services of worship. The Court of Appeal found that the employment tribunal had not erred in concluding that the Church of England's doctrinal position was to be found in a statement of Pastoral Guidance from the House of Bishops in conjunction with the Church's canonical view of marriage.[50] While judges would be acting beyond their

[40] See now Equality Act 2010, Sch 9, para 2. Like religion, sexual orientation is a 'protected characteristic' under the Equality Act 2010 and hence discrimination in matters of employment on this ground is generally unlawful.
[41] Equality Act 2010, Sch 9, para 2(5).
[42] Equality Act 2010, Sch 9, para 2(6).
[43] Lord Sainsbury of Turville: 'we had in mind a very narrow range of employment: ministers of religion, plus a small number of posts outside the clergy, including those who exist to promote and represent religion', HL Debs, col 779, 17 June 2003.
[44] *R (on the application of Amicus et al) v Secretary of State for Trade and Industry* [2004] EWHC 860 (Admin), paras 114–27, per Richards J, holding that the equivalent earlier provision was consistent with the Equality Framework Directive and was not invalid.
[45] *Reaney v Herford Diocesan Board of Finance* (2007) ET Case No 1602844/2006 (17 July 2007).
[46] 'The Claimant would be in one of the small number of jobs which would be closely associated with the promotion of the Church. The Claimant would have been promoting religion in the way in which it has been suggested the regulations are meant to encompass' (ibid at 102).
[47] ibid at 103–04.
[48] ibid at 105–07.
[49] *Pemberton v Inwood* [2018] EWCA Civ 564.
[50] ibid 62–63.

competence in assessing the soundness of such doctrinal positions by adjudicating between rival claims, the *Pemberton* decision illustrates how they can nonetheless ensure that those exceptions do not become de facto exemptions by assuring themselves that there is a basis for doctrinal claims.

Indeed, a recent decision from the European Court of Justice affirms that judicial supervision of this kind is required in areas to which EU equality law applies.[51] In a preliminary ruling on a reference from a German Federal Labour Court concerning the correct approach to the exception in Article 4(2) of the Equality Framework Directive for churches and religious ethos organisations,[52] the CJEU held that the principle of effective judicial review must apply.[53] While courts should not assess the legitimacy of the ethos of the organisation, they were expected to determine 'whether the occupational requirement imposed by the church or organisation … is genuine, legitimate and justified, having regard to that ethos'.[54] Consequently there had to be an 'objectively verifiable' 'direct link between the occupational requirement imposed by the employer and the activity concerned'.[55] Furthermore, the occupational activity had to be sufficiently important for the manifestation of that ethos or the exercise by the church or organisation of its right of autonomy.[56] Moreover, the organisation was obliged to show in the particular case that 'the supposed risk of causing harm to its ethos or to its right of autonomy is probable and substantial'.[57] Accordingly, it was not open to member states to provide in their law that the need for the exception was to be determined by the religious organisation itself and any such national provision had to be interpreted in the light of the principle of effective judicial supervision and, if this was not possible, to be disapplied.

The CJEU's approach is in line with that adopted by the European Court of Human Rights in balancing religious autonomy with other rights in which the Strasbourg court has in effect taken on the role of verifying that the domestic courts have undertaken the proportionality analysis with sufficient rigour and without undue deference to religious group interests.[58] The appropriateness of such balancing is considered next.

---

[51] Case C-414/16 *Egenberger v Evangelisches Werk fur Diakonie und Entwicklung eV* EU:C:2018:257 (Grand Chamber, 17 April 2018).

[52] Art 4(2) states: 'Member States may maintain national legislation in force at the date of adoption of this Directive or provide for future legislation incorporating national practices existing at the date of adoption of this Directive pursuant to which, in the case of occupational activities within churches and other public or private organisations the ethos of which is based on religion or belief, a difference of treatment based on a person's religion or belief shall not constitute discrimination where, by reason of the nature of these activities or of the context in which they are carried out, a person's religion or belief constitute a genuine, legitimate and justified occupational requirement, having regard to the organisation's ethos. This difference of treatment shall be implemented taking account of Member States' constitutional provisions and principles, as well as the general principles of Community law, and should not justify discrimination on another ground'.

[53] *Egenberger* (n 51) at 55 and 59.

[54] ibid at 61.

[55] ibid at 63. Pursuit of 'an aim that has no connection with that ethos or with the exercise by the church or organisation of its right of autonomy' would not be legitimate' (at [66]).

[56] ibid at 65.

[57] ibid at 67.

[58] *Obst v Germany* App no 425/03 (ECtHR, 23 September 2010); *Schüth v Germany* (2011) 52 EHRR 32. *Siebenhaar v Germany* App no 18136/02 (3 February 2011); *Fernandez Martinez v Spain* (2015) 60 EHRR 3.

VI. Weighing Conscience Claims Against Other Interests

If it is accepted that conscience claims should be judicially recognised in the ways outlined so far, what, if any, are the limits to recognition? In recent decades proportional balancing has emerged as the dominant method of human rights adjudication – a move reflected in the belated adoption by the European Court of Human Rights in *Eweida* of it as the preferred method for reconciling religion and belief and other interests, at least in an employment context.[59] On the whole this move is to be applauded in the case of religion and belief as reflecting a generous approach to when the right is engaged and offering the potential (not always actualised to date) of allowing for more systematic and structured consideration of the relevant interest, in which the onus is on the state to justify limitation of the right. This section will adopt a generally more sceptical approach, however, of its applicability to freedom of conscience claims.

In theory, when it comes to the weighing of conscience against other social interests and other people's rights under human rights law the difference between conscience and religion and belief is of some importance. This is because the text of Article 9 ECHR and Article 18 ICCPR refer to a right to *manifest* one's religion or belief (subject to limitations) but only a right to freedom of conscience. From this most writers conclude that there is no right to manifest one's freedom of conscience.[60] While this conclusion appears faithful to the drafting of these instruments it also creates a series of difficulties. Nor does it seem to have proved much of an obstacle in practice to courts proceeding on the basis that individuals have a right to express their conscience, which can be limited according to other factors.

The difficulty with distinguishing religion and belief on the one hand and conscience on the other is neatly expressed by Carolyn Evans: 'Many people come to their beliefs by following their conscience and their conscience is, in turn, shaped by the nature of those beliefs'.[61] Moreover, if a juridical distinction has to be drawn it would seem to follow that the religiously informed conscience should be better protected (through a limited right to be manifested) than the non-religious conscience. This does not comport well with the invariably cited statement that freedom of thought, conscience and religious is a precious right for non-believers. That apparent inconsistency may, however, be cancelled out by the right to manifest one's *beliefs* – assuming this to be to be sufficiently broad to include non-religious questions of conscience.

In fact, the practice of the European Court of Human Rights suggests that it does not pay undue attention to these distinctions. That may be because in the past the Court frequently applied a restrictive approach to when Article 9(1) was engaged under the well-known dictum from the *Arrowsmith* case that not every action motivated or inspired by a belief

---

[59] *Eweida* (n 17) para 83: 'Given the importance in a democratic society of freedom of religion, the Court considers that, where an individual complains of a restriction on freedom of religion in the workplace, rather than holding that the possibility of changing job would negate any interference with the right, the better approach would be to weigh that possibility in the overall balance when considering whether or not the restriction was proportionate'. See also: *Obst v Germany* (n 58); *Schüth v Germany* (n 58); *Siebenhaar v Germany* (n 58).

[60] C Evans, *Freedom of Religion under the European Convention on Human Rights* (Oxford, Oxford University Press, 2000) 52.

[61] ibid, 52–53.

is a practice that manifests it.[62] So, in the case of conscience claims by pharmacists, in its brief admissibility decision in *Pichon and Sajous v France*, the European Court of Human Rights found that the conviction for refusal to sell contraceptives that had been medically prescribed did not interfere with the pharmacists' Article 9 rights. The Court said:

> [A]s long as the sale of contraceptives is legal and occurs on medical prescription nowhere other than in a pharmacy, the applicants cannot give precedence to their religious beliefs and impose them on others as justification for their refusal to sell such products, since they can manifest those beliefs in many ways outside the professional sphere.[63]

That decision pre-dates the change of approach of the European Court of Human Rights in *Eweida* and it is likely that were it to be decided again today it would be on the basis that there was a justified limitation under Article 9(2), because of the rights and freedoms of others. Indeed, even before *Eweida*, a markedly more nuanced position was adopted by the Court in *RR v Poland*, where it stated:

> States are obliged to organise the health services system in such a way as to ensure that an effective exercise of the freedom of conscience of health professionals in the professional context does not prevent patients from obtaining access to services to which they are entitled under the applicable legislation.[64]

This appears to impliedly acknowledge that Article 9 is in play[65] and avoids some of the obvious questions begged by the *Pichon and Sajous* decision about 'imposition' of the pharmacists' views and whether freedom to manifest views in other contexts is a reason to deny the right to do so in one's employment.

So far there is no evidence that the Court applies its post-*Eweida* approach to Article 9 only to manifestation of *religious* beliefs. Clearly, one option would be to retrace the steps to *Arrowsmith* and to develop instead a more robust distinction between conscience, belief and religion. The developing right of conscientious objection to military service would perhaps be the most obvious field in which such a distinction could emerge, but to date there is no sign of the Court treating non-religious pacifists differently to religious ones. Moreover, to do so would seem anomalous and discriminatory.

Paradoxically the only attempt to develop a more systematic distinction between religion and belief and conscience comes in a partially dissenting judgment by Judges Vucinic and De Gaetano in one of the *Eweida* group of cases, *Ladele v UK*, and it turns the conventional analysis referred to above on its head. The judges noted that conscience is protected under Article 9(1) but is 'conspicuously absent' from the limitations available to Member States in Article 9(2).[66] From this they concluded that conscience, once a certain threshold is reached, is an absolute right (similar to the *forum internum*) which cannot be qualified (inter alia, with respect to the rights of others) in the way that religious manifestation more

---

[62] *Arrowsmith v UK* (1981) 3 EHRR 218. The majority of the Commission found that the applicant's distribution of leaflets calling on soldiers not to serve in Northern Ireland were not a protected manifestation of her pacifist beliefs because the leaflets in question reflected political arguments rather than pacifism as such.

[63] *Pichon and Sajous v France* App no 49853/99 (Commission Decision, 2 October 2001).

[64] *RR v Poland* App no 27617/04 (ECtHR, 26 May 2011).

[65] Admittedly, however, Art 9 was not directly considered by the Court (which found breach of Arts 3 and 8 in the case of a woman suffering repeated delay in accessing prenatal screening).

[66] *Eweida* (n 17) Partially Dissenting Opinion of Judges Vucinic and De Gaetano, at 2.

generally might be. Following this logic they found that Ms Ladele had a right to follow her conscience on a moral matter and that, since this was an absolute right, there was consequently no requirement to engage in any kind of balancing exercise in consideration of sexual orientation rights. Her fundamental human right to exercise moral conscience could not be trumped by an 'abstract' right. Predictably the latter choice of terms has drawn criticism, although, paying careful attention to the Convention jurisprudence on sexual orientation equality, it is not indefensible.[67] However, it is the argument about the fundamental nature of conscience which is the focus here.

Interestingly, the history of the development of the right of conscientious objection before the UN Human Rights Committee shows the Committee having progressively moved to the same approach. In *Yeo-Bum Yoon and Myung-Jin Choi v Republic of Korea*[68] the Committee decided, for the first time, that lack of alternative civilian service to military conscription breached Article 18 of the Covenant. Bearing in mind that a large number of states had introduced schemes of alternative service to accommodate conscientious objectors to compulsory military service, it found that Korea had not adequately demonstrated why this was impossible in its case without compromising national security. Accordingly, it could not rely on Article 18(3) to limit the right.[69] This reasoning could not easily account for the application of Article 18 to non-religious conscientious objectors,[70] whose right to manifest their beliefs was not explicit in the text. The approach of treating conscientious objection as a manifestation of the right of religion and belief also left open the possibility that a state might in future be able to justify its refusal to accommodate conscientious objectors under Article 18(3). However, as Sir Nigel Rodley of the HRC later pointed out, since claims of conscientious objection were most likely to arise against the background of existential threats to the state this possibility had 'a certain lack of reality'. He argued instead that because of the value of sanctity of life the 'right to refuse to kill must be accepted completely' and therefore Articles 18(1) and 18(2) were a more appropriate basis for the right of conscientious objection.[71] Subsequently in *Jeong et al v Republic of Korea* the HRC accepted the force of these points and found by a majority that the complainants' conviction and sentence for refusing to be drafted amounted to an infringement of their freedom of conscience, in breach of Article 18(1), rather than by way of unjustified restriction on external manifestation.[72] In the later decision of *Young-kwan Kim and others v Republic of Korea*,

[67] I Leigh and A Hambler, 'Religious Symbols, Conscience and the Rights of Others' (2014) 3 *Oxford Journal of Law and Religion* 2–24.

[68] *Yeo-Bum Yoon and Myung-Jin Choi v Republic of Korea*, CCPR/C/88/D/1321-1322/2004, UN Human Rights Committee, 23 January 2007.

[69] 'Freedom to manifest one's religion or beliefs may be subject only to such limitations as are prescribed by law and are necessary to protect public safety, order, health, or morals or the fundamental rights and freedoms of others.'

[70] See *Eu-min Jung, Tae-Yang Oh, Chang-Geun Yeom, Dong-hyuk Nah, Ho-Gun Yu, Chi-yun Lim, Choi Jin Taehoon Lim, Sung-hwan Lim, Jae-sung Lim and Dong-ju Goh v Republic of Korea*, Comm Nos 1593 to 1603/2007 (adopted 23 March 2010), UN Doc CCPR/C/98/D/1593-1603/2007, finding violations of Art 18 where a number of the complainants had no specific religious basis for their conscientious objection.

[71] *Atasoy and Sarkut v Turkey*, Comm Nos 1853/2008 and 1854/2008, UN Doc CCPR/C/104/D/1853-1854/2008 (2012).

[72] *Jeong et al v Republic of Korea* Communications no 1642-1741/2007 (Human Rights Committee, 27 April 2011).

the Committee acknowledged that the implication of its approach was to treat some forms of conscientious objection as absolute and others[73] as only entitled to qualified protection.[74]

The concept of overlapping protection, in which some conscientious positions receive full protection and others only a qualified protection that is defeasible by other interests, gains some support from the way different types of conscience claim are often treated in practice. There is broad consensus that some acts against one's conscience are so serious that the individual's protection against them should be absolute. Being compelled to kill another person contrary to one's beliefs about the sanctity of human life falls into this category (whether the beliefs are religiously derived or not). This helps to explain the protection in many legal systems and under human rights law for conscientious objection to military service. On the other hand, conscience-based beliefs about marriage or sexual conduct have tended to be treated by courts as subject to qualified protection, where, among other considerations, the rights and freedoms of others need to be proportionally balanced.[75]

This is not to say that such balancing is unproblematic either. There has also been a regrettable tendency on the part of the Strasbourg court to refer to the 'rights and freedoms of others' in a loose and generalised way.[76] This can be seen in the existing Convention jurisprudence in which conscience has come into conflict with the interests of others. The text of the Convention itself is unhelpful since it does not specify what is to count as a 'right' or 'freedom' in the various limitation clauses (especially Articles 8(2), 9(2) and 10(2)). In fuller discussions elsewhere I have argued in favour of a reversibility test which would require the Court to ask whether another identifiable victim would have an admissible Convention claim if the state were to 'reverse' the outcome by giving priority to the less favoured right. If such a victim cannot be identified then the test suggests that no legitimate aim for a restriction exists. It follows that there is no need to consider questions to do with the legal quality or proportionality of the restriction. This is not the place for a full recapitulation of the argument but, in summary, the reversibility test helps to prevent the undisciplined growth of limitations to rights, helps promote consistent and symmetrical interpretation of Convention rights, and maintains the priority of Convention rights over other legal interests. Some prominent examples of 'balancing' by the European Court of Human Rights of freedom of thought, conscience and belief and other rights are shown to be spurious by careful application of this test.[77]

The relevance of the reversibility test can be briefly demonstrated by illustrating its potential applicability to the *Ashers Baking* ('Gay Cake') case recently decided by the

---

[73] Such as objections to compulsory schooling and payment of taxes.

[74] *Young-kwan Kim and others v Republic of Korea* (Comm no 2179/2012 (14 January 2015), CCPR/C/112/D/2179/2012.

[75] See, eg *Eweida* (n 17) [106], dealing with the claim brought by Ms Ladele; *In the Matter of Marriage Commissioners Appointed under The Marriage Act, 1995*, 2011 SKCA 3 (10 January 2011); *Dichmont v Newfoundland and Labrador (Government Services and Lands)* 2015 NLTD (G) 14.

[76] *cf* J Bomhoff, 'The Rights and Freedoms of Others: The ECHR and its Peculiar Category of Conflicts between Fundamental Rights' in Eva Brems (ed) *Conflicts Between Fundamental Rights* (Antwerp-Oxford, Intersentia, 2008).

[77] I Leigh, 'Reversibility, Proportionality and Conflicting Rights: *Fernández Martínez v Spain*' in S Smet and E Brems (eds), When Human Rights Clash at the European Court of Human Rights: Conflict or Harmony? (Oxford, Oxford University Press, 2017) 218–41; I Leigh and A Hambler, 'Religious Symbols, Conscience and the Rights of Others' (2014) 3 *Oxford Journal of Law and Religion* 2–24; I Leigh, 'Damned if they do, Damned if they don't: the European Court of Human Rights and the Protection of Religion from Attack' (2011) 17 *Res Publica* 55–73.

UK Supreme Court.[78] The interest here is on the Convention rights arguments, rather than on the applicability of discrimination law to the appeal.

In the Supreme Court the bakery argued that even if discrimination law applied to its refusal to supply the cake with the message 'Support Gay Marriage', the legislation should be interpreted compatibly with their rights under Articles 9 and 10 ECHR or, if such an interpretation was not possible, be treated as ultra vires. Conversely, the Equality Commission argued that the legislation had already struck a balance between the competing rights that the courts should defer to and that the appellants' Article 9 and 10 claims were limited by the rights and freedoms of others. In that context it is important to clearly identify what the competing rights are. The bakers contended that to treat their refusal to supply the cake with the message supporting same-sex marriage as unlawful discrimination was a form of compelled speech, contrary to Articles 9 and 10 of the Convention.

How should the claim that to do so would offend the bakers' conscience be treated? On the one hand, the bakers argued that they were asked to positively endorse something they found to be immoral. This perhaps put them in a stronger position than a business that refused service to a same-sex couple on grounds of conscience.[79] On the other hand, the endorsement point is open to the objection that bakers are not normally understood to identify with the message they ice, whether the message contains birthday or anniversary greetings or support for a football club.[80] This is partly a question of whose viewpoint the law should adopt – that of an onlooker[81] or of the person concerned. Normally, however, courts are reluctant for good reason to go behind the beliefs of a religious claimant if satisfied that they reach a minimal threshold of cogency, seriousness, coherence and importance. The recent Convention jurisprudence shows the Court tending to take such statements at face value where the actions are 'directly motivated' by the applicant's religious beliefs[82] and, consequently, treating Article 9 as engaged, but (as noted above) this is coupled with a preparedness to apply the limitations under Article 9(2) in a loose or generous way for the state's benefit. It is not surprising, then, that the Supreme Court accepted that it was the baker's own view that to supply the cake with the message in support of gay marriage would be contrary to their conscience that was determinative.[83]

If it is accepted that fulfilling the cake order involved the bakery or its directors identifying with the message, then being required to do so in the case of a message that they disagreed

---

[78] The county court found that a bakery had breached equality legislation by its refusal, in accordance with the proprietors' Christian beliefs, to supply a cake for a campaign event with slogan in favour of same-sex marriage: *Lee v Ashers Baking Co Ltd & Anor* [2015] NICty 2. For discussion see R Wintemute, 'Message-Printing Businesses, Non-Discrimination and Free Expression: Northern Ireland's "Support Gay Marriage" Cake Case' (2015) 26 *King's Law Journal* 348. The Northern Ireland Court of Appeal rejected an appeal, holding that the bakery had directly discriminated on grounds of sexual orientation and political opinion: *Lee v McArthur & Ors*, [2016] NICA 29. The Supreme Court held that there was no sexual-orientation discrimination. It also found that to the extent that there was any discrimination on the basis of political belief, enforcing the anti-discrimination legislation against the bakery would breach the religious freedom (Art 9) and negative freedom of expression (Art 10) of the owners of the bakery. *Lee v Ashers Baking Company Ltd & Ors* (Northern Ireland) (n 20).

[79] Such refusals are likely to be dismissed as a straightforward claim for exemption from legal obligations because of disagreement with the law: *cf* Baroness Hale in *Bull v Hall* (n 14) at 37.

[80] *Lee v McArthur & Ors* [2016] NICA 29, at 67.

[81] Wintemute, 'Message-Printing' (2015) 353–55 argues in favour of the viewpoint of a reasonable onlooker.

[82] See, for example, *Eweida* (n 17) at 103 (refusal of marriage registrar to conduct civil partnership ceremonies) and 108 (refusal to provide sex counselling to same-sex couples).

[83] *Lee v Ashers Baking Company Ltd & Ors* (n 20), at 54.

with would undoubtedly constitute an interference with their freedom of expression. Equally, approached from the direction of the directors' conscience[84] the same applies – this is the basis, after all, for the earliest conscience provisions, allowing a person to affirm rather than swear a religious oath in court or as a condition of public office. The European Court of Human Rights has repeatedly found that a requirement to swear a religious oath violates Article 9.[85]

Could it be argued, though, even accepting that freedom of speech or freedom of thought, conscience and religion was engaged, that it should be limited in the interests of the rights and freedoms of others under Article 9(2) or 10(2)? It is here that the reversibility test is potentially helpful in clarifying what rights or interests are at stake. It would be a mistake to start from the premise that what is involved is a clash between freedom of conscience and equality rights. This is an inaccurately wide formulation which is likely to lead to an unsound conclusion. There is no general Convention right to be protected against discrimination by private persons in the provision of goods and services. Article 14 of the ECHR applies only to discrimination by *states* in relation to *the enjoyment of Convention rights*. Protocol 12 (which the UK has not signed in any event) is wider but still stops short of requiring states to prohibit discrimination by private parties.[86] Some Council of Europe states have legislated on discrimination in the provision of goods or services by private suppliers, but many have not. Those that have not could not be said to be in breach of the Convention. Equally, EU law does not require states to prohibit discrimination in the provision of goods and services on grounds of age, disability, religion or belief, or sexual orientation.[87] It is clear then that if there were no equality legislation applicable in Northern Ireland to goods and services Mr Lee would have not have a Convention rights claim arising from the refusal of the cake order.

The distinction between rights under national legislation and human rights *stricto sensu* ought to be highly pertinent when considering ostensible conflicts of rights in cases such as this. The effectiveness of protection under the Convention would be undermined if rights under national legislation were able to prevail over those rights chosen for special protection under the ECHR. It is a regrettable feature of both the Strasbourg and domestic jurisprudence, however, that too often in the past courts have failed to be alert to this distinction.[88]

---

[84] The European Court of Human Rights has been reluctant to recognise that commercial organisations as such have rights under Article 9: JC Norton, *Freedom of Religious Organisations* (Oxford, Oxford University Press, 2016), 179–180. In *Asher's Baking* the Supreme Court held that to hold the company liable on this basis would 'effectively negate' the appellants' Convention rights: *Lee v Ashers Baking Company Ltd & Ors* (n 78 above), para 57. This is discussed in more detail by Frank Cranmer in his contribution to this volume.

[85] *Buscarini v San Marino* (2000) 30 EHRR 208; *Alexandridis v Greece*, App no 19516/06 (ECtHR, 21 February 2008); *Dimitras v Greece*, App nos 42837/06, 3269/07, 35793/07 and 6099/08 (ECtHR, 3 June 2010).

[86] *Explanatory Report to the Protocol 12 to the Convention for the Protection of Human Rights and Fundamental Freedoms* (Council of Europe, 2000), para 25.

[87] A longstanding proposal to extend it in this way in the 'Horizontal Directive' has not been implemented: European Commission, 'Proposal for a Council Directive on Implementing the Principle of Equal Treatment between Persons irrespective of Religion or Belief, Disability, Age or Sexual Orientation' COM (2008) 0426 final.

[88] For example in *Bull v Hall* (n 14) deciding that the Christian guesthouse owners' rights (with regard to manifesting their belief in the immorality of sex outside heterosexual marriage) were limited by the rights and freedoms of others under Art 9(2). The Supreme Court did not engage in any systematic analysis of what the overriding rights were from a Convention point of view. At para 5 of her judgment Baroness Hale refers in general to the applicability of appellants' rights under Arts 8 and 14, but in the later section dealing with the applicability of the Human Rights Act 1998 bases the discussion on their rights under the ordinary law instead (ibid at 44). See also Lord Toulson and Lord Neuberger at 72 and 85 respectively, concurring.

The Supreme Court in *Ashers Baking* found that there had been no sexual orientation discrimination by refusing to bake a cake with the slogan 'Support Gay Marriage' so the Court did not have the opportunity to resolve an ostensible conflict of rights. Even if it had found that there had been sexual orientation discrimination, it is nonetheless worth empha-sising the political nature of the event for which the cake was intended. The legislation on same-sex marriage does not apply to Northern Ireland and there can be little doubt that to oppose its introduction is squarely within the range of political discourse, highly protected under Article 10.[89] From this point of view the respondent was free to promote his message for a change in the law but the appellants, just like anyone else, could not be compelled to assist him. Adopting a reversibility analysis, there is no Convention right to be supplied with a cake with a message, still less a political message with which the supplier disagrees.

This argument is consistent with the Supreme Court's treatment of political belief discrimination in *Ashers Baking*.[90] It found that the message in support of gay marriage was prima facie indissociable from Mr Lee's political beliefs and so raised the question of whether he had been directly discriminated against on grounds of those beliefs. Baroness Hale found, however, that while the bakery could not refuse service because of the customer's sexual orientation or support of gay marriage,

> that important fact does not amount to a justification for something completely different – obliging them to supply a cake iced with a message with which they profoundly disagreed. In my view they would be entitled to refuse to do that whatever the message conveyed by the icing on the cake. ... The fact that this particular message had to do with sexual orientation is irrelevant.[91]

If, as I have argued, the courts were to be substantially more cautious in reaching for balanc-ing as a way of defeating potentially undesirable claims, there could be a prospect that the floodgates would open to unmeritorious applicants and 'conscience creep' would lead to an anarchical situation. There are several responses that can be made to this understandable concern. Firstly, proportional balancing may indeed be appropriate for a narrower category of cases. Conscientious objection claims by medical professionals spring to mind as a field in which this type of contextual, fact-sensitive approach would be suitable. Where countries at the one pole entirely deny conscientious objection so that a pro-life midwife in Sweden is unable to find work[92] or, at the other pole, allow it so freely that women are impeded from their legal entitlement to access abortion, as in Italy and Poland,[93] it seems entirely correct to balance the two rights in a context-sensitive way.

---

[89] *Castells v Spain* (1992) 14 EHRR 445.

[90] Discrimination on grounds of political belief is an under-explored aspect of the Art 14 jurisprudence. In *Redfearn v United Kingdom* [2013] IRLR 51 (ECtHR) the European Court of Human Rights found that the absence of a remedy for employment discrimination on the basis of political opinion or membership infringed Art 11, in the case of dismissal of an employee who had been elected as a British National Party councillor. His Art 14 claim was admissible but was not determined in the light of the Court's finding on Art 11. Assuming, however, that political belief discrimination falls within the scope of Art 14, the reversibility argument made above about sexual orientation would, apply in the same way: a state is not required by the Convention to make such discrimination unlawful in the case of the private supply of goods and services and so 'the rights and freedoms of others' do not arise under Art 9(2) or 10(2). The legislative prohibition in Northern Ireland is certainly unusual, if not unique, in the Council of Europe.

[91] *Lee v Ashers Baking Company Ltd & Ors* (Northern Ireland) (n 20) at 55.

[92] As in the case of Ellinor Grimmark. BBC, 'Swedish Anti-Abortion Midwife Loses Court Case' (BBC News, 13 April 2017).

[93] Parliamentary Assembly of the Council of Europe, Resolution 1763 (2010). See Explanatory Memorandum, 'Women's Access to Lawful Medical Care: the Problem of Unregulated Use of Conscientious Objection', Doc 11757 (Rapporteur C McCafferty).

Secondly, if there is an increase in resort to conscience claims it may be partly in response to the perception that existing religious freedoms claims are being too lightly treated by the courts in a way that invariably results in defeat whenever an obstacle is encountered, such as a conflicting societal interest or the claim that the state is acting to protect the rights of others.[94] Religious affiliation is frequently characterised as a matter of individual choice – with the implication that it is less worthy of protection than other rights. Arguably, claimants have been forced to respond to religious illiteracy on the part of society and the courts by enunciating more clearly the nature and consequences of their beliefs and to find new legal ways of presenting their arguments. A more rigorous judicial approach to conflicting rights in religion cases might incidentally disincentivise some conscience claimants.

Thirdly, proportionality is not the only way to limit over-broad conscience claims in any event. There are other tools available. It is open to a court to apply the existing requirements that beliefs must attain a certain level of cogency, seriousness, cohesion and importance[95] and that there must be a sufficiently close and direct nexus between the act and the belief[96] to fall within Article 9 more stringently to debar tenuous conscience claims. Although, as noted above, the European Court of Human Rights uses these tests sparingly, one can see how such reasoning could potentially deal with some instances where the claim is that the person's conscience would be violated if they were made to some degree complicit in the actions of other people that it would be immoral for they themselves to undertake. There is also the possibility in cases of contrived conscience claims of defeating them by (sparing) use of a sincerity test.[97]

VII. Conclusion

The question of how courts approach conscience claims is assuming greater significance and is likely to continue to do so due to a variety factors. These include the increasing pluralism of Western societies which make it less likely than in the past that legislation can be framed to accommodate the variety of beliefs and practices existing in these societies. At the same time, against the combined background of the Culture Wars and of 9/11 and its aftermath, religion has become toxic for many liberal legislators. As a consequence they seem less inclined than in previous decades to provide conscience clauses when enacting reforming legislation.[98] The side-effect is that claimants look to the courts for protection instead. Conscience claims are no longer the preserve of conscripted soldiers. They are increasingly made by public officials, healthcare professionals and even bakers. Judicial activism may itself be part of the cause. Where the courts engage in progressive or innovative

---

[94] For example, *SAS v France* [2014] ECHR 695.

[95] *Bayatyan* (n 25) at 110.

[96] *Eweida* (n 17) at 82.

[97] A Hambler, 'Establishing Sincerity in Religion and Belief Claims: a Question of Consistency' (2011) 13 *Ecc L J* 146–56.

[98] Note, for example, the refusal to grant more than temporary exemption for Catholic adoption agencies from the Equality Act 2010.

constitutional interpretation of rights, for example to assisted suicide or same-sex marriage, one effect may be to create new crises of conscience for existing professionals.[99]

In this chapter it has been argued that the courts should embrace conscience claims both for normative and doctrinal reasons. At the normative level the frequently voiced objections to conscience claims – that they involve special treatment of certain groups that somehow violates the rule of law or that claimants are privilege-seekers – have been shown to rest on misunderstandings. Equal treatment does not require uniformity. The reverse is the case in fact, once it is accepted that conscience burdens some individuals in a way that it would be unjust not to recognise. Legal doctrine reflects this position and there is a clear duty on courts in human rights law when the right of freedom of conscience is engaged to make appropriate provision where the legislature has failed to do so.

On the other hand, the fear that by doing so the courts would open the floodgates to anarchy underestimates the extent to which courts currently supervise the boundaries of conscience claims both by individuals and groups under exceptions and exemptions. As noted above, conscience claims are increasingly made in response to newly introduced rights and services under progressive law reform, whether by the legislature or the judiciary. Here the question of how to reconcile conscience with other societal interests and the rights and freedoms of others arises. It should not be assumed that proportional balancing is the correct or best way to resolve all such potential conflicts. Indeed, in some situations on careful analysis it is unlikely to be applicable and the right of freedom of conscience will be unqualified. Even where conscience rights are qualified there may be more appropriate alternatives, involving more careful examination of whether either freedom of conscience or the ostensibly conflicting right is properly engaged. However, there is likely to remain a smaller group of conscience claims – including those by healthcare professionals – where proportional balancing is unavoidable and appropriate.

---

[99] As with physician assisted suicide in Canada (*Carter v Canada (Attorney General)* [2015] SCC 5) or same-sex marriage in the US in *Obergefell et al v Hodges, Director of Ohio Department of Health et al*, Supreme Court of the United States, 576 US, 26 June 2015 and South Africa in *Minister of Home Affairs and Another v Fourie*, Case CCT 60/04, 1 December 2005 [2005] ZACC 19 (although the judgment in *Fourie* also seems to have been the catalyst for inclusion in the subsequent legislation of a right of conscientious objection: Civil Union Act 2006, s 6; *Fourie* at 159).

7

The Difference between Illegitimate Conscience and Misguided Conscience: Equality Laws, Abortion Laws and Religious Symbols

YOSSI NEHUSHTAN AND STELLA COYLE*

I. Introduction

When the liberal state, through its legislative body, the executive or judiciary, decides whether to accommodate conscientious objections, normally by exempting the objector from the application of a legal norm or policy, it can apply one of two approaches: a content-neutral approach or a content-based approach.

A content-neutral approach would be a specific implementation of neutral liberalism. According to any perception of neutral liberalism, when the state decides whether to tolerate views, beliefs or 'conceptions of the good', it should ignore the values that ground the moral reasons for people's behaviour.[1] The state can only take into account neutral considerations, such as the potential risk to public order or to general public interests, and the amount of harm that may be caused to rights and interests of others. Within the context of conscientious objection, when the neutral state decides whether to accommodate the objection, it must ignore the content of the conscience or the content of the moral values that grounded the objection. The neutral state cannot, of course, completely avoid making value-based decisions. When it takes into account the amount of harm that may be caused to rights and

* School of Law, Keele University. Our thanks are due to Megan Davidson for her excellent research assistance and to John Adenitire for his insightful and extremely helpful comments. The argument about the importance of the content of the conscience in cases where conscientious objections rely on unjustly intolerant, morally repugnant and illegitimate values, is developed in detail in Y Nehushtan, 'Conscientious Objection and Equality Laws: Why the Content of the Conscience Matters' (2019) *Law and Philosophy* (forthcoming). Here we focus on the cases where the conscientious objection relies on misguided yet legitimate values, ie the cases of abortion laws and religious symbols.

[1] For this approach see: J Rawls, *Political Liberalism* (New York, Columbia University Press, 1993) 192–93; B Ackerman, *Social Justice in the Liberal State* (New Haven, CT, Yale University Press, 1980) 11; R Dworkin, *Taking Rights Seriously* (Cambridge, MA, Harvard University Press, 1977) 266, 273; R Dworkin, *A Matter of Principle* (Oxford, Oxford University Press, 1985) 191–92; R Dworkin, *Sovereign Virtue: The Theory and Practice of Equality* (Cambridge, MA, Harvard University Press, 2000) ch 6; T Nagel, *Equality and Partiality* (Oxford, Oxford University Press, 1995); B Barry, *Justice as Impartiality* (Oxford, Oxford University Press, 1995); W Kymlicka, *Multicultural Citizenship: A Liberal Theory of Minority Rights* (Oxford, Clarendon Press, 1995).

interests of others, a value-based decision must be made as to which rights people actually have. And when the neutral state takes into account the harm that may be caused to general public interests or public goods, these interests and goods need to be identified – and this must entail value-based decisions. In terms of general public interests, it is important to acknowledge the common presumption that religion is a human good, even if the liberal state professes to be secular. This presumption is reflected in international and domestic human rights charters.[2] Nevertheless, religion is normally not treated in law as valuable as such. The protections granted to religious belief and expression are normally grounded more in the recognition that religious believers can be vulnerable – or that their religious belief is valuable to them – regardless of them being wrong from the secular state's (possible) point of view. It is this that renders the standard liberal approach a content-neutral one.

A content-based approach, on the other hand, requires the state to evaluate the moral soundness and moral legitimacy of the conscience or the moral values that ground the conscientious objection. A content-based approach does not have to be a liberal approach. It can be non-liberal or anti-liberal. However, for the purpose of this chapter it will be assumed that the state is a liberal state and that as a liberal state it can only choose between a content-neutral approach, as an implementation of neutral liberalism, and a liberal, content-based approach, as an implementation of what may be called perfectionist-liberalism or substantive-liberalism.

As opposed to neutral liberalism, perfectionist theories hold that the state has a duty or at least a right to promote well-being or human flourishing by supporting and protecting certain values and ways of life. It demands that the state acts, or refrains from acting, in order to create and maintain legal and social conditions that best enable its subjects to pursue valuable and worthwhile lives rather than any kind of life. In a nutshell, any perfectionist political or moral theory holds that some ideals of human flourishing are sound whereas others are not; that the state is justified in favouring the former; and that there is no general moral principle that forbids the state from favouring sound values, even when these values are controversial, as long as these values are indeed sound.[3] The liberal framework views certain principles, particularly autonomy and equality, to be necessary for human flourishing. These axioms can be regarded as self-evident in liberalism, and it is in this context that such values can be described as 'sound'.

Choosing between neutral liberalism and perfectionist liberalism is necessary in order to define the limits of liberal tolerance towards conscientious objections. Accommodating conscientious objection, typically by granting conscientious exemptions from the application of the law or of administrative policies, is usually the outcome of tolerance.

---

[2] See for example Art 18 of the UN's Universal Declaration of Human Rights and Art 9 of the European Convention on Human Rights.

[3] For this approach see: J Raz, *The Morality of Freedom* (Oxford, Clarendon Press, 1986); R Abel, *Speech and Respect: Hamlyn Lectures Series* (London, Sweet & Maxwell, 1994) esp ch 4; G Sher, *Beyond Neutrality: Perfectionism and Politics* (Cambridge, Cambridge University Press, 1997); S Wall, *Liberalism, Perfectionism and Restraint* (Cambridge, Cambridge University Press, 1998); C Brettschneider, *When the State Speaks, What Should It Say?: How Democracies Can Protect Expression and Promote Equality* (New Jersey, Princeton University Press, 2012); S Macedo, 'Transformative Constitutionalism and the Case of Religion: Defending the Moderate Hegemony of Liberalism' (1998) 26 *Political Theory* 56, 58, 76; G Watt, 'Giving unto Caesar: Rationality, Reciprocity and Legal Recognition of Religion' in R O'Dair and A Lewis (eds), *Current Legal Issues: Law and Religion* (Oxford, Oxford University Press, 2001), 54.

Here, tolerance is understood as refraining from harming the 'other' although the tolerant person has good reasons (in his opinion) to harm that 'other'. The tolerant person makes an adverse judgement about another person, the adverse judgement provides the tolerant person with reasons to harm the other, but the tolerant person restrains himself and avoids harming the other. These three elements of (a) adverse judgement, (b) reasons for causing harm and (c) restraint, differentiate the concept of tolerance and the attitude of tolerance from concepts such as respect, acceptance or indifference.

The principle of tolerance better explains both the practice of accommodating conscientious objection by granting conscientious exemptions and the attitude of those who grant the exemptions. Typically, granting conscientious exemptions from a legal rule which is not morally neutral presupposes that the state does not share the conscientious objector's values or his or her way of balancing between values, or believes it would be unbearable and indeed intolerable if everyone shared the objector's kind of conscience and reasoning. Otherwise, the exemption would have been the general rule rather than the exception to it.[4]

If granting conscientious exemptions – or more generally – accommodating conscientious objection is in most cases the outcome of tolerance, then the practice of granting conscientious exemptions is closely related to the complex question of the limits of tolerance. And if the state is generally a liberal state, the exact question will be that of the limits of liberal tolerance. These limits can be decided by applying one of the two possible theories that were described above: neutral liberalism or perfectionist liberalism.

In this paper it will not be argued that the legislature should take a moral stand and should apply a content-based approach when deciding whether to accommodate conscientious objections. Rather, it will be argued that the legislature *does* take this moral stand. The arguments will focus on how exactly the legislature takes this moral stand – and how should courts apply this moral stand – by offering a distinction between conscientious objections that rely on unjustly intolerant, morally repugnant and illegitimate values; and objections that rely on misguided yet legitimate values.

II. Conscientious Objection and Illegitimate Values: Equality Laws

A. Why the Content of the Conscience Matters

As made clear by Peter Jones in chapter three, in most cases of conscientious objection, both in the UK and in the European Court of Human Rights, the courts consistently apply a mostly neutral rhetoric, while almost completely ignoring the content of the relevant conscience. In these cases the courts avoid, almost completely, making any normative judgement about the content of the relevant conscience. Instead, they decide the cases before them while relying

---

[4] For a detailed argument according to which granting conscientious exemptions is normally an expression of tolerance see: Y Nehushtan, 'What Are Conscientious Exemptions Really About?' (2013) 2 *Oxford Journal of Law and Religion* 393. For a critical discussion of the argument that the principle of tolerance better explains the practice of granting conscientious exemptions, see: J Adenitire, 'Conscientious Exemptions: From Toleration to Neutrality; From Neutrality to Respect' (2017) 6 *Oxford Journal of Law and Religion* 268.

mostly on content-neutral justifications.[5] If the legislature, however, takes a moral stand in cases of conscientious objection, then both the legislature and the courts should do so by differentiating between two types of cases:

- Type 1: claims for exemption or accommodation that are directly based on repugnant, unjustly intolerant, anti-liberal and ultimately illegitimate values. This type of case will be briefly discussed below within the context of conscientious objection to equality laws.

- Type 2: claims that are based on values that may be irrational or morally misguided but are not necessarily unjustly intolerant or morally illegitimate. This type of case includes, for example, wearing religious dress or symbols in the workplace, and refusal to perform abortion or to provide contraception.

Normative evaluation of the content of the conscience provides a weighty reason (though not necessarily a conclusive one) for not tolerating type 1 and for tolerating type 2 under certain conditions. A normative evaluation does not always rule out the application of neutral considerations. A normative evaluation may require the content of the conscience to be added to the overall considerations. In some cases, where the content of the conscience is grossly repugnant and utterly illegitimate, then neutral considerations need not apply.

B. Conscientious Objection and Equality Laws

Cases of type 1 include conscientious objections that rely on unjustly intolerant and illegitimate values such as homophobic or racist views and unjust discriminatory practices (eg a refusal to provide services to homosexuals; excluding women from the public or political sphere; 'separate but equal' practices, and so on). Four recent UK cases are good examples of cases of type 1: *Ashers Baking* (refusal to sell a 'gay marriage' cake),[6] *Bull* (refusal to let a bed-and-breakfast room to a gay couple),[7] *Ladele* (refusal to register a civil partnership between a gay couple),[8] and *McFarlane* (refusal to counsel same-sex couples on sexual matters).[9] All these cases are based on a claim for exemption or accommodation that has been made in light of the Equality Act 2010 (or similar legislation), which prohibits discrimination on the ground of sexual orientation.

Notwithstanding important differences between these cases, they all share one crucial point. In all four cases the refusal to provide a service relied on an adverse judgement that the conscientious objector made about gay people. In three of the four cases (*Bull*, *Ladele* and *McFarlane*) a service was denied to gay couples because they were gay. In the

[5] J Maher, 'Eweida and Others: A New Era for Article 9?' (2014) 63 *International & Comparative Law Quarterly* 213; R Sandberg, 'Laws and Religion: Unravelling *McFarlane v Relate Avon Limited*' (2010) 12 *Ecclesiastical Law Journal* 361; P Cumper and T Lewis, '"Public Reason", Judicial Deference and the Right to Freedom of Religion and Belief under the Human Rights Act 1998' (2011) 22 *King's Law Journal* 131; M Hill and R Sandberg, 'Is Nothing Sacred? Clashing Symbols in a Secular World' (2007) *Public Law* 488; N Gibson, 'Faith in the Courts: Religious Dress and Human Rights' (2007) 66 *Cambridge Law Journal* 657.
[6] *Lee v Ashers Baking Company Ltd & Ors (Northern Ireland)* [2018] UKSC 49.
[7] *Bull and another (Appellants) v Hall and another (Respondents)* [2013] UKSC 73.
[8] *Ladele v London Borough of Islington* [2009] EWCA (Civ) 1357.
[9] *McFarlane v Relate Avon* [2010] EWCA Civ 88.

fourth case (*Ashers Baking*) a service was denied not because of the identity of the customer but because of his views (ie supporting gay marriage), yet the reason for denying the service was an adverse judgement that the conscientious objector made about gay people.

Discrimination against gay people, because they are gay, relies on intolerant, anti-liberal and illegitimate values. More importantly, moral disagreements about whether this discrimination does in fact rely on illegitimate values are of little significance here. This is so because by enacting equality laws the liberal state, through the legislature, has already expressed its view that discrimination against gay people does rely on illegitimate values. The state decided the limits of liberal tolerance by relying on content-based rather than content-neutral considerations. Equality laws set an underlying moral principle according to which less favourable treatment just because of a protected characteristic is basically indefensible.[10]

Within the context of providing services to the public, equality laws have two purposes. The narrow purpose is to prevent service providers from discriminating against customers while relying on their protected characteristics, thus to protect customers from being discriminated against because of their protected characteristics. The broader purpose is to prevent service providers from acting upon their discriminatory views when they provide services to the general public, thus preventing service providers from refusing to provide a service if the refusal relies on an adverse judgement about others (non-customers) because of their protected characteristics.

With regard to both purposes, the consequences of the discriminatory act are in fact irrelevant. Discriminatory acts that result from an adverse judgement about others because of their protected characteristics are inherently immoral and illegal regardless of their actual consequences in each and every specific case. Service providers are not allowed to act upon their discriminatory views – and the existence of harm or offence in a particular case is plainly irrelevant. If the purpose of equality laws is broader than preventing harm or offence to – in our case – customers, and if the purpose is to prevent service providers from acting upon their discriminatory views when they provide a service to the general public, then a refusal to provide a service because the service provider holds discriminatory views about gay people, for example, is illegal regardless of whether the customer is or is not gay. Put differently, and according to a proper reading of the Equality Act 2010 and similar statutes, acting upon an intolerant, morally illegitimate conscience is illegal because of the content of the conscience and regardless of the consequences of the discriminatory act.

These purposes of equality laws also explain why conscientious objectors should not be exempted from these laws. When equality laws include protected characteristics (and in the cases mentioned above, sexual orientation) they take a moral view on this issue, which almost always contradicts other moral views that some people hold. The prohibition on discriminating against others on the basis of their sexual orientation is not aimed at enlightened people who would never consider discriminating against lesbian, gay, bisexual and

---

[10] This is the underlying principle behind the Equality Act 2010, notwithstanding the provisions allowing for *indirect* discrimination on the grounds of a protected characteristic, if it is a proportionate means of achieving a legitimate aim. Indirect discrimination will normally not result from conscientious objection that relies on discriminatory values (unless, of course, the indirect discrimination aims to conceal these discriminatory values). If the content of the conscience that dictates the discriminatory act relies on discriminatory values, that would normally be a case of direct discrimination which is always prohibited as a result of a value-based liberal approach.

transgender (LGBT) people, nor is it mainly aimed at those who discriminate against LGBT people because of mere preferences or interests. It is aimed at homophobes and those who have moral reasons for discriminating against LGBT people. From the tolerant-liberal state's point of view, it makes no sense to exempt from equality laws the same people who are the reason for enacting such laws.

C. Conscientious Objection, Equality Laws and Religious Belief

As to the common clash between the principle of equality and freedom of religion, equality laws – and most notably the Equality Act 2010 – create a clear hierarchy of rights according to which equality decides the limits of freedom of religion. When freedom of religion and the principle of equality clash, there are only two options: either freedom of religion allows religious believers to discriminate against others or equality defines the limits of freedom of religion. Equality and autonomy are arguably the basis of all other human rights. Humans have rights as humans, and they are all equally human.[11] They have rights so they could be free to be the (partial) authors of their life without fear of sanctions, being manipulated or threatened, and thus to be autonomous. Therefore the limits or the scope of all human rights, including freedom of religion, are defined inter alia by equality and autonomy itself. More specifically, freedom of religion ends when it leads to an unjust discrimination against others.[12] The question of whether exercising freedom of religion *unjustly* discriminates against others cannot be answered without subscribing to a comprehensive moral or political theory. It cannot be answered in a coherent and satisfactory way by subscribing to neutral liberalism. It can only be answered by subscribing to either the religious point of view or to the liberal-humanist-secular point of view. If the relevant anti-discrimination legislation entrenches liberal-humanist-secular values it will be incoherent if it does not create a hierarchy of rights according to which equal treatment sets the limits of freedom religion. This helps to explain why the courts have struggled in their attempts to resolve the conflict between religion and sexual orientation in equality law. The courts' emphasis on the secular state[13] is of limited value if the judgments nevertheless proceed on the illusory basis of content-neutral considerations. It appears that courts are nervous of explicitly recognising the need for a hierarchy of rights where equality is the determining factor.

The argument about hierarchy of rights may lead to a broader question: should religious belief be a concern of equality law at all? Answering this question in the negative results, yet again, in equality trumping freedom of religion, but this time – not because equality is placed higher in the hierarchy of rights, but because equality statutes exclude or should exclude freedom of religion from the discourse of rights or from the balance of harms, at least in part. The question of the relevancy of religious belief within the context of

---

[11] For a recent critical discussion of the view that human beings possess human rights 'simply in virtue of being human', see RN Fasel, '"Simply in Virtue of being Human"? A Critical Appraisal of a Human Rights Commonplace' (2018) *Jurisprudence* (forthcoming).
[12] For a similar view see F Raday, 'Culture, Religion and Gender' (2003) 1 *International Journal of Constitutional Law* 663, 701.
[13] See for example *MacFarlane* (n 9) at 22 per Laws LJ.

equality law arises in two ways: first, from the argument that religious belief is a choice;[14] and second, from the partly related argument that distress (a feeling that one dislikes having) ensuing from beliefs ought to be treated differently from other kinds of distress, namely those that relate to one's identity.[15] A full discussion of these arguments is beyond the scope of this paper, but they are nonetheless worth acknowledging. To consider the first argument, one can accept that the unequal impact of a law may be a prima facie indication of that law's unfairness; for example, a conservative religious registrar might experience the legal requirement to conduct same-sex marriage ceremonies as particularly difficult. However, more substantiation is needed, beyond his or her feelings, to show exactly why the law is unfair or discriminatory. Under a liberal legal framework, claims for equality should be reserved for rules that treat people differently on the basis of characteristics (such as sexual orientation). If religious belief is characterised as a chosen preference rather than a characteristic (and we do not necessarily subscribe to this view), it should make no equality claim. Instead, the religious should bear the consequences of their chosen, preferred belief. This possible argument raises a few difficulties that will not be discussed here.

The second argument builds on the first argument. When considering the difficulty experienced by those who deeply hold discriminatory values, it is helpful to recognise the distinction between distress that is mediated by belief and distress that is mediated by one's identity. Equality law should protect against only the latter type of distress. The distress argument is related to the choice argument because both acknowledge that people bear some personal responsibility for how long they have distressing feelings and how intense they are. Further, it may be argued that it would be disingenuous to describe belief-mediated distress as a harm, either to the individual religious discriminator, or to our axiomatic liberal principles of autonomy and equality. Some argue that the very word 'harm' has a tendency to 'slither',[16] enabling individuals to say they have suffered harm whenever something happens that they would prefer not to have happened.

An example of this 'slithering' is the attempt to extend the notion of harm to include the worsening of a person's condition via a worsening of their status. Lilian Ladele and Gary McFarlane lost their jobs because of their refusal to provide services to gay people (civil partnership ceremonies and sex therapy to gay couples respectively), and the Bulls had to sell their hotel as a result of their refusal to let double rooms to same-sex couples. According to Thomson, it is not an infringement of someone's condition per se to cause them to lose their job (unless the loss is caused by an infringing act such as spreading lies about them), because 'the gravamen of the charge against one who causes a status worsening lies in the means used. If those means are no infringement of a claim, then causing the status worsening is not either. Thus status worsenings are not themselves harms'.[17] On this view, the refusal of the claims made by Ms Ladele, Mr McFarlane and the Bulls did not amount to harm, either to them as individuals or to the liberal principles of autonomy and equality.

---

[14] See for example Sedley LJ's characterisation in *Eweida v British Airways plc* [2010] EWCA Civ 80, [40] of religious belief as a choice, and also Brian Barry, *Culture and Equality: An Egalitarian Critique of Multiculturalism* (Cambridge, MA, Harvard University Press, 2002); Peter Jones, 'Religion and Freedom of Expression' (2011) 17 *Res Publica* 1.

[15] See J J Thomson, *The Realm of Rights* (Cambridge, MA, Harvard University Press, 1990).

[16] ibid 260.

[17] ibid 266.

We do not, however, have to subscribe to the 'lack of harm' argument in order to maintain the hierarchy of rights with regard to equality and freedom of religion. We could agree that harm was in fact caused in the cases mentioned above but to add that the harm is justifiable. The cases of *Ladele, McFarlane, Bull* and *Ashers Baking*, may be perceived as cases where the religious believers were indirectly discriminated against. Bearing in mind the purpose of equality laws, and correctly applying core liberal principles, will result in a conclusion that the harm caused in these cases is proportionate and therefore justified. Any other conclusion will reflect an Orwellian argument according to which imposing the duty not to discriminate on those who wish to discriminate is itself prohibited discrimination. The following section elaborates on this point.

D. 'Discrimination' Against Those Who Wish to Discriminate Against Others

A common argument made either explicitly or implicitly by many is that the court should at least appreciate that those who are prevented from discriminating against others, even though their conscience or religion prescribes such discrimination, are or may be the ones who are being discriminated against.[18]

Two different tests can be applied here in order to refute this argument. The first is the intention/motive test, which is a neutral one. This test asks who was the first who restricted (in the broadest sense possible) the freedom of others – or discriminated against others – because of a negative opinion about these others or their values. The second is a content-based test that gives priority to liberal values over non-liberal ones.

If we apply the intention/motive test to the *Ashers Baking* case, for example, we will find that the buyer did not aim to discriminate against religious-Christian cake-sellers because of their religion or religious belief. He did not treat them differently because of their religious belief or indeed at all. His initial purpose was not to limit their freedom of religion because he made an adverse judgement about their identity or their values. The sellers, however, did exactly that. They refused to serve a customer because of the adverse judgement they made about gay people as such, and as a result, about the customer's views.

The neutral intention/motive test according to which we ask who was the first who treated others differently merely shifts the burden of proof. It is for those who were the first to discriminate to justify their acts. Such justification may be found if the discriminator acts upon liberal values and as a reaction to an act or a demand which is based on anti-liberal, morally repugnant values. The purpose of equality legislation is to prevent discrimination based on protected grounds. Confusingly, one of these protected grounds is religion. This is confusing because religious belief is quite often the reason for a discriminatory approach against others. Moreover, religious belief is presumably the only protected ground that can itself be a reason for discriminating against others.[19]

---

[18] For this argument see: Maher, 'Eweida and Others' (2014) 231–32; R Sandberg (n 5 above) 363; J Rivers 'The Secularisation of the British Constitution' (2012) 14 *Ecclesiastical Law Journal* 371, 383.

[19] A McColgan, *Discrimination, Equality and the Law* (Oxford, Hart Publishing, 2014) 136.

But religious belief is merely a belief.[20] Unless it is argued that religious belief should be singled out for special, positive treatment – and that would be incompatible with any meaningful version of liberalism and with the principle of equality itself – equality laws should be interpreted in the following way: discriminating against religious people only because they are religious, while completely ignoring the content of their religious belief or the general content of their religion may be morally wrong and also illegal. At the same time, religious belief should almost never form a valid legal reason for discriminating against others unless we are willing to allow all those who are morally committed to discriminatory views to act upon these views and to discriminate against others. And that would obviously be a death sentence for all equality laws. This explains why arguing that preventing people from discriminating against others, even though their conscience or religion prescribes such discriminating, is in fact discrimination – is an Orwellian argument. Such an argument empties equality laws of their content and purpose and leads to a legal permission to discriminate merely because one deeply holds discriminatory values.

E. Equality Laws and the Importance of the Conscientious Objector's Values

Equality laws are not and cannot be neutral. They reflect a content-based moral decision about the importance and weight of the principle of equality vis-à-vis other rights or interests. This also means that from the state's point of view, conscientious objection to equality laws always relies on unjustly intolerant and morally illegitimate values. As will be shown shortly, this is not the case with regard to cases of type 2.

When the state, for example, grants exemptions from equality laws to religious organisations, the state morally disapproves the religious conscience that prescribes discrimination against protected groups (most commonly on the basis of sex, sexual orientation and religion). If the state perceived the religious discriminatory conscience as morally desirable, it would not have enacted equality laws to begin with. It is true that exemptions from equality laws are often granted only to religious organisations. This may lead to perceiving these exemptions as an expression of favouritism rather than tolerance. This perception is only partly true. Religious organisations do get special, positive treatment within the context of equality laws. But the true meaning of this favouritism is that religious organisations are the only ones that are being tolerated by the state. This unique mixture of favouritism and tolerance does not contradict the argument that granting conscientious exemptions is almost always an expression of tolerance, and that equality laws express a content-based moral stand about the relative importance of the principle of equality.

The distinction between cases of type 1 and cases of type 2 reflects a view that those who object to the law for conscientious reasons and whose conscience does not rely on unjustly intolerant and illegitimate values or beliefs have a stronger case (other things being equal) to be granted conscientious exemptions. The content of the conscience should be taken into account by the courts, along with other relevant considerations, if the liberal state has already decided, through its legislature, to eliminate the availability of bad options, to

---

[20] In *Eweida*, Sedley LJ went further and characterised religious belief as a choice. See *Eweida* (n 14) [40].

discourage people from making bad choices – choices that are unjust because they interfere with autonomy and equality – and to not tolerate illiberal, unjustified intolerance.

Various kinds of moral disagreement (or other types of disagreement) should be tolerated by the state, whereas other kinds of disagreement should not. In order to distinguish the two, a value-based examination of the conscience in question must be made. In the following section, we will focus on cases of type 2, justify their categorisation to this type and prescribe the state's proper response to these cases while differentiating these cases from cases of type 1. Two paradigmatic cases will be used as primary examples: wearing religious symbols in the workplace and objection to perform abortions.

III. Conscientious Objection and Misguided yet Legitimate Values

Here, the claim for exemption, accommodation and in any event, tolerance, is based on values or practices that may be irrational or morally misguided but are not necessarily unjustly intolerant or morally illegitimate. Religious or conscientious objection of this type is quite common and includes, for example, refusal to perform abortion or to provide contraception;[21] to wear safety helmets;[22] to work on the religious day of rest;[23] to receive or allow medical treatment (eg blood transfusions, as is the case with Jehovah's Witnesses);[24] to perform compulsory military service;[25] or even to use the internet.[26]

The above examples are not all of one kind. The fact that these examples of conscientious or moral objection are all included in type 2 does not imply that they give rise to similar problems or that they should be treated equally by the state. These examples are included in type 2 because the conscientious or moral objection in all of them does not result from values that necessarily run against core values of liberalism. It also does not result from unjustly intolerant views or morally repugnant values. They do rely on irrational beliefs or morally misguided values, at least from the state's point of view, but this is not a sufficient reason for the tolerant-liberal state not to tolerate them.

A refusal to wear safety helmets, a refusal to work on the religious day of rest and a refusal to receive or allow medical treatment and so on – and as far as they rely on religious values or reasons – are all irrational because religion itself and religious belief are irrational, in the sense that they are based on faith, not reason.[27] Yet irrationality, unlike profound

---

[21] For an ECtHR's refusal to grant exemption to pharmacists who refused to sell contraception see: *Pichon and Sajous v France App n 49853/99* (Commission Decision, 2 October 2001).

[22] S Poulter, *Ethnicity, Law and Human* Rights (Oxford, Oxford University Press, 1998) ch 8.

[23] R Gavison and N Perez, 'Days of Rest in Multicultural Societies: Private, Public, Separate' in P Cane, C Evans and Z Robinson (eds), *Law and Religion in Theoretical and Historical Context* (Cambridge, Cambridge University Press, 2008) 186.

[24] R Singelenberg, 'The Blood Transfusion Taboo of Jehovah's Witnesses: Origins, Development and Function of a Controversial Doctrine' (1990) 31 *Social Science and Medicine* 515.

[25] *Bayatyan v Armenia* (2012) 54 EHRR 15.

[26] *Blackburn & Anor v Revenue & Customs* [2013] UKFTT 525 (TC), where two beekeepers had won the right not to file their VAT returns online after claiming that to do so was contrary to their religious belief.

[27] We will not try to defend the argument that religious belief is inherently irrational. For a view that what distinguishes religious belief is that it is based on faith, not reason, see: T Macklem, 'Faith as a Secular Value' (2000) 45

immorality, is not a sufficient reason for an intolerant response to conscientious objection. Parents' refusal to allow medical treatment to their children is morally misguided and should not be tolerated by the state – but not because of the content of the (normally religious) conscience. It should not be tolerated because it results in harming others, sometimes even causing death to others. There is nothing in the content of the misguided belief that blood transfusion is morally or religiously prohibited that is intolerant, illiberal or morally illegitimate. The moral content of the conscience is utterly misguided and irrational but it is the consequences of acting upon this conscience (ie unjustly harming others) that require the state not to accommodate this specific conscientious objection. With the absence of such consequences, a refusal of a blood transfusion, to wear a safety helmet or to work on the religious day of rest do not challenge core liberal values, do not express unjust intolerant values and are not morally illegitimate in and of themselves. Therefore, unlike objecting to equality laws that prohibit discriminating against others because of who they are, the content of the conscience in these cases can't form a weighty reason for not tolerating it. It does not follow, however, that the content of the conscience is irrelevant. The cases of wearing religious dress in the workplace and the refusal to perform abortions exemplify this point.

A. Religious Symbols

Wearing religious symbols in the workplace or presenting religious symbols in the public sphere are two notable examples of a claim for exemption, accommodation or merely respect, which indirectly expresses misguided yet morally legitimate views. We do not wish to address in full the complex issue of religious symbols in the liberal state.[28] We will also ignore religious dress such as the burka or the niqab, which symbolise oppression, subjection and exclusion (and we will not defend this assertion here).[29] The discussion here will

---

McGill Law Journal 1, 133. For a different view about the rationality of religious commitment (rather than religious faith) see R Audi, *Rationality and Religious Commitment* (Oxford, Oxford University Press, 2011). For the possibility that believing in something that cannot be proved may still be reasonable see D Richards, *Toleration and the Constitution* (New York, Oxford University Press, 1986) 75–77. For the argument that religious belief or simply religion is grounded in reason, see, for example, J Finnis, *Natural Law and Natural Rights*, 1st edn (Oxford, Oxford University Press, 2011) 378–88. It is interesting to note that the argument about the irrational nature of religion was adopted by the House of Lords in *R (Williamson and Others) v Secretary of State for Education and Employment* [2005] UKHL 15, [23], where Lord Bingham stated that 'typically, religion involves belief in the supernatural. It is not always susceptible to lucid exposition or, still less, rational justification'. And see also in *McFarlane v Relate Avon Ltd* [2010] EWCA Civ 880, [23]–[24], where Lord Laws contrasted the objective grounds of the law with the subjective opinion of religious believers, 'incommunicable by any kind of proof or evidence'.
[28] For a detailed discussion about this subject see: S Ferrari and S Pastorelli (eds), *Religion in Public Spaces: A European Perspective* (London, Routledge, 2012); P Weil, 'Lifting the Veil of Ignorance' [2004] *Progressive Politics* 2; G van der Schyff and A Overbeeke, 'Exercising Religious Freedom in the Public Space: A Comparative and European Convention Analysis of General Burqa Bans' (2011) 7 *European Constitutional Law Review* 424; E Howard, *Law and the Wearing of Religious Symbols* (London, Routledge, 2012); A Vakulenko, 'Islamic Headscarves and the European Convention on Human Rights: An Intersectional Perspective' (2007) 16 *Social and Legal Studies* 183; M Hill, 'Legal and Social Issues Concerning the Wearing of the Burqa and Other Head Coverings in the United Kingdom' in A Ferrari and S Pastorelli (eds), *The Burqa Affair Across Europe* (London, Routledge, 2013) 77; L Vickers 'Religion and the Workplace' (2015) 14 *The Equal Rights Review* 106.
[29] For some insight into the reasoning behind this assertion, see the judgment of Lady Hale in *R (on the application of Begum) v Headteacher and Governors of Denbigh High School* [2006] UKHL 15.

focus on religious symbols or dress (such as the cross, the Star of David, the star and crescent, the yarmulke or the hijab), which merely indicate that a person holds a religious belief. Within this scope, we will also illustrate a few conditions for tolerating religious symbols in the public sphere. The discussion will also clarify how this case is different from cases of type 1 that were described above (claims for exemption or accommodation directly based on illegitimate, intolerable values).

The *Eweida* case[30] will be used as a referencing point for the main arguments, yet these arguments also apply to similar cases as well. In *Eweida* the dispute followed restrictions placed by employers on wearing a visible cross around the neck.[31] The question here would be: do employees in the private sector have a right to wear visible religious symbols?

Religious symbols are, well, symbols. As such they convey a certain message. The exact content of this message depends on variable factors and may change according to the circumstances. For the purpose of this paper, the question can be narrowed down to: which message is being conveyed by a person who wears a religious symbol or religious dress? Here, too, the answer may depend on varied circumstances. A person may decide to wear a religious symbol or dress for various and complex reasons. However, and within almost all monotheistic religions, one particular message is almost always present, either implicitly or explicitly, and it is always conveyed to all others. This message goes as follows: 'I believe that God exists. I believe in one particular God or religion, and I believe that all who have different beliefs are wrong'.[32] So when Eweida wore a small yet noticeable cross while providing services for customers, Eweida conveyed the following message: 'I believe that God exists. I believe in Christianity, and I believe that all non-Christians and non-religious people are wrong'. For Eweida, this may not be the main reason for wearing a cross. It might be the case that this was not the message Eweida in fact wanted to convey. It might be the case that for her (and many others) wearing a religious symbol is no more than a personal statement of love towards God or a symbol of commitment to God or of gratitude to God. But this is beside the point because those who wear the Christian cross do believe that God exists, do believe in Christianity and, if they take their religious views seriously, they also believe that all non-Christians and non-religious people are wrong. Regardless of any other possible motives or messages, this is what the cross always symbolises. This is what it reveals about those who wear it, whether they made a conscious decision to convey such a message or not.

It is not argued here that all symbols, including religious symbols, always have objective meanings. More often than not the meaning of a symbol is context-dependent and its subjective meaning may vary. The point made here is more modest: common religious symbols and religious dress which can be found in majority or minority religions in the 'Western world' (eg the cross, the Star of David, the star and crescent, the yarmulke or the hijab) do have one common meaning on top of any other subjective meaning that may vary

---

[30] *Eweida v United Kingdom* (2013) 57 EHRR 8.

[31] In this case, and before the dispute came before the courts, the employer (British Airways) changed its policy, allowing the display of some religious and charity symbols, including, for example, the cross and the Star of David.

[32] And here we wish to ignore the relatively rare cases, certainly within the major religions, where religious believers concede that there are other valid religions (or Gods). Our focus is on the monotheistic and creedal religions.

according to the circumstances and the context. This common meaning reflects the way in which almost all those who see the symbol understand it. It also reflects the attitude of almost all those who wear the symbol or present it. This attitude includes making an adverse judgement about those who do not share the religious person's views.

At this point a distinction should be made between making adverse judgements about others, having intolerant views, and acting upon these views. Making adverse judgements about others is not the same as having intolerant views. All those who think that they are right about a certain moral value also think that those who disagree with them are wrong. That would be the adverse judgement that they make about these erroneous others (or their views, or both). This, however, is not an intolerant state of mind. Equating intolerant state of mind with having an opinion about moral issues will render the term 'intolerance' meaningless. Intolerant states of mind and intolerant views are classified as such when the adverse judgement which is made about others provides one with reasons to harm, offend or refrain from assisting others. An intolerant act is classified as such when one acts upon these reasons (for example, by refusing to provide services to others, as in the case of conscientious objection of type 1).

This explains why wearing a religious symbol is always an expression of an adverse judgement which is made about others. Religious persons, if they take their religion and their religious beliefs seriously, have to make some kind of adverse judgement about 'others' (agnostics, atheists, antitheists and those who believe in the 'wrong' religion) and they make their adverse judgement because of the others' views. Wearing a religious symbol makes sure that all others will know that the one who wears the symbol makes an adverse judgement about them, whether the person who wears the religious symbol intended to convey this message or not.

Wearing religious symbols may also be an expression of intolerant views, if the adverse judgement which is made about others gives the religious person reasons to harm, offend or refrain from assisting others. And yet, this does not make wearing a religious symbol an intolerant act. Wearing a religious symbol will be an intolerant act only if the adverse judgement mentioned above gives the religious person reasons to offend, intimidate or harm others, and only if the religious person acts upon these reasons when they decide to wear or present the religious symbol. Put differently, wearing a religious symbol will be an intolerant act only if the person who wears that symbol wears it with the intention to offend, intimidate or harm others – and as a result of making an adverse judgement about others. This is almost never the case. Thus, wearing a religious symbol is not necessarily an act of intolerance yet it does reflect making adverse judgements about others and may reflect having intolerant views about others.

This still does not mean that wearing religious symbols should be prohibited or restricted. Making adverse judgements about other people's values should always be legal. Expressing intolerant views, and even acting on them, should normally be legal. Under certain circumstances they may not be socially tolerated in various ways but only in exceptional cases should they not be tolerated by the law. Intolerant views are merely the result of one being committed to one's values – and these values may not be unjustly intolerant. Intolerant views are not inherently morally wrong. Subscribing to perfectionist-liberal views must entail making adverse judgements about non-liberal views or people; subscribing to secular, humanist views must entail making adverse judgements about religion and perhaps religious people as well; and subscribing to a religious view must entail making adverse judgements about non-religious views and at times non-religious people. The alternative to a complete and consistent avoidance of making adverse judgements about other people's views is having no views of our own. Therefore, there is nothing inherently wrong in making adverse judgements about others. These adverse judgements may also give us reasons to treat others less favourably. That would mean that we now hold intolerant views about others, but there is nothing inherently wrong in having intolerant views or even in acting upon one's intolerant views about others (or their views). It will only be wrong if this intolerance is unjust. The question of whether intolerance is or is not justified is answered by liberalism itself. If autonomy is the main reason for tolerating others, then unjustified intolerance would be intolerance that causes unjust harm to others or that unjustly limit their freedom or autonomy as decided from a perfectionist-liberal perspective.[33] Expressing religious views and acting upon these views may, but do not have to be, unjustified intolerance. Accordingly, wearing religious dress and exhibiting religious symbols are normally not unjustified intolerant acts even though they may convey unjustly intolerant values.

The intolerant views that are expressed by wearing a cross, for example, so far as they express a commitment to a certain belief and a rejection of contradictory beliefs may be very mildly intolerant. They do express positive views about a certain set of religious beliefs and they do express some adverse judgement about those who think differently – but this is well within the zone of intolerant yet legitimate views that should be tolerated by the law and society. Holding a set of moral values and making adverse judgements about those who think differently reflects a desirable state of mind as opposed to moral relativism.

The problem therefore lies elsewhere. The problem is in fact twofold: first, the problem lies in the intolerant nature of religion and in the distinction between the private and the public sphere. Second, the problem also lies in the different treatment that is given to pro-religion symbols comparing to anti-religion symbols, and in the public-popular response to both types of symbol. Again, this is an indication of the societal presumption of religion as a human good.

As to the exact intolerant nature of religion: religion is not merely intolerant in the same way as other ideologies or sets of moral values are. All comprehensive ideologies are intolerant towards contradictory ideologies and values. Religion, however, is *unjustly* intolerant – as far as its content (values, morality, decrees, laws, etc) is unjustly intolerant – which is almost always the case. This unjust intolerant nature of religion, which was described in detail elsewhere and will not be repeated here,[34] provides the tolerant-liberal state with reasons not to tolerate religion in a proportional manner.[35] While every comprehensive theory or ideology is intolerant by its nature, religion is uniquely and unjustly intolerant, and in a way that poses unique challenges to the tolerant-liberal state. If this is true (and we will not defend this argument here), religious symbols may not be allowed to be displayed in certain places (the workplace, state institutions, 'public' institutions, etc) even when the symbol itself does not directly convey illegitimate, unjustly intolerant values, and even if the person wearing the symbol does not intend to convey unjustly intolerant views – as was the case in *Eweida*,

---

[33] For a detailed discussion of this approach see: Y Nehushtan, *Intolerant Religion in a Tolerant-Liberal Democracy* (Oxford, Hart Publishing, 2015) ch 3.
[34] ibid ch 5.
[35] ibid 198, 201.

for example. This is so because religion is inherently and unjustly intolerant and because the liberal state should not support or endorse, directly or indirectly, intolerant ideologies or sets of beliefs.

The liberal state should also consider the need to avoid shaping the public sphere according to religious values even when they are not necessarily unjustly intolerant. Allowing religious symbols in the public sphere creates an accommodating atmosphere that in turn may strengthen cultural, social and political religious tendencies and religion itself. A tolerant-liberal state should not create an accommodating atmosphere for ideologies, including religious ones, that are unjustly intolerant and anti-liberal by their nature.

A possible response to this secular, anti-religious approach would be that tolerating religious symbols in the public sphere rather than banning them better corresponds to the notion of an open and pluralistic society.[36] This response confuses liberalism with neutrality or with lack of commitment to substantive liberal values. Tolerance and pluralism may be valuable principles but they do have limits. The tolerant-liberal state should tolerate and does tolerate non-liberal, misguided, challenging, disturbing and worthless views and ways of life. The tolerant-liberal state, however, should not rush to compromise tolerance and pluralism by allowing symbols that convey anti-liberal, unjustly intolerant and anti-pluralist ideologies in the public sphere.

This understanding of the nature of religious symbols and the proper response to them is fairly close to what is often called 'active secularism', according to which 'all aspects of political and public life must be free from any religious influence'.[37] According to this approach the state has an extremely weak reason to prohibit wearing or displaying religious symbols in the private sphere. However, the state does have a weightier reason, yet not necessarily a prevailing one, to prohibit wearing or displaying religious symbols in the public sphere, including in the workplace.[38]

There is more to be said about the reasons for excluding religious symbols from the public sphere, and from the workplace, but we will refrain from elaborating on this point mainly because the intolerant nature of religion is probably not a decisive reason for excluding religious symbols from the public sphere and the workplace. It is a reason that should be taken into account but it does not necessarily decide the outcome. Religious symbols may be allowed in the public sphere and the workplace after all if anti-religious symbols are accorded the same status and protection. Thus, whether one is or is not convinced by the soundness of the link between the intolerant nature of religion and the need to exclude religious symbols from the public sphere is of less importance. The more important point is that of the equal treatment that should be granted to both religious and anti-religious symbols and sentiments.

---

[36] A Steinbach, 'Burqas and Bans: the Wearing of Religious Symbols under the European Convention of Human Rights' (2015) *Cambridge Journal of International and Comparative Law* 29, 42.

[37] ibid 39; D McGoldrick, 'Religion in the European Public Square and in the European Public Life: Crucifixes in the Classroom?' (2011) 11 *Human Rights Law Review* 451, 457; S Poulter, 'Muslim Headscarves in School: Contrasting Legal Approaches in England and France' (1997) 17 *Oxford Journal of Legal Studies* 43, 50.

[38] It should be noted though that the view that the right to be free from exposure to manifestations of religion or belief by others in the public sphere was recognised by the ECtHR only in *Lautsi v Italy* [2009] ECHR 1901 – a decision that was immediately and unfortunately overruled in *Lautsi and Others v Italy* [2011] ECHR 2412. See also: CK Roberts, 'Interpreting Freedom from Religion: a Step Too Far?' in *Law & Religion UK*, 15 June 2016, at www.lawandreligionuk.com/2016/06/15/interpreting-freedom-from-religion-a-step-too-far.

This aspect of the subject gives rise to questions pertaining to equality, fairness and tolerance. Despite what has been said above about 'active secularism' and the need to not tolerate religious symbols in the public sphere, and especially in the workplace, such symbols may be tolerated after all, provided that symbols that convey opposite views are also allowed. As was noted earlier, wearing a religious symbol or dress in the workplace normally conveys the following message: 'I believe that God exists. I believe in one particular God or religion, and I believe that all who have different beliefs are wrong.' Expressing this view in the public sphere, including the workplace, can only be allowed if all religious believers – as well as atheists and especially antitheists – are allowed to exercise the same right. This means that if a service provider or an employee is allowed to wear a visible cross in the workplace, his fellow antitheist worker should be allowed to exhibit a visible slogan that states, for example, 'Good without God'. If a lecturer is allowed to wear religious dress in the classroom, his fellow antitheist lecturer should be allowed to wear a T-shirt with a slogan that states 'There is no God', or 'God is dead'.

The immediate response to the above would probably be that while wearing religious symbols or religious dress is being done in good faith and with no intention to offend others, antitheist symbols or expressions are provocative by their nature and do result from a will to offend others. This possible response is misguided for three reasons. First, it fails to appreciate how offensive or troubling religious symbols are to atheists and antitheists, regardless of any intention to offend them; second, and more importantly, it fails to appreciate the sincere and deep commitment that antitheists have to their secular, humanist and anti-religion values; third, and most importantly, it mistakenly equates (a) acting while foreseeing a certain result (here offending others) with (b) intention to offend others. These three reasons are simultaneously discussed below.

Classifying anti-religion symbols as provocation and in fact as an expression of unjust intolerance results from a misguided view according to which doing X while knowing that others will be offended by X always entails an intention to offend. This view is mistaken because it fails to distinguish between intentional result and incidental result – a critical distinction from the moral perspective.[39] It is especially important within the discourse of tolerance. It would be false to argue that when the harm caused by an act is unavoidable or highly predictable, the performer is to be considered intolerant (or 'provocative') if he or she does not refrain from the action. The intolerant person causes harm because they make adverse judgements about others. Classifying an act as intolerant depends on this being the primary reason or at least a reason that is necessary for committing the harmful act. When an adverse judgement about others is only one of the reasons for not avoiding an act that one would have done regardless of this adverse judgment, the actor is not to be considered intolerant but inconsiderate or disrespectful.

Therefore, accusing antitheists of being provocative merely because they express publicly their deeply held moral values results from the fact (and it is a fact) that antitheists know that some religious people will be offended if antitheist views are openly expressed (and by

---

[39] We are aware that in many jurisdictions (including in England and Wales) the *mens rea* requirement in criminal law relies on a legal assumption according to which foreseeing that a certain behaviour will lead to a certain result is equivalent to intending that result. We will not try to evaluate the moral validity of this legal assumption here. It is clear, however, that all too often we do foresee the result that is likely to follow from our behaviour (eg dropping out from our University studies, which we know that will definitely upset our parents) yet we do not avoid this behaviour, for many possible reasons, and despite lack of intent to cause the likely result.

the same token, because almost no one thinks that antitheists may be offended or troubled by religious symbols, exhibiting religious symbols is hardly ever perceived as provocation). However, knowing that others may be offended by a certain expression, and intending to offend those others are not quite the same thing. A woman may know that some orthodox religious people may be deeply disturbed by her 'indecent' appearance when she walks on the high street, but it would be ridiculous to accuse that woman of being provocative or of having an intention to offend others if she decides to put on 'indecent' clothes after all – and if she would have done so even if it did not trouble anyone. Gay people must know that showing affection to their partners in public will offend or deeply disturb homophobes but it would be misguided to accuse gay couples of being provocative merely because they show their affection in public if they would have done so even if it did not trouble anyone. Antitheists also know that expressing their views will offend others, but since they would have expressed their views even if they were not offending anyone they cannot be accused of having an intention to offend. Religious people also know (or should know) that expressing their religious views (eg through wearing a religious symbol) may disturb others, but since they would have expressed their views even if they were not disturbing anyone (and only if this is the case) they cannot be accused of having an intention to offend.

Religious expressions, including religious symbols and dress are, by definition, anti-antitheism. They convey a message that contradicts the deepest beliefs of a minority group – as atheists and antitheists are still a small minority in all democratic states.[40] Religious people and those who are indifferent to religion may find it hard to believe, but many atheists and antitheists who take their moral beliefs seriously are troubled and disturbed when they are exposed to religious symbols. For atheists and antitheists, religious symbols represent or may represent irrationality, intolerance and persecution, to name a few. A helpful illustration of this was given by the author and broadcaster Christopher Hitchens in a debate with a US religious broadcaster. When asked if he were walking alone at night and saw a group of men approaching, he would feel safer knowing that they were returning from a prayer meeting, Hitchens responded in the negative:

> Just to stay within the letter 'B', I have actually had that experience in Belfast, Beirut, Bombay, Belgrade, Bethlehem, and Baghdad. In each case I can say absolutely, and can give my reasons, why I would feel immediately threatened if I thought that the group of men approaching me in the dusk were coming from a religious observance.[41]

Many atheists and antitheists do not respect either religious symbols or religion generally. They merely tolerate the exhibition of religious symbols because they respect other people's right to express their misguided views. But this attitude can only be sustainable under a regime of reciprocity. Namely, only if religious people, society and the law are willing

---

[40] It is estimated that atheists comprise 2–13% the world's population, whereas people who have no religion comprise 10–22% of the world's population: *The Global Religious Landscape A Report on the Size and Distribution of the World's Major Religious Groups as of 2010* (Pew Research Centre, The Pew Forum on Religion and Public Life, 2012). Available at www.pewforum.org/2012/12/18/global-religious-landscape-exec. In the UK, the Office for National Statistics report, 'Religion in England and Wales 2011', highlights the findings of the most recent census (2011): '14.1 million people, around a quarter of the population in England and Wales, reported they have no religion in 2011'. Available at www.ons.gov.uk/peoplepopulationandcommunity/culturalidentity/religion/articles/religioninenglandandwales2011/2012-12-11.

[41] C Hitchens, *God is Not Great: How Religion Poisons Everything* (London, Atlantic Books, 2007).

to tolerate the antitheist view – the view that God does not exist or that religion is simply wrong – and when this view is expressed openly in the workplace. These views should be allowed whenever religious symbols are allowed (with the exclusion of places of worship) and only if these views are allowed to be openly expressed should the exhibition of religious symbols also be allowed.

There are in fact only two acceptable options here. Either both religious symbols and anti-religious symbols are allowed in the public sphere and in the workplace or neither type of symbol is allowed. A decision that neither is allowed will not be an unreasonable one. Deciding that the workplace, as well as some other public places, should be both religion-free and antitheism-free may be a reasonable decision that can easily be justified (though we will not aim to do it here).[42] So is the decision that both religious and anti-religion symbols and expressions should be allowed. This conclusion underlies the main difference between conscientious objection of type 1 and conscientious objection (or claims for accommodation) of type 2.

In cases of type 1, the conscientious or moral objection relies on unjustly intolerant and illegitimate values (eg perceiving gay people as inferior because of who they are). Also, the objection finds its expression in a discriminatory act (eg a refusal to provide a service). In cases of type 2, however, the conscientious or moral objection, or demand for accommodation, relies on misguided and at times intolerant yet morally legitimate values (mere belief in a certain religion). Also, the objection does not find its expression in discriminatory acts but rather in mere (symbolic and indirect) expressions of intolerant, religious values. Wearing a religious symbol or religious dress does not necessarily imply that the religious person also holds unjustly intolerant and morally illegitimate values. It certainly implies that the person is religious, thus may subscribe to a set of intolerant values, but it does not necessarily follow that that person holds unjustly intolerant and morally illegitimate views, or that they are willing to act upon these views. More specifically, a person who wears a cross in the workplace may or may not make an adverse judgement about gay people, for example, and may or may not act upon this judgement. Therefore, the mere wearing of the cross, troubling as it may be for antitheists, does not necessarily convey morally illegitimate values and does not in and of itself deny others of rights or interests because of their identity, or at all. This makes it easier for the liberal-tolerant state to tolerate religious symbols and dress in the public sphere, under certain conditions. The same cannot be said about a refusal to provide a service based on perceiving others – because of who they are – as inferior.

B. Abortions

The controversial refusal to perform abortions, assist the abortion procedure, prescribe contraception or perform euthanasia also falls within type 2. It should be noted from the

---

[42] For a recent affirmation of this view see Case C-157/15 *Achbita v G4S Secure Solutions NV* [2017] 3 CMLR 21, Opinion of AG Kokott. In this case, a female employee was not allowed to wear a hijab at work. The employer prohibits employees from wearing any visible religious, political or philosophical symbols at work. The Advocate General found this policy legal. The court accepted this view and concluded that the ban does not constitute direct discrimination if it is founded on a general company rule prohibiting visible political, philosophical and religious symbols in the workplace and not on stereotypes or prejudice against one or more particular religions or against religious beliefs in general. The ban, however, may constitute indirect discrimination that may be justified (and was justified in this case) by applying the proportionality principle.

outset that the moral legitimacy or the legality of anti-abortion, anti-contraception or anti-euthanasia laws is irrelevant when we evaluate the moral legitimacy of the conscientious objection to perform these acts. This will be explained in more detail below.

A refusal to perform abortions (or prescribe contraception or perform euthanasia) may be, but not necessarily, based on religious values. Such a refusal does not rely on unjustly intolerant or morally illegitimate values as it does not result from an adverse judgement that is made about others because of who they are or because of their identity (which explains why cases of type 2 differ from cases of type 1). A refusal to perform abortion normally relies on the view that the foetus is a human being. Since the foetus is perceived as a human being abortion is being equated with murder. These assertions and their implications can be disputed but there is nothing in these assertions which is unjustly intolerant, morally illegitimate or even anti-liberal. This argument requires further clarification. The argument that a conscientious or moral objection to perform abortion (or to prescribe contraception or perform euthanasia) does not result from intolerant, morally illegitimate or anti-liberal values is true only if the sole claim here is not to take part (either directly or indirectly) in these practices. If all that the objectors wish is to distant themselves from an act that is being perceived as murder, there is nothing in the content of their conscience or moral belief – and in acting upon this conscience or moral belief – that can be perceived as unjustly intolerant, morally illegitimate or anti-liberal.

Things are utterly different if the same conscience or moral belief (according to which performing abortion, using contraception and performing euthanasia are in fact acts of murder) results in enacting a law or deciding a policy that prohibits others from having or performing abortions or euthanasia, or using or prescribing contraception. Such a policy is clearly unjustly intolerant, anti-liberal and thus morally illegitimate. It is intolerant because it results from an adverse judgement that is being made about others (because of their values and behaviour) and because this adverse judgement is a sufficient reason to harm others by preventing them from acting according to their interests as they perceive them. Such a policy is also anti-liberal as it unjustly limits people's autonomy – and here we subscribe to the view that we do not intend to justify, that denying people the right to die, to use contraception or to have an abortion is in fact an unjust violation of their autonomy.

If we focus on cases of conscientious objection, the distinction between cases of type 1 and cases of type 2 becomes more evident. In cases of type 1 an individual objects to a law the purpose of which is to express and enforce a moral stand regarding a moral issue. Within the context of equality laws, for example, the state decides that even though making an adverse judgement about others because of who they are is legal (and rightly so) it is illegal to act upon this judgement by treating people differently and because of their protected characteristics. This is a moral stand and as such it is rejected by many who hold discriminatory moral values. It will make equality laws (or any other laws that aim to enforce moral values) completely redundant if people are exempted from the application of such laws because they morally object to their content.

Things are completely different in cases of type 2. Laws that allow abortions or performing euthanasia do not necessarily take a moral stand for abortions and euthanasia (things may be different regarding the use of contraception). They take a moral stand with regard to autonomy and the ability to choose. When the state allows abortions or euthanasia, the state does not necessarily wish to encourage these practices. The state does not necessarily think that having an abortion or deciding to die is morally right (as opposed to treating people equally, for example, which is always perceived by equality laws as morally right). The state merely allows people to choose to behave in a way that the state presumably thinks is not morally wrong. The state may also think that it has no role in preventing people from making decisions about core issues that are part of their private life, regardless of the value or the wisdom of these decisions.

When the state allows abortions, euthanasia or contraception use, it also does not have to take a moral stand against those who choose not to have abortions or euthanasia or use contraception. As to the conscientious objectors who refuse to perform abortions or euthanasia or provide contraception, the state may think that their conscience results from misguided values but not necessarily from repugnant, illegitimate values. More importantly, exempting physicians and pharmacists from the general duty to provide a medical service does not necessarily make the laws that allow abortion, euthanasia and contraception redundant. It does not compromise the moral stand which is reflected in these laws. It does not necessarily and inherently compromise the state's commitment to its liberal values. Thus, from this narrow perspective only (and while ignoring numerous other relevant considerations) the tolerant-liberal state has no content-based reasons to refuse granting exemptions in cases of type 2.

Even though the reasons for refusing to grant exemptions in cases of type 2 are not content-based, it does not follow that these reasons are or should be purely neutral. In our case, these reasons may not be content-based as they are detached from the content of the conscience of the objector – but they may be value-based in the sense that they may reflect the state's moral view as to the need to allow women to have full and easy access to abortion and contraception. Therefore, if granting exemptions to those who object to performing abortion would put at risk the provision of a safe and accessible abortion service available to all pregnant women who need and want it, this would be a compelling reason to either refuse granting these exemptions or to refuse employing those who object to performing abortion. This is so because allowing women to have abortions (safely and easily) is the morally superior view. It is the morally superior because of well-known, yet obviously controversial reasons, which will not be discussed here, and there is no need to discuss these reasons here because even if one rejects these reasons, the state did not. By enacting laws that allow women to have abortions the state in fact subscribes to the view that enabling autonomy and allowing women to choose whether to have abortions is the morally superior view. Moral consistency requires the state to tolerate conscientious objections to laws which reflect the state's moral view up to the point where the ability to achieve the moral aim of the law is threatened. It is worth emphasising here that even though we are pro-choice, we accept that refusal to perform abortions does not rely on morally repugnant values, and that the refusal does not (inherently or necessarily) involve making an adverse judgement about women as women. Content-neutral considerations can therefore be applied in order to balance harm, as long as the guiding principle – that women continue to have easy and affordable access to abortion – is not jeopardised.

If the state does take a moral stand for allowing abortions, this also means that the state merely tolerates, rather than respects, the view that abortions are morally repugnant. The state thinks that those who hold the view that abortions are morally repugnant are wrong; otherwise it would not have allowed abortions at all. The state then must hope that those who hold this view will not be sufficiently powerful to decide the general policy in this matter. The state will also be willing to tolerate the objection to performing abortions insofar as the abortion procedure is still easily accessible. This descriptive argument has more general implications as it exemplifies the link between the discourse of tolerance and content-based or value-based legal and moral discourse. Accordingly, when courts wrongly equate granting conscientious exemptions with respecting objectors rather than tolerating them, the courts may also ignore the crucially important content-based or value-based considerations.

The Extra Division of the Inner House's decision in *Doogan* is a good example of ignoring both the discourse of tolerance and the relevant content-based and value-based arguments. In *Doogan*, Lady Dorrian submitted, within the context of abortion laws, that the right to conscientious objection

> is given because it is recognised that the process of abortion is felt by many people to be morally repugnant … it is a matter on which many people have strong moral and religious convictions, and the right of conscientious objection is given out of respect for those convictions and not for any other reason.[43]

This neutral stand, according to which those professionals who conscientiously object to abortion are granted conscientious exemptions merely because they perceive abortions as morally repugnant, is partly accurate and only within the narrow abortion context.[44] It is almost always inaccurate outside this context because under current law, and with regard to most cases, it is not sufficient for a conscientious objector to find X morally repugnant in order to be exempt from complying with a law that demands doing X. Something is missing from this reasoning, otherwise the right to conscientious objection, or the right to be granted conscientious exemptions, would have been given to all sincere conscientious objectors and we know that this is not the case. The court's view may also be morally dubious outside of the abortion context because people should not be exempt from the law, even when they sincerely think that X, which is required by the law, is morally repugnant, if their objection to X is in fact morally repugnant, as is the case in objecting to equality laws, for example. People may sincerely think that inter-racial or same-sex marriage is morally repugnant. This cannot be sufficient reason, or valid reason at all, to allow racist and homophobic people to refuse to provide services to inter-racial or same-sex couples. The liberal state, by enacting equality laws, has already decided that racist and homophobic discriminatory acts are immoral and therefore illegal. This moral stand must be kept, especially when the law is being challenged by conscientious objectors who rely on a repugnant conscience that was the reason for enacting equality laws to begin with.

Even though the neutral moral reasoning in *Doogan* can be justified within the abortion context, it does have troubling implications. It is not surprising that the neutral stand in *Doogan* was followed by a descriptive argument that the right to conscientious objection is given to those who object to abortion for moral or religious convictions 'out of respect for

---

[43] *Greater Glasgow Health Board (Respondents) v Doogan and another (Appellants) (Scotland)* [2013] CSIH 36, [38]. For a similar, morally neutral argument within the context of the *Doogan* case, see: R Ekins, 'Abortion, Conscience and Interpretation' (2016) 132 *LQR* 6, 7: 'one might reasonably presume that Parliament respects moral and religious convictions and will be slow to impose on any person a duty to participate in an act he or she views as gravely wrong'.

[44] It is partly accurate because even within the context of abortion, conscientious exemptions are not always granted on-demand, but rather they depend on referring the patient to a professional who is willing to perform the procedure. See below in the text to fn 46.

these convictions'. If we respect other people's moral convictions merely because they hold these convictions, and if we do that while granting them conscientious exemptions, the discourse is inevitably neutral. However, if we perceive granting conscientious exemptions as an expression of tolerance rather than that of respect (as we should do) then the discourse inevitably becomes non-neutral. We do not respect other people's morally misguided conventions, and we do not respect them precisely because they are misguided. By enacting laws which allow abortions the state has already decided that perceiving abortion as morally repugnant is in fact morally misguided; otherwise the state would not have enacted the permissive abortion law to begin with. We may be willing, however, to tolerate the objector's morally misguided convictions and to exempt them from the law under certain conditions. Two of these conditions are (1) the objector's convictions are not morally illegitimate and (2) the ability to achieve the aim of the law to which the objectors (wrongly) object will not be affected by granting the exemptions.

A possible counter-argument may be that laws that allow abortions may in fact express tolerance towards abortions and towards those who wish to have them or perform them. Put differently and in theory, the legislature may hold a moral view against abortions yet may also be willing to tolerate those who think differently by allowing them to act upon their morally misguided views, ie to have and to perform abortions. Here, the state, by its laws, in fact tolerates the act that it permits. At the same time the law respects and morally endorses those who morally object to the act that the law permits – and the law does that by granting the objectors exemptions from the application of the law.

While this state of affairs is theoretically possible, it is politically unrealistic. When the political majority strongly holds moral convictions it tends to enact legal norms that reflect these convictions. This is generally true, and perhaps especially true, with regard to those who hold anti-liberal, religious or 'conservative' views. It will be refreshing to have a legislature that allows abortions while strongly holding the view that abortions are morally repugnant. Thus – and for all practical purposes – when the law sets a legal rule that reflects moral convictions it is reasonable to assume that the legislature holds the very same convictions rather than contradictory ones. Contradictory convictions may be accommodated by way of creating exceptions and qualifications to the general rule but normally not by formulating the rule itself.

This is, therefore, the nature of the link between the discourse of tolerance and content-based or value-based legal and moral discourse. Content-based and explicit value-based considerations are, however, normally missing from UK case law. The case of *Doogan* will again be used as the most recent and clear example. In *Doogan*, midwives objected to delegating, supervising and supporting staff to participate in and provide care to patients throughout the termination process. The hospital, however, took the view that this did not constitute the provision of one-to-one care to patients and that the petitioners could be required to do it.[45] The Supreme Court's decision in *Doogan*, much like the Extra Division of the Inner House's decision, is morally and legally sound but the judicial reasoning fails to indicate the relevant value-based or content-based considerations that grounded the decision.

---

[45] *Doogan* (n 43) [19].

Apart from deciding the case before it, the court also made the following general statement about conscientious objection in healthcare cases:

> Whatever the outcome of the objectors' stance, it is a feature of conscience clauses generally within the health care profession that the conscientious objector be under an obligation to refer the case to a professional who does not share that objection. This is a necessary corollary of the professional's duty of care towards the patient. Once she has assumed care of the patient, she needs a good reason for failing to provide that care. But when conscientious objection is the reason, another health care professional should be found who does not share the objection.[46]

Two points can be made here. First, even though the court in *Doogan* explicitly avoided evaluating the broader implications of its decision[47] and preferred to focus on 'the construction of the statute'[48] (as if it is possible to do so while ignoring the broader social context), the above quote does put forward an implied pre-condition for granting conscientious exemptions: the conscientious objector is under an obligation to refer the case to a professional who does not share that objection. This may mean that if there is no other professional who is willing to treat the patient (while providing equally quick, accessible, affordable and professional treatment), a conscientious exemption will not be granted.[49] That would be an example of applying what we called 'value-based' considerations rather than 'content-based' considerations. When this implied pre-condition is read in light of the court's ruling that the right to conscientious objection does not cover 'things done before the course of treatment began, such as making the booking before the first drug is administered',[50] it becomes clear that the court took a moral stand according to which conscientious objections to taking part in the abortion procedure will only be tolerated if it does not affect women's rights to easy and quick access to this procedure.

The fact that the court did not explicitly express this moral stand may lead to concluding that the Supreme Court arbitrarily limited the scope of the right to conscientious objection to performing abortions without due regard for its consequence.[51] Judicial transparency and a more explicit, content- or value-based reasoning might have revealed that the decision was not arbitrary after all. The judicial decision implicitly took a perfectionist-liberal, moral point of view, according to which morally misguided objections to performing abortions or supporting the abortion process may only be tolerated and accommodated if it does not frustrate the general, moral purpose of the general legal rule: giving women a true choice when they decide whether to have an abortion.

Second, the 'alternative professional' policy, which requires the conscientious objectors to refer the patient to a professional who is willing to perform the procedure, can be morally

---

[46] ibid [40] (Lady Hale).

[47] ibid [27]: 'we are not equipped to gauge what effect either a wide or a narrow construction of the conscience clause would have upon the delivery of that service, which may well differ from place to place. Our only safe course is to make the best sense we can of what the section actually says'. See also ibid [25]: 'It is also not for this court to speculate upon the broader consequences of taking a wide or a narrow view of the meaning of section 4'.

[48] ibid [33]: 'This is, as already stated, a pure question of statutory construction'.

[49] For a different view see Ekins, 'Abortion' (2016) 8: 'One should reject flatly any suggestion that the conscience clause is limited, beyond its express terms, by the policy of maintaining a safe and accessible abortion service'. Ekins also argues that the conscientious objector is in fact under no duty to refer an abortion case to a professional who does not share that objection (p 11).

[50] *Doogan* (n 43 [37]).

[51] As was argued by Ekins (n 43) 10.

valid only if the conscientious or moral reason for refusing to treat a patient does not rely on unjustly intolerant, morally illegitimate values. Refusing to take part in an abortion process would be a good example for such a refusal. Refusing to treat patients because of their identity, political views or moral views (and for conscientious reasons) surely cannot be accommodated by referring the case to a professional who does not share that objection. This, again, underlies the difference between cases of type 1 and cases of type 2.

IV. Conclusion

If accommodating conscientious objections is almost always an expression of tolerance, then deciding whether to accommodate conscientious objections means deciding the limits of tolerance. The starting point of the article was that the liberal state must and does take a moral stand in cases of conscientious objection. The state, through its legislature, takes a content-based approach and evaluates the moral soundness and moral legitimacy of the conscience or the moral values that ground the conscientious objection. The state does so by differentiating between two types of cases:

- Type 1: claims for exemption or accommodation that are directly based on repugnant, unjustly intolerant, anti-liberal and ultimately illegitimate values.
- Type 2: claims that are based on values that may be irrational or morally misguided but are not necessarily unjustly intolerant or morally illegitimate.

Normative evaluation of the content of the conscience provides a weighty reason (though not necessarily a conclusive one) for not tolerating type 1 and for tolerating types 2, under certain conditions.

The liberal state should not hurry to compromise its liberal values when they are expressed in value-based legislation by applying neutral tests and granting exemptions to those who do not share these values. Such compromises will make the law, and core liberal values, redundant. It should be easier for the liberal state to apply neutral tests when it considers granting exemptions to those who, for conscientious reasons, object to laws that do not reflect liberal values (eg safety laws that impose a duty to wear helmets) or to those who object to laws that contradict their conscience, yet their conscience does not reflect intolerant and anti-liberal values (eg an objection to performing abortions). The liberal state does not have to grant exemptions in cases that fall within these categories, as further considerations should also be taken into account, but the fact that granting exemptions in these cases does not run against core liberal values is a reason not to refuse granting exemptions. Equality laws, however, do not fall in either of these categories.

The normative argument according to which the judiciary must take a moral rather than a neutral stand in cases of conscientious objection is complemented by a descriptive argument according to which the legislature often does take a moral stand when it enacts the law from which an exemption is sought. Not all laws reflect a moral stand regarding their content, at least not a moral stand that relies on a comprehensive moral or political theory, but when the law does reflect such a moral stand it will be morally inconsistent if the courts refuse to take the same moral stand when deciding whether to grant conscientious exemptions as a judicial remedy to those who object to the law for conscientious reasons.

8

Conscientious Objection, 'Proper Medical Treatment' and Professionalism: The Limits of Accommodation for Conscience in Healthcare

MARY NEAL*

I. Introduction

In recent years there has been a marked increase in academic interest in the phenomenon of conscientious objection (CO) in healthcare. The resulting literature, which is already substantial and continually expanding, reflects a spectrum of opinion on the practice, ranging from support through mere toleration to barely disguised (and occasionally open) hostility. Despite some forceful academic opposition, however,[1] most scholars who engage with the issue recognise the appropriateness of accommodating CO at least to some extent. The usual way of explaining why it is necessary and/or desirable to accommodate CO involves citing the need to protect individuals from being obliged to violate their *moral integrity* in the course of performing their professional roles. The meaning of 'moral integrity' is itself the subject of detailed philosophical debate,[2] and is not my focus in this chapter: here, I presuppose that 'a physician's interest in moral integrity is a very important interest that has substantial moral weight'[3] and that the primary reason for

* School of Law, University of Strathclyde. I first presented the paper on which this chapter is based at 'Conscience in Law and Medicine: A Half-Day Symposium' at the Anscombe Bioethics Centre, Oxford on 12 April 2018, and I am grateful to David A Jones, Toni Saad and others who were present at that event for helpful discussion of the main themes. I would also like to thank my frequent co-author and collaborator Sara Fovargue of Lancaster University for our frequent (and often vigorous) conversations about conscience, including discussion of the themes explored in this chapter.
[1] See, eg J Savulescu, 'Conscientious Objection in Medicine' (2008) 332 *British Medical Journal* 294; U Schuklenk and R Smalling, 'Why Medical Professionals have no Claim to Conscientious Objection Accommodation in Liberal Democracies' (2017) 43 *Journal of Medical Ethics* 234; and A Giublini, 'The Paradox of Conscientious Objection and the Anemic Concept of "Conscience": Downplaying the Role of Moral Integrity in Healthcare' (2014) 24 *Kennedy Institute of Ethics Journal* 159.
[2] Mark Wicclair's defence of the 'identity conception' of moral integrity in the healthcare context includes helpful discussion of a range of views: MR Wicclair, 'Conscientious Objection in Healthcare and Moral Integrity' (2017) 26 *Cambridge Quarterly of Healthcare Ethics* 7.
[3] MR Wicclair, 'Is conscientious objection incompatible with a physician's professional obligations?' (2008) 29 *Theoretical Medicine and Bioethics* 171, 176.

accommodating and exercising CO is that we recognise the value of moral integrity and wish to respect and preserve it.

No one supports an *unlimited* right to CO, however; all of us who recognise the need to protect professionals against violations of integrity also recognise that we cannot simply allow each individual professional complete liberty to decide which parts of her role she will perform. A principal concern uniting writers across the spectrum of opinion, therefore, is the issue of *limiting* accommodation for conscience: which conscience claims, if any, do we regard as valid and wish to accommodate, and which do we wish to exclude, and what criteria can be used to tell between the two? Among sympathetic commentators, this concern has generated an ongoing discussion in which various suggestions regarding the appropriate parameters of CO are proposed and debated. At the sceptical/hostile end of the spectrum, it is claimed that it is *impossible* to defend CO in a limited way, so that allowing it inevitably opens the floodgates to an ever-increasing tide of refusals in the absence of any way of excluding those that are spurious. My argument in this chapter is a contribution to the sympathetic project of attempting to identify defensible parameters for CO.

In any discussion of CO, it is helpful at the outset to distinguish the latter practice from 'conscience' in the wider sense. Although there are various theories of what conscience is, and a range of suggested definitions, I understand conscience to be a faculty that enables us to direct, reflect on, and assess – both prospectively, contemporaneously, and retrospectively – the way we exercise our moral agency (in 'exercises' of moral agency I include our attitudes and the ethical positions we hold/advance, as well as speech, actions and omissions). As such, to the extent that the practice of healthcare necessarily (and perhaps routinely) involves decision-making that contains a moral element (as many writers on conscience have claimed it does[4]), the consciences of health professionals will, inevitably, be engaged across a wide range of practice areas. There is extensive scope for overlap between the exercise of conscience in this broad sense, and the exercise of other kinds of judgements that professionals make in the course of their roles, such as judgements about best interests, futility, and any judgement which doesn't simply involve what Miola has called 'technical medical skill'.[5]

CO is, and ought to be, a much narrower phenomenon, however. Almost all of those who argue that CO ought to be accommodated within healthcare, myself included, recognise that there must be limits on that accommodation. The debate then becomes one about what the appropriate limits are, and there are various suggestions about how to draw them. One possibility is that we could restrict CO to a narrow range of treatments. Another is that we can limit CO according to the nature of the practitioner's potential involvement: for example, allowing professionals to opt out only of 'direct' or 'hands on' involvement,[6] and perhaps requiring a practitioner who is *un*willing to provide a particular treatment to arrange for the patient seeking it to see another practitioner who *is* willing (the so-called

---

[4] See, eg A Asch, 'Two Cheers for Conscience Exceptions' (2006) 36 *Hastings Center Report* 11; and D Weinstock, 'Conscientious Refusal and Health Professionals: Does Religion Make a Difference?' (2014) 28 *Bioethics* 8.

[5] J Miola, *Medical Ethics and Medical Law: A Symbiotic Relationship* (Oxford, Hart Publishing, 2007) 13.

[6] *Greater Glasgow Health Board v Doogan* [2014] UKSC 68.

'duty to refer', sometimes known as the 'conventional compromise'[7]). Another family of suggestions is that we should only accommodate those objections that pass tests of reasonableness and/or genuineness.[8] Many writers endorse a combination of these suggestions. In this chapter, I want to make a very specific suggestion: namely, that CO should be accommodated only in relation to a narrow category of activity, which I will call 'liminally proper' medical treatment.

I will begin by describing the spectrum of proper medical treatment and the concept of liminally proper treatment as a category within that spectrum, and will then explain how I think combining this concept with justifications based on 'moral integrity' can help to clarify the proper scope of conscientious objection in healthcare. I will argue that the concept of liminally proper treatment can illuminate some of the key issues in academic debates about conscience. Most importantly, it delineates the range of activities in which CO should be accommodated: in doing so, it answers questions about the proper *scope* of CO and whether (and how) CO can be limited, and addresses concerns about so-called 'conscience creep'.[9] But it can also help us navigate debates about the *reasonableness* of conscience claims, and in an overarching sense, the idea of liminally proper treatment also contributes to debates about the compatibility of CO with healthcare *professionalism*.

II. The Spectrum of 'Proper Medical Treatment'[10]

The spectrum of proper treatment and the category of liminally proper treatment within it are fundamental to my arguments about CO throughout this chapter, so it is necessary to set these ideas out thoroughly before going any further.

The phrase 'proper medical treatment' has appeared in case law since at least the second half of the nineteenth century.[11] In the majority of cases in which it has been used since then, judges have used the phrase simply to denote the treatment that is appropriate for a patient's condition. But in two landmark judgments handed down by the UK House of Lords in early 1993, 'proper medical treatment' was cited (on both occasions by Lord Mustill) in a way that seemed to assign a more substantive, analytical role to the idea. In the first of the two cases, *Airedale NHS Trust v Bland*,[12] Lord Mustill mused:

> How is it that … a doctor can with immunity perform on a consenting patient an act which would be a very serious crime if done by someone else? The answer must be that bodily invasions in the course of proper medical treatment stand completely outside the criminal law.[13]

[7] D Brock, 'Conscientious refusal by physicians and pharmacists: who is obligated to do what, and why?' (2008) 29 *Theoretical Medicine and Bioethics* 187.

[8] See, eg RF Card, 'Reasons, reasonability and establishing conscientious objector status in medicine' (2017) 43 *Journal of Medical Ethics* 222.

[9] JD Cantor, 'Conscientious objection gone awry: restoring selfless professionalism in medicine' (2009) 360 *New England Journal of Medicine* 1484, 1485.

[10] The spectrum and categories set out in this section were originally proposed in M Neal, 'Locating Lawful Abortion on the Spectrum of Proper Medical Treatment' in S Fovargue and A Mullock (eds) *The Legitimacy of Medical Treatment: What Role for the Medical Exception?* (London, Routledge, 2015), 124. The discussion here draws extensively on that earlier analysis, refines it, and applies it to the issue of conscientious objection for the first time.

[11] *Symm v Fraser and Another* (1863) 3 F&F 859.

[12] [1993] AC 789.

[13] ibid at 891.

Just over a month later, in the case of *R v Brown*,[14] which concerned sado-masochistic activity between consenting adult men, Lord Mustill enumerated a number of 'special exceptions' to the general rule that consent cannot form a defence to criminal charge of causing actual bodily harm or wounding. One of the exceptions he acknowledged, which was not directly relevant to the case in hand, was 'proper medical treatment':

> Many of the acts done by surgeons would be very serious crimes if done by anyone else, and yet the surgeons incur no liability. Actual consent, or the substitute for consent deemed by the law to exist where an emergency creates a need for action, is an essential element in this immunity; but it cannot be a direct explanation for it, since much of the bodily invasion involved in surgery lies well above any point at which consent could even arguably be regarded as furnishing a defence. Why is this so? The answer must in my opinion be that proper medical treatment, for which actual or deemed consent is a prerequisite, is in a category of its own.[15]

In these passages, Lord Mustill understood himself simply to be *articulating* a 'medical exception' to the criminal law which already existed. As his Lordship observes, such a medical exception is necessary because, although consent can make *minor* touchings lawful, many of the intrusions that happen in the course of providing healthcare are too significant to be rendered lawful by consent alone; they 'lie well above any point' at which consent could provide a defence. The lawfulness of these more significant intrusions therefore depends upon the operation of the medical exception. Apart from the dicta quoted above, however, the courts' engagement with the medical exception has been minimal;[16] and apart from a seminal article by Penney Lewis in 2012,[17] it was also 'largely overlooked in the medical law literature'[18] until it was subjected to sustained scrutiny in a collection of academic essays published in 2015.[19] One result of this academic inattention has been that the relationship between 'the medical exception' and 'proper medical treatment' – which is important for the purposes of the present argument – was never clearly explained. Put simply, the landscape of 'proper medical treatment' includes much more than just the serious intrusions that rely on the medical exception for their lawfulness. It also includes many things that are less intrusive – and so are lawful on the basis of consent alone – and others that are not physically intrusive at all, like consultation, visual examination, prescribing, advice, and so on. The relationship between the two concepts might therefore be summarised by saying that the medical exception performs a legitimising function in relation to *some* but by no means *all* 'proper medical treatment'.

In my own contribution to the 2015 collection,[20] my interest was not so much in the operation of the 'medical exception' at the boundary between the lawful and the unlawful, but rather in exploring everything on the 'lawful' side of the line, to see what further distinctions, if any, could be drawn. At the time, I noted that 'little attention seems to have

---

[14] [1994] 1 AC 212.

[15] ibid at 266.

[16] In subsequent cases, courts have tended simply to use the phrase or quote Lord Mustill's dicta without any further elaboration. See, eg *Ms B v An NHS Hospital Trust* [2002] EWHC 429 (Fam); *Re A (Children) (Conjoined Twins)* [2000]; *Secretary of State for Defence v AW* [2010] UKUT 317 (AAC); *R v BM* [2018] 2 Cr App R 1.

[17] P Lewis, 'The Medical Exception' (2012) 65 *Current Legal Problems* 355.

[18] C Purshouse, 'Review of Sara Fovargue and Alexandra Mullock (eds), *The Legitimacy of Medical Treatment: What Role for the Medical Exception?* London, Routledge, 2016' (2016) 24 *Medical Law Review* 303, 303.

[19] Fovargue and Mullock, *The Legitimacy of Medical Treatment* (2015).

[20] Neal, 'Locating Lawful Abortion' (2015) 124.

been paid so far to gradations of properness *within* the landscape of the lawful'.[21] Suspecting that it might be possible to observe various *degrees* of properness, I began by trying to identify what the features of a 'paradigm case' of proper medical treatment would be, and working from there to identify other categories of treatment which were more or less 'proper' depending on how well they mapped onto that paradigm. Ultimately, I identified three categories within the range of lawful medical treatment: treatment that is *paradigmatically* proper; treatment that is *clearly* proper; and treatment that is *liminally* proper. The latter category, liminally proper treatment, is the one that interests me in terms of its potential for clarifying debates about CO, but it is important to understand how this category is constituted and how it contrasts with paradigm and clear proper treatment before moving on to apply it to CO.

A. Paradigmatically Proper Treatment

I have argued previously that the *paradigm case* of proper medical treatment is constituted where 'treatment is carried out with the consent of the patient and for the patient's therapeutic benefit'.[22] This formulation is an adaptation of Lord Denning's dictum in *Bravery v Bravery*[23] that 'ordinary' surgery is 'done for the sake of a man's health, with his consent'.[24]

There are two distinct elements here: consent, and therapeutic value. Here, 'consent' signifies the consent of the patient herself (and so assumes a patient with capacity). I will use 'therapeutic value' to describe interventions with the potential for health-related benefit, ie interventions aimed at the management, care, and/or prevention of disease and disorder. So on what basis can the paradigm case of proper medical treatment be said to comprise these two elements?

Consent belongs in the paradigm, in my view, because of the dominance of the principle of respect for autonomy in medical law and ethics.[25] The requirement for consent is one of the main ways in which that principle is given effect. Lord Mustill noted in *Bland* that 'consent is normally an essential element in proper medical treatment'.[26] He elaborated:

> [T]he consent of the patient is so important ... because it is usually essential to the propriety of medical treatment. Thus, if the consent is absent, and is not dispensed with in special circumstances by operation of law, the acts of the doctor lose their immunity ... If the patient is capable of making a decision on whether to permit treatment and decides not to permit it his choice must be obeyed, even if on any objective view it is contrary to his best interests. A doctor has no right to proceed in the face of objection, even if it is plain to all, including the patient, that adverse consequences and even death will or may ensue.

A few weeks later, in *Brown,* his Lordship referred again to 'proper medical treatment, for which actual or deemed consent is a prerequisite'.[27] The requirement for consent is

---

[21] ibid at 127.

[22] ibid at 128.

[23] [1954] 1 WLR 1169 (CA).

[24] ibid at 1180.

[25] TL Beauchamp and JF Childress, *Principles of Biomedical Ethics*, 4th edn (Oxford, Oxford University Press, 1994).

[26] *Airedale NHS Trust v Bland* [1993] AC 789, 892 (per Lord Mustill).

[27] *R v Brown* [1994] 1 AC 212 at 266.

wide-ranging: it is now well-established in law that an adult patient with capacity has 'an *absolute* right to choose whether to consent to medical treatment',[28] and that this right to choose 'exists notwithstanding that the reasons for making the choice are rational, irrational, unknown or even non-existent'.[29] The requirement is also capable of trumping other important legal and ethical considerations: when a patient has capacity, her autonomy will be respected (as noted in Lord Mustill's dictum above) even where her autonomous choice places her life in danger,[30] and even where it risks not only her own life, but also the life of a viable foetus.[31] The fact that consent is indispensable where it is possible indicates that consent is the ideal; the 'gold standard' that we seek wherever possible.

Therapeutic value is also paradigmatic, because of the widespread understanding that healthcare exists to provide health-related benefits to patients. The physician patient relationship has traditionally been regarded as a 'healing relationship',[32] and relationships and encounters between health professionals and patients as 'therapeutic' relationships and encounters.[33] The British Medical Association, for example, refers to the 'normal therapeutic role' of the doctor.[34] Moreover, while scholars disagree regarding the ends and goals of medicine (and I will return to this theme later), all plausible suggestions seem to cite the provision of health-related benefits.[35] As Wicclair has noted,

> it is plausible to maintain that healing is associated with the concept of medicine (or any credible conception of it), and it is arguable that an individual who is not committed to that end fails to qualify as a physician, let alone a virtuous one.[36]

Given all of this, it makes sense to regard treatment provided with the patient's consent and directed at a healing or therapeutic outcome as *paradigmatically* proper. The majority of treatment falls into this category: whenever a patient with capacity consents to treatment for his/her own benefit, the treatment is paradigmatically proper.

B. Clearly Proper Treatment

Obviously, a large number of well-accepted healthcare interventions do not correspond to the paradigm just described, and treatment can, of course, still be lawful, and ethical, when one or other element of the paradigm is absent. When consent is impossible because a patient lacks capacity, various patient-focused consent substitutes are possible. Adults with the legal power to do so can give consent on behalf of young children, or other adults who lack capacity; treatment in emergencies can be justified by appeal to the doctrine of necessity; or treatment can be provided on the basis that it is in the 'best interests' of a

---

[28] *Re T (Adult: Refusal of Medical Treatment)* [1992] EWCA Civ 18 per Lord Donaldson (emphasis added).
[29] ibid at 3.
[30] *Re T* (n 28); see also the discussion of autonomy trumping sanctity of life in *Bland* (n 26).
[31] *St George's Healthcare NHS Trust v S* [1998] 3 All ER 673.
[32] ED Pellegrino, 'Toward a Reconstruction of Medical Morality' (2006) 6 *The American Journal of Bioethics* 651, *passim*.
[33] British Medical Association, *Medical Ethics Today: The BMA's Handbook of Ethics and Law* (Oxford, Wiley, 2012), *passim*.
[34] ibid 690.
[35] See also L Frith, 'What do we mean by "Proper" Medical Treatment?' in Fovargue and Mullock (n 10) 32.
[36] Wicclair, 'Is conscientious objection incompatible?' (2008) 174.

patient with a long-term or permanent incapacity. In a very limited number of cases, the patient-focused consent substitute is the authorisation of a court,[37] or power granted under legislation.[38] All of these modes of justification, although still patient-centred in the sense that they are concerned with the patient's good, or interests, are nevertheless 'alternative' in the sense of being departures from, or substitutes for, the *ideal* of informed consent. As such, these are not *paradigmatic* cases of proper treatment. Nevertheless, it is both necessary and desirable that we be able to intervene therapeutically in cases where patients cannot give their consent. It is desirable, for example, that health professionals be able to treat children with their parents' consent, to perform emergency surgery on a patient who is rushed to hospital while unconscious, or to administer antibiotics to a patient with dementia who has a bacterial skin infection. Therapeutic treatment where consent is impossible but is substituted by another *patient-centred* safeguard is not subject to serious doubts about whether it is the kind of thing that health professionals should be involving themselves in: although it does not map on to the paradigm of proper medical treatment, therefore, it is nevertheless *clearly* proper.

C. Liminally Proper Treatment

My main focus in this chapter is on a third category – 'liminally proper treatment'. So when is treatment liminally proper? Here, the element of consent is not the issue. I have claimed that where consent is absent, but its absence is compensated by an alternative patient-centred justification (such as necessity or best interests), treatment is *clearly* proper. If consent is possible, but is not obtained, then any intervention on the patient is *improper*.[39] Thus, liminality does not arise because of an issue with the consent element of the paradigm, but rather because of a question mark over the second element of the paradigm: the *therapeutic value* or therapeutic potential of the intervention.

In some liminal cases, the issue is that there is room for disagreement about whether the procedure is genuinely therapeutic (according to the meaning set out above). In these cases, controversy might arise either because it is disputed that the patient's condition is a disease or disorder, or because the proposed treatment is risky or experimental. These sorts of issues arise in relation to what Penney Lewis has called 'new or controversial

---

[37] Court authorisation is required for non-therapeutic sterilisation of patients with incapacity. Where the procedure *is* therapeutic – for example, to deal with a medical condition such as excessive menstruation or cancer – the relevant patient-focused consent substitute is 'best interests', and no court authorisation is necessary: see J Herring, *Medical Law and Ethics*, 5th edn (Oxford, Oxford University Press, 2014) 281.

[38] In the UK, mental health legislation empowers doctors to treat mentally ill patients non-consensually in very limited circumstances. This power only applies in relation to treatment of the person's mental disorder itself; it is not a wide-ranging power to treat the patient without her consent. The relevant statutory provisions are in s 58 of the Mental Health Act 1983 (which allows compulsory treatment in England and Wales on the basis of a 'second opinion' from an appointed doctor who has consulted with professionals involved in the person's treatment) and Part 7 of the Mental Health (Care and Treatment) (Scotland) Act (which provides for Compulsory Treatment Orders in Scotland).

[39] With the very limited exception of non-consensual treatment under mental health legislation described above at n 38. Where legislation provides authority, this authority functions as a patient-focused consent substitute and renders treatment 'clearly proper'.

medical procedures', like 'cosmetic surgery; circumcision and genital mutilation; contraceptive sterilization; organ donation; non-therapeutic research; gender reassignment surgery; and amputation for body integrity disorder'.[40]

Abortion is another example of a practice in which therapeutic value is arguably often absent. It has been acknowledged that 'in the vast majority of cases ... the request for abortion is not grounded primarily in medical factors,'[41] but is sought and provided primarily for 'social' reasons. Such abortion must be regarded as liminally proper, on my analysis, due to the question mark over its therapeutic value (I discuss this in more detail later). Questions also arise about therapeutic value in relation to practices like assisted suicide and euthanasia. In these cases, we can reasonably ask whether a life-ending intervention can logically be beneficial, given the lack of a beneficiary (since the person who *would* have been the beneficiary is extinguished by the intervention). Because this question deserves to be taken seriously,[42] these practices' potential for health-related benefit is necessarily contestable; this in turn means that the practices, where lawful, are liminally proper.

Thus, the liminal category consists of interventions where the potential for health-related *benefit* is absent, uncertain, or contested. It also includes some interventions that have been recognised as proper medical treatment although they are positively *harmful* – either because they harm the patient without any possibility of benefit at all, or because whatever benefit they offer cannot outweigh the harm caused. Living kidney donation is the example that comes most readily to mind: while the intervention on the *recipient* is obviously therapeutic, the intervention on the *donor* to remove her organ obviously results in a significant reduction of function and the increased health risks associated with having only one healthy kidney. So how does such an intervention come to be regarded as proper treatment, and permitted by law, despite this?

In discussing the medical exception, Penney Lewis observed that when treatment is permitted in spite of absent or contested therapeutic potential for the patient, its authorisation involves some kind appeal (explicit or implicit) to 'public good' considerations. As Lewis puts it, 'The therapeutic intention or intention to benefit the patient may be absent because the intention is to benefit another, or society'.[43] She acknowledges that 'The public focus of the justification may be implicit or explicit'.[44]

It is for those advocating the recognition of a non-therapeutic practice as 'proper treatment' to advance the necessary public interest justification and appeal to the relevant 'public goods', but in the case of living kidney donation, these 'goods' will presumably include altruism and the desirability of saving life; in the case of abortion, arguments include the 'good' of bodily autonomy and the harm of having to remain pregnant against one's will. Arguments for decriminalising assisted suicide and euthanasia often refer to the 'goods' of minimising suffering, being compassionate, and respecting choice/autonomy in relation to intimate decisions. The role of public good claims in bringing non-therapeutic practices and actions within the scope of 'proper medical treatment' is important in terms of the link between liminality and conscientious objection, discussed further below.

[40] Lewis, 'Medical Exception' (2012) 355.
[41] S Sheldon, 'The Abortion Act's Paternalism Belongs to the 1960s' *The Guardian* (22 March 2012) www.theguardian.com/law/2012/mar/22/abortion-act-needs-reform.
[42] I will explore this issue further in future work.
[43] Lewis (n 17) 359.
[44] ibid 361.

Figure 8.1 The spectrum of proper medical treatment determined by therapeutic value

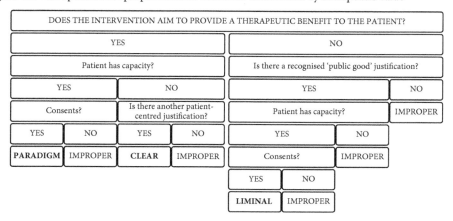

D. A Central Case: Abortion

Obviously, abortion is the major context in which the issue of CO arises, and it was in relation to abortion that I first began to develop my idea of a spectrum of proper treatment.[45] I argued then that abortion was 'paradigmatically proper' when consent was present and the abortion was performed with the clear purpose of producing a health benefit. Abortion is currently permitted by the law in Scotland, England and Wales on any one or more of the following grounds:[46]

A. that the continuance of the pregnancy would involve risk to the life of the pregnant woman, greater than if the pregnancy were terminated;[47]
B. that the termination is necessary to prevent grave permanent injury to the physical or mental health of the pregnant woman;[48]
C. that the pregnancy has not exceeded its 24th week and that the continuance of the pregnancy would involve risk, greater than if the pregnancy were terminated, of injury to the physical and mental health of the pregnant woman;[49]
D. that the pregnancy has not exceeded its 24th week and that the continuance of the pregnancy would involve risk, greater than if the pregnancy were terminated, of injury to the physical and mental health of any existing children of the family of the pregnant woman;[50]

---

[45] Neal (n 10).

[46] The convention of lettering the statutory grounds A–G is used by the Department of Health & Social Care in England and Wales and the equivalent reporting body in Scotland when reporting the abortion statistics annually. See, eg *Abortion Statistics, England & Wales: 2017* (Department of Health & Social Care, 2018). Schedule 1 of the Abortion Regulations 1991 No 499 uses the letters A–E, and Schedule 1 of the Abortion (Scotland) Regulations 1991 No 460 (S41) uses A–G. Grounds A–E inclusive must be certified by two registered medical practitioners, whereas Grounds F and G (the emergency grounds) require certification by a single practitioner.

[47] Abortion Act 1967, s 1(1)(c).

[48] Abortion Act 1967, s 1(1)(b).

[49] Abortion Act 1967, s 1(1)(a).

[50] Abortion Act 1967, s 1(1)(a).

E.   that there is substantial risk that if the child were born it would suffer from such physical or mental abnormalities as to be seriously handicapped;[51]

F.   that the termination is immediately necessary to save the life of the pregnant woman;[52] and

G.   that the termination is immediately necessary to prevent grave permanent injury to the physical or mental health of the pregnant woman[53]

Several of these grounds explicitly cite 'health' as the reason for authorising the procedure, and grounds A, B, F, and G seem straightforwardly therapeutic. Nevertheless, not all abortions provided under the Act are *necessarily* 'therapeutic' in terms of the paradigm I have described. It is difficult to see how an abortion provided *only* on the basis of ground D or E could be regarded as therapeutic *for the woman herself*. But there is also a question mark around the therapeutic value of ground C, the so-called 'social ground', which accounts for upwards of 95 per cent of abortions in the UK, year on year. This ground is also expressed in therapeutic language, but to quote Ann Furedi, CEO of the UK's largest abortion provider, BPAS: 'We all know, if we are honest, that ground C is a kind of code for "it's an unwanted pregnancy"'.[54] And as Sally Sheldon, a prominent pro-choice academic, has observed: 'in the vast majority of cases … the request for abortion is not grounded primarily in medical factors'.[55]

In relation to ground C, then, what we seem to have, by abortion providers' and pro-choice campaigners' own account, is therapeutic *rhetoric*, but a non-therapeutic reality. And if abortion were to be completely decriminalised and made available 'on request' (as is being advocated by campaigners at the time of writing), so that it was no longer being provided even *nominally* on therapeutic grounds, this would further undermine the link between abortion and therapeutic value.

Significantly, contemporary public debates about abortion contain many claims and counterclaims about the status (or not) of abortion as 'healthcare' or 'treatment'. For example, the campaign to decriminalise abortion in the UK calls for abortion to be regulated 'by the same robust regulatory and ethical frameworks which govern all other medical procedures in the UK',[56] and launching a Home Office review into the desirability of legislating for 'buffer zones' around abortion clinics, the then Home Secretary Amber Rudd said that 'it is completely unacceptable that anyone should feel harassed or intimidated simply for exercising their legal right to healthcare advice and treatment'.[57] Pro-choice campaigners in the US habitually refer to abortion as 'women's reproductive healthcare',[58] and the incoming

[51] Abortion Act 1967, s 1(1)(d).
[52] Abortion Act 1967, s 1(4).
[53] Abortion Act 1967, s 1(4).
[54] A Furedi, 'Are there too Many Abortions?' (2008/09) *Abortion Review Special Edition: Abortion and Women's Lives* (Papers from the BPAS conference, London, 25–26 June 2008) 3, www.abortionreview.org/images/uploads/AR_SpecialEdition_2.pdf.
[55] Sheldon 'Paternalism' (2012).
[56] We Trust Women, 'About the Campaign' at www.wetrustwomen.org.uk/about-the-campaign.
[57] Press Association, 'UK Mulls Tougher Laws to Protect Women from Abortion Clinic Protesters' *The Guardian* (26 November 2017) at www.theguardian.com/world/2017/nov/26/abortion-clinics-uk-mulls-tougher-laws-to-protect-women.
[58] To give just one example, the National Women's Law Center lists 'abortion' under 'Health Care and Reproductive Rights' section on its website at nwlc.org/issue/health-care-reproductive-rights.

President of Planned Parenthood Federation of America (the country's largest abortion provider) has recently stated, 'Having a physician as the head of Planned Parenthood, it is a sign that what we are doing is mainstream medical care. Why is it not?'[59] Conversely, opponents of abortion frequently *deny* that abortion is healthcare or treatment. To give one recent example, during the recent Eighth Amendment referendum campaign in the Republic of Ireland, a group of general practitioners signed a letter criticising the government's draft abortion legislation in the following terms:

> In circumstances where the draft abortion law specifies that the role of the GP will be 'carrying out the termination of pregnancy' at the request of the patient, without the need for any reason to be given by the patient, there is no way such a proposal could be described as 'healthcare'. The government's legislative proposal in the event of the referendum passing would also permit abortion, including on mental health grounds, up to 24 weeks in pregnancy. Again, these vague and ill-defined grounds for abortion do not constitute evidence-based healthcare.[60]

In light of public disagreement about whether or not abortion is 'treatment', and the non-therapeutic reality of the overwhelming majority of abortions (those provided exclusively on grounds D or E, and almost all of those provided solely on ground C), it seems reasonable to conclude that most abortions can be located within the liminal category of proper medical treatment. The law in the UK already allows CO in relation to these abortions,[61] while excluding CO in relation to abortion that is paradigmatically therapeutic (although not explicitly on that basis, of course).[62] As such, my approach would support accommodating CO in relation to the same procedures as UK law currently does, albeit for different reasons.

E. An Anomalous Case: Infant Male Circumcision

Before moving on, I want to note one example that is difficult to categorise on my model: namely, the practice of infant male circumcision (IMC). Opinion is divided regarding whether the benefits of this practice outweigh its risks,[63] but even among those who accept that it is non-therapeutic, disagreement persists about whether it can be ethical. On the one hand, Margot Brazier writes that 'Although medical opinion may not necessarily regard [IMC] as positively beneficial, it is in no way medically harmful if properly performed'.[64] On the other, Michael Thomson and Marie Fox criticise 'continued professional willingness to tolerate the non-therapeutic, non-consensual excision of healthy tissue'.[65] If we regard

---

[59] Dr Leona Wen, incoming head of Planned Parenthood, in an introductory video on the organisation's website at www.plannedparenthood.org/about-us/our-leadership/dr-leana-wen.

[60] D Young, '120 GPs sign No Vote Letter Arguing Abortion "without Reason" not Healthcare', *Irish News* (24 May 2018) at www.irishnews.com/news/republicofirelandnews/2018/05/24/news/120-gps-sign-no-letter-arguing-abortions-without-reason-not-healthcare-1338299.

[61] Abortion Act 1967, s 4(1).

[62] Abortion Act 1967, s 4(2).

[63] M Frisch and BD Earp 'Circumcision of Male Infants and Children as a Public Health Measure in Developed Countries: A Critical Assessment of Recent Evidence,' (2018) 13 *Global Public Health*, 626.

[64] M Brazier, *Medicine, Patients and the Law* (London, Penguin, 1992) 350.

[65] M Fox and M Thomson, 'A Covenant with the Status Quo? Male Circumcision and the New BMA Guidance to Doctors' (2005) 31 *Journal of Medical Ethics* 463.

IMC as offering a therapeutic benefit significant enough to justify the intrusion, and if we take the consent of the parents as a valid patient-centred safeguard, then on my model it would appear to be 'clearly proper'. If we regard it as having no therapeutic benefit, however (or not enough to justify the level of intrusion), or as intolerably risky/harmful, then even parental consent ought to be insufficient to bring it even into the *liminal* category of 'proper treatment'. The issue is further complicated by 'public good' claims about IMC's religious significance, the value of respecting religious freedom, and the 'good' of community membership and belonging.

When we compare the example of IMC (understood as non-therapeutic) with the paradigm case of proper medical treatment, we see that in IMC, *both* elements of the paradigm are being substituted: patient consent is substituted by parental consent, and therapeutic value is replaced with claims about public goods or interests. On my model, where *neither* element of the paradigm case is present, we are not dealing with proper medical treatment at all. Nevertheless, IMC is lawful in many jurisdictions including the USA (where it is routine for male infants in many parts of the country) and the UK, although there are campaigns to outlaw it in some northern European countries, and a ban is currently being considered in the Danish Parliament.[66]

Figure 8.2 The spectrum of proper medical treatment with examples

	CONSENT OF PATIENT	OTHER PATIENT-CENTRED JUSTIFICATION (BEST INTERESTS, NECESSITY, CONSENT OF PARENT)
THERAPEUTIC VALUE FOR PATIENT	PARADIGM *Eg* – *All therapeutic interventions involving a consenting adult with capacity*	CLEAR *Eg* – *Therapeutic intervention on a young child or a patient with dementia* – *Emergency surgery on an unconscious patient* – *Court authorised sterilisation of person with incapacity* – *Treatment under mental health legislation*
'PUBLIC GOOD' JUSTIFICATION	LIMINAL *Eg* – *Living organ donation* – *Non-therapeutic abortion*	LIMINAL or IMPROPER? *Eg* – *Infant male circumcision*

---

[66] M Busby, 'Danish Parliament to Consider Becoming First Country to Ban Circumcision of Boys', *The Independent* (3 June 2018) at www.independent.co.uk/news/world/europe/denmark-boyhood-circumcision-petition-danish-parliament-debate-a8381366.html.

F. Summary

Before turning to apply all of this specifically to the context of CO, it is useful to recap what I have claimed so far. My first main claim has been that, although the limited academic literature on proper medical treatment has focused on the operation of the 'medical exception' in drawing a line between the lawful and the unlawful, there is also analytical work to be done in categorising what lies on the lawful side of that line. Specifically, I have proposed that we understand the landscape of 'proper medical treatment' as a spectrum comprising gradations of properness, and I have made a series of claims about how the categories within that spectrum are constituted. In *paradigm* cases of proper treatment, the patient herself has consented to an intervention that has the potential for therapeutic benefit *to her*. In *clear* cases of proper treatment, the therapeutic element of the paradigm is still present, but the consent element is substituted by another patient-centred justification (proxy consent, necessity, or best interests) because the patient lacks capacity and consent is therefore impossible. There is also, I have argued, a *liminal* zone of proper medical treatment, containing practices or individual cases in which therapeutic value is absent or contested, and where the status of the practice as 'proper' depends instead upon explicit or implicit claims about public good or public interest.

It is not part of my project here to describe the content of the liminal category comprehensively; the content of the category itself will inevitably be contested. However, I have already suggested that it might include much abortion, as well as practices like gender reassignment surgery and assisted reproduction for people who are not affected by fertility issues; it will also include assisted suicide and euthanasia wherever these practices are lawful. It must be emphasised that my claim here is *not* that these practices are not proper; rather, it is that when they are lawful, they occupy a contested realm *within* the spectrum of what is proper.

Importantly, the content of the liminal category will not remain constant, but will evolve. Emerging treatments that are risky or controversial will become new additions to the category, while other previously liminal practices will move out of the liminal realm and into the 'clearly proper' category as they become less risky, or as normalisation takes effect. Some activities are likely to remain contested over the long term: 'life issues', for example, or interventions that are perceived to be aimed at preference-satisfaction rather than the management, care, or prevention of disorders. But what counts as liminally proper treatment will develop over time, and on my model, this means that new things will inevitably join the range of practices to which CO is available, and others will cease to be appropriate contexts for objection.

III. Restricting Conscientious Objection to Liminally Proper Treatment

A. 'Lawfulness' and 'Properness'

Often, arguments against accommodating CO cite the 'lawfulness' of treatment as a reason why someone employed as a health professional ought to be willing to provide it. Christian

Fiala et al, for example, complain that 'Reproductive health care is the only field in medicine where societies accept the argument that the "freedom of conscience" of health care professionals (HCPs) and institutions can limit a patient's access to a *legal* medical treatment'.[67] In their view, CO should really be called 'dishonourable disobedience' because it violates 'the right to *lawful* healthcare'.[68] Very recently, Fiala and Joyce Arthur have emphasised law and lawfulness in questioning the permissibility of CO: 'In effect, the state is allowing objectors to personally boycott democratically-decided laws, usually for religious reasons, without having to pay any price for it. But why should doctors be given a privileged exemption from otherwise valid laws …?'[69] Similarly, Julie Cantor has insisted that 'Physicians should support an ethic that allows for *all legal options*' and should be prepared to 'cast off the cloak of conscience when patients' needs demand it'.[70]

It is of the nature of CO that it is practiced in relation to treatments that are lawful because, as Sara Fovargue and I have noted, CO operates 'as a bulwark against expectation, and where a practice is *un*lawful and there is no expectation that reasonable HCPs will engage in it, the "shield" of [CO] is unnecessary'.[71] Thus, Daniel Weinstock's description of CO as a 'claim to be exempted from delivering legal medical services'[72] is accurate. What I have tried to show so far in this chapter, however, is that the landscape of 'lawful treatment' is not homogenous; we can recognise gradations of properness within it. Within the category of 'liminally proper treatment' are practices whose status *as* treatment is debatable, because their therapeutic value is, *at best*, in doubt and this therapeutic deficit is compensated by appeals to the 'public good' or 'public interest'. But claims about the public good or interest are inevitably contested and negotiable, and insofar as examples of liminally proper treatment are justified by reference to such claims, they adopt that element of controversy.

'Lawful treatment' is not a flat, undifferentiated landscape, but rather a spectrum of categories, and the liminal category is a category in which interventions, although legally permitted, are quite appropriately negotiated, debated and subject to differences of moral opinion. The fact of legalising or decriminalising a practice obviously does not settle outstanding *ethical* disagreement; and that disagreement will carry on in a number of settings, not least the professional environment(s) where the lawful but ethically contested practice is to be carried out.

The approach proposed here offers a response to those who claim that professionals should be willing to provide any treatment that happens to be lawful. It allows us to distinguish different degrees of properness within the range of what is lawful, allowing for different responses to these different degrees of properness. If the status of an intervention *as* proper treatment is debatable, it is *not* obvious that all professionals should be willing to perform it.

---

[67] Fiala et al, 'Yes We Can' (2016) 21 *The European Journal of Contraception and Reproductive Health Care* 201, 201 (emphasis added).
[68] ibid (emphasis added).
[69] C Fiala and JH Arthur, 'There is no Defence for "Conscientious Objection" in Reproductive Health Care' (2017) 216 *European Journal of Obstetrics & Gynecology and Reproductive Biology* 254, 255.
[70] Cantor, 'Conscientious objection gone awry' (2009) 1485 (emphasis added).
[71] S Fovargue and M Neal, 'In "Good Conscience": Conscience-Based Exemptions and Proper Medical Treatment' (2015) 23 *Medical Law Review* 221, 229.
[72] D Weinstock, 'Conscientious Refusal and Health Professionals: Does Religion Make a Difference?' (2014) 28 *Bioethics* 8, 12.

B. 'Moral Integrity' as (Insufficient) Justification for CO

But what about the role of *moral integrity* in justifying CO? I mentioned earlier that the case for accommodating CO usually involves arguing that moral integrity is valuable and worth preserving, and that we must allow CO so that individuals are not forced to *violate* their moral integrity by sharing in moral responsibility for what they consider to be serious wrongdoing. The view that accommodation of CO is necessary because of the need to protect integrity has been described as a 'dominant'[73] and 'uncontroversial'[74] view in the academic literature on conscience, and I have endorsed the idea of a strong connection between conscience, moral agency and integrity in my own previous work.[75] But if moral integrity is the ground-level justification for accommodating CO, how does this square with my proposal that we accommodate CO only in relation to liminally proper treatment, given that the moral integrity of individual professionals may also be at stake in *non*-liminal cases?

The answer must be that moral integrity alone cannot delimit the extent of permissible CO. Although it seems axiomatic that a genuinely *conscientious* objection will necessarily involve a wish on the part of the objector to hold the line on a matter she regards as ethically serious, it is frankly impossible to verify that this is so in every case. Moreover, as noted already, although the standard way of justifying CO is to appeal to moral integrity, this is invariably accompanied by an acknowledgment that CO cannot be available every time a professional might plausibly claim that her moral integrity is at stake, and that some defensible way of limiting it is necessary. It would be practically impossible – not to mention highly undesirable on professional and ethical grounds – to give professionals a blanket entitlement to opt out of tasks purely by claiming that participation would violate their moral integrity. If CO is to fit within a workable system of healthcare, instead of representing a fatal stumbling block to such a system, it must operate within certain parameters, and not amount to what Wicclair has called 'conscience absolutism'.[76]

Consider what we might term 'purely moral' objections: objections that involve claims about morality (and perhaps about risks to moral integrity), but make no claims – either explicit or implicit – about the nature of treatment, or healthcare, or the proper role of the health professional. An example of such an objection might be the objection of a doctor, on religious grounds, to examining patients of the opposite sex. This kind of objection stands outside of healthcare, in conflict with it; it does not advance the enterprise of healthcare as a whole. It might be argued that it is worthwhile to accommodate such objections where possible if the challenges they present are outweighed by the benefits of retaining the services of doctors with those religious beliefs. But if we do choose to accommodate the objection for this sort of reason, what we are doing is entering into a trade-off, effectively saying to the objector: 'we will accommodate your objection because although the objection *itself* does

---

[73] C McLeod, 'Taking a Feminist Relational Perspective on Conscience' in J Downie and JJ Llewellyn (eds) *Being Relational: Reflections on Relational Theory and Health Law* (Vancouver, UBC Press, 2012).

[74] A Giubilini 'Conscientious Objections and Medical Tribunals' (2016) 42 *Journal of Medical Ethics* 78.

[75] M Neal and S Fovargue, 'Conscience and Agent-Integrity: A Defence of Conscience-Based Exemptions in the Health Care Context' (2016) 24 *Medical Law Review* 544.

[76] MR Wicclair, *Conscientious Objection in Health Care: An Ethical Analysis* (Cambridge, Cambridge University Press, 2011) ch 2.

not benefit the enterprise of healthcare in any way (and in fact harms it), we are willing to absorb this harm in order to benefit from your continued employment in *other* ways'.

By contrast, objections to liminal treatment *themselves* add value to the enterprise of healthcare. As noted above, liminally proper treatment *invites* disagreement, and those who exercise CO are participating in this legitimate disagreement. When CO relates to treatment in the liminal realm, then, it is not an abrogation or a contradiction of professionalism. On the contrary, a professional who exercises CO in relation to a liminal practice is participating in the legitimate process of contesting the status of such practices and reaching a conclusion. CO is one valid way of engaging with the category of liminally proper treatment, and dissent is just as much a contribution to the discussion as is willingness to participate.

Moreover, when we theorise CO by reference to liminally proper treatment, we locate the practice of CO *within* the norms and language of the healthcare professions, and of healthcare law and ethics, referring to concepts, ideas and principles that are intelligible by those who are being asked to respect the objector's position. This is important, because a major anxiety expressed by opponents of CO is the worry that CO is too subjective; too dependent on private, hidden reasons that may seem idiosyncratic and are often unarticulated and inaccessible to others. The objector is seen as someone deviating from professional standards of behaviour, standing outside the realm of professionalism and its norms, and speaking, if at all, in a foreign language. CO is seen not as something that *pertains* to professionalism, but as something that conflicts with it and denies it.[77] But when we explain CO by reference to liminally proper treatment, we locate the objector, and CO as a practice, *within* the parameters of professional discourse and professional norms, speaking to the professional community in its own language and engaging in the legitimate process of exploring and debating the boundaries of professional activity. Importantly, I am not claiming here that *individual objectors* do, or should, actually use this kind of language when expressing their objections; but rather, that those who theorise, regulate and adjudicate CO should do so.

IV. Some Clarifications

A. Distinguishing My Approach from Those That Prioritise 'Professional Values'

Across the spectrum of academic opinion on CO, arguments about the legitimacy and scope of CO include frequent references to 'professional values', 'values internal to the profession', 'the ends (or goals) of healthcare' and other similar formulations. At the sceptical end of the spectrum, there are frequent assertions that 'private' or 'personal' values have no place in professional practice and must not be allowed to shape interactions between professionals and their patients. For some, this means that CO should not be allowed at all; see, for example, Schuklenk and Smalling's insistence that there is no moral claim to CO because

---

[77] See, eg R Baker, 'Conscience and the Unconscionable' (2009) 23 *Bioethics* ii; also Savulescu, 'Conscientious Objection' (2008) and Cantor (n 9).

professionals must not be permitted 'to subvert the objectives of the professions they voluntarily joined'.[78] Others are willing to tolerate *only* those objections that correspond to or are consistent with the values of the relevant profession; according to Martha Swartz, for example, 'There should be a presumption against the validity of conscientious objection based on personal, as opposed to professional, values by health care professionals'.[79]

Writers who are less sceptical or even supportive of CO also attempt to delineate the acceptable scope of CO by reference to 'the core values of the profession'[80] or the 'norm of medicine'.[81] Fovargue and I have previously criticised such attempts on various grounds, including that: (i) the ends/goals of medicine are expressed too vaguely to provide any concrete guidance about whether particular practices are compatible with them or not; (ii) there is no clear demarcation between 'personal' and 'professional' values; (iii) even if we could draw such a line, the compartmentalisation of the personal and the professional would be inimical to the very 'personal integrity' that CO is supposed to safeguard; and (iv) where 'professional values' refers to the ethical guidance drawn up by a professional body for its members, we need to be willing to question the basis on which the body claims its normative authority (and its claims to trump the demands of individual conscience). In relation to the latter point, we wondered whether CO might be an important tool by which dominant discourses can be critiqued and contested.[82]

So I am unconvinced by 'professional values' accounts of the limits of CO. Yet there are superficial similarities between the claims of some of the writers at the more tolerant end of that spectrum and the approach I am advancing here, making it important that I spell out the distinctions between my proposal and theirs. Zuzana Deans, for example, distinguishes between what she regards as impermissible objections, where 'an individual's views that are *external* to the pursuit of the profession prevent her from providing a service',[83] and permissible objections in which

> a professional considers that to provide a certain service or treatment would endanger not only her personal integrity, but also her professional integrity because she is being asked to do something that she sincerely believes the profession is mistaken to support given the fundamental ethos and pursuit of the profession. This type of conflict is important to recognize, and the moral objection should be heard by the profession.[84]

This sounds similar to my claim about the benefit of casting CO in a language that is intelligible to those who are being asked to respect the objector's refusal to participate; the reference to a sincere belief that the profession is mistaken also seems to come close to (if not to go as far as) my claim that the 'treatment' status of activity in the liminally proper zone is debatable, and a proper subject of professional disagreement. Likewise, while Wicclair acknowledges that the general *reason* for accommodating claims is the preservation of moral integrity,

---

[78] Schuklenk and Smalling, 'Conscientious Objection Accommodation in Liberal Democracies' (2017) 3.

[79] MS Swartz, '"Conscience Clauses" or "Unconscionable Clauses": Personal Beliefs Versus Professional Responsibilities' (2006) 6 *Yale Journal of Health Policy Law & Ethics* 269, 349–50.

[80] Z Deans, 'Conscientious Objection in Pharmacy Practice in Great Britain' (2013) 27 *Bioethics* 48.

[81] TC Saad and G Jackson, 'Testing Conscientious Objection by the Norm of Medicine' (2018) 13 *Clinical Ethics* 9.

[82] Neal and Fovargue 'Conscience and Agent-Integrity' (2016) 559–69.

[83] ibid (emphasis added).

[84] ibid.

he attaches the *condition* that 'an appeal to conscience has significant moral weight only if the core ethical values on which it is based correspond to one or more core values in medicine'.[85] I have agreed that the 'ground-level' justification for CO is the need to respect and protect integrity, but have also argued for restricting its scope to the liminal zone. So how does what I am saying here differ qualitatively from the positions of commentators like Deans and Wicclair?

The key difference is that the limits I advocate refer not to 'core values' (either of the profession or of healthcare/medicine as an enterprise) but to the idea that some lawful treatment is 'liminally proper', which in turn depends specifically on a deficiency in therapeutic benefit and compensation by public good considerations. Instead of looking at the objection and asking whether *that* is based on values internal or external to healthcare, my approach does almost the converse: it distinguishes a category of *treatment* on the basis that it is ultimately grounded in factors external to healthcare (specifically, in external claims about 'public goods') and regards such treatment as essentially contestable (and open to objection) for that reason.

So, rather than looking to see whether an objection is grounded in some acceptable (to whom?) interpretation of the 'values of the profession' or the 'goals of healthcare' (notions which are inescapably vague), my approach focuses on the much narrower, more muscular, and everyday notion of 'therapeutic benefit' which, although it too can be disputed (as is assumed by the very notion of liminality central to my thesis here), is nevertheless much less abstract and mercurial than the other types of idea. Instead of asking whether a particular *refusal* proceeds upon a valid or invalid *philosophical position*, my approach asks whether a particular *practice* is aimed (or not) at providing therapeutic benefit to patients. If not, and it is permitted instead on the basis of essentially contestable notions of 'public good' or 'public interest', it is reasonable and legitimate for professionals to take (and act upon) the position that they wish not to be involved in it.

B. Distinguishing My Approach from 'Reasonableness' Tests

Deans argues that 'if a professional does not want to carry out a certain service, *she must surely have to give a good account of her reasons* for this, and her reasons must be acceptable to the profession'.[86] Schuklenk notes that 'the principle that objectors ought to explain themselves … is supported by numerous authors'.[87] Notable examples of authors who support subjecting conscience claims to versions of a 'reasonableness test' include Robert Card, Morten Magelssen and Thomas Cavanaugh.[88] Although different authors' proposals differ markedly, the general idea is that by deploying such tests, we can weed out indefensible

---

[85] MR Wicclair, 'Conscientious Objection in Medicine' (2000) 14 *Bioethics* 205, 217.

[86] Z Deans, 'Pharmacy Practice in Great Britain' (2013) 53 (emphasis added).

[87] U Schuklenk, 'Conscientious Objection in Medicine: Accommodation Versus Professionalism and the Public Good' (2018) 126 *British Medical Bulletin* 47, 50.

[88] See, eg Card 'Reasons' (2017); M Magelssen, 'When Should Conscientious Objection be Accepted?' (2012) 38 *Journal of Medical Ethics* 18; and TA Cavanaugh, 'Professional Conscientious Objection in Medicine with Attention to Referral' (2010) 9 *Ave Maria Law Review* 189.

claims, and/or prevent unmanageable expansion of the range of practices covered by conscience rights. Card, for example, proposes that professionals be required to explain their conscientious positions to a Medical Conscientious Objection Review Board which will judge their claims according to a standard of what Card calls 'reasonability' (taking into account factors including whether the professional's position is genuine, whether it reflects one of the person's 'core' values, whether it is based on empirical error, whether it causes 'needless and unwarranted harm' to others, and whether it creates a barrier to the timely provision of care in an emergency), and either grant or withhold 'conscientious objector' status.

Such suggestions tend to involve expecting *individual objectors* to demonstrate the reasonableness of their own particular objections, and this has always seemed problematic to me, for a variety of reasons that Fovargue and I have enumerated elsewhere. In particular, we have expressed concern that such processes might unfairly disadvantage those who are less confident, articulate or comfortable discussing their religious and moral views with a panel of 'experts'.[89] We also share Jason Marsh's concern that it might be *impossible* to establish the 'reasonableness' of religious-based positions, in particular, since these are grounded not in reason, but in supernatural beliefs. Furthermore, as Schuklenk points out, adjudicating on the reasonableness or otherwise of religious and moral positions may also conflict with 'The need for the secular state to remain neutral with regard to the validity or otherwise of these ideologies and individual convictions'.[90] He notes that the courts in the United States – and other jurisdictions – have shied away from engaging in 'reasonableness tests', quoting the US Supreme Court:

> What principle of law or logic can be brought to bear to contradict a believer's assertion that a particular act is 'central' to his personal faith? Judging the centrality of different religious practices is akin to the unacceptable 'business of evaluating the relative merits of differing religious claims'.[91]

It seems fairer to individuals, and more manageable for those running health services, to address reasonableness at the level of the *practice* rather than at the level of the individual. The approach I propose here would identify a category of activity (the liminal zone of proper treatment) within which it is reasonable to disagree, and recognise a right to object to practices that fall within that category, instead of scrutinising the reasonableness of each individual objector/objection. This amounts to a sort of 'built-in reasonableness test'. Since the ground-level justification for allowing CO is still a concern to preserve moral integrity, my approach also builds in a presumption that objections will be moral in nature, albeit not *purely* moral in the sense described above in section III B above. However, my approach does not consider that there is anything to be gained by attempting to *ensure* in individual cases that the objection is moral, or reasonable, since this would be so easy for unscrupulous objectors to simulate, and yet unduly difficult for genuine, but less well-educated, less confident, or less articulate objectors to prove.

---

[89] Fovargue and Neal (n 71) 235–37.
[90] Schuklenk 'Conscientious Objection in Medicine' (2018) 50.
[91] *Employment Division, Dept of Human Resources of Oregon v* Smith [1990] 494 US 872, 887 per Scalia J, cited in Schuklenk (ibid) 50.

C. 'Liminally Proper': Practice-Level, Case-by-Case or Both?

Throughout this chapter, I have focused on the fact that 'liminally proper' status can be determined at the level of whole *practices* where therapeutic benefit is contested or absent, and debatable claims about the 'public good' are being used – either explicitly or implicitly – to bring the practice within the rubric of 'healthcare' (and perhaps even to make it lawful at all). But might it also be possible to decide that a particular *individual* intervention is 'liminally proper' because of the circumstances in which it is performed, even though in other circumstances the same intervention might constitute paradigmatically or clearly proper treatment?

Stephen W Smith has argued, in a series of recent articles, that in addition to the more familiar examples involving beginning of life issues, we can also describe as 'conscience claims' those cases where professionals seek to opt out of treating patients beyond the bounds of what is meaningfully therapeutic *for that patient*.[92] Smith calls these 'bridge too far' cases; cases in which an intervention which might be entirely appropriate in another context is considered to be a 'bridge too far' for a particular patient, given the patient's prognosis and circumstances. Importantly, Smith explicitly distinguishes these cases from cases covered by 'predictable, generalisable rule-based conscientious objection',[93] and simply proposes that we recognise the claim of the professional to be allowed to opt out of involvement in interventions of this kind as a 'claim of conscience'.[94]

It seems uncontroversial to me that 'conscience' (as opposed to CO) is involved in these cases – the practice of healthcare is widely acknowledged to be a profoundly moral enterprise in which the consciences of professionals are engaged at every turn.[95] But although Smith does not make the claim that these cases involve CO *as such*, I think his work raises a question which my model must confront: namely, whether liminality (and therefore the permissibility of CO) is only determinable at the whole-practice level, or whether it can also be determined on a case-by-case basis.

I have previously suggested that many 'bridge too far' interventions cannot even be liminally proper:

> Individual interventions that belong in this category might include burdensome interventions upon dying patients (for example, the resuscitation of a patient who is terminally ill and close to death, or the aggressive treatment of an infection in a dying patient with antibiotics which cause unpleasant side effects. Insofar as such interventions cause suffering which is not outweighed by any meaningful gain in comfort or enhanced life expectancy, they … may be outside the boundaries of proper medical treatment.[96]

I say they 'may be' outside the boundaries because arguably, there may be exceptional cases in which these ostensibly improper interventions may be justified in the patient's

[92] SW Smith, 'A Bridge Too Far: Individualised Claims of Conscience' (2015) 23 *Medical Law Review* 283.
[93] ibid at 283.
[94] ibid, *passim*.
[95] See, eg ED Pellegrino, 'Commentary: Value Neutrality, Moral Integrity, and the Physician' (2000) 28 *Journal of Law, Medicine & Ethics* 78; see also Asch, 'Two Cheers for Conscience Exceptions' (2006) and Weinstock, 'Conscientious Refusal and Health Professionals' (2014).
[96] Neal (n 10) 131.

best interests: for example, where a dying patient is resuscitated in order to enable a much wished-for last goodbye with a loved one who is known to be on their way to the bedside. Absent such exceptional circumstances, however, interventions that are on balance harmful, and often performed in circumstances where capacity is impaired, would appear not even to be liminally proper, since there appears to be no plausible 'public good' claim to be made in their defence. And if they are straightforwardly improper (ethically impermissible) on my model, there ought to be no question of any expectation that professionals will undertake them, and thus no need for the shield of CO.

But for argument's sake, would it *matter* if liminality (and so the permissibility of CO) could be determined on a case-by-case basis as well as at the whole-practice level? It might matter if the benefits I have claimed for my model are benefits that accrue *only if* liminality is always determined at the whole-practice level. In discussing reasonableness tests, above, I claimed that it was an advantage of my approach that it was not necessary to determine the reasonableness of each individual objection. Might this particular benefit be diluted if it were *also* possible to decide liminality and allow for CO in individual cases? Arguably not: in these cases, too, the determination of 'reasonableness' would be built into the prior decision about whether or not the *intervention* was, in fact, liminal. And there is another reason why the existence of liminal *interventions* could have, at most, a limited impact on my model: namely, that the majority of instances of CO would still involve practices for which it was predetermined that the *practice* was liminal and that CO was therefore applicable, like abortion. To be clear, however: most of what Smith calls 'bridge too far' interventions would be improper, not liminally proper, on my model (meaning there would be no need to consider CO).

The other benefits I have claimed for my approach – the benefits of explaining CO by reference to a spectrum of proper medical treatment, theorising it in terms intelligible to the professions, and understanding it as a legitimate professional position instead of 'dishonourable disobedience' – accrue regardless of whether the permissibility of CO is decided at the level of whole practices or individual interventions.

V. Conclusion

In this chapter I have described a spectrum of proper medical treatment that includes a category within which the properness of treatment can be regarded as 'liminal' (existing at the boundary of the spectrum of the proper) due to absent/contested therapeutic benefit and explicit or implicit appeal to 'public good' factors. I have argued that it is in relation to practices in this liminal category that CO ought to be accommodated. The approach proposed here is distinguishable from approaches which seek to delineate the parameters of CO by citing 'core professional values' or 'the goals of healthcare' (or similar). In addition, insofar as it might be regarded as containing a built-in reasonableness test, I have argued that my approach is preferable to models which impose tests of reasonableness at the individual level.

Whereas lawfulness is an all-or-nothing property, the 'properness' of treatment can be understood as a scalar property, existing on a spectrum. This can help to explain why, contrary to the claims of some critics of CO, not all lawful treatment is necessarily entitled to the same degree of support from health professionals. Practices in the liminal category are legitimately debated, negotiated and objected to, including by professionals in the context of their professional roles.

Smith has observed that '*conscience* must be inward-facing. A decision of conscience is about the conduct of the person claiming conscience. Conscience is about *my* actions, not the actions of other people'.[97] The primary reason we allow CO is because we accept that it is sometimes necessary for a professional to be able to extract herself from involvement in something she considers to be seriously wrong and thereby protect herself from sharing in moral responsibility for serious wrongdoing (as she sees it). This is what I mean when I say that respect for moral integrity and concern for its preservation is still the 'ground level justification' for CO on my model. But whereas *conscience* may well be inward-facing, *conscientious objection* is certainly not, or at least not exclusively. It is a public act, a professional position, and an act of participation: participation in debates at and around the boundaries of 'proper medical treatment'.

---

[97] SW Smith, 'Individualised Claims of Conscience, Clinical Judgement, and Best Interests' (2018) 26 *Health Care Analysis* 81, 83 (emphases added).

9

The Art of Living with Ourselves: What Does the Law Have to do with Conscience?

GERALD CHIPEUR QC AND ROBERT CLARKE

'Atticus, you must be wrong.'

'How's that?'

'Well, most folks seem to think they're right and you're wrong ...'

'They're certainly entitled to think that, and they're entitled to full respect for their opinions,' said Atticus, 'but before I can live with other folks I've got to live with myself. The one thing that doesn't abide by majority rule is a person's conscience.'

— Harper Lee, *To Kill a Mockingbird* (1960)

I. Introduction

Freedom of conscience is one of the least understood of all rights protected by the European Convention on Human Rights (the 'Convention'). And yet the Convention is not alone in enshrining this rather enigmatic right – it has attracted the protection of every major human rights treaty since its notable inclusion in both the preamble to, and the first Article of, the Universal Declaration of Human Rights in 1948. At a national level, it has appeared in constitutions around the world, from Albania to Zimbabwe. However, despite its apparent ubiquity, it is seldom invoked in litigation, and therefore has rarely been subjected to meaningful judicial analysis.

There are two principal reasons why freedom of conscience appears to be an awkward outlier among the more familiar cadre of human rights. The first is the philosophical complexity of the concept itself, particularly when compared to more accessible concepts such as freedom of expression. The underlying notion of conscience is one which can be hard to neatly define, transcending the bounds of law into philosophy, psychology, sociology and theology. Secondly, even when we can assume a common understanding of what conscience is, the legal – and practical – implications of facilitating freedom of conscience can lead to hesitancy.

Compounding these two primary considerations is the fact that, historically, freedom of conscience has most commonly been situated among a triad of related rights within the treaties. These cousins – freedom of religion, freedom of thought and freedom of belief – have much in common with freedom of conscience, but are not synonymous. Courts – both in Strasbourg and domestically – have often been content to rely on freedom of religion or belief in cases which perhaps would have been best understood – and evaluated – as conscience claims.

This blurred understanding of freedom of conscience is now being refined in the United Kingdom and elsewhere through the crucible of legislative debate[1] and through judicial deliberation. Recent years have seen an array of claimants seek protection: from business-owners[2] to civil servants,[3] and health care professionals[4] to religious organisations.[5] In the legislative sphere, politicians have long recognised the importance of 'conscience votes' by which elected representatives are free to vote in line with their convictions unconstrained by the pressure of party whips and party lines. Between 1997 and 2015, there were more than 100 free votes[6] in the House of Commons on topics as diverse as the Hunting Bills, Lords reform, the Human Fertilisation and Embryology Bill, and the Act introducing same-sex marriage.[7]

There have been various attempts to define the protections and limits of freedom of conscience but there remains no unified approach and significant disagreement as is evident from this volume alone. This chapter will draw together a number of emerging strands to advance an understanding of conscience which is worthy of protection, and a legal approach to achieving that protection while addressing the most common objections.

In the first part of this chapter, we will review the foundations of conscience to make clear that the legal approach that follows stands on a historically and philosophically solid foundation. We will then go on to propose a test in three major parts for identifying, and evaluating, conscience claims. The effect of this will be to make clearer the divisibility and particularity of the (nonetheless related) cluster of rights protected under Article 9 of the European Convention.

---

[1] For example, Baroness Cumberlege introduced a conscience clause into the Marriage (Same Sex Couples) Bill (2013–2014) which received significant debate. See HL Deb 8 July 2013, vol 747, col 39.

[2] See, eg, *Lee v Ashers Baking Company Ltd & Ors (Northern Ireland)* [2018] UKSC 49 and *Masterpiece Cakeshop v Colorado Civil Rights Commission*, 584 US ___ (2018).

[3] See, eg, the case of the French mayors who sought an opt out from Le Conseil Constitutionnel in relation to conducting marriages for same-sex couples (Conseil Constitutionnel Decision 2013-353 QPC of 18 October 2013); the case of Islington registrar Lilian Ladele whose objection to the officiating of civil partnership ceremonies reached the European Court of Human Rights (*Eweida and Others v UK* (2013) 57 EHRR 8); and the case of the county clerk for Rowan County in Kentucky, Kim Davis, who declined to issue marriage licences to same-sex couples (*Miller v Davis*, 667 F App'x 537 (6th Cir 2016)).

[4] *Grimmark and Steen v Sweden* (ECtHR, pending); *Jachimowicz v Sauherad Municipality* HR-2018-1958-A (case no. 2018/199) (Supreme Court of Norway).

[5] See, eg, the Canadian cases of *Smith and Chymyshyn v Knights of Columbus and others* 2005 BCHRT 544, concerning the hire of a church hall; *Canadian Centre for Bio-Ethical Reform v Peterborough (City)* [2016] OJ No 4626; *Canadian Centre for Bio-Ethical Reform v Hinton (Town)* [2017] AJ No 347, concerning the availability of advertising space.

[6] House of Commons Library, *Free Votes in the House of Commons since 1997* (Parliamentary Information Lists, Number 04793, 15 November 2016). www.researchbriefings.files.parliament.uk/documents/SN04793/SN04793. pdf. Although there is no formal system for the recording of free votes, this parliamentary report compiles information based on comments by Ministers and in the media given that parties will usually announce when they will not be whipping the vote.

[7] The Second Reading of the Marriage (Same Sex Couples) Bill on 5 February 2013 was reported to be a free vote. ibid.

One assumption which will run through this chapter is that the maximisation of freedom of conscience is both an individual[8] and societal good.[9] Others have made this case and we seek to build upon this foundation by advancing a novel test for the juridical examination of conscience-based claims. There needs to be an assessment of whether we are comfortable with permitting exceptions to laws of general application on the basis of what are often painted as subjective and opaque inclinations.

In the course of advancing the three-stage test, we will pre-empt and respond to popular counter-arguments, including the argument that allowing for freedom of conscience could result in chaos (the 'anarchy' argument), that any exemptions amount to religious privilege (the 'privilege' argument), that conscience is already protected under freedom of religion (the 'confluence' argument), that any separate protection would not make a material difference (the 'no benefit' argument), and the narrower argument that conscience cannot be a licence to offend other important rights and interests (the 'limiting' argument).

II. What is Freedom of Conscience?

It is clear that conscience is something which has straddled the secular and the religious and has, since at least the fifth century BC, embraced the idea of a split person – a tension within.[10] Richard Sorabji has noted that 'the very gradual secularization [in the eighteenth century] of the idea of conscience was, I believe, a resecularization, because the early Greek views of conscience were themselves comparatively secular'.[11] Indeed, drawing on the work on John Locke,[12] it has been argued that conscience is

> not a *source* of moral law, but it applies moral knowledge – whether that knowledge is shaped by religious beliefs or not … Christians believe it is a witness to the existence of God's law and a foreshadowing of God's judgment, but everyone may experience it as an internal sense of right and wrong. These descriptions are different perspectives on the same faculty.[13]

The source, functioning and effect of this concept have been wrestled with by philosophers through the ages including Immanuel Kant, who understood conscience to be 'an internal court in man'. Anticipating the response that such a fusion of the judicial functions could be open to attacks as to impartiality, he asserted 'all duties of a man's conscience will, accordingly, have to think of someone other than himself … as the judge of his action, if conscience is not to be in contradiction with itself'.[14] Gandhi too recognised the idea of an external constraining force in conceding that he would feel compelled to act contrary to his non-violent principles if he could not otherwise save the life of a girl: 'God would not forgive me

---

[8] P Lenta, 'Freedom of Conscience and the Value of Personal Integrity' (2016) 29 *Ratio Juris* 246.

[9] R Vischer, *Conscience and the Common Good: Reclaiming the Space Between Person and State* (Cambridge, Cambridge University Press, 2009).

[10] R Sorabji, *Moral Conscience Through the Ages* (Chicago, University of Chicago Press, 2014).

[11] ibid 6.

[12] J Locke, *An Essay Concerning Human Understanding*, (PH Niditch ed, Cambridge, Cambridge University Press, 1975).

[13] NS Chapman, 'Disentangling Conscience and Religion' (2013) 4 *University of Illinois Law Review* 1457, 1490.

[14] I Kant, *Metaphysics of Morals* (Mary Gregor tr, Cambridge, Cambridge University Press 1991).

if, on the Judgment Day, I were to plead before him that I could not prevent these things from happening because I was held back by my creed of non-violence'.[15]

This understanding is reflected in the more recent dissenting opinion of Judges Vučinić and De Gaetano of the European Court of Human Rights (ECtHR) in *Eweida and Others v UK* that conscience 'enjoins a person at the appropriate moment to do good and to avoid evil'.[16] Indeed, the law already anticipates this by making all manner of exceptions, even against countervailing considerations such as individual safety or the cohesiveness of the education system, based on matters of conscience. In the case of Sikhs riding a motorcycle, Parliament decided that the principal reason driving the mandatory helmet legislation – safety of the rider – was insufficient to extend the requirement to those for whom it might pose a moral or religious conflict.[17]

It is clear that conscience can both compel action and inaction. In the classic case of conscientious 'objectors' to military service, it is usually seen as a refusal to abide by the requirements of a national conscription or service law. Conversely, the case of a Muslim requiring a particular diet could perhaps more accurately be characterised as a positive obligation of conscience. That is a more holistic way of viewing conscience: not merely as a right to 'object' to certain things, but as the usually thoroughly unproblematic desire to live life in accordance with what we each believe to be right and wrong.

Therefore, problems tend to arise only in the relatively unusual circumstances where the law of the land either compels a person to do something that they believe they cannot, or requires them to abstain from something that they believe is morally compelled. It is important to bear this in mind in any discussion of freedom of conscience. The vast majority of the time, the majority of people are able to live their lives without conscientious difficulty. This does not mean that a framework for responding to the relatively few cases that arise is unimportant, but rather it is all the more necessary to provide resolution in instances of true conflict, knowing that this will be the exception. Indeed, even those few people finding themselves in this kind of situation may wish for an easier life where painful choices did not arise, but to compromise when they do would be a form of betrayal of self. Indeed, a colloquial appeal to conscience is that 'I couldn't live with myself if I …'

It is here where a distinction between religion and conscience can be blurred, as many will have an understanding of conscience informed by their religious beliefs. For the Christian, this is reflected in Romans 14:

> I know and am persuaded in the Lord Jesus that nothing is unclean in itself, but it is unclean for anyone who thinks it unclean … So do not let what you regard as good be spoken of as evil. Whoever thus serves Christ is acceptable to God and approved by men … Everything is indeed clean, but it is wrong for anyone to make another stumble by what he eats … Blessed is the one who has no reason to pass judgment on himself for what he approves. But whoever has doubts is condemned if he eats, because the eating is not from faith. For whatever does not proceed from faith is sin.[18]

[15] MK Gandhi, *Collected works* (New Delhi, Publications Division Government of India, 1978) vol 71, 225.

[16] *Eweida and Others v UK* (2013) 57 EHRR 8, at 2 (joint partly dissenting opinion of Judges Vučinić and De Gaetano).

[17] A bill exempting Sikhs from this requirement was debated in 1975: The Motor-Cycle Crash Helmets (Religious Exemption) Act 1976. See, eg the speech of Mr Sydney Bidwell, HC Deb 28 January 1975, vol 885, cols 222-5.

[18] Romans 14:14–23, English Standard Version.

Here the Apostle Paul comments on the responsibilities of the strong to the weak. The conflict is between a stronger believer who has become convinced that no food remains unclean, and a believer who has not come to this position. How then should the strong (or powerful) act? Paul's answer is unambiguous. They should not ride roughshod through the weaker conscience (as mistaken as it may be), but should defer to it. The section contains two striking and connected aspects of the Christian understanding of conscience. Firstly, that conscience can be mistaken. But secondly, that it is nonetheless sacrosanct.

For whatever disagreement there may be as to the precise parameters of conscience, perhaps the clearest area of application is in matters concerning life and death, given the high stakes involved. In the case of abortion, many people of faith believe that it is morally wrong to end a life, once conceived. While their belief may find its source in religion, it may also be based on a philosophical understanding of the development and dignity of the human person from conception. That belief would not (and should not) be limited to people of faith, with many more doctors than those who are religious expressing a conscientious objection to abortion.[19]

This is an area of classic moral controversy in which conscientious conflicts might reasonably be anticipated and where laws are passed to do just that in anticipating the conflict. For example, when the Abortion Act 1967 was before Parliament, the position of doctors was hotly debated. As a result, section 4 of the Act is very clear in providing that no person is under any duty to participate in 'any treatment authorised by [the] Act to which he has a conscientious objection'. And when the Human Fertilisation and Embryology Act 1990 was debated, not only was that bill subject to a free vote for Parliamentarians, but language was included to protect those with a conscientious objection to 'any activity governed by this Act'.[20]

Similarly, in every country that has introduced euthanasia legislation, the right of doctors and other medical professionals to refuse to participate in causing death has been protected. Policies seeking to remove this protection have been robustly challenged.[21] In another area that has given rise to legal challenges, South Africa has adopted specific protections to exempt government employees from performing same-sex ceremonies on the grounds of conscience, religion or belief.[22] And at least 21 EU countries provide conscience protections for medical professionals in the context of abortion in law, with others protected by professional guidelines and practice.[23]

There is a clear recognition that when Parliament legislates in morally controversial areas, consideration must be given to those who may be placed in a difficult position by the legislation. Conscience protections therefore exist at a national level to protect the consciences

---

[19] See, eg, *Plattform 'Ärtze für das Leben' v Austria* App no 10126/82 (ECtHR, 21 June 1988), in which the European Court of Human Rights recognises a pro-life position as protected. This argument is well developed by Anderson and Girgis in their portion of J Corvino, S Girgis, R Anderson, *Debating Religious Liberty and Discrimination* (Oxford, Oxford University Press, 2017).

[20] Human Fertilisation and Embryology Act 1990, s 38.

[21] See, eg, *The Christian Medical and Dental Society of Canada v College of Physicians and Surgeons of Ontario* [2018] ONSC 579, now on appeal to the Court of Appeal.

[22] Civil Union Act 2006, s 6 (South Africa). See also *Reference re: Same-Sex Marriage* [2004] 3 SCR 698, 721–23 in which the Supreme Court of Canada required a similar exemption for 'religious' officials.

[23] Amicus Brief of ADF International in the case of *Linda Steen v Landstinget i Jönköpings Län*, T 2153-15, p 16. Available at adfinternational.org/wp-content/uploads/2018/01/linda-steen-amicus-brief.pdf.

of religious and non-religious people on the rare occasions when they find themselves in conflict with the law of the land on a matter of moral significance.

Yossi Nehushtan and Stella Coyle, in chapter seven of this volume, argue that conscience should be tolerated but only to the extent that Parliament has prescribed such an accommodation. They argue that a content-based approach entitles the state to evaluate things like the 'moral soundness' and 'legitimacy' of a belief, and only in some cases make an exemption as an act of toleration.[24] This is a version of the privilege argument. One problem with this approach is that the nature of freedom of conscience is such that this kind of narrow interpretation does not make sense. In the same way that Parliament cannot conceive of every possible application of a law, thus necessitating interpretation by the courts, Parliament similarly cannot anticipate how that same law may sit conscientiously for everyone it may affect. If we accept that freedom of conscience is generally good, then our laws should, and indeed do,[25] seek to maximise the protection it is afforded rather than starting from a place of having presumed to exhaustively define the possible protections. In addition, the idea that the State somehow definitively proclaims new moral orders with each legislative Act is at odds with Parliament's view of itself as well as the courts' view of the legislature.[26] At a philosophical level, for the state to discourage 'intolerant' views circularly results in the state only tolerating a narrow range of views – arguably the definition of intolerance.

Still, the view that exemptions granted by Parliament constitute the extent of conscientious protection in UK law is one some have found attractive. However, that view is neither consistent with a proper understanding of conscience itself, as set out above, nor the current state of the law.

Courts in the United Kingdom are bound to consider the impact of the European Convention by virtue of section 6(3)(a) of the Human Rights Act 1998. That means that they must secure freedom of conscience as protected by Article 9, and that Article is not limited to the discrete areas in which Parliament has chosen to legislate.

Perhaps the most salient example, albeit in a different national context, is that of *Bayatyan v Armenia*[27] in which a man had been convicted for refusing military service. Mr Vahan Bayatyan had sent a letter to the Armenian Government indicating the nature of his objection – relating to his pacifist convictions as a Jehovah's Witness – and indicating that he was ready to perform alternative civilian service. The prosecutor responded by charging him with a number of offences, including draft evasion. He was convicted and sentenced to 18 months' imprisonment.

Even that custodial term was insufficient for the prosecutor who appealed the sentence seeking a heavier punishment on the grounds of the 'social danger of the crime'. The appellate court agreed and increased his punishment to two and a half years. Bayatyan, a 20-year-old

---

[24] See also Y Nehushtan 'What Are Conscientious Exemptions Really About?' (2013) 2 *Oxford Journal of Law and Religion* 393.

[25] For an argument that the current British Medical Association (BMA) guidance for doctors fails to recognise the full breadth of conscience protections afforded to doctors, see especially: J Adenitire, 'The BMA's guidance on conscientious objection may be contrary to human rights law' [2017] 43 *Journal of Medical Ethics* 260.

[26] J Adenitire, 'Conscientious Objections: From Toleration to Neutrality; From Neutrality to Respect' (2017) 6 *Oxford Journal of Law and Religion* 268, in which the editor of this volume makes the argument that Parliament is constitutionally incompetent to express toleration or otherwise for conscience.

[27] *Bayatyan v Armenia* (2012) 54 EHRR 15.

man at the time, served about ten months before he was released on parole. He filed a claim with the European Court of Human Rights that same day under Article 9.

The Lower Chamber of the ECtHR was not receptive to his claim, explaining that Article 4 of the Convention, which provides that 'no one shall be required to perform forced or compulsory labour', specifically anticipated that there were some states which did not have a right to object on grounds of conscience. The case was referred to the Grand Chamber which came to a different conclusion on viewing the matter through the prism of the rights guaranteed by Article 9 instead:

> [P]luralism, tolerance and broadmindedness are hallmarks of a 'democratic society'. Although individual interests must on occasion be subordinated to those of a group, democracy does not simply mean that the views of a majority must always prevail: a balance must be achieved which ensures the fair and proper treatment of people from minorities and avoids any abuse [by the] dominant. Thus, respect on the part of the State towards the beliefs of a minority ... group ... by providing them with the opportunity to serve society as dictated by their conscience might, far from creating unjust inequalities or discrimination as claimed by the Government, rather ensure cohesive and stable pluralism and promote religious harmony and tolerance in society.[28]

That principle is now relatively uncontroversial, but at the time marked a significant departure from the then existing case law of the Commission.[29] This new understanding, which has been followed since,[30] clearly delineates conscience as a separate ground, moving away from the practice of listing in an undifferentiated manner the cluster of related rights protected by Article 9. The language used by the Grand Chamber also sets out a principle that could readily be applied in other areas. The recognition that requiring someone to use lethal force can impermissibly conflict with their conscience is a general principle that could have ready application in, for example, the field of healthcare.

The ECtHR has continued to develop this principle. For example, *Papvasilakis v Greece* concerned a man who objected to military service, not on grounds of his religious convictions but on broader pacifist convictions.[31] The Court had no difficulty in determining that there was nonetheless an interference with his rights under Article 9[32] and found that Greece had violated the Convention in failing 'to comply with their positive obligation under Article 9 of the Convention to ensure that interviews of conscientious objectors by the special committee are conducted in conditions guaranteeing procedural efficiency and the equal representation required by [law]'.[33]

In one of its leading decisions on Article 9, *Eweida and Others v United Kingdom*,[34] Judges Vučinić and De Gaetano reasoned, in a partly dissenting opinion, that there is

---

[28] ibid 126.

[29] In *GZ v Austria* App no 5591/72 (Commission Decision, 2 April 1973) the Commission had stated that it was up to the Member States as to whether or not to permit conscientious objection.

[30] *Erçep v Turkey* App no 43965/04 (ECtHR, 22 November 2011); *Bukharatyan v Armenia* App no 37819/03 (ECtHR, 10 January 2012); *Tsaturyan v Armenia* App no 37821/03 (ECtHR, 10 January 2012); *Fethi Demirtaş v Turkey* App no 5260/07 (ECtHR, 17 January 2012); *Savda v Turkey* App no 42730/05 (ECtHR, 12 June 2012); *Tarhan v Turkey* App no 9078/06 (ECtHR, 17 July 2012); *Buldu and Others v Turkey* App no 14017/08 (ECtHR, 3 June 2014).

[31] Indeed, conscientious objection was widely accepted in the First World War in Britain for religious, but also moral, objections. *Papvasilakis v Greece* App no 66899/14 (ECtHR, 15 September 2016).

[32] ibid at 50.

[33] ibid at 66.

[34] *Eweida* (n 16).

a fundamental difference between freedom of religion and freedom of conscience. In their view, freedom of conscience could not be subject to the same limitations as freedom of religion:

> [O]nce that a *genuine* and *serious* case of conscientious objection is established, the State is obliged to respect the individual's freedom of conscience both positively (by taking reasonable and appropriate measures to protect the rights of the conscientious objector) and negatively (by refraining from actions which punish the objector or discriminate against him or her). Freedom of conscience has in the past all too often been paid for in acts of heroism, whether at the hands of the Spanish Inquisition or of a Nazi firing squad.[35]

This is a more robust protection of conscience than will be advanced in this chapter, but is helpful in both demarcating the issues in *Ladele*'s case as being conscience-based issues, and the need for a higher standard of protection.

The Convention is not alone in protecting conscience. Even before its drafting, the Universal Declaration of Human Rights – described as the foundational instrument of the entire human rights movement[36] – recognised in its first Article that human beings are endowed with reason and conscience.[37] Conscience was considered sufficiently important in the reconstruction of Europe following two world wars that it featured prominently in this aspirational text. It was also incorporated into Article 18 of the International Covenant on Civil and Political Rights (ICCPR), according to which 'everyone shall have the right to freedom of thought, conscience and religion'. The body established to monitor compliance with the Covenant stresses the 'far reaching and profound' nature of this right in its General Comments No 22 and

> draws the attention of State Parties to the fact that the freedom of thought and the freedom of conscience are protected equally with the freedom of religion and belief. The fundamental character of these freedoms is also reflected in the fact that this provision cannot be derogated from, even in time of public emergency.[38]

Similar language exists in the Charter of Fundamental Rights of the European Union in Article 10 and in resolutions of the European Parliament.[39] Turning to the Organization for Security and Co-operation in Europe, its Guidelines for Review of Legislation Pertaining to Freedom of Religion or Belief note that states should seek to resolve the 'many circumstances where individuals and groups, as a matter of conscience, find it difficult or morally objectionable to comply with laws of general applicability'.[40]

In conclusion, freedom of conscience is protected – as a general right – in all major human rights treaties and has been interpreted by the ECtHR as protecting an individual

---

[35] ibid at 3.

[36] P Alston, R Goodman, HJ Steiner, *International Human Rights in Context: Law, Politics, Morals* (Oxford, Oxford University Press, 2007) 136.

[37] Universal Declaration of Human Rights 1948, Art 1.

[38] UNCHR 'General Comment No. 22: Article 18 (Freedom of Thought, Conscience or Religion)' (1993) UN Doc CCPR/C/21/Rev.1/Add.4, para 1.

[39] See European Parliament, 'Resolution on the situation of Christians in the context of freedom of religion' (20 January 2011) P7_TA(2011)0021.

[40] OSCE/ODIHR Advisory Panel of Experts on Freedom of Religion or Belief in consultation with the European Commission for Democracy through Law, 'Guidelines for Review of Legislation Pertaining to Freedom of Religion or Belief' Adopted by the Venice Commission at its 59th Plenary Session, 18–19 June 2004.

who finds themselves in moral (and not necessarily religious) conflict with the law of the land. Our modern understanding resonates with the historic philosophical understanding of conscience as being a split person within directing us to do what is right. The next section will advance a three-stage test that seeks to legally identify and evaluate conscience claims with a view to answering the pragmatic – rather than principled – objections to conscience protections.

III. Evaluating Conscience

Having recognised that it is right to call conscience for what it is, the question of how such claims should be identified and protected arises. One view is that they should simply be amalgamated with the broader category to which these claims belong, with any analysis being a mirror image of the well-established analysis of other claims under Article 9 – that any interference is only justified if it pursues a legitimate aim by proportionate means.

There are two principal reasons as to why we suggest a more specific approach is warranted. Firstly, the mirror image approach does not help in identifying which claims are conscience claims, rather than freedom of religion or belief claims, and so is still prone to the same lack of precision as the historical approach of the ECtHR. Secondly, given that conscience claims cannot be identified in this way, it is also not possible to offer any enhanced level of protection such as we suggest should be extended to these claims affecting the moral integrity of a person.

The framework we will advance contains three distinct stages. The first stage is an evaluation of whether the claim arises as a result of a constraining moral framework. Having established this context to the claim, the second stage involves a detailed look at the facts to decide whether they genuinely disclose a serious moral conflict, both from the perspective of the genuineness of the claimant's claim, and the absolute governmental necessity of the proposed restriction. The final stage is a truly robust attempt at accommodating the person in question, allowing exceptions to a general rule where such an exception would not defeat the purpose of the rule.

A. The Threshold Question

The first stage of the test we propose is one which the claimant must overcome. It requires conscience claimants to demonstrate the existence of a constraining moral framework. It is a direct response to the anarchy argument. This says that given the existence of a conscientious conflict cannot easily be proved, people would be able to do precisely what they want and disobey any and every statutory or contractual obligation simply by raising a flag of convenience masquerading as conscience.

The primary issue with this criticism is that conscience has never been understood as a solely individualistic construct. The very root of the word in Latin comes from *conscientia*, which represents the idea of shared, or common, knowledge. Rather than being purely individualistic, conscience is inherently community-based. It may not be one's immediately proximate community that is concerned, but the binding force of conscience on an individual stems from the fact that there is a framework outside of oneself by which one feels constrained.

This external, or at least outward-facing, constraint goes some way to explain the often very high cost that individuals are willing to pay in order to live in accordance with their conscience. A mere personal whim would likely not generate that sort of allegiance. People generally have an aversion to self-harm. And yet asserting a conscience claim will usually involve some degree of sacrifice. Even assuming that conscience is protected in the way anticipated in this chapter, there may well be social stigma, retaliation or the fear of adverse treatment which follows the exercise of this right. Indeed, both historically and more recently,[41] conscientious objectors have faced a real risk of imprisonment and yet maintained their position, such was the force of the constraint upon their behaviour. Of course, the fact that someone is willing to face prison in order to pursue a certain course of conduct is not reason alone to exempt them, but it is another way of seeing the external forces at work which take someone outside of themselves to act in a way which they know may come at a significant personal cost.

Beyond the existence of the threshold, it is not a court's role to assess the validity of the framework, but simply the existence and relevance of it.[42] The key question for a tribunal at this stage is to ascertain the source of the conscience claim. A mere personal desire – which may be very strong, and the contravention of which may result in personal feelings of disgust – is inadequate to satisfy this test.

There are two elements to this preliminary assessment. The first is that there is the presence of a moral framework. The second is that the framework is relevant to the subject matter at hand. These are both objective considerations. It is not sufficient that someone feels as though they are subscribing to a moral framework, or that there is a link between the motivated behaviour and the framework, or that the framework is in fact moral rather than, say, preferential. Given that this part of the test is intended to eliminate spurious claims that do not reach the level of gravity intended to be protected under laws guaranteeing freedom of conscience, it is appropriate that this first stage acts as an objective filter.[43] For example, in the case of someone asserting that they conscientiously believed they must wear green to their place of employment every day contrary to a corporate dress code, the question would be 'why?'. If the answer is because the individual likes green, or thinks they look best in green, that would be a purely personal preference and their claim would fall at this threshold stage.

By contrast, take the example of a medical practitioner conscientiously objecting to abortion. If they are asked why, in the cases of which we are aware, they would usually ascribe this to their beliefs about the sanctity of human life, beginning as they understand it at conception. The source would be catechetical teaching or a philosophy of life, demonstrating an external framework. If, however, they object simply because they 'do not like'

---

[41] W McGurn, 'Why Must Kim Davis Be Jailed? A Federal Judge Chose the Nuclear Option Instead of Finding a Reasonable Accommodation' (*The Wall Street Journal*, 7 September 2015).

[42] This is the existing, and traditional, position. Peter Jones finds some support for this in ch 3 of this volume, ultimately concluding it is pragmatically justified, even though not out of principle.

[43] See *Ktunaxa Nation v. British Columbia (Forests, Lands and Natural Resource Operations)* 2017 SCC 54 in which the Supreme Court of Canada held that freedom of conscience and religion protect the rights of individuals, not deities.

abortion, then, despite the obvious difference in gravity, the situation would be much closer to the first hypothetical.

This can be seen in practice at one of the United Nations treaty monitoring bodies. The Human Rights Committee,[44] in interpreting the ICCPR, has considered that 'a belief consisting primarily or exclusively in the worship and distribution of narcotic drugs cannot conceivably be brought within the scope of Article 18 of the Covenant'.[45] Under this matrix, although a claimant may be able to argue that their desire to use or distribute narcotic drugs is motivated by a belief, it is going to be difficult to identify a moral framework to which that attaches in all but the most specific of cases. However, while it may be difficult, the individualised nature of conscience means that we do not have to look far to find a counter example.

Perhaps the clearest example is found in the US case of *Employment Division v Smith*,[46] which was one of the cases that ultimately led to the Religious Freedom Restoration Act of 1993 (RFRA). In *Smith*, two Native Americans were fired from positions as drug counsellors after ingesting the psychoactive drug peyote during religious ceremonies long practised in the Native American Church. At the time, the State of Oregon criminalised possession of peyote, with no defence for religious usage. After a number of appeals, the case ended up at the US Supreme Court, which ruled that:

> [I]f prohibiting the exercise of religion is not the object of the [law] but merely the incidental effect of a generally applicable and otherwise valid provision, the First Amendment has not been offended … To make an individual's obligation to obey such a law contingent upon the law's coincidence with his religious beliefs, except where the State's interest is 'compelling' – permitting him, by virtue of his beliefs, 'to become a law unto himself,' – contradicts both constitutional tradition and common sense. To adopt a true 'compelling interest' requirement for laws that affect religious practice would lead towards anarchy.[47]

One can clearly see the anarchy argument at play. This decision, of 17 April 1990, was subject to considerable criticism from across the political spectrum and led Congress to pass RFRA less than three years later. RFRA provides that 'Government shall not substantially burden a person's exercise of religion even if the burden results from a rule of general applicability, except' where it 'furthers a compelling governmental interest' and is the 'least restrictive means of furthering that … interest'.[48]

During the passage of RFRA, the argument that it could lead to a tyranny of the minority was advanced. In debates relating to conscience, arguments about one driven to murder by conscience are often deployed. And yet the 'conscientious murderer' is a straw man.[49] This stage of the test requires an external moral framework that is relevant to the action or inaction concerned and excludes the insane and the anarchistic.

The requirement for the existence of a moral framework explains why many of the cases that have come before the courts, and many of the hypotheticals that can be generated, relate

---

[44] A United Nations Treaty Monitoring Body under the provisions of Art 28, International Covenant on Civil and Political Rights.

[45] *MAB, WAT and J-AYT v Canada* Communication No. 570/1993 (Human Rights Committee, 8 April 1994), UN Doc CCPR/C/50/D/570/1993.

[46] *Employment Division v Smith* 494 US 872 (1990).

[47] ibid 885.

[48] 42 US Code § 2000bb-1(a) and (b).

[49] See Chapman, 'Conscience and Religion' (2013) 1492.

to religious adherents. The practical reality is that many of those asserting a conscience claim will be religious, though it is important to say that is not necessarily so.

The realms of freedom of religion and freedom of conscience are related, but not synonymous. For example, a request for permission to construct a religious building may well be sound in religious freedom protections, but perhaps not in conscience. Similarly, it is not possible to simply say that any claim relating to, for example, worship will be grounded in freedom of religion; or that any claim by an atheist will be a conscience claim. It also follows that there may be situations in which the 'same' claim in different circumstances will fall under different heads of protection. There is an individuality to this. It is not possible in the way that might be most attractive to lay down bright lines as to claims that would always be considered claims of conscience and those that would be considered claims of religious freedom. This is the confluence argument – that any protection for conscience is unnecessary, as conscience wholly coincides with religion or belief.

For example, the actions of someone exploring a religion, without committing to it, would appear to fall more readily under freedom of religion rather than freedom of conscience. Indeed, it is true that 'someone with religious beliefs may come to a conscientious judgment about a particular course of conduct without consciously basing that judgment on religious beliefs, and a coreligionist may come to the same judgment by consciously drawing on religious beliefs'.[50]

The US Supreme Court has perhaps more accurately encapsulated the overlapping but distinct nature of conscience and religion in two cases considered in the 1960s which also provide a cogent response to those who argue that conscience is purely religious. The first, *Seeger*,[51] concerned an exemption from the military draft on the part of three men who did not have a belief in a Supreme being, at least in the orthodox sense, and were thus outside the scope of the exemption then available under section 6(j) of the Universal Military Training and Service Act.

The US Supreme Court found itself seeking to evaluate a belief which 'occupies a place in the life of its possessor parallel to that filled by the orthodox belief in God'.[52] If the beliefs were not required by God, the US Supreme Court sought to evaluate whether it occupied a similarly fundamental place in the moral understanding of the individual. This is consistent with Kant's view of conscience as an external constraint, and the understanding of conscience that we have relied upon as being the moral voice directing action.

The issue returned to the US Supreme Court only a few years later in *Welsh*.[53] Elliot Ashton Welsh II objected to performing military service but specifically indicated that his objection was *not* grounded in religious belief. Building on the *Seeger* precedent the Supreme Court ruled that conscientious objection was available to 'all those whose consciences, spurred by deeply held moral, ethical, or religious beliefs, would give them no rest or peace if they allowed themselves to become a part of an instrument of war'.[54]

---

[50] ibid 1491.
[51] *United States v Seeger* 380 US 163 (1965).
[52] ibid 166.
[53] *Welsh v United States* 398 US 333 (1970).
[54] ibid 344.

Similarly, in Canada, the Supreme Court has held that 'in a free and democratic society … freedom of conscience and religion' should be broadly construed to extend to conscientiously-held beliefs, 'whether grounded in religion or in a secular morality'.[55]

It is important to note what the court is *not* being asked to consider at this stage. Specifically, it is not the court's role to assess the validity of any moral framework, but rather the existence, and relevance, of it.[56] Courts are legally incompetent to determine whether something is morally right or morally wrong given the moral neutrality of the state.[57] However, when it comes to evaluating the existence of a constraining moral framework, courts are used to evaluating similar concepts in the context of claims of freedom of religion. In those cases, the court does not investigate the validity of a religion, but instead evaluates the claim by reference to such characteristics as the objective coherence of the belief espoused and the subjective sincerity of the believer.

In the leading case of *Grainger plc v Nicholson*,[58] the Employment Appeal Tribunal (EAT) was asked whether a belief about climate change was a protected belief under the Employment Equality (Religion or Belief) Regulations 2003. In that context, Burton J said that a philosophical belief must (a) be genuinely held; (b) be a belief and not merely an opinion based on the present state of information; (c) relate to a weighty and substantial aspect of human life and behaviour; (d) attain a certain level of cogency, seriousness, cohesion and importance; and (e) be worthy of respect in a democratic society and not conflict with the fundamental rights of others.

In the case of our threshold assessment of whether the claimant can demonstrate the existence of a constraining moral framework, the court should similarly seek to identify whether the framework is one that has a sufficient level of cogency, seriousness, cohesion and importance. For example, a claim based on a moral framework purporting to regulate the temperature of an office environment may lack the level of seriousness to be considered a constraining moral framework.

Element (a) is also dealt with in our test, but under the second stage (below), given that it is not so much an element which negates the conscientious nature of the claim as one which, in the particular circumstances, means the claim is not in fact made out. Element (c) would seem to be implicit in the requirement that there be a constraining moral framework. Element (e), insofar as it is a balancing of sorts against the rights of others, is dealt with in the second and final stages of our test – having identified with precision the interests at stake. However, a standalone test that a claim be worthy of respect is inappropriate for the same reasons as outlined above in the context of Nehushtan and Coyle's argument on toleration. In borrowing from the existing jurisprudence surrounding religion or belief, we introduce some certainty to this otherwise novel test, as well as transparency in the reasoning of cases which are more properly cases of conscience.

---

[55] *R v Morgentaler* [1988] 1 SCR 30, 37.

[56] See *R (on the application of Begum) v Headteachers and Governors of Denbigh High School* [2006] UKHL 15, [2007] 1 AC 100.

[57] See J Martínez-Torrón, 'Protecting Freedom of Conscience Beyond Prejudice' in S Ferrari (ed), *Routledge Handbook of Law and Religion* (London, Routledge, 2015) 200.

[58] *Grainger plc v Nicholson* [2010] IRLR 4.

B. Genuine Presence of a Serious Moral Conflict

Having established that there is a constraining moral framework in play, this second stage of our test evaluates whether there is the genuine presence of a serious moral conflict. A conflict has two sides, and this stage evaluates the robustness of both sides with a view to maximising freedom of conscience. If either side is found wanting, there is no conflict and the remaining side must prevail. There are therefore two parts to this assessment, the first being subjective, and the second objective.

The first part draws on *Eweida and Others v UK*[59] in evaluating the claimant's case. *Eweida* clarified that manifestation (of a religion or belief) is not limited to acts which are a mandatory part of the practice of the religion or belief in question. Rather:

> [T]he existence of a sufficiently close and direct nexus between the act and the underlying belief must be determined on the facts of each case. In particular, there is no requirement to establish that he or she [the applicant] acted in fulfilment of a duty mandated by the religion in question.[60]

At its simplest, this amounts to a requirement that the act in question is *in fact* motivated by the belief advanced. It seems unobjectionable that, when considering a claim of conscience, the act or objection made must *in fact* flow from that conscience framework.

Significantly, this is a subjective test. There can be no other way of evaluating this that would not undermine the understanding of conscience as set out in the first part of this chapter. If conscience is the judge sitting on one's shoulders, there would be little relief for a court to hold that there is in fact no conscientious difficulty in a situation where one feels conflicted.[61] Of course, given the threshold test, cases that arrive at this juncture will already concern a matter of moral significance and so will already be about more than mere feeling. In passing this second hurdle, a conscience claimant will have evidenced, objectively, that there exists a moral framework capable of motivating the behaviour in question (stage 1, above), and that, in fact, their behaviour is an outworking of the framework (stage 2).

Thereafter, having established a prima facie case of conscience, the burden shifts to the respondent – often the state. It must demonstrate that the interference that has given rise to the dispute is absolutely necessary to pursue a legitimate state interest. This is language borrowed from both the Strasbourg and the American jurisprudence and differs, with reason, from the Article 9 lexicon of 'pursuing a legitimate aim'. One of the principle reasons for this is to highlight the different, higher, standard that this represents. Those state interests can be seen in Article 9(2) which, notably, already lists fewer qualifications than any of the other qualified articles under the Convention.[62]

In *Eweida*, the Court also revisited the proportionality assessment and rejected the argument that someone should simply resign to avoid an interference with their Convention rights. That was the position the National Secular Society advanced before the ECtHR in

---

[59] *Eweida* (n 16).

[60] ibid at 82.

[61] This approach contrasts slightly with the argument set out by Peter Jones in ch 3 of this volume, aligning more closely with the approach of Paul Billingham in ch 4.

[62] See generally, C Evans, *Freedom of Religion under the European Convention on Human Rights* (Oxford, Oxford University Press, 2001) 137.

Eweida: 'freedom to resign is the ultimate guarantee of freedom of conscience'.[63] The Court's refusal to accept this submission removed a 'trump card' that had been played by governments and employers until then.

This imposition of a *robust* proportionality analysis is to be favourably contrasted with an otherwise increasingly broad approach that the Strasbourg Court has taken to necessity. In its case law, the balancing test is the most complex stage. The test has varyingly been described as the requirement of proportionality, the existence of a pressing social need and a consideration of less restrictive means. The standards in this legal mixing pot have been described as 'so interdependent, none ... can be examined convincingly in isolation'.[64]

In *SAS v France*,[65] the Grand Chamber of the ECtHR wrestled with the question of a nationwide criminal prohibition on full-face coverings, including the Muslim burqa. The applicant, a 24-year-old Muslim woman, argued before the Court that 'according to a well-established feminist position, the wearing of the veil often denoted women's emancipation, self-assertion and participation in society, and that ... it was not a question of pleasing men but of satisfying herself *and her conscience*' (emphasis added).[66] She further argued that 'her aim was not to annoy others, but to feel at inner peace with herself'.[67] In her submission, the French prohibition could not be considered necessary as any supposed aim could be achieved by less restrictive means. Similar arguments were made by a number of third-party intervenors.

In response, the government argued that the measure, which it accepted was a limitation, was necessary for public safety, and secondly for protecting the rights and freedoms of others by ensuring 'respect for the minimum set of values of an open and democratic society'. These were explained as including 'the observance of the minimum requirements of life in society', equality between men and women, and human dignity.[68]

In upholding the ban, the Court first dismissed the government's argument that the ban could be justified on the grounds of public safety insofar as it applied to all people in all places at all times. The Court found that it was disproportionate to any specific identifiable threat. Moreover, the Court expressed doubt that security considerations had been at the forefront of the minds of the framers of the law. However, the ban *could* be justified on the grounds of the notion of *vivre ensemble* – living together – as a dramatic recasting of the 'rights and freedoms of others' under Article 9(2).[69]

---

[63] Submissions on behalf of the National Secular Society in *Eweida* (n 16) para 29. Available at www.secularism.org.uk/uploads/nss-intervention-to-european-court-of-human-rights.pdf.

[64] M Evans, *Religious Liberty and International Law in Europe* (Cambridge, Cambridge University Press, 1997) 322.

[65] *SAS v France* (2015) 60 EHRR 11.

[66] ibid at 77.

[67] ibid at 12.

[68] ibid at 77 and 82.

[69] ibid at 157. The Supreme Court of Canada accepted the reasoning behind the ban on the Muslim burqa when it allowed law societies in Canada to deny approval of a law school at Trinity Western University because a statement of faith was required of students. *Law Society of British Columbia v Trinity Western University* 2018 SCC 32; *Trinity Western University v Law Society of Upper Canada* 2018 SCC 33. Both the European Court of Human Rights and the Supreme Court of Canada balanced the interests of individuals with the rights and freedoms of citizens. Those courts should instead have balanced the interests of the state with the right and freedoms

The Court thus approached the public safety argument with healthy scepticism, while affording the state a wide deference on the objective of living together in harmony.[70] We describe the scepticism as healthy, as it should not be sufficient for a state to merely plead a permissible ground for interference. It must be demonstrated that the measure is in fact necessary to achieve the objective in question. While the Court recognised that the notion of living together is a flexible notion with a 'resulting risk of abuse,'[71] it chose to reserve the more stringent analysis for the necessity stage.[72] We are suggesting a more robust interrogation of the aim advanced, even before considering necessity, to ensure that it does in fact fall within the permissible and exhaustive list, and that the interference is capable of achieving the aim.

On the subsequent question of necessity, perhaps the best Convention analogue is found under Article 2, the right to life. This is an absolute right under the Convention from which no derogation is possible. The Convention indicates that life may be taken in the narrowest of circumstances and only when it is *absolutely necessary*.[73] That was first interpreted by the Strasbourg Court in *McCann and Others v United Kingdom*[74] to mean 'a stricter and more compelling test of necessity must be employed than that normally applicable'.[75]

Comparison of conscience claims to the right to life is helpful not only because it is an example of a higher level of protection being afforded to a Convention right, but also because of the gravity of many of the areas which give rise to claims of conscience. Conscience often concerns matters of life and death in areas such as abortion, the death penalty, military service, euthanasia and embryo-destructive research. The fact that the state is held to a higher standard in these kinds of contexts is a powerful argument for holding the state to at least an equal standard when it wants to compel a citizen to do that to which the citizen morally objects.

This produces a necessity test which demands an evaluation of any less restrictive means,[76] an aspect of proportionality rarely expanded upon by the ECtHR, but an important part of the US RFRA jurisprudence. For example, in the case of *Burwell v Hobby Lobby Stores, Inc*[77] the US Supreme Court ruled that a closely held for-profit corporation could be exempt from a law of general application on the basis of deeply held religious beliefs. The case concerned the so-called contraceptive mandate that required employers to provide health care cover, including certain contraceptives. Four of these contraceptives were objected to on the basis that they can act as abortifacients. The US Supreme Court ruled that, although

---

of citizens. It is important to note that Trinity Western University responded to the Supreme Court of Canada by accommodating non-believers. On 14 August 2018, the President of Trinity Western University announced that the statement of faith was no longer required of students, but would be optional.

[70] A Portaru, 'The "Rights and Freedoms of Others" vs. Religious Manifestations: Who Wins at the ECtHR?' in W Benedek, F Benoît-Rohmer, M Kettemann, B Kneihs and M Nowak (eds), *European Yearbook on Human Rights 2015* (Oxford, Intersentia, 2015).

[71] *SAS v France* (n 65) at 122.

[72] The Court did a similar thing in *Dakir v Belgium* App no 4619/12 (ECtHR, 11 July 2017).

[73] European Convention on Human Rights, Art 2(2).

[74] *McCann and Others v United Kingdom* (1995) 21 EHRR 97.

[75] ibid at 147.

[76] See also E Brems and L Lavrysen, 'Don't Use a Sledgehammer to Crack a Nut: Less Restrictive Means in the Case Law of the European Court of Human Rights' (2015) 15 *Human Rights Law Review* 139.

[77] *Burwell v Hobby Lobby Stores, Inc.* 573 US ___ (2014), 134 S Ct 2751.

the government may have a compelling interest in providing access to these contraceptive methods, the mandate on employers was not the least restrictive means of achieving that end. This was because accommodations had been allowed for non-profit entities, and there was no reasonable basis to distinguish between the two types of entity.

Approaching a case like *SAS v France* through this lens would result in the court adopting a sceptical approach to the idea of 'living together'. In noting that this is not a permissible limitation under Article 9(2), it may mark the end of the enquiry and, with nothing on the counterbalance, the conscience claim would prevail. If the state could truly demonstrate that its concern is the rights and freedoms of others, it would have to do so convincingly by reference to what those rights are. Moreover, it would have to demonstrate how a nation-wide criminal prohibition (a relatively restrictive means)[78] is the least restrictive method of achieving that objective.

By far, the most common challenge in recent cases dealing with religious freedom is some formulation of anti-discrimination law – weighed in the balance as the right of others to be free from discrimination. This is the limiting argument. Within this volume, that is one of the strongest difficulties identified by Moon. He argues that conscience can be protected (in the case of religious objectors) where the public interest will not be significantly compromised, but that 'religious beliefs about civic issues such as homelessness, same-sex marriage, and reproductive rights can neither be excluded nor insulated from political decision-making. On these issues, the state is not, and cannot be, neutral'.[79]

Conscientious accommodation seems to attract the most significant opposition within the commercial space. Indeed, that has been the area in which a number of business-owners in the West have been pursued, including the Bull family who ran a small bed and breakfast in Cornwall.[80] In that case, the Christian owners maintained a policy of only letting double-bedded rooms to married couples. At the relevant time, it was only possible for opposite-sex couples to be married. A same-sex couple had booked a double room and, upon arrival, were told of the policy and that it would only be possible to take a twin room. The couple brought a claim of direct and indirect sexual orientation discrimination in the provision of goods and services under the Equality Act (Sexual Orientation) Regulations 2007.[81] The couple rejected an offer made by Mr and Mrs Bull to reimburse the additional expense of finding alternative accommodation and a modest sum for the inconvenience.[82] They were successful at first instance and also at the Court of Appeal, which found direct discrimination. The Court of Appeal also found that any interference with the hoteliers' rights under Article 9 was proportionate and in pursuit of a legitimate governmental objective.

The Supreme Court dismissed an appeal against this ruling, holding that it was key that the same-sex couple were in a civil partnership. Given that this was to be treated as like a marriage, and given the correspondence between the effect of the hotel's policy and

---

[78] The ECtHR has been rightly reluctant to accept blanket bans as justified, see, eg *Hirst v UK (No 2)* (2006) 42 EHRR 41.

[79] See ch 5 in this volume, text to n 18.

[80] *Bull and another v Hall and another* [2013] UKSC 73, [2013] 1 WLR 3741.

[81] ibid at 3. The Supreme Court noted that 'all of this legislation has since been replaced (for a case such as this) by the Equality Act 2010, but the principles, concepts and provisions with which we are concerned have remained the same'.

[82] ibid at 11.

a protected characteristic, Lady Hale, writing for the majority, held that it was a case of direct discrimination.[83]

In going on to consider indirect discrimination, it was common ground between the parties that the question for the Court was whether indirect discrimination could be justified. Lady Hale thought it difficult to see how this 'could ever be justified' – a conclusion which did not change following consideration of the relevant Article 9 authorities. Aidan O'Neill QC, for the Bulls, argued that there existed a duty of reasonable accommodation. Lady Hale was 'more than ready to accept that the scope for reasonable accommodation is part of the proportionality assessment, at least in some cases'.[84]

In this context, brief consideration was given to the two Canadian cases of *Eadie and Thomas v Riverbend Bed and Breakfast and others (No 2)*[85] and *Smith and Chymshyn v Knights of Columbus and others*.[86] These cases both concerned a refusal, based upon religious convictions, to provide a bedroom in a bed and breakfast in the former and a wedding reception venue in the latter. The UK Supreme Court considered that these cases could 'provide some comfort' to Mr and Mrs Bull, but very quickly considered that they 'cannot get round the fact that United Kingdom law prohibits them from doing as they did'.[87] Specifically, the Court considered that any accommodation was impossible for the same reasons that even indirect discrimination could not have been justified.

Lady Hale has subsequently questioned that outcome, wondering whether the decision was 'something of a relief or whether we would be better off with a more nuanced approach'.[88] Speaking to the Law Society of Ireland in 2014, she questioned why someone should not be afforded a reasonable accommodation where there is 'no competing equality right in play' and concluded: 'I am not sure that our law has yet found a reasonable accommodation of all of these different strands. The story has just begun'.[89]

The approach we outline provides one solution to this critique. It does not have to simply be a case as to which of multiple protected characteristics shall prevail. In many cases, we would argue that the only counterbalance is a generalised interest in combatting discrimination. That was the case, for example, for Lillian Ladele in *Eweida*. No same-sex couple had made a complaint and, given the size and scheduling possibilities of the London Borough of Islington, no one was going to be refused service. The counterweight in that case was expressed as the Borough's commitment to equal opportunities. As sensible as such a policy may be, the general aim cannot overcome (and is not undermined by) a conscience claim.[90] It cannot overcome a conscience claim on our analysis, as it is pitting a fundamental right,

---

[83] Note also that the case was due to be heard alongside the similar case of *Black & Anor v Wilkinson* [2013] EWCA Civ 820, [2013] 1 WLR 2490 which concerned a same-sex couple who were *not* in a civil partnership. In that case, the Court of Appeal had expressed the view that, had they not felt bound by the decision in *Bull v Hall*, they would have likely found the discrimination to be indirect, but not justified. However, this appeal was not pursued at the Supreme Court.

[84] *Bull v Hall* (n 80) at 47.

[85] *Eadie and Thomas v Riverbend Bed and Breakfast and others (No 2)* 2012 BCHRT 247.

[86] *Smith and Chymshyn v Knights of Columbus and others* 2005 BCHRT 544.

[87] *Bull v Hall* (n 80) at 50.

[88] Lady Hale, 'Freedom of Religion and Belief' (Annual Human Rights Lecture to Law Society of Ireland, 13 June 2014), 17. Available at www.supremecourt.uk/docs/speech-140613.pdf.

[89] ibid 20.

[90] This was, for example, the conclusion of the US Supreme Court in *Boy Scouts of American v Dale* 530 US 640 (2000).

properly asserted, against a vague aspiration, however meritorious it may be. This does not undermine that aspirational objective, as the prohibited discrimination remains prohibited in all but the carefully defined cases where a claim of conscience has been established. Moreover, there are *already* exemptions afforded to (non-commercial) religious organisations under the Equality Act 2010, so the existing position is already more nuanced than the absolutist nature of this counterargument would suggest.[91]

Some commentators have accepted the argument that general interests in countering discrimination should be inadequate counterweights, but instead point to the idea of dignitary harm in specific cases involving individuals. Without using that term, Lady Hale draws on the idea in *Bull*. It is the idea that allowing otherwise impermissible discrimination causes non-pecuniary harm to the person or persons being discriminated against.

The first thing is to recognise that to the extent there is dignitary harm on one side, there is certainly a similar claim on the other side on the part of someone who is going to be forced by the state to do something with which they cannot abide. However, we are on dangerous territory when the state enters into the business of attempting to protect feelings. This much was recognised in the successful campaign to have section 5 of the Public Order Act 1984 amended to remove the criminalisation of 'insulting' language. It chills freedom of expression and ultimately shuts down ideas that may today be in the minority and disfavoured, but tomorrow lead to our awakening or some other significant discovery. How true this is of conscience. For the same reason that we do not simply want to permit only 'pleasant' expression – society is at its best when those with differing beliefs are able to co-exist in accordance with conscience.

Moreover, there is at times shorthand to the framing of these issues on the question of 'clashing rights' which can unhelpfully obscure the reality. For example, Nehushtan and Coyle, in their contribution to this volume, argue that 'homophobic or racist views and unjust discriminatory practices (eg refusal to provide services to homosexuals …)'[92] are 'illegitimate' views. However, if used to describe the cases in which these issues have arisen, that would be a significant mischaracterisation. In *Ashers Baking*,[93] for example, it is clear that the bakery did not, and would not, decline service on the grounds of the customer's sexual orientation. Rather, the cake requested included a message on the top reading 'Support Gay Marriage' which was a message that the bakery felt they could not, in good conscience, endorse or promote. That is a markedly, and legally, different position from the one in which a vendor excludes a group of people based on a protected characteristic.

While some, including Andrew Koppelman, have accepted that 'there have been no claims of a right to simply refuse to deal with gay people',[94] this compelling, but straw man, argument persists. Similar arguments were made by the State of Colorado in seeking to defend its punishment of cake artist Jack Phillips whose case was recently decided by the US Supreme Court in *Masterpiece Cakeshop v Colorado Civil Rights Commission*.[95] However, in contrast to the position taken by the State in *Ashers*, Colorado accepts that

---

[91] Equality Act 2010, Sch 23, s 2.
[92] Chapter 7 of this volume.
[93] *Lee v Ashers Baking Company Ltd & Ors (Northern Ireland)* [2018] UKSC 49.
[94] A Koppelman, 'Gay Rights, Religious Accommodations, and the Purposes of Antidiscrimination Law' [2015] 88 *South California Law Review* 619, 643.
[95] *Masterpiece* (n 2).

an unconscionable message *would be* sufficient to allow the service provider to decline the order – they simply dispute there is messaging inherent in a wedding cake:

> Indeed, in cases involving requests to create cakes that feature specific designs or messages that are offensive to the vendor, Colorado law dictates a different result … [U]nder Colorado law, '[a]n African-American baker may decline to create a custom cake celebrating the racist ideals of a member of the Aryan Nation' and 'a Muslim baker may refused to create a custom cake denigrating his faith for the Westboro Baptist Church.' … Phillips himself may not be compelled to create 'cakes with offensive written messages' such as 'anti-American or anti-family themes, atheism, racism, or indecency.'[96]

In the United Kingdom, the judgment in *Bull* laments that 'we do not normally allow people to behave in a way which the law prohibits because they disagree with the law. But to allow discrimination against persons of homosexual orientation … because of a belief, however sincerely held, would be to do just that.'[97] The fact that neither of these cases related to an adverse judgment about gay people is evident from the record in both cases.

It could reasonably be argued that if the ECtHR were to apply the legitimate aim and necessity test in a more rigorous way, then this deviation would be unnecessary. Nonetheless, it is clear that the ECtHR prefers a more permissive approach under the existing Article 9 jurisprudence.[98] In order to achieve a higher level of protection for conscience within Article 9, a differential must be introduced which is hereby done by pressing the state on how the measure achieves an enumerated (and non-generalised) aim, and by insisting that it is truly the least restrictive way of achieving it.

C. Robustly Attempted Accommodation

The third and final stage of any conscience adjudication is to evaluate whether there has been a robust attempt to accommodate the person in question. By this stage, the person will have demonstrated that their behaviour is genuinely motivated by a constraining moral framework and the state will have demonstrated that it has an actual legitimate (enumerated) aim in maintaining its rule which is no more restrictive than is necessary to achieve that aim. This is the most individualised stage of the test where an individual arrangement may be able to maximise conscience without undermining the effect of a generally desirable law.

Lucy Vickers, in chapter ten of this volume, highlights the influential actors that have advocated for a duty of reasonable accommodation. She reviews the existing models in operation in North America, considering that the US model provides only a very weak form of protection. By contrast, she accepts that the Canadian model provides more robust protection but ultimately concludes that the introduction of a duty of reasonable accommodation would likely make no material difference to the outcome of conscience claims

---

[96] Brief of the Colorado Civil Rights Commission in *Masterpiece Cakeshop Ltd and Jack Phillips v Colorado Civil Rights Commission, Charlie Craig and David Mullins*, 29 November 2017, pp 11–12 (citations omitted).

[97] *Bull v Hall* (n 80) at 37.

[98] See also J Gerards, 'How to Improve the Necessity Test of the European Court of Human Rights' [2013] 11 *International Journal of Constitutional Law* 466.

and could, in any event, already be read into our existing indirect discrimination test which considers essentially the same factors. This is the no benefit argument. We reach a different conclusion for three principal reasons, each of which can be seen through the lens of the Court of Appeal decision in *Ladele*.

Firstly, anti-discrimination law is principally concerned with mandating the same treatment between similar persons whereas cases of conscience are about providing for *different* treatment for individuals. For example, in *Ladele*, the Court of Appeal considered that the tribunal had fallen into error on the question of direct discrimination because 'It cannot constitute direct discrimination to treat all employees in precisely the same way'.[99] In forcing conscience claims into the realm of indirect discrimination, a number of secondary difficulties, identified by Vickers, then arise, including the issue of group disadvantage and the thorny issue of the identification of relevant comparators. Anti-discrimination law is grounded in premises unsuited to conscience claims.

Secondly, in the context of the assessment we have outlined in this chapter, courts *would* likely reach different conclusions when compared with outcomes under existing indirect discrimination law. For example, the Court of Appeal in *Ladele* identified as an error of law the conclusions of the tribunal on the relevant comparator. The Court of Appeal thought it to be 'another registrar who refused to conduct civil partnership work because of antipathy to the concept of same sex relationships but which antipathy was not connected [to] or based upon his or her religious belief'.[100]

That leaves a conscience claimant in the unattractive position of only finding relief where someone without their conscientious convictions would have been accommodated. That is both wrong in principle and illogical. By contrast, in our assessment, on the facts in *Ladele*, the employer may have failed at the second stage of our test when required to demonstrate that compelling Lillian Ladele to officiate same-sex partnerships was the only way of serving their 'Dignity for All' policy. In circumstances in which there had been no complaints from service users, where she had already been accommodated for some time, and where other authorities had easily accommodated individuals, it would seem difficult for the state to make it through even to this third step – but assuming that it could, the obvious accommodation could then not be ignored according to any measure of robustness.

Thirdly, Vickers weighs what she accepts would be the additional clarity and transparency against the legal uncertainty that would arise with the introduction of a new legal doctrine, particularly one so fact-sensitive. Of course, with any legal developments in a common law jurisdiction, the parameters are mainly fleshed out as they are tested through development of the case law. However, any uncertainty that exists, either in the short term due to novelty or the longer term due to individuality, is mitigated by the way this will require these kinds of disputes to be resolved.

By way of example, in Ladele's case, the employee appointed to carry out the investigations was one Mr Daniels. In the course of his investigation, he disclosed confidential information about action the council was proposing to take with the internal LGBT forum in violation of council policy, and considered a letter from Ms Ladele, described by the EAT as 'thoughtful and temperate', as in itself an act of gross misconduct.[101] These incidents,

---

[99] *Ladele v London Borough of Islington* [2009] EWCA Civ 1357, at 29.
[100] ibid at 39.
[101] *Islington v Ladele* [2008] UKEAT 0453/08/1912, at 77.

among others, resulted in two judges of the European Court of Human Rights considering that 'a combination of back-stabbing by her colleagues and the blinkered political correctness of the Borough of Islington (which clearly favoured "gay rights" over fundamental human rights) eventually led to her dismissal'.[102]

Where an employer knows they will have to explain, in the cold light of a courtroom, why there was no lesser alternative and why there was no accommodation available, a greater proportion of these cases will be resolved in the workplace. Individual accommodations are almost always best devised by those closest to the circumstances in question, rather than the kind of actions taken by Islington, which seemed geared towards the claimant's dismissal rather than accommodation. In the case of *Ladele*, the existing law resulted in a victory before the Employment Tribunal which was reversed by the EAT and Court of Appeal. At the European Court of Human Rights, her case divided the judges. What is clear about the existing jurisprudence is that it is far from clear.

Moreover, the concept of individual accommodation is not unknown to UK law and would therefore not be a wholly novel introduction. Disability law provides an example of a duty which encourages individualised solutions and is not as easily defeated as the 'no benefit' argument suggests is inevitable. An explicit duty to reasonably accommodate was established for the first time in EU law in the Employment Equality Directive, but only in relation to disability. Article 5 of the Directive states that 'reasonable accommodation shall be provided ... unless such measures would impose a disproportionate burden on the employer'. The reasonable adjustment model means that employers must take measures to enable a person with a disability to work and advance up to the point that those measures impose a disproportionate burden on the employer. This is in many ways the same model, outlined by Vickers, in the US and Canada. The decisive question is always then one of threshold – where does 'reasonableness' stop?

That EU law concept is transposed into UK law in the form of a requirement to make 'reasonable adjustments'. The Equality and Human Rights Commission in the UK provides guidelines on what might be a reasonable adjustment that is instructive. For example, the Commission indicates that adjustments may include, 'structural or other physical changes such as widening a doorway, providing a ramp or moving furniture'. While this likely would not have cross-applicability in the case of conscience, an example is also provided of 'allocating some of the worker's duties to another worker', and transferring certain work 'away from a worker whose disability involves severe vertigo', or 'altering the worker's hours'.[103] This appears to go well beyond the 'undue hardship' threshold in Title VII of the US Civil Rights Act which Vickers concludes is 'fairly easy to override ... in practice'.[104]

Perhaps one of the most interesting parts comes towards the end of the guidance. It says that, 'in some situations, a reasonable adjustment will not work without the co-operation of other workers. Your other staff may therefore have an important role in helping make sure that a reasonable adjustment is carried out in practice. You must make sure that this happens'. This stands in stark contrast to the decision of *Burns v Southern Pacific*

---

[102] *Eweida* (n 16) at 5.

[103] Equality and Human Rights Commission, 'Guidance on Workplace Adjustments' (12 July 2016). Available at www.equalityhumanrights.com/en/multipage-guide/employing-people-workplace-adjustments.

[104] See ch 10 of this volume, text to n 44.

Transportation Co,[105] cited by Vickers, in which an employer merely had to demonstrate that non-objecting employees would be imposed upon in order to refuse an accommodation.[106]

There are a significant number of cases that could be resolved if a robust attempt at individualised accommodation were to be made, even when implicating an important interest, identified at Stage 2 of our test. We already accept that even some ordinarily reasonable public interests may be subjugated to the demands of conscience in the context of motorcycle helmets, religious attire and more. And even in more complex cases, such as *Ladele* and *McFarlane*, Vickers in this volume recognises that if it had been desirable 'alternative ways to accommodate the religious employees' objections were easily identifiable'.[107] Courts should not be quick to accept a respondent's argument that no accommodation is possible.[108]

UK law, and employers, are therefore already familiar with the concept of reasonable accommodation albeit with respect to a different protected characteristic. There are also harbingers of this doctrine in the case law of the ECtHR.[109] The Court has been willing to consider that the *motivation* for law-breaking is a relevant consideration for the authorities in terms of response. *Thlimmenos v Greece*[110] concerned someone seeking qualification as an accountant who had been convicted of insubordination for refusing military service in 1983. The Court found the Greek authorities had violated Article 14, read in conjunction with Article 9, holding:

> [T]he applicant's exclusion from the profession of chartered accountants did not pursue a legitimate aim. As a result, the Court finds that there existed no objective and reasonable justification for not treating the applicant differently from other persons convicted of a serious crime.[111]

It is the second part that is most interesting. Until this point, the Court had considered that Article 14 prohibited the state from treating people in analogous situations differently without justification. Here, the Court decided that equality sometimes means treating different situations differently, rather than simply applying the same standard across the board. The context was relatively serious – the effect of a criminal conviction (though not the fact of it) – and the Court held that Greece should have mitigated the impact given its conscientious context.

Similar allowances have been made in a line of cases dealing with the Roma. *Munoz Diaz*[112] concerned a woman of Roma origin who complained of the refusal to grant her a survivor's pension as her marriage, conducted according to Roma rite, was not recognised by the authorities. In finding in the applicant's favour, the Court took 'the view that, whilst the fact of belonging to a minority does not create an exemption from complying with marriage laws, it may have an effect on the manner in which those laws are applied'.[113]

---

[105] *Burns v Southern Pacific Transportation Co* 589 F 2d 403 (9th Cir 1978).

[106] The Canadian model is similar to the UK disability model: both employers and employees must participate in providing a reasonable accommodation. See, eg, *Central Okanagan School Board v. Renaud* [1992] 2 SCR 970.

[107] See ch 10 of this volume, text to n 11.

[108] M Hill, '*Reasonable Accommodation: Faith and Judgment*' (2016) EUI Working Paper RSCAS 2016/07. Available at www.cadmus.eui.eu/bitstream/handle/1814/38810/RSCAS_2016_07.pdf;sequence=1.

[109] A Power-Forde, 'Freedom of Religion and "Reasonable Accommodation" in the Case Law of the European Court of Human Rights' (2016) 5 *Oxford Journal of Law and Religion* 575.

[110] *Thlimmenos v Greece* (2001) 31 EHRR 411.

[111] ibid at 47.

[112] *Muñoz Díaz v Spain* App No 49151/07 (ECtHR, 8 December 2009).

[113] ibid at 61.

In both of these examples, the European Court recognised that the conscientious context of law-breaking can be relevant to a possible legal accommodation required in response to the general rule. This is not to say that a conscientious conviction is the same as a disability, but the model of protection, being enhanced and individualistic, provides a helpful model to address the argument that any change would reduce legal certainty.

Interestingly, the doctrine has also attracted the attention of Lady Hale, president of the UK Supreme Court. In Lady Hale's 2014 speech, mentioned above, she questioned whether, 'we [should] be developing, in both human rights and EU law, an explicit requirement upon the providers of employment, goods and services to make reasonable accommodation for the manifestation of religious and other beliefs? And even vice versa?'[114] This thinking has crept into her judicial decision-making. It can be seen in the case of *Bull v Hall*,[115] outlined above, and in the Scottish midwives case.[116]

Turning then to the criticism as to legal certainty, the best response is to look at what level of legal certainty currently exists. In the case of check-in worker Nadia Eweida, she succeeded at the Employment Tribunal, then lost before the EAT, with which the Court of Appeal largely concurred. She then won at the European Court of Human Rights. The approach outlined in this chapter, for whatever it may lack in certainty, compensates in clearer legal reasoning and practical fact-specific solutions.[117]

IV. Conclusion

In conclusion, the existing jurisprudence both nationally and from the Strasbourg Court is currently inadequate to deal with conscience claims. As exemplified by Lady Hale's judgments and extra-judicial speeches, there is an appetite for a better balance. Under the existing law, we lack a means of determining what is a conscience claim and what is not. But the law requires that where a measure fails as indirectly discriminatory, it must be replaced by a non-discriminatory measure.[118] Reasonable accommodation provides the remedy in the form of an adjustment to eliminate the discriminatory impact without compromising the measure's general purpose.

The history of protection against discrimination based upon disability illustrates the value and desirability of the reasonable accommodation model. Until 2010, indirect discrimination protection did not extend to disability, which was only protected by the duty to make reasonable adjustments. When the Equality Act 2010 extended the protection from indirect discrimination to disability, there was no consequent repeal of the duty of reasonable adjustment, which now sits side by side, providing an exception to a valid general rule.

---

[114] Lady Hale (n 88) 16.

[115] *Bull v Hall* (n 80).

[116] *Greater Glasgow Health Board v Doogan and another* [2014] UKSC 68, [2015] 1 AC 640.

[117] An advantage also identified by European Commission funded research into the application of reasonable accommodation beyond the field of disability: E Bribosia and I Rorive, 'Reasonable Accommodation Beyond Disability in Europe?' (2013). Available at www.ec.europa.eu/justice/discrimination/files/reasonable_accommodation_beyond_disability_in_europe_en.pdf.

[118] Equality and Human Rights Commission, 'Religion or belief: is the Law Working?' (2 December 2016). Available at www.equalityhumanrights.com/en/publication-download/religion-or-belief-law-working.

Some of these cases generate more controversy than others. For example, in cases concerning anti-discrimination law, there are those who understandably ask what public good is served in effectively allowing an exemption from such laws in the circumstances set out above. And yet, properly construed, these cases do not undermine anti-discrimination legislation at all. In all the cases mentioned above, not one person was seeking the right to discriminate against customers based upon a protected characteristic. All those claimants said they would serve anyone regardless of their sexual orientation. Rather, in the cases which we are aware of, the refusal has not been based on the identity of the customer, but on the message to be promoted. This chapter outlines a test to limit accommodation to those claims that are based on a conscientious belief. Claims of conscience often come with a high social, if not legal, cost given the anti-majoritarian nature of conscience. There will be no slippery slope to mass civil disobedience.

Despite the cost, there remains a conscientious line which an individual is entitled to draw. Indeed, there are many much lesser reasons a provider may still legitimately draw that line – because they do not want to promote a particular football team on a cake, because they took offence at how a customer addressed them, or because of a long-running neighbourhood feud. That is not to say those situations are precisely alike, but they are much closer than the analogy that sometimes lazily gets drawn between, for example, the cake cases and the laws of Jim Crow which did legitimise invidious discrimination based simply upon a protected characteristic.[119]

One objection is that a model of reasonable accommodation would make no practical difference to the outcome of these sort of cases, it being simply a different way of conducting the balancing test that is already part of the Strasbourg and British case law.[120] In our view, that is an incorrect starting point. It is, rather, preferable to start with the question of whether these are in fact conscience claims. And if they are conscience claims (and we suggest a way of so determining), then the fact that a new analysis would not result in a different outcome does not take away from the fact that it is right to call something what it is.

That said, this approach would almost certainly result in different outcomes. A clearer framework would undoubtedly be of benefit given the ambiguity of existing provisions. Indeed, a recent parliamentary inquiry into freedom of conscience in connection with the provision of abortion services heard a

> substantial body of evidence which suggests that there is increasing pressure on healthcare practitioners with such a conscientious objection to participate in abortions, both directly and indirectly, regardless of their moral and ethical views … Evidence received by the APPG indicated that fair and proper application of the Conscience Clause depends too much upon the attitude and discretion of healthworkers' individual managers or teaching staff.[121]

---

[119] See, eg M Williams, 'Masterpiece Cakeshop Reminds Me of Jim Crow. We Can't Create New 2nd-Class Citizens' *USA* Today (McLean, 5 December 2017).

[120] See ch 10 in this volume. *cf* K Alidadi, *Religion, Equality and Employment in Europe: The Case for Reasonable Accommodation* (Oxford, Hart, 2017).

[121] All Party Parliamentary Pro-Life Group, 'A Report into Freedom of Conscience in Abortion Provision' (July 2016). Available at www.conscienceinquiry.uk/wp-content/uploads/2016/12/Pro-Life-APPG-Freedom-of-Conscience-in-Abortion-Provision.pdf.

Human rights protect the weak from the strong. Nowhere is that more true than in the context of conscience, where an individual has found himself at odds with the state. No one should be asked to compromise conscience. Were a conscientious objection to become the majority view, we might expect that to be reflected by a change in the law in due course, indeed, such has been the case with exemptions to compulsory military service. Those that would find themselves objecting will therefore usually be a politically powerless minority. This is the main reason that freedom of conscience has generally been developed through the decisions of courts, rather than the acts of the legislature. Indeed, as Sorabji's account makes clear, there were times when Christians needed to appeal to freedom of conscience as a minority, and times when it was instead the 'heretics' and 'unbelievers' who prayed in aid of conscience against an ascendant church.[122] Both the powerful and powerless, the beneficiaries and the benefactors, should therefore unite in their defence of a doctrine that protects the space for disagreement and cooperation within a civil society.

---

[122] Sorabji, *Moral Conscience* (2014) chs 2–3.

Comparative Questions in the Law
of Conscientious Exemptions

10

Conscientious Objections in Employment: Is a Duty of Reasonable Accommodation the Answer?

LUCY VICKERS[1]

The aim of this chapter is to consider how conscience claims are best addressed in the context of employment. The current mechanism for protecting those who raise conscience claims at work is through a non-discrimination claim under the Equality Act 2010. In what follows, the non-discrimination model for managing conscience claims will be assessed, and its shortcomings identified. The chapter then asks whether basing claims on a duty of reasonable accommodation would improve the protection for those with conscientious objections to carrying out aspects of their jobs. By comparing the position in North America where such claims are dealt with under a duty of reasonable accommodation, the conclusion is reached that while this is an effective means of protection, it is not preferable to the indirect discrimination model. Instead, it is concluded that conscience claims can be adequately protected at work through the current legal framework.

I. Conscientious Objection and Indirect Discrimination

Requests to be exempt from carrying out work-related tasks to which the claimant holds a conscientious objection[2] are currently treated as cases of indirect discrimination, with the exception of special rules applying in the context of abortion and human embryology.[3] Indirect discrimination is defined as the application of a provision, criterion or practice in relation to religion or belief which applies to those who do not share the religion or belief, but which puts or would put persons of the religion or belief in question at a particular disadvantage compared to others, and which cannot be shown to be a proportionate means

---

[1] For more on the issues discussed in this chapter, see L Vickers, *Religious Freedom, Religious Discrimination and the Workplace*, 2nd edn (Oxford, Hart Publishing, 2016) chs 6 and 7.

[2] It is assumed in what follows that conscientious objections are based on religion or belief.

[3] Section 4(1) of the Abortion Act 1967 states: 'no person shall be under any duty ... to participate in treatment authorised by this Act to which he has a conscientious objection'. Similar terms can be found in s 38(1) Human Fertilisation and Embryology Act 1990.

of achieving a legitimate aim.[4] A neutral practice that is required of all staff but which puts persons who hold a conscientious objection[5] to carrying out the task at a disadvantage compared with others would therefore give rise to a potential claim of indirect discrimination; any refusal to accommodate a request for exemption from the work task will therefore need to be justified. Cases have involved diverse matters, including objections to joining the rota for cleaning the office fridge,[6] and requests to be excused from offering a service to gay and lesbian clients.[7] Other examples, which have been reported in the press, include requests from shop workers to be exempt from serving alcohol.[8]

The concept of indirect discrimination, with its requirement that any refusal to allow conscientious objection be justified, provides a flexible mechanism through which diverse claims can be assessed. Any assessment of proportionality will need to consider all the facts of the case, such as the ease with which others can be found to cover for the task without disadvantage or disruption to others, whether the individual can be redeployed to other duties, and how central the task is to the job in question. For example, exemption for a university lecturer from serving alcohol or meat products at a reception for new students would seem to be relatively simple to accommodate and so it would be unlikely for any refusal to be justified; the request does not relate to a core aspect of the job, and it will be relatively easy to find an alternative person to serve the refreshments. In contrast, it would be proportionate to refuse to accommodate a butcher who refused to handle meat, or a publican who refused to serve alcohol.

However, assessing proportionality is not always easy, and can involve careful deliberation on the part of the court to determine the correct balance between the interests of the employer in running an effective business and the religious interests of the member of staff with the conscience claim. An additional layer of complexity arises when the conscientious objection to a work-related task has been on grounds which themselves are discriminatory against others. For example, cases involving marriage registrars who wish to be exempted from carrying out civil partnerships or same-sex marriage; or involving staff who refuse to shake hands with clients of the opposite sex on religious grounds. These cases are treated as potentially indirectly discriminatory; the requirement to carry out the civil partnership or to shake hands with clients is a neutral requirement, which causes disadvantage to the particular religious employee because he or she cannot comply for religious reasons, and so the requirement will need to be justified as a proportionate means to achieve a legitimate aim.

Two cases have come before the UK courts where staff had conscientious objections to performing aspects of their jobs, for reasons which themselves involved discrimination

---

[4] Section 19 Equality Act 2010. The wording of the Directive is: 'where an apparently neutral provision, criterion or practice would put persons of a particular religion or belief … at a particular disadvantage compared with other persons' unless it can be justified: Art 2(2).

[5] While objections would not need to be religious they are likely to be linked to beliefs of a serious nature, such as to be classified as beliefs under the legislation. Less serious objections, of a type that would be unlikely to be classified as based on belief, are also unlikely to be classified as 'conscientious objections' either.

[6] *Chatwal v Wandsworth Borough Council* [2011] UKEAT 0487_10_0607.

[7] *Ladele v Islington Borough Council* [2009] EWCA Civ 1357; *McFarlane v Relate Avon Ltd* [2010] EWCA Civ 880.

[8] See for example R Mendick, 'Muslim staff at Marks & Spencer can Refuse to Sell Alcohol and Pork' (*The Telegraph*, 21 December 2013) at www.telegraph.co.uk/finance/newsbysector/retailandconsumer/10532782/Muslim-staff-at-Marks-and-Spencer-can-refuse-to-sell-alcohol-and-pork.html.

on other grounds. In *Ladele v Islington Borough Council*[9] Ladele sought to be excused from carrying out civil partnerships on the basis of her religious beliefs, but permission was refused. Similarly, in *McFarlane v Relate Avon Ltd*[10] McFarlane claimed that he was discriminated against for refusing, on religious grounds, to provide psychosexual therapy to same-sex couples. The Court of Appeal in *Ladele* held that the refusal to accommodate the request to be exempt from carrying out civil partnerships was justified as the employer was entitled to rely on its policy of requiring all staff to offer services to all service users regardless of sexual orientation. The decision in *McFarlane* was determined fairly briefly and followed *Ladele*: the employer's requirement that McFarlane offer therapy to all clients regardless of sexual orientation was potentially indirectly discriminatory as it put him at a disadvantage, but it was justified as a proportionate means to achieve equality on other grounds. The outcome of the two cases was upheld by the ECtHR on a similar basis: the restriction on religious freedom was justified as a proportionate means to protect the equality rights of others.

The cases illustrate the indeterminacy of indirect discrimination claims. Although both the domestic and European Court decided that the employers' refusal to allow the employee's conscientious objection, it is possible of course to imagine a different outcome of the balancing exercise, particularly given that alternative ways to accommodate the religious employees' objections were easily identifiable. For example, staff could be allowed to swap clients informally, or in Ladele's case the employer could have not designated her as a civil partnership registrar, and thus precluded her from conducting the civil partnership ceremonies.[11] Indeed, in *Ladele* the Court of Appeal was clear that it was not criticising the decision by some councils to accommodate similar requests from marriage registrars. Instead, proportionality was assessed fairly broadly, using a wide range of factors including the fact that she was employed in the public sector, and that her job was of a secular nature.[12]

As with indirect discrimination cases generally, the decisions in *Ladele* and *McFarlane* were based on the balancing of competing interests to achieve what the court assessed was a proportionate outcome. The proportionality approach contained within the indirect discrimination framework allows for cases to be determined with sensitivity to the individual facts of the case as well as broader contextual factors. For example, a court can give

---

[9] *Ladele v Islington Borough Council* [2009] EWCA Civ 1357; then heard with *Eweida and Others v UK* (2013) 57 EHRR 8.

[10] *McFarlane v Relate Avon Ltd* [2010] EWCA Civ 880.

[11] See C McCrudden, 'Marriage Registrars, Same-sex Relationships, and Religious Discrimination in the European Court of Human Rights' in S Mancini and M Rosenfeld (eds), *The Conscience Wars: Rethinking the Balance between Religion, Identity, and Equality* (Cambridge, Cambridge University Press, 2018). He suggests that if Ladele had not been designated as a civil partnership registrar, there would be no adverse impact on equality of opportunity for same-sex couples. There may, however, be an infringing of the dignity of same-sex couples if Islington were to allow staff to opt out of offering them a service.

[12] *Ladele* (n 9) at 52. An additional factor in Ladele's case was that she was already in post when the civil partnerships were introduced and so she had not applied for a job which she knew she could not perform; arguably she should not lose her job when the job had changed around her. However, although the job had changed during her employment, it is worth noting that changes in work tasks are often introduced by employers, particularly in response to technological or legal developments, and this does not usually give rise to rights for employees to continue to work in their previous roles. It is arguable that the new methods of working in Ladele's case were too radical in nature to be seen as part of her original contractual obligations. Yet, the fact remains that there is no inherent right for an employee to assume that her job cannot change.

weight, as it did in *Ladele* and *McFarlane*, to an employer's interest in setting its own ethos, as well as recognising interests such as economic efficiency and whether the workplace is public sector or private sector.

A. The Benefits and Disadvantages of the Indirect Discrimination Model

The cases of *McFarlane* and *Ladele* provide clear examples of how an indirect discrimination model can work to protect those with a conscientious objection to carrying out aspects of their work. They also illustrate some of the limitations of the model. In particular, its flexibility and fact-sensitive decision-making gives rise to the charge that the law lacks certainty and is too indeterminate. It remains hard to predict in any particular case whether a particular conscience claim should be allowed by an employer or not.

i. Solitary Conscience Claims

An additional limitation of the indirect discrimination model has arisen in respect of individual conscience claims, where the beliefs on which the claim is based are not shared by others. Indirect discrimination claims have usually been understood as a mechanism for addressing group disadvantage, with the focus on neutral rules which put a group (women, a religious group, etc) at a disadvantage compared with others not in that group. The wording of the Equality Act 2010 thus requires that the applicant must show that a neutral requirement is imposed which 'puts or would put' persons of the same religion at a particular disadvantage. The wording rarely creates difficulties in relation to sex and race discrimination, where there will always be others in the same group as the applicant. However, in the context of religious discrimination, the restriction can be significant. If an individual has a personal religious or philosophical belief which gives rise to a personal conscientious objection to carrying out an aspect of the job, it may be the case that others will also need to be disadvantaged if the applicant is to come within the indirect discrimination protection.

This issue was raised in the domestic hearings in *Eweida v British Airways*.[13] Eweida was a member of the check-in staff for British Airways, who was refused permission to wear a cross over her uniform, as this was in breach of its uniform policy. Her indirect discrimination claim was unsuccessful, because the refusal to accommodate the request of a single believer was not covered by the indirect discrimination protection, which required a group disadvantage. The definition states that a neutral requirement (here the requirement not to wear visible jewellery) be imposed which 'puts, or would put, *persons* of the same religion at a particular disadvantage (emphasis added)'. This suggested that more than one person must hold the belief. As Eweida was the only person identified in the proceedings who held the particular belief, there could be no indirect discrimination. The result of this ruling is that individual believers who do not share their beliefs with others are not protected by the indirect discrimination provisions in the Equality Act.[14]

---

[13] *Eweida v British Airways* [2010] EWCA Civ 80. See the comment on the EAT decision in L Vickers, 'Indirect Discrimination and Individual Belief: *Eweida v British Airways plc*' [2009] *Ecclesiastical Law Journal* 197.
[14] This approach is confirmed in *Chatwal v Wandsworth Borough Council* [2011] UKEAT 0487_10_0607.

However, it is unclear whether this limit on indirect discrimination still applies follow-ing the decision of the ECtHR in *Eweida v UK*[15] that Eweida's dismissal breached her right to freedom of religion or belief under Article 9 ECHR. McCrea suggests that solitary believers are not protected under indirect discrimination provisions, even though they are protected under the human rights framework of the ECHR.[16] In reaching this conclusion he refers to the decision of Sedley LJ in the Court of Appeal hearing in *Eweida*, in which he suggests there is 'no indication that the Directive intended either that solitary disadvantage should be sufficient … or that any requirement of plural disadvantage must be dropped'.[17] Sedley LJ also refers to the fact that Disability Discrimination Act 1995 was designed to create individual claims and uses special wording to do so, implying that the wording of the indirect discrimination provisions cannot therefore have been designed to cover individual claimants.

However, although indirect discrimination has its roots in addressing group disad-vantage, this should not mean that it cannot develop to protect individuals who suffer disadvantage as well. After all, the parent Directive 2000/78 is worded in the conditional tense, suggesting that it could apply to hypothetical claimants.[18] Sedley LJ's reference to the Disability Discrimination Act 1995 ignores the fact that under the Equality Act 2010 all forms of indirect discrimination are protected using the same wording, without special protection for individual disability claims. Yet the Equality Act 2010 is not usually under-stood to have removed the protection against indirect discrimination from individual disabled people; this suggests that the definition of indirect discrimination as contained in s 19 Equality Act can be read to include protection for solitary believers. Such a reading would also accord with the ECtHR decision.[19]

Reading the provisions of the Equality Act to comply with the ECtHR decision in *Eweida* involves reading 'puts *or would put* persons with whom B shares the [religion or belief] (emphasis added)' at a disadvantage to mean 'would put persons of the religion or belief at a disadvantage *were there to be any*'. Although this argument was put to the Court of Appeal in *Eweida*, it was not accepted, on the basis that 'the argument loads far too much on to the word "would"'.[20]

The position following later cases remains somewhat unclear. The point was discussed in *Mba v London Borough of Merton*,[21] where the Court of Appeal recognised that the protec-tion of freedom of religion under Article 9 does not require that the claimant first establish a group disadvantage. Nonetheless, it held that this would not mean that the Equality Act 2010 should be interpreted so as to enable indirect discrimination to apply to individual claimants.[22] At first, it seems that, after *Mba*, group disadvantage still needs to be shown

---

[15] *Eweida* (n 9).
[16] R McCrea, 'Singing from the Same Hymn Sheet? What the Differences between the Strasbourg and Luxembourg Courts Tell Us about Religious Freedom, Non-Discrimination, and the Secular State' (2016) 5 *Oxford Journal of Law and Religion* 183–210.
[17] *Eweida* (n 13) at 15.
[18] See also N Bamforth, M Malik and C O'Cinneide (eds) *Discrimination Law, Theory and Context* (London, Sweet and Maxwell, 2008) 307–08.
[19] In accordance with s 3 Human Rights Act 1998.
[20] *Eweida* (n 13) at 17.
[21] *Mba v London Borough of Merton* [2013] EWCA Civ 1562.
[22] ibid at 34–35.

for claims of indirect discrimination under the Equality Act. However, the point was not definitively dealt with in the case, as the question of group disadvantage had been conceded on the facts; moreover, as Lord Justice Vos confirmed, this issue was not fully argued.[23] The point therefore still seems to be left open, and it is arguable that despite the Court of Appeal's approach in *Eweida* and *Mba*, indirect discrimination should cover individual disadvantage, particularly given that the parent Directive 2000/78 is worded solely in the conditional.[24]

There are some clear advantages to the requirement of group disadvantage;[25] in particular it would avert the danger that discrimination claims could be generated by a wide range of behaviours linked to individual beliefs.[26] However, there are clear disadvantages too, not least the fact that it leaves individual believers unprotected when it comes to manifesting their beliefs at work. Allowing individual indirect discrimination cases under the Equality Act 2010 would mean that the protection would accord with Article 9, and protect the conscience claims of those who do not share their beliefs with others, and who cannot make claims directly under the Human Rights Act 1998.[27] After all, allowing indirect discrimination to be used in individual conscience cases would not mean that employers would need to accommodate any and all conscience claims: any refusal which is potentially indirectly discriminatory will still need to be justified.

ii. Clarity of the Provisions

Apart from the problems of protecting individual conscience claims through indirect discrimination, there are some additional limitations to the model: it is not, on the face of it, obvious that conscience claims can be brought under this mechanism; and it could lead to a levelling down of protection for other equality grounds.

The fact that indirect discrimination provides a level of protection for those with conscientious objections to work tasks may well not be apparent to those not well versed in discrimination law. It requires claimants to know that the requirement to undertake the task is a 'provision, criterion or practice' and that their objection puts them at a disadvantage. In practice, it will usually not be claimants who recognise this, but their lawyers! Thus the fact that legal protection exists will not be evident to most of those who have a conscientious objection to performing specific work tasks.

iii. Levelling Down

The concern about the risk of 'levelling down' protection for other grounds arises because of the need to ensure consistency as between different strands of equality law in the application of indirect discrimination.[28] Section 19 Equality Act 2010 relies heavily on the notion of

---

[23] ibid at 41.

[24] See also Bamforth et al, *Discrimination Law* (2008) 307–08.

[25] See for example, R Allen and G Moon, 'Substantive Rights and Equal Treatment in Respect of Religion and Belief: Towards a Better Understanding of the Rights, and their Implications' (2000) *EHRLR* 580, 601.

[26] *Eweida* (n 13) at 18.

[27] Although religion and belief are protected under Art 9 ECHR, individual employees in the private sector cannot make direct claims under the Human Rights Act 1998.

[28] SB Lahuerta, 'Taking EU Equality Law to the next level: in search of coherence' (2016) 11 *European Labour Law Journal* 348.

proportionality, and this allows for contextual interpretation which can take into account all the circumstances of the particular case. In the context of sex or race discrimination, the test for proportionality is strict: the means chosen for achieving that legitimate aim must correspond to a real need on the part of the undertaking, must be appropriate with a view to achieving the objective in question and must be necessary to that end.[29] For example, costs or inconvenience would not be acceptable as justification for indirect sex discrimination, but these factors could help justify indirect religious discrimination. If the different grounds of discrimination are meant to be interpreted similarly, a decision that economic cost can justify religious discrimination could result in a finding that the same were true of sex or race discrimination.

One solution to this problem would be to allow a hierarchy to develop whereby different grounds of equality are explicitly given different levels of protection. However, such an approach would be contentious.[30] An alternative is to introduce separate protection for religion or belief, to avoid any 'cross contamination' of standards of protection. If a separate legal mechanism were to be used, designed to address religious claims, it may also be more easily understood by users. The obvious contender for such a new legal mechanism is the duty of reasonable accommodation, and to this I now turn.

II. The Reasonable Accommodation Model

The reasonable accommodation model creates an obligation on employers to accommodate requests from employees for changes to working conditions, as long as it is reasonable to do so. The mechanism puts the onus on the employee to seek the accommodation, which the employer would then be under an obligation to agree, unless it is reasonable not to do so. Accommodations based on conscience would include requests to be exempt from performing particular work tasks. For example, Ms Ladele's claim would be recast as a request that her refusal to perform civil partnerships be granted (accommodated) by the employer.

The concept of accommodation is already part of domestic disability discrimination law, with its duty on employers to make reasonable adjustments to the workplace. This recognises the fact that changes to the workplace to allow full participation by disabled people will need to be very individualised. The focus therefore needs to be on adapting workplaces to the individual needs of disabled people. As with the variety of experiences of disability, religious practices and conscience claims can vary widely, and so a personalised duty of reasonable accommodation for religious needs may well be thought an appropriate way forward to improve the protection of religious interests at work.

The concept certainly has received significant academic support, on the basis that it can improve protection for religion or belief in employment,[31] and help reduce the

---

[29] Case 170/84 *Bilka-Kaufhaus v Weber von Hartz* [1986] ECR 1607-1631 [1986], at 607.

[30] The creation of a 'hierarchy' of equality rights is something which was warned against in the Commission's 'Explanatory Memorandum' to the Directives: *Proposal for a Council Directive: Establishing a General Framework for Equal Treatment in Employment and Occupation* COM (1999) 565 final, 6.

[31] See ch 9, part III, of this volume; see also M Gibson, 'The God "Dilution"? Religion, Discrimination and the Case for Reasonable Accommodation' (2013) 72 *Cambridge Law Journal* 578; Christians in Parliament, *Clearing the Ground: Preliminary Report into the Freedom of Christians in the UK* (London, 2012) available at www.eauk.org/current-affairs/publications/upload/Clearing-the-ground.pdf; K Alidadi, 'Reasonable accommodations for religion and belief: Adding value to Art.9 ECHR and the European Union's anti-discrimination approach to employment?'

inconsistency and incoherence currently identified within EU equality law.[32] Moreover, to the extent that the concern regarding individual claims remains valid, it would be overcome by the creation of a duty of reasonable accommodation.

A duty of reasonable accommodation was suggested for the UK by the Independent Review of the Enforcement of UK Anti-Discrimination Legislation.[33] It has more recently been proposed as a way to manage religious interests in the work place by the think tank Res Publica.[34] Lady Hale has also give it her support, although within the framework of indirect discrimination law, stating that she is 'more than ready to accept that the scope for reasonable accommodation is part of the proportionality assessment, at least in some cases'.[35] In addition, at European level, the EU funded *Religare* project[36] recommended in its final report that a legally enshrined right to reasonable accommodation of religion or belief at work would fill the gaps in existing legal protection and better meet the needs of religious employees. To this can be added an EU Parliamentary Assembly resolution,[37] inviting states to seek reasonable accommodations in order to guarantee effective equality in terms of freedom of religion; and the support of the UN Special Rapporteur on freedom of religion or belief.[38] Gerald Chipeur QC and Robert Clarke, in their contribution to this volume, are also strong advocates of this model.

In order to assess whether the introduction of a duty of reasonable accommodation would provide a better mechanism for protecting conscientious objection within the employment context, it is worth considering its operation in two other jurisdictions.

A. The Duty of Reasonable Accommodation in the United States of America

In the USA, anti-discrimination provisions are contained in Title VII of the Civil Rights Act 1964.[39] In addition, government workers are protected against religious discrimination under the Constitution, and many individual states have their own human rights laws which cover discrimination. Title VII includes a duty of reasonable accommodation and is the focus of what follows.

(2012) 37 *European Law Review* 693; E Bribosia, J Ringelheim, and I Rorive, 'Reasonable Accommodation for Religious Minorities – A Promising Concept for European Antidiscrimination Law?' (2010) 7 *Maastricht Journal of European and Comparative Law* 137.

[32] Lahuerta, 'Taking EU Equality Law to the next level' (2016).

[33] B Hepple, M Coussey and T Choudhury, *Equality: A New Framework – The Report of the Independent Review of the Enforcement of UK Anti-Discrimination Legislation* (Oxford, Hart Publishing, 2000).

[34] J Orr, *Beyond Belief: Defending Religious Liberty through the British Bill of Rights* (London, Res Publica, 2016).

[35] Per Lady Hale, *Bull & Anor v Hall & Anor* [2013] UKSC 73 at 47; Lady Hale 'Religion and Sexual Orientation: The Clash of Equality Rights' (Yale Law School, 7 March 2014) available at www.supremecourt.uk/docs/speech-140307.pdf.

[36] Information about the project is available at www.religareproject.eu.

[37] Council of Europe Parliamentary Assembly, 'Freedom of Religion and Living Together in a Democratic Society' (Res 2017, 30 September 2013). Available at assembly.coe.int/nw/xml/XRef/Xref-XML2HTML-en.asp?fileid=22199&lang=en.

[38] UNCHR, Interim Report of the Special Rapporteur on Religion and Belief (2014) UN Doc A/69/261, which focused on tackling religious intolerance and discrimination in the workplace.

[39] 42 USC § 2000e-2.

The Civil Rights Act did not originally contain a duty of reasonable accommodation. However, soon after its enactment, it was felt that an amendment was required to make clearer that religious freedom requires the protection of religious practice or observance, as well as the protection of belief itself, and so it was amended to include a duty on the employer to accommodate the religious practices of employees, as long as to do so did not cause undue hardship to the employer.[40]

The provisions cover all forms of accommodation, and would include the types of request that arise from conscientious objection. The duty requires that religion be accommodated unless there is undue hardship, interpreted to mean that, if accommodation is to be required, there must be no more than *de minimis* cost, either in terms of financial cost or in terms of disruption, or administrative inconvenience.[41] As a result of the low level of hardship required, employers are left with a rather slender duty to accommodate.

Although the level of hardship that needs to be shown is very low, there are some limits on what can be undue hardship such as to limit the duty of accommodation. Any hardship must operate on the conduct of the employer's business.[42] It must create some form of economic hardship, and cannot be merely hardship of a spiritual nature. For example, in *Townley Engineering*,[43] where the employer sought to run the business as a Christian, faith-operated business, weekly mandatory devotional services were held during working time, and the employer sent out gospel tracts with outgoing mail and printed Bible verses on invoices. The employers argued that accommodating an atheist employee by excusing him from attendance at the weekly service would cause 'spiritual' hardship to the company as it would 'chill' their religious purposes. The court accepted that spiritual hardship could exist, but held that the restriction in the legislation to hardship in the conduct of the business ruled out the use of non-economic harm to justify a refusal to accommodate religion.

Excluding spiritual hardship may make it harder to override the duty to accommodate, but the low level of economic hardship required still means it is fairly easy to override the duty in practice. The main parameters of the duty of accommodation were set out in two cases before the Supreme Court, both involving members of the Worldwide Church of God. In *Trans World Airlines, Inc v Hardison*[44] a clerk in the stores department of TWA asked to change his hours to avoid working from sunset on Friday until sunset on Saturday. The shift system at TWA was operated on a seniority basis, agreed through a collective bargaining system. At first, Hardison's request was accommodated, as he had sufficient seniority to enable him to be given his requested shifts in accordance with the collectively agreed system. However, after being moved to a new part of the business he lost seniority, and could no longer arrange shifts to suit his religious beliefs. The union was unwilling to agree a waiver of the seniority system to enable his beliefs to be accommodated, and TWA would not allow him to work a four-day week as that would mean incurring the additional expense

---

[40] The amendment was made to the definition of religion: The term 'religion' includes all aspects of religious observance and practice, as well as belief, unless an employer demonstrates that he is unable to reasonably accommodate to an employee's or prospective employee's religious observance or practice without undue hardship on the conduct of the employer's business; 42 USCA § 2000e j. Failure to offer reasonable accommodation can make the employer liable for punitive damages.
[41] *Ansonia Board of Education v Philbrook* 479 US 60 (1986).
[42] 42 USCA § 2000e j.
[43] *Townley Engineering* 859 F 2d 610 (9th Cir 1988).
[44] *Trans World Airlines, Inc v Hardison* 432 US 63 (1977).

of employing an extra worker for Saturdays. When he was dismissed, the court had to determine whether a reasonable accommodation had been available for Hardison. The Supreme Court ruled that the options available to the employer (overriding the seniority system that had been agreed with the union, or allowing Hardison to work a four-day week at extra cost to the employer) would have imposed undue hardship on the employer. The Court took the view that to override a seniority system would mean denying one member of staff's preference in favour of another's preference, and would not be reasonable. Overall, they ruled, the employer does not need to take on more than *de minimis* costs in order to offer reasonable accommodation.

The second case, *Ansonia Board of Education v Philbrook*,[45] involved a request to use 'personal business' leave to supplement leave for religious observance, so as to enable the applicant to take sufficient paid days off for religious observance. The employer would not allow the paid 'personal leave' days to be taken for this purpose. The employer was only prepared to accommodate the request for extra leave by allowing Philbrook to take unpaid leave. The question which arose was whether the employee has to accept a reasonable offer of accommodation once it is offered (here the unpaid leave) or whether he can claim that a failure to offer his preferred accommodation (here the paid 'personal business' leave) is unreasonable. The Supreme Court held that once the employer has shown that a reasonable accommodation has been offered, the employer's duty ends. The fact that an employee can identify an alternative accommodation which he or she would prefer does not change matters: the employer is under no obligation to offer the employee the least disadvantageous accommodation available.[46] There is a requirement on the employee to be flexible in accepting an accommodation if it is reasonable, even if he can identify less disadvantageous accommodations.

The combined effect of *Hardison* and *Philbrook* is that, although a duty to accommodate exists, it is so easily overridden that employees' religious interests are given very little practical protection. Once a countervailing interest is identified, the duty on the employer to accommodate religion tends to give way. In this respect, the level of accommodation required for religious claims can be contrasted with that required in disability cases, where undue hardship is defined to mean an action requiring significant difficulty or expense.[47]

In religion and belief cases, it would seem, then, that what is given with one hand via the duty of accommodation is taken away with the other via the low level of hardship needed to fulfil the duty.[48] In effect, changing the mechanism for protecting conscience claims from a non-discrimination approach to a reasonable accommodation approach is not a panacea; the duty of reasonable accommodation is only as strong as the standards of reasonableness applied.

However, even though the standard of hardship is set low in the USA, with only *de minimis* hardship required, employers are required to make some attempt at accommodation.

---

[45] *Ansonia* (n 41).

[46] In reaching this conclusion, the Supreme Court disregarded guidelines produced by the US Equal Employment Opportunity Commission (EEOC) that suggested that where there is an alternative accommodation which does not cause hardship, the employer should offer the one which least disadvantages the religious employee. See also *EEOC v Ilona of Hungary* 108 F 3d 1169 (7th Cir 1997).

[47] Amercians with Disabilities Act (1990) 42 USC Sec 12111 (10).

[48] See, further, JD Prenkert and JM Magid, 'A Hobson's Choice Model for Religious Accommodation' (2006) 43 *American Business LJ* 467.

One matter which can give rise to hardship to the employer is a negative reaction to any accommodation by other staff. The cases are not always consistent on this issue. On the one hand, a refusal by other staff to accept a religious practice can give rise to undue hardship for the employer, and can give grounds to refuse to accommodate. Thus, in *Wilson v US West Communications*[49] a Catholic employee, who wore a badge with a picture of an aborted foetus on it as part of a vow to be a 'living witness' against abortion, was dismissed because her colleagues found the badge offensive. The court held that the duty to accommodate did not require an employer to allow an employee to impose her views on others. On the other hand, any hardship to the employer must be real, and cannot be purely hypothetical. Thus, in *Burns v Southern Pacific Transportation Co*[50] the employer argued that to accommodate a Seventh Day Adventist's conscientious objection to paying union dues would cause dissention among workers, leading to inefficiency. This was rejected by the court, which stressed that undue hardship requires more than just proof that some employees would grumble. The employer would need to show that other employees were imposed upon, or that the work routine would be disrupted.[51]

The duty of reasonable accommodation has been used in the US in the context of conscientious objection to work tasks, although the hardship caused to employers in having to make special arrangements in the assignment of work will usually mean that requests do not have to be accommodated. Moreover, the matching duty on religious employees to be flexible and to accept the accommodations offered by the employer[52] also means that they will find it difficult to claim that a failure to allocate tasks according to religious preference is unlawfully discriminatory. Accommodations such as allowing voluntary swaps of tasks, or offering to redeploy are reasonable,[53] although this will only be feasible where the employer is large enough and skills are transferable. In the case of medical staff who wish to avoid providing medical care such as abortion, they would also be expected to refer patients to staff who will provide the service. Where the reallocation of work is not practical, dismissal can be lawful. Thus, in a case reminiscent of *McFarlane*, where a counsellor refused, for religious reasons, to counsel clients who were homosexual or who were involved in extra-marital relationships, dismissal was not discriminatory: it would not be possible to determine in advance whether such an issue may arise in a counselling relationship, and to allow staff to opt out of some tasks would lead to an uneven distribution of work among colleagues.[54]

Some employees in the US have claimed that they have religious objections to participating in training or complying with workplace diversity policies, particularly where they believe it requires them to condone homosexuality. Employers have not generally been required to accommodate such objections. The need to promote diversity and tolerance within the workplace has been seen as legitimate, and the hardship caused to an employer if he is prevented from promoting such a culture at work is seen to override any duty to

---

[49] *Wilson v US West Communications* 58 F 3d 1337 (1995).
[50] *Burns v Southern Pacific Transportation Co* 589 F 2d 403 (9th Cir 1978).
[51] See also *Tooley v Martin-Marietta Corp* 648 F 2d 1239 (1981), and *Townley Engineering* (n 43).
[52] *Ansonia* (n 41).
[53] *Shelton v University of Medicine and Dentistry of New Jersey* 223 F 3d 220 (2000).
[54] *Bruff v North Mississippi Health Services* 244 F 3d 495 (2001).

accommodate religion. Thus in *Peterson v Hewlett Packard*[55] Peterson's refusal to desist from displaying Bible verses denouncing homosexuality in response to posters celebrating the diversity of the Hewlett Packard workforce led to his dismissal. This was held not to be discriminatory: to require the employer to stop the diversity programme would have amounted to undue hardship.

Interestingly, the courts have allowed some accommodation of religious views which are critical of homosexuality, where to do so does not lead to any active discrimination against other workers. For example, *Buonanno v AT&T Broadband LLC*[56] involved an employee who was required to sign a diversity statement which stated that he 'valued' the differences among people. He claimed that this required him to make a statement which was supportive of homosexuality, even though this was incompatible with his religious view that homosexuality was sinful. He was prepared to sign an alternative statement agreeing to value the fact that there are differences between people (as opposed to valuing the differences themselves). Given that the employee in question had no intention of discriminating against or being disrespectful towards homosexual staff, and that a form of words which was compatible with the employer's diversity policy could have been found, the court determined that the employee's religious objections to the standard diversity statement should have been accommodated. The employer's refusal to investigate the possibility of an alternative wording amounted to a failure to accommodate: investigating a minor amendment to the wording of the statement would not cause undue hardship to the employer. It was significant to the decision that Buonanno was not asking to be exempt from the duty to respect others in the workplace. Indeed, he was prepared to sign a statement which involved a commitment to respect others. However, he was not prepared to sign a statement with which he disagreed, on religious grounds. In terms of balancing interests, Buonanno's freedom of conscience could be accommodated as long as he was prepared to respect the diversity policy of the company in practice.

The cases illustrate that a range of fairly low-level accommodations can be found to be reasonable by the courts, but the duty stops well short of creating anything like a right to conscientious objection to work tasks. However, the duty does achieve some measure of protection for religious interests at work, as it requires that employers make an attempt to accommodate. Although only *de minimis* hardship is required, it must be real and not merely hypothetical. In effect, the onus is put on the employer to show that they have thought about trying to accommodate and have actual reasons why to do so would be difficult. Moreover, the duty provides a mechanism whereby employees will feel free to request an accommodation, and means that conscience claims must be considered by the employer, who may only reject them where they clash with other interests.

B. The Duty of Reasonable Accommodation in Canada

The legal protection against discrimination in Canada is provided within a federal legal system, with equality provisions contained in the legislation of the relevant province. All provinces, municipal and federal governments are also subject to the Canadian Charter

---

[55] *Peterson v Hewlett Packard* 358 F 3d 599 (9th Cir 2004).
[56] *Buonanno v AT&T Broadband LLC* 313 F Supp 2d 1069 (2004).

of Rights and Freedoms, and the Canadian Human Rights Act,[57] which contain general non-discrimination guarantees. Although this creates a number of different religious equality provisions, most follow the same basic model, and although the wording of the various provisions differs, this seems to make little difference to the outcome of cases.[58]

Discrimination on grounds of religion is unlawful. An exception exists where there is a bona fide occupational requirement to be of the particular religion. In some provinces there is an explicit requirement on employers to accommodate the religious employee up to the point of undue hardship.[59] Other provinces do not have an explicit requirement, but the overall protection is very similar: the Supreme Court case law makes clear that there is an overarching duty to accommodate up to the point of undue hardship, and the duty can be understood to form part of the non-discrimination duty. In order to show that an employer's requirements are necessary, it must be shown that the employer cannot accommodate the employee's request for variation in the work rules, without undue hardship.[60]

Early Canadian cases took a similar approach to the USA, with the view that requiring that an employer bear anything more than a *de minimis* cost was 'undue hardship' (and therefore not required of an employer).[61] However, the law has developed so that employers are required to go further to accommodate religious practice,[62] while still acknowledging that it can be acceptable for the employee to bear some of the costs of religious practice. Factors that can be taken into account in assessing whether there is undue hardship include financial cost, disruption of a collective agreement, problems of morale of other employees, interchangeability of workforce and facilities, size of employer and the ease with which the workforce can be adapted.[63] Although the list of factors which can justify failure to accommodate is extensive, the Canadian duty to accommodate is stronger than that in the USA. The decision in *Meiorin*[64] confirmed that accommodation will be required unless it is impossible to do so without undue hardship. Although case law shows that a higher level of accommodation is required in the Canadian courts, it should be noted that the *Meiorin* test is not that if an accommodation is possible it must be offered: the test remains subject to undue hardship. Only if it is possible to accommodate *without undue hardship* will accommodation be required. If it is possible to accommodate, but to do so imposes undue hardship, then the accommodation will not be required.

Although the duty of accommodation does not require all religious requests to be granted, failing to consider options for accommodation may result in a discrimination finding. Once a potential accommodation has been identified by an employee, the employer

---

[57] RSC 1985, c H-6. The Canadian Human Rights Act has less impact as it only applies to the few federally regulated industries such as banking, shipping, federal public service, post office, etc.

[58] More detail, particularly on the separate provincial laws, can be found in W Tarnopolsky and W Pentney, *Discrimination and the Law* (Toronto, Carswell, 2005).

[59] See Manitoba Human Rights Code s 9, which contains a duty of reasonable accommodation.

[60] *British Columbia (Public Service Employee Relations Comm) v BCGEU* [1999] 3 SCR 3 ('Meiorin') and confirmed in *British Columbia (Superintendent of Motor Vehicles) v British Columbia (Council of Human Rights)* [1999] 3 SCR 868 ('Grismer'). In some provinces, the exception only applies to religious organisations operating in a not-for-profit environment.

[61] *Froese v Pine Creek School Division No 30*, M Rothstein QC, 28 December 1978 (Man Bd Adjud) (unreported).

[62] *Central Okanagan School District No 23 v Renaud* [1992] 2 SCR 970, a case involving dismissal for refusing to work days designated as holy by the employee's religion.

[63] *Central Alberta Dairy Pool v Alberta (Human Rights Commission)* [1990] 2 SCR 489.

[64] *British Columbia (Public Service Employee Relations Comm) v BCGEU* [1999] 3 SCR 3 ('Meiorin').

effectively becomes under an obligation to consider an accommodation. In *Qureshi v G4S Security Services*[65] the employer rejected the applicant once it learnt of his need for time off to pray for an hour every Friday. The Human Rights Tribunal of Ontario held this was discriminatory. It confirmed that the duty to accommodate has both a substantive and procedural component, and that there was a duty on the employer to take adequate steps to assess and explore accommodation options once it was aware of the potential need for accommodation: there was no need to wait for a request from the employee. Failure to meet the procedural requirement to consider accommodation could be sufficient to establish discrimination, although on the facts, the tribunal also found that there was no undue hardship: the claims about hardship were vague and speculative, and no clear evidence had been provided.

A number of specific exceptions allow staff to refuse to undertake certain work tasks. For example, professional bodies, such as physicians, make explicit allowance for their members to conscientiously object to performing abortions,[66] and section 3 of the Civil Marriage Act recognises that officials of religious groups are free to refuse to perform marriages that are not in accordance with their religious beliefs. However, as in the UK, religious individuals employed as civil marriage commissioners are not given exemption from performing same-sex marriage.[67]

In more general terms, claims for conscientious objection to performing particular work tasks will be dealt with as a matter of accommodation. In *Moore v British Columbia (Ministry of Social Services)*,[68] a financial aid worker was dismissed for refusing to grant a client financial aid for an abortion, because of religious objections to abortion. The Human Rights Council decided that as the employer had taken no steps to accommodate her religious views, Moore had suffered religious discrimination. For example, requests of the type refused by Moore were relatively infrequent, and other workers could have been asked to deal with them. What is interesting about the case is that, although it was suggested that Moore should have removed herself from the client's case (rather than taking it on and then refusing assistance), it did not place much responsibility on the employee to avoid the problem of clashes between religious scruple and compliance with the employer's reasonable job requirements.[69] The issue was not discussed because it was clear that no attempt to accommodate had been made. However, it may well be that in some cases the onus will pass to the employee not to undertake work which he or she is unable fully to perform on religious grounds.

Canadian courts put an onus on both parties to compromise when it comes to accommodating religion at work. Employers are required to do more than merely show that there is some impact upon their business: they can be required to tolerate some level of

---

[65] *Qureshi v G4S Security Services* 2009 HRTO 409 (CanLII).

[66] See for example, College of Physicians and Surgeons of Ontario, '*Professional Obligations and Human Rights*' (March 2015) at www.cpso.on.ca/policies-publications/policy/professional-obligations-and-human-rights. The obligation to refer patients to other staff who will provide the service has been challenged on religious freedom grounds: CBC News, 'Doctors make Charter Challenge on Right to Refuse Care on Religious Grounds' (CBC News, 24 March 2015) at www.cbc.ca/news/canada/ottawa/doctors-make-charter-challenge-on-right-to-refuse-care-on-religious-grounds-1.3006462.

[67] *In the matter of Marriage Commissions* [2011] SKCA 3.

[68] *Moore v British Columbia (Ministry of Social Services)* (1992) 17 CHRR D/426.

[69] See W Tarnopolsky and W Pentney, *Discrimination and the Law* (Toronto, Carswell, 2005) para 6.2(d).

inconvenience or expense. To this extent, the approach in Canada can be contrasted with that in the USA. The Canadian courts have recognised equally that it is acceptable to allow some cost on the employee's part, thus achieving a reasonable balance between the interests of the religiously observant employee and the needs of the employer.

However, as with the position in the USA, any additional protection for religious interests provided by a duty to accommodate is only strong if that duty cannot be easily overridden. The 'undue hardship' standard can be easily met in the US; the Canadian duty is stronger, as 'undue hardship' is harder to show. What this shows is that the level of protection provided does not necessarily depend on the legal framework: whether there is a duty to accommodate or a duty not to discriminate indirectly, the strength of the protection will be determined by the scope of the proportionality or 'hardship' review. Nonetheless, although a duty of accommodation does not necessarily lead to a change in the level of protection provided, there may be other reasons for introducing an approach to the protection of conscience claims through a duty of reasonable accommodation, as discussed below.

III. Is a Reasonable Accommodation Model a Better Way to Deal with Conscientious Objection?

It is sometimes assumed that a change to a reasonable accommodation model would lead to a different outcome in cases such as *Ladele*.[70] Just as some doctors are able to refuse to perform abortions, with patients referred elsewhere, so, Ms Ladele's request not to perform civil partnerships could be readily accommodated. She could have not been designated a civil partnership registrar, or she could have arranged for other staff to perform civil partnerships in her place. Such accommodation was indeed offered by other councils, so it was entirely practicable. This raises the question of whether such an approach would be a preferable means to deal with conscientious objections at work.

The first question that arises when addressing the question of whether or not it would be beneficial to introduce a duty of reasonable accommodation in the UK is whether such a duty would merely replicate the protection that already exists. After all, the indirect discrimination provisions of the Equality Act 2010 already amount, in effect, to a duty of reasonable accommodation in practice. As seen in *Ladele* in the domestic hearing under the Equality Act, the employer's requirement that all staff perform civil partnerships put members of staff with a conscientious objection to doing so at a particular disadvantage, and so the requirement had to be justified as a proportionate means of achieving a legitimate aim. The case can thus be reframed as a reasonable accommodation claim, but the assessment of whether a failure to accommodate was reasonable would effectively be determined by considering the same matters as when determining whether it was proportionate.

The fact that a duty of reasonable accommodation can be read into our understanding of indirect discrimination was effectively accepted by Lady Hale in *Hall v Bull* where it was suggested that the extent to which it is reasonable to expect the employer to accommodate the employee should be taken into account in the overall proportionality assessment.[71]

---

[70] Gibson, 'The God "Dilution"?' (2013); McCrudden, 'Marriage Registrars' (2018).
[71] *Bull & Anor v Hall & Anor* [2013] UKSC 73 at 47.

This inherent link between reasonable accommodation and indirect discrimination is also implicitly accepted in *Achbita v G4S*,[72] where the CJEU suggested that it could take into account whether the employer had tried to find alternative work for the employee when assessing proportionality. The requirement to engage in some dialogue to see if there are other roles that the employee could fulfil creates a level of obligation on employers to try to accommodate religious employees in other roles, whilst stopping short of creating a separate duty to accommodate.

It seems then that the creation of a separate and explicit duty of reasonable accommodation would not materially change the level of protection available for religion or belief in the workplace. Framing such a request as one for the accommodation which cannot be unreasonably refused does not add additional protection to that available using the indirect discrimination provisions.[73] Taking the case of *Ladele* as an example again, the question whether Ms Ladele could refuse to carry out civil partnerships will not turn on whether the protection is framed as indirect discrimination or reasonable accommodation, but instead will be determined by whether a court decides that a refusing to allow her conscientious objection is justified, or (what amounts to the same question, albeit framed differently) whether it is unreasonable.[74]

It can clearly be seen from the consideration of the North American experience that there is nothing inherent in the use of the term 'reasonable' in place of the term 'proportionate' or 'justified' which guarantees any specific level of protection. The two jurisdictions use the same framework, the duty of reasonable accommodation, but the standards of protection vary, as the different courts assess 'undue hardship' differently. It may be the case that Canadian courts have provided a greater degree of accommodation for religious conscience, but this cannot be due to its use of a particular legal mechanism, or else the US would have the same levels of protection. If the Canadian courts were to use an indirect discrimination approach it could just impose a stricter notion of justification to achieve the same levels of protection. It is thus not the legal mechanism which affects the level of protection for conscience claims, but more the question of judgment applied by the courts.

If the legal framework does not seem to effect the level of protection afforded, why then might one argue for the creation of a duty to accommodate? Reasons relate to procedural matters such as the burden of proof; clarity and ease of use; and the symbolic and practical implications of separating the legal treatment of religious equality from other equality grounds.

First, in relation to discrimination, although the burden of proof is favourable to individuals claiming that they have been discriminated against, the onus remains on the claimant to show that a requirement has been imposed that puts him or her at a disadvantage. The burden then shifts to the employer to justify the requirement. In contrast, with a duty of reasonable accommodation, the employee merely has to ask for an accommodation and the employer will then need to show that any accommodation would be unreasonable. There is no need to identify others who are also disadvantaged, in fact no need to find comparators

[72] Case C-157/15 *Achbita v G4S Secure Solutions NV* [2017] 3 CMLR 21.
[73] Assuming, as argued above, that indirect discrimination can be used by individual claimants.
[74] A Stein, 'Reasonable Accommodation for Religion and Belief: Can it be Accommodated in EU Law without an Express Duty?' in M-C Foblets, K Alidadi, JS Neilsen and Z Yanasmayan, (eds) *Belief, Law and Politics: What Future a Secular Europe?* (Farnham, Ashgate, 2014).

at all. The creation of an individualised duty of reasonable accommodation suggests that each case can be assessed on its own merits, with a personalised assessment,[75] and without the need for generalised group disadvantage. Thus, using a duty of reasonable accommodation approach is not only easier from the point of view of initiating a claim, but it also avoids the difficulties discussed above surrounding the question of whether there needs to be a group disadvantage.[76] In addition, the duty of accommodation also makes clear that it can be used for one off claims rather than ongoing changes to work.

Second, the duty of accommodation may be more intuitive and straightforward for employees to use.[77] It is clear on its face that it creates rights for the employee with regard to religion and belief at work. This overcomes the problem identified above, that it may not be apparent to those not well versed in discrimination law that indirect discrimination can offer them any legal protection. The creation of a discrete 'right to reasonable accommodation' would make the existence of the right much more visible and therefore more accessible to employees and employers.

The creation of a separate duty of reasonable accommodation may also be more accessible to workers because they find it less confrontational to frame religion or belief requests in terms of a request for accommodation rather than as a claim of indirect discrimination.[78] Instead of having to allege that their employer has discriminated against them, religious employees may feel more comfortable merely requesting an accommodation. Such an approach could lead to more open dialogue about religion or belief in the workplace, as claims would feel less like allegations of wrongdoing made about the employer, and would therefore be more likely to lead to constructive dialogue and compromise.[79]

Yet, although a move to a duty of reasonable accommodation may look as if it will result in greater clarity and ease of use for employees, such an outcome is not inevitable. Although a duty may seem to provide clarity, the creation of a special duty of reasonable accommodation for religion and belief at work could result in some misconceptions. Certainly while on the face of it, the duty of accommodation seems clearer, the level of hardship that would be needed before an accommodation is said not to be reasonable has not been determined, and litigation is likely to be required before any real clarity is achieved.[80] Even then, if the duty of accommodation results in more individualised, case-by-case assessment of requests, then clarity for employers and employees may be elusive in practice. As Pitt points out,[81] employment tribunals may struggle for consistency on when an accommodation is reasonable. Decisions are likely to vary, with no appeal allowed on the factual conclusions reached by tribunals as long as they have properly directed themselves. The lack of clarity in the level of accommodation required (added to inherent lack of clarity regarding the meaning of the key terms of 'religion' and 'belief') means that the true scope of any proposed duty of reasonable accommodation of religion and belief is very hard to anticipate.

---

[75] See Alidadi, 'Reasonable accommodations for religion and belief' (2012).

[76] If a group is required before a claim can be made, this also raises the question of how the members of that group should be identified. See F Ast, 'Reflections on the Recognition of a Right to Reasonable Accommodation in EU Law' in Foblets et al, *Belief, Law and Politics* (2014).

[77] Alidadi (n 31).

[78] ibid; Gibson (n 31).

[79] See P Edge and L Vickers, 'Review of Equality and Human Rights Law relating to Religion or Belief' Research Report 97 (London, EHRC, 2015).

[80] ibid.

[81] G Pitt, 'Taking Religion Seriously' (2013) 42 *Industrial Law Journal* 398.

Although what is required under a duty of reasonable accommodation should eventually become clear, it is not evident that any such clarity would be unqualifiedly positive. Most of those calling for the introduction of a duty of accommodation have assumed that it would lead to increased protection for employees with a religion or belief.[82] However, this is not necessarily the case, as the level of protection would depend on the level of hardship required before an accommodation would be said to be unreasonable and so not required. Moreover, even if greater protection were to result, whilst popular with some,[83] many others would not support an increase in the protection of religion and belief at work.[84] In particular, there is concern that by framing the protection for religious practice at work as a duty to accommodate, an onus is put on the employer to acquiesce to requests. As Pollock suggests, the emphasis is on reaching a compromise, even of 'splitting the difference', rather than on looking objectively at whether a practice puts a particular religious group at a disadvantage, and whether it can be justified as a proportionate means of achieving a legitimate aim. Moreover, any pressure to compromise brings with it the concomitant concern that religions with greater demands will be granted greater accommodation.

The fact that it is not clear from the nature of the mechanism itself whether a duty of reasonable accommodation could lead to greater protection than the indirect discrimination mechanism reveals the lack of any clear theoretical underpinning for the duty of accommodation. Although the aims of anti-discrimination law is an area of extensive academic debate,[85] the parameters of our equality norms are long established; courts are fairly clear about the scope of the law, and how to balance the respective rights of employees and employers. In contrast, a theoretical underpinning for the duty of accommodation of religion at work is less well developed. On the one hand, it can be understood to form part of the general non-discrimination law, in which case one might expect that the standard of reasonableness will remain very close to that of justification and proportionality under indirect discrimination. On the other hand, its theoretical basis may come from the ECHR, with its focus on religion as a key aspect of pluralism, and respect for cultural diversity and traditions.[86] Indeed, development of a duty of reasonable accommodation would be consistent with the decision of the ECtHR in *Thlimmenos v Greece*.[87] Here it was accepted

[82] Alidadi (n 31).

[83] See for example Christians in Parliament, *Clearing the Ground* (2012); see also some of the responses cited in M Mitchell and K Beninger (with E Howard and A Donald), *Religion or Belief in the Workplace and Service Delivery* (Manchester, Equality and Human Rights Commission, 2015).

[84] See responses in some of the workshops reported in Edge and Vickers, *Review of Equality and Human Rights Law* (2015). See also D Pollock, Personal Memorandum of Evidence to the Commission on Religion and Belief in British Public Life, available at www.thinkingabouthumanism.org/wp-content/uploads/2014/12/Commn-on-R+B-in-Public-Life-David-Pollock-evidence.pdf; and Commission on Religion and Belief in British Public Life, *Living with Difference: Community, Diversity and the Common Good* (Cambridge, The Woolf Institute, 2015).

[85] See for example, D Hellman and S Moreau (eds), *Philosophical Foundations of Discrimination Law* (Oxford, Oxford University Press, 2013); T Khaitan, *A Theory of Discrimination Law* (Oxford, Oxford University Press, 2015); I Solanke, Discrimination as Stigma: A Theory of Discrimination Law (Oxford, Hart Publishing, 2016); S Fredman, Discrimination Law (Oxford, Oxford University Press, 2002); B Hepple, 'The Aims of Equality Law' in C O'Cinneide and J Holder (eds), *Current Legal Problems* (Oxford, Oxford University Press, 2008). See also N Fraser, 'Rethinking Recognition' (2000) 3 *New Left Review* 107, and C Taylor, *Multiculturalism and the Politics of Recognition* (Princeton, Princeton University Press, 1992).

[86] *Moscow Branch of the Salvation Army v. Russia* (2007) 44 EHRR 46, at 61. See McCrudden (n 11).

[87] *Thlimmenos v Greece* (2001) 31 EHRR 15. Note, however, that the case law of Art 9 ECHR does not impose a duty to accommodate religion at work. See *Ahmad v UK* (1981) 4 EHRR 126 and *Stedman v UK* (1997) 23 EHRR CD168, both confirmed in *Kosteski v The Former Yugoslav Republic of Macedonia* [2006] ECHR 403.

that failure to accommodate religious difference resulted in unequal treatment, because it amounted to a refusal to treat different people differently. However, the ECtHR has only recently accepted that the right to freedom of religion of belief may survive entry to the workplace. Its jurisprudence on the right to conscientious objection at work is not well developed, having largely been based on conscientious objection in the context of military service. There may therefore be little by way of guidance available to courts as they find their way to establishing what is reasonable in the work context.

The arguments in favour of creating a new duty of accommodation, while backed by some in Europe,[88] thus remain contentious. Any perceived advantages for religious individuals, such as clarity and ease of use, are, on closer examination, fairly fragile; and furthermore, any move to increase the protection for religion at work would certainly not be supported by all.

Thus far, the arguments in favour and against the introduction of a duty of reasonable accommodation for religion or belief at work have focused on practical issues such as the burden of proof, perceptions regarding clarity in the law, and the effect that a different framework may have on workers seeking to have a religious practice accommodated. In addition to these practical issues, there is also the question of the symbolism of the creation of a separate duty of reasonable accommodation, given that the duty does not of itself create any greater or lesser protection than that provided by indirect discrimination. The creation of a separate framework for religious interests in the workplace could be seen as granting special status to such claims, thereby privileging religion over other interests; and views will certainly differ as to whether this is a good outcome.[89] However such a suggestion does presume that the special protection will be greater protection, yet as has been seen in the discussion of the USA above, there is nothing inherent in the creation of a duty of accommodation that means that this will be the case. Thus if special treatment is given to conscience claims at work, it should not necessarily be assumed to be privileging religion: if the threshold of reasonableness is set low, special treatment could just as easily lead to reduced protection.

Indeed, it may be that separate protection should be introduced for religion and belief, not because it will create stronger protection, but in order to signal clearly that religion and belief should be treated differently from other equality grounds. This is due to the risks to other areas of equality law of protecting all protected characteristics according to the same standards, as set out above. In effect creating a separate duty of reasonable accommodation would remove the danger of 'cross fertilisation' from religious discrimination claims into other areas of equality law.

IV. Conclusion

The introduction of a duty of reasonable accommodation has been suggested as a preferred mechanism for protecting conscience claims at work by Gerald Chipeur QC and Robert Clarke in their chapter in this volume, by the Council of Europe Parliamentary Assembly

---

[88] See Council of Europe Parliamentary Assembly, 'Freedom of Religion' (2013).
[89] See Pollock, *Personal Memorandum* (2015); and Pitt, 'Taking Religion Seriously'(2013).

resolution,[90] the UN Special Rapporteur on freedom of religion or belief,[91] and the Independent Review of the Enforcement of UK Anti-Discrimination Legislation.[92] Yet, in more the recent reviews of the effectiveness of the law protecting religion and belief in UK, neither the Equality and Human Rights Commission, nor the Commission on Religion and Belief in British Public Life have taken this line.[93] Instead they have concluded that the law on indirect discrimination is sufficient to deal adequately with religion or belief claims.

The main reason for this approach is their confidence that the current legal regime is largely effective in protecting religion or belief at work. Moreover, any difficulties courts or employers do face with regard to conscience claims are not overcome by a change of legal framework. Any difficulty just shifts location. For example, although there is some indeterminacy in indirect discrimination when it comes to assessing whether the refusal of a request is justified, there is equally likely to be indeterminacy when a court or employer decide whether the refusal of accommodation is reasonable. Returning to the *Ladele* case, it does not really make any difference whether the conscience claim is cast as indirect discrimination or reasonable accommodation, or indeed, as in her ECtHR case, as a case of freedom of religion or belief, the court still has to undertake a balancing exercise and reach a considered judgment as to whether she can rely on conscientious objection to same-sex relationships to be excused from a part of her job. The use of the term 'reasonable' in place of the term 'proportionate' or 'justified' does not guarantee any greater or lesser level of protection.

At least by relying on indirect discrimination to determine conscience claims in the workplace, courts will be able to draw on their long experience of assessing indirect discrimination claims. The concept of proportionality is well developed in the UK, in EU law and in the jurisprudence of the ECHR. A full assessment of how proportionality can be used to achieve a fair balance between the interests of the employers and employees cannot be given here,[94] but suffice to say, the concept allows for a nuanced assessment of a wide range of factors that may arise in a case, both individualised fact sensitive matters, and broader contextual factors. Thus, by remaining within a non-discrimination framework, courts can draw on their long experience of upholding and promoting equality when assessing proportionality.

In conclusion, conscience claims in the workplace are best protected by the established law on indirect discrimination, which is sufficient to provide appropriate and balanced protection for religion and belief in the workplace. Indirect discrimination based on a the notion of proportionality offers a means to reach an equilibrium whereby individuals' protection for conscience claims at work can co-exist with the rights of others.

[90] Council of Europe Parliamentary Assembly (n 37).
[91] See also Orr, *Beyond Belief* (2016) and the EU *Religare* project (n 36).
[92] B Hepple et al, *Equality* (2000).
[93] EHRC, *Religion or Belief: Is the Law Working?* (London, EHRC, 2016); Commission on Religion and Belief in British Public Life (n 84).
[94] For more detail see Vickers, *Religious Freedom* (2016) ch 3.

11

Who Should Give Effect to Conscientious Exemptions? The Case for Institutional Synergy

JOHN ADENITIRE*

I. Introducing the Allocation Problem: Conscientious Objection to Officiating Same-Sex Marriages

This chapter is developed on the background of an evolving practice in various jurisdictions of granting conscientious exemptions. As will be shown at various points throughout this chapter, the type of claims made by conscientious objectors vary widely. Sometimes objectors claim that they have a legal right not to perform acts made mandatory by their employment (eg work on Sundays or during religious festivities) or by a statute (eg mandatory military conscription). Sometimes individuals claim that they have, or should have, a legal right to positively perform acts which are normally illegal on the basis that their conscience compels them to (eg assist someone in committing suicide). On other occasions they claim that a whole social group should not be required to comply with legal obligations that contradict the beliefs which are constitutive of that group (eg certain churches not to be required to officiate same-sex marriages). Jurisdictions differ in their responses to these claims to exemption.

It is not the main purpose of this chapter to make a case in favour or against the granting of exemptions to conscientious objectors in any one particular case.[1] Rather, the main focus of this chapter is what will be called the 'allocation problem': why and how to allocate to one or the other institution of government the responsibility of giving effect to a conscientious exemption?

---

*Thanks are due to Professor David Feldman who read and commented on several versions of this chapter which was initially destined for, but did not make it into, my doctoral dissertation. Readers interested in the institutional consequences of conscientious exemptions should also consider Y Nehushtan, 'The Case for a General Constitutional Right to be Granted Conscientious Exemption' (2016) 5 *Oxford Journal of Law and Religion* 230.

[1] A preliminary case in favour of granting conscientious exemptions generally has been made in J Adenitire, 'Conscientious Exemptions: From Toleration to Neutrality; From Neutrality to Respect' (2017) 6 *Oxford Journal of Law and Religion* 268 and specifically in the context of the Islamic veil in J Adenitire, 'SAS v France: Fidelity to Law and Conscience' [2015] *European Human Rights Law Review* 78. This is further developed in ch 13 Part II in this volume.

It is necessary to illustrate the complexities of the allocation problem before attempting to address it. This is done here by reference to exemptions sometimes granted to those who object to officiating same-sex marriages. The mechanisms through which this exemption has been recognised have varied across jurisdictions and an analysis of these offers a useful means to explore the allocation problem.

Take the US case of the County Clerk for Rowan County, Kim Davies, who refused, based on her religious conscience, to sign or allowed to be signed by her deputies, certificates which would enable same-sex couples to marry. Her request to be exempt from performing her duties as an elected servant of the state was rejected by the Kentucky District Court[2] and, after unsuccessfully seeking from the US Supreme Court (USSC) a stay of the District Court's order obliging her to sign the certificates,[3] she was imprisoned for about a week for refusing to comply with order.[4]

Kim Davies' claim was considered, inter alia, under the Kentucky Religious Freedom Restoration Act (KRFRA) which mirrors the Federal Religious Freedom Restoration Act of 1993[5] (RFRA). It reads:

> Government shall not substantially burden a person's freedom of religion. The right to act or refuse to act in a manner motivated by a sincerely held religious belief may not be substantially burdened unless the government proves by clear and convincing evidence that it has a compelling governmental interest in infringing the specific act or refusal to act and has used the least restrictive means to further that interest. A 'burden' shall include indirect burdens such as withholding benefits, assessing penalties, or an exclusion from programs or access to facilities.[6]

KRFRA is a legislative act which prohibits the government from substantially burdening a person's religious conscience unless the government can prove that it has created that burden in pursuit of a compelling governmental interest and has used the least conscience-burdening means to achieve that interest. Importantly, a court of law can assess whether the legal test has been satisfied and can provide an exemption to the conscientious objector.

KRFRA is therefore a legislature-created mechanism which allocates to the judiciary the task of giving effect to the right to exemption for conscientious objectors. The allocation is however done in a special way: the legislature does not deal itself with the conflict between the right to exemption and the right, in this case, for same-sex couples to marry. Instead the legislation can be viewed as allocating the resolution of such conflicts to the judiciary through the 'compelling governmental interest' test. This has some important institutional implications: whatever one might think about the outcome of the Kim Davies case, criticism of, or praise for, its outcome will be directed to the courts, not the legislature. This raises the question of institutional legitimacy of courts in resolving conflicts of rights. This in turn may lead one to question whether the legislature's decision to allocate this task to the judiciary, rather than to deal with it itself, was a wise one.

---

[2] *Miller v Davis* [2015] Dist Court Civil Action No 15-44-DLB.

[3] *Miller v Davis* (No 15A250) (USSC).

[4] A Blinder and Ri Pérez-Peña, 'Kim Davis, Released from Kentucky Jail, Won't Say If She Will Keep Defying Court' (*The New York Times*, 8 September 2015) at www.nytimes.com/2015/09/09/us/kim-davis-same-sex-marriage.html?_r=2.

[5] 42 US Code §§ 2000bb-1.

[6] Chapter 446.350 of the Kentucky Revised Statutes.

A different legal mechanism could have been employed in the Kim Davies case. The UK's legislature predicted, in the Marriage (Same Sex Couples) Act 2013, that a conflict between conscience and marriage equality might arise and proposed its own resolution of that conflict. Under s 1(3)–(5) it provided that the clergy of the Church of England and the Church of Wales is exempt from complying with the obligation to officiating same-sex marriages. It also exempted, under s 2, other religious organisations and individuals involved in the religious rites of marriage if these have a conscientious objection. However, it explicitly excluded, in s 2(4), registrars from the exemption clauses. Had the Kim Davies case arisen in the UK, the outcome would have been determined by a clear legislative balancing of rights, not a judicial one. The institutional implications would have been different. Criticism of, or praise for, the outcome of the case would be best directed to the legislature rather than courts. Furthermore, the institutional legitimacy question would take a different form: is the legislature the best institution for deciding whether conscience should prevail over the right to marriage equality for same-sex couples?

There is another mechanism under which the Kim Davies issue could have been considered. Consider a submission made in the Court of Appeal for Saskatchewan, Canada, in the *Marriage Commissioners Reference case*.[7] The case concerned the constitutional validity of possible legislative amendments that would allow marriage commissioners to refuse to perform same-sex marriages. The following scheme was proposed:

> What if the request for the services of a marriage commissioner involved completion of a form indicating, not just the time and place of the proposed ceremony, but also the genders of the two people planning to marry? ... Assume too that the Director operated a simple internal system whereby a commissioner who did not want to perform same-sex marriage ceremonies because of his or her religious beliefs could make that fact known to the Director. ... the Director's office could reply to a request for marriage services by privately taking into account the religious beliefs of commissioners and then providing, to the couple planning to marry, a list of commissioners in the relevant geographical area who would be available on the planned date of the wedding and who would be prepared to officiate. The accommodation of commissioners who did not want to be involved in a same-sex ceremony would not be apparent to the couple proposing to wed and there would be no risk of the couple approaching a commissioner and being refused services because of their sexual orientation.[8]

Such a system, it was said in the case, was in operation at least in Toronto.[9] Unlike the RFRA or the UK Marriage Act, this scheme avoids explicit conflicts of rights. Marriage commissioners with a conscientious objection are accommodated without that having any visible impact on the marriage rights of same-sex couples (that is on the assumption that there are enough non-objecting commissioners available to officiate). It is clear that this scheme would point to a different outcome in the Kim Davies case: had the scheme been in operation in Kentucky, she would not have had to go to court to justify her view and would have continued in her job without ever going to prison. In fact, possibly only very few people other than the director of the scheme would need to know of her convictions.

Note, however, how the scheme has very different institutional implications. Praise for, or criticisms of, this solution are not to be addressed to either the legislature or courts but to

---

[7] *In the Matter of Marriage Commissioners* 2011 SKCA 3.
[8] ibid 86.
[9] ibid 87.

the public administration. This may be puzzling if one holds dear to the dichotomy, sometimes exposed in the literature, that the ultimate responsibility for rights is to be allocated either to the judiciary or the legislature or a combination of both.[10] This literature often looks with scepticism at the capacity of the public administration, which is an emanation of the executive branch, to protect rights. Such scepticism may sometimes be warranted. However, the ingenuity (whether or not justified) of this solution to the Kim Davies scenario could not be achieved without the exercise of executive discretion and a degree of behind-the-scenes handling which would be generally inappropriate in either legislatures or courts.

It seems, then, that there are at least three possible frameworks which could be adopted for dealing with the Kim Davies scenario. Further analysis of these schemes will be considered in the following sections. However, for now the analysis undertaken suffices to show the complexity of the allocation problem. The adoption of any of the three frameworks reveals that different institutional considerations have to be weighted. The first scenario, the one modelled around the RFRA, requires an assumption that the judiciary is an appropriate institution which has the legitimacy and expertise for dealing with conflicts between important rights. In certain jurisdictions this assumption is granted by the existing legal framework. The US, for example, has a strong tradition of the judiciary being the final decision-maker of what fundamental rights require and there is a culture of the other institutions accepting its findings. The USSC's finding in *Obergefell*[11] that there is a constitutional right for same-sex couples to marry has been accepted by the executive despite its controversial social and legal implications.[12] In New Zealand, by contrast, there is a long tradition of Parliamentary Sovereignty and the judiciary is not allowed, even under the New Zealand Bill of Rights Act 1990, to invalidate or refuse to apply legislation which is inconsistent with the rights protected under the Bill of Rights.[13] Therefore, the assumption underlying the KRFRA model would not go unchallenged.

The second model (ie the UK's Marriage Act), whereby Parliament resolves conflicts of rights and specifies criteria, would fit more comfortably with the legal tradition in New Zealand where the legislature and the executive have a strong mandate for rights protection (vis-à-vis courts).[14] The underlying assumption in this scheme is that the

---

[10] The literature is voluminous and no attempt is made here to summarise it. In the UK the school of thought associated with the idea of strong judicial responsibility in matter of rights takes its cue from TRS Allan. See, for example TRS Allan, *The Sovereignty of Law: Freedom, Constitution, And Common Law* (Oxford, OUP, 2015). UK proponents of strong political responsibility in matter of rights are, among others, Adam Tomkins and Richard Bellamy: A Tomkins, *Our Republican Constitution* (London, Hart Publishing, 2005); R Bellamy, *Political Constitutionalism: A Republican Defence of the Constitutionality of Democracy* (Cambridge, Cambridge University Press, 2007). Certain theorists, such as CJS Knight and Stephen Sedley, have argued for shared responsibility: CJS Knight, 'Bi-Polar Sovereignty Restated' (2009) 68 *Cambridge Law Journal* 361; S Sedley, 'Human Rights: A Twenty-First Century Agenda' [1995] *Public Law* 386.

[11] *Obergefell v Hodges* (2015) 135 SCt 2584.

[12] In a press release, President Barack Obama welcomed the decision in a public speech made on the same day the judgment was released. See 'Remarks by the President on the Supreme Court Decision on Marriage Equality' (*whitehouse.gov*, 26 June 2015) at www.whitehouse.gov/the-press-office/2015/06/26/remarks-president-supreme-court-decision-marriage-equality.

[13] Under the New Zealand Bill of Rights Act 1990, s 4, courts are explicitly denied the power to invalidate or not apply enactments which are inconsistent with the rights protected under the Bill of Rights.

[14] Under s 7 of the New Zealand Bill of Rights Act 1990, the Attorney-General is to report to Parliament of inconsistencies between proposed legislation and the rights guaranteed in the Bill of Rights. The reports do not bind Parliament who may legislate disregarding the reports.

legislature has adequate legitimacy or expertise, plausibly grounded in its democratic mandate, to adequately consider conflicts between important rights and determine how they are to be resolved. Again, this assumption will not be accepted universally. Critics may point to the less than ideal records of certain legislatures in upholding rights, especially when those rights are claimed by individuals, such as criminals or foreigners, coming from social groups which are not traditionally well championed by parliamentary representatives.[15]

The third model, with its reliance on accommodation mechanisms adopted by the public administration, assumes that the public administration is in fact willing to accommodate public servants' consciences. This is not a given. The UK case of *Ladele*[16] shows that not all public bodies are willing to accommodate their employees' consciences. In that case Islington Borough Council decided that it was not prepared to allow its registrar to object to officiating civil partnerships for same-sex couples. It considered that doing so would amount to unjustifiable discrimination against same-sex couples. The Council's view was unsuccessfully challenged in the UK Court of Appeal and in the ECtHR.[17] The Court of Appeal, for example, stated that even under the ECHR

> Ms Ladele's proper and genuine desire to have her religious views relating to marriage respected should not be permitted to override Islington's concern to ensure that all its registrars manifest equal respect for the homosexual community as for the heterosexual community.[18]

The analysis above, centred on the Kim Davies case, indicates the depth of the allocation problem. It should be clear by now that the responsibility for giving effect to conscientious exemptions may be allocated to different institutions and implemented in several ways. Whatever choice is made will have an impact on the possible substantive outcomes of the claim, on the authority of the institution tasked with considering the issue, and may or may not challenge the canons of the existing legal tradition, in particular the existing rules of institutional competence.

The complexity of the allocation problem runs much deeper than the Kim Davies case study could show. The reason is that in that instance the focus was on a particular type of conscientious objection which had its own specific issues. In particular, Kim Davies's claim to be exempt from performing her duty was bound to conflict with the right of same-sex couples. This is not necessarily always the case with all kinds of conscientious objection claims. An employee conscientiously objecting to joining a trade union (as under the UK's Industrial Relations Act 1971)[19] does not normally interfere with the rights of others.

---

[15] The standard example here is the consistent refusal by the UK Parliament to grant voting rights to prisoners despite various rulings, in the ECtHR and the UK Supreme Court, that such refusal violates human rights. See *Hirst v United Kingdom* (2006) 42 EHRR 41. and *R (on the application of Chester) v Secretary of State for Justice* [2014] AC 271. However, it seems that the UK government has now conceded that prisoners on a temporary licence may now be allowed to vote. See the statement of the Secretary of State for Justice, David Lidington, in HC Deb 02 November 2017, vol 630, col 1007.

[16] *Ladele v London Borough of Islington* [2009] EWCA Civ 1357.

[17] The claimant in *Ladele* was also unsuccessful in the ECtHR in *Eweida and Others v UK* (2013) 57 EHRR 8.

[18] *Ladele* (n 16) at 55.

[19] Section 9 provides that '(1) Any worker who – (a) (…) (b) objects on grounds of conscience both to being a member of a trade union and to paying contributions to a trade union in lieu of membership of it, may propose to the trade union that, instead of paying such contributions, he should agree to pay equivalent contributions to a charity to be determined by agreement between him and the trade union'. This section was repealed by section 1 of Trade Union and Labour Relations Act 1974.

This objection may trigger other kinds of problems such as undermining the effectiveness of collective bargaining through trade unions if too many employees claim the right. But this consideration will have different institutional implications from those of the Kim Davies case. The trade union scenario does not raise the same issues of institutional legitimacy required to balance two conflicting rights. Instead, it raises a more straightforward case of monitoring that not too many people are claiming the right.

From the above it follows that in order to start solving the allocation problem one ought to understand that claims of conscientious objection may vary in kind and each may give rise to specific issues which may be best resolved if allocated to one institution rather than another. Furthermore, there might be general considerations common to all kinds of conscientious objection claims which may inform the exercise of allocating to one institution or another the task of giving effect to conscientious exemptions. It would be useful then to catalogue those general considerations and analyse how they affect the allocation problem. This will be the task undertaken in part III of this chapter.

However, it is also possible that the solution to the allocation problem is affected by other considerations which are not specific to conscientious objection claims but affect rights more generally. In the Kim Davies case there was much talk about institutional legitimacy and expertise, especially in the context of resolving conflicts between two conflicting rights. Conflicts of rights do not only arise in the context of claims of conscientious objection but are a recurring feature of rights more generally. It is possible, then, that a more general theory of the proper role of institutions in matters of rights may inform solutions to the specific issues raised by the allocation problem. Consequently, it would be useful to develop a more general normative theory of the proper role of institutions in rights discourse and then see how that theory informs the solution to the allocation problem. This will be the task undertaken in the next part of the chapter where the idea of institutional synergy is explored: the idea that all three branches of government have a valuable role to play in giving effect to rights; even though, pessimistically, all institutions are likely to deliver suboptimal outcomes in matters of rights, optimistically, they may compensate each other's weaknesses while abiding within their constitutional roles.

II. Institutional Synergy as the Lodestar to the Solution to the Allocation Problem

A. Universal Scepticism about Institutions

It may be possible to formulate a theory about institutions which gives pride of place to a particular institution – let's say legislatures – in the protection of fundamental rights and then use that theory to critique jurisdictions whose practices diverge from that theory.[20] That theory would inform possible solutions to the allocation problem: a legislature-centred theory would embrace the approach that we have observed, for example, in the UK's Marriage (Same Sex Couples) Act 2013 where the legislature directly engaged with,

---

[20] See above n 10 for some examples of such theories.

and gave its own resolution of, the conflicts between the right to exemption and marriage equality. Such a theory would treat with a good measure of scepticism the framework of the RFRA where judges are called upon to determine whether the public interest or other people's rights should prevail over the conscientious scruples of objectors. This chapter will not argue that one institution should be preferred to the other for the two following reasons.

First, a solution to the allocation problem needs to be adaptable to different legal traditions and constitutional arrangements. Because, as observed, different legal traditions have established different mechanisms of institutional protection for rights (we have compared the tradition in New Zealand to the US tradition), a rigid theory that gave pride of place to the protection of rights to one institution would not be able to accommodate a jurisdiction that gave pride of place to another institution. Such a theory would only be able to advocate fundamental reforms in the diverging jurisdiction rather than provide solutions which are compatible with that jurisdiction's existing framework.

Second, a solution to the allocation problem needs to be informed by an attitude of scepticism about institutions. The scepticism about institutions has two components. The first – call it the natural fallibility trait – says that given that institutions are operated by human beings, who are by nature fallible, institutions may fail, in reasoning or outcome, in their assigned task to deliver optimal outcomes in issues of rights. The second – call it the structural fallibility trait – says that because institutions are designed to fulfil different functions they necessarily have pre-determined structural sets of strengths and weaknesses. Giving effect to rights requires a variety of conditions which no one institution is likely to satisfy by itself.

The natural fallibility trait is, it is admitted, a weak objection to developing a theory which gives pride of place to a particular institution. All institutions are likely to be equally affected by the problem of human fallibility. Nevertheless, while being a weak objection for scepticism about any one particular institution, the natural fallibility trait remains a valid reason for universal institutional scepticism, given that all institutions are operated by fallible human beings. This deep scepticism does not lead to advocating that institutions should never be allocated the responsibility to deal with rights issues. Rather, universal institutional scepticism says that whichever institution is given the responsibility for deciding a rights issue one may always encounter sub-optimal outcomes occasioned by human error or bad faith.

Universal institutional scepticism is reinforced by the structural fallibility trait. This says that institutions have pre-determined structural sets of strengths and weaknesses by constitution and therefore giving pride to one institution is likely to lead to some disappointments. As will be explored in more detail in part III, legislatures, for example, are unlikely to have the resources to legislate to cater for the wide variety of possible claims of conscientious objection. Likewise, courts can only deal with those cases that come before them and can do very little to pre-empt breaches of rights. The public administration may find informal solutions to clashes between the right to conscientious objection and other fundamental rights; however, as illustrated in the Kim Davies case study, these are likely to be disputable and the object of legal controversies. Allocating the responsibility for rights to any single institution therefore appears to lead to inevitable shortcomings in the challenging project of upholding rights in a satisfactory manner.

A way of embracing the conclusion of universal institutional scepticism is to state that, given that institutions may disappoint in one way or another, one should look for the least worst option. This may have been the rationale for John Griffith's political constitutionalism: his scepticism about objective solutions to conflicts between rights coupled with a deep-seated distrust of bearers of institutional power led him to advocate the championing of the political process over the legal one for essentially pessimistic reasons. Politicians, he argued, at least can be more easily removed from office than judges when they fail to deliver optimal outcomes.[21] One may, however, adopt a more optimistic, but equally sceptical, attitude. One may instead look for a way to ensure that institutions compensate for one another's weaknesses. This technique is 'institutional synergy'.

B. Institutional Synergy[22]

What is being advocated here is that the outcome to universal institutional scepticism should be an optimist outlook whereby institutions, using their own specific strengths, are able to remedy each other's shortcomings. There is no reason to believe that such synergetic relationship between institutions cannot take place without advocating fundamental reforms of the existing legal culture of a particular jurisdiction. In New Zealand, for example, the constitutional structure does not allow judges to strike down legislation on human rights grounds.[23] Rather than reject or approve this, a theory grounded in institutional synergy takes it as a simple matter of fact and devises solutions around it. It will look, for example, at the way other institutions, such as legislatures or the executive, may capitalise on their existing institutional powers to better protect rights. It will also investigate how courts may, with their perceived limitations, contribute to the task at hand.[24]

Institutional synergy should be seen as a method of finding solutions to problems, not as a solution in itself. It says that we should explore how institutions, as we find them in a given jurisdiction, may compensate for each other's weaknesses in resolving any given issue of rights. Institutional synergy may fail as a working method: none of the institutions in a given jurisdiction may be committed to upholding rights. If that is the case then the validity of institutional synergy as a working method should be the least of our worries. Institutional synergy may however deliver positive outcomes even in those scenarios which we thought deeply unsatisfactory. This is because under this view one may look even to the executive, usually depicted as prone to authoritarianism and abuse of power,[25] as a possible institution

---

[21] 'A further advantage in treating what others call rights as political claims is that their acceptance or rejection will be in the hands of politicians rather than judges and the advantage of that is not that politicians are more likely to come up with the right answer but that, as I have said, they are so much more vulnerable than judges and can be dismissed or at least made to suffer in their reputation': JAG Griffith, 'The Political Constitution' (1979) 42 *The Modern Law Review* 1, 18.

[22] This idea has greatly benefited from engagement with scholars promoting a model of collaboration between institutions in rights discourse. PA Joseph, 'Parliament, the Courts, and the Collaborative Enterprise' (2004) 15 *King's Law Journal* 321. E Carolan, 'Dialogue Isn't Working: The Case for Collaboration as a Model of Legislative–Judicial Relations' (2016) 36 *Legal Studies* 209.

[23] See n 13.

[24] For example, in the New Zealand context, the recent indication that judges may have the jurisdiction to issue a formal declaration of inconsistency, similar to the UK's s 4 HRA declaration of incompatibility, should be welcomed. See *Taylor v Attorney-General* [2015] NZHC 1706.

[25] Griffith, 'The Political Constitution' (1979) 16. He says that 'Governments are too easily able to act in an authoritarian manner'. Similarly, Allan, *The Sovereignty of Law* (2015) 208. '[T]he court's powers of supervision of administrative agencies and executive public authorities may be understood to derive from its inherent jurisdiction to prevent the abuse of power, defending the rights of those affected.'

to remedy the failures of the other institutions in matters of rights. Take, for example, the absolute prohibition in the UK of assisted suicide.

While suicide is legal in the UK, assisting someone to commit suicide may be punished with a sentence of up to 14 years.[26] This absolute prohibition may be generally motivated by laudable intentions to protect particularly vulnerable people who may request assistance in suicide for undue reasons. However, as the *Nicklinson* case reminds us, the prohibition encroaches on the rights of certain disabled individuals who are mentally competent and free from undue external pressures but who, given their condition, cannot perform suicide without assistance.[27] The UK Supreme Court has held that this absolute prohibition interferes with the right to private life of these disabled and mentally competent individuals.[28] Five out of nine judges of the court asserted that the interference might ultimately constitute a violation of the ECHR. However, the Court refused to issue a declaration of the incompatibility with the ECHR because it did not think it was legitimate for it to do so. In fact Lords Neuberger, Mance, Wilson, Reed and Clarke were of the view that Parliament ought to consider the question of the compatibility with human rights of the absolute ban of assisted dying before any judicial intervention. At the time of the decision, the UK Parliament was in fact considering the Assisted Dying Bill which, if enacted, would have legalised assisted dying in very limited circumstances. Lord Sumption and Hughes would leave this decision to Parliament entirely because it involved courts dealing with a morally charged question the resolution of which was best suited to a democratically elected institution. Lady Hale and Lord Kerr, in the minority, would have granted the declaration of incompatibility sought on the ground that doing otherwise would amount to an abdication of the duty placed on courts by the Human Rights Act to assess the compatibility of legislation with the ECHR.

The UK Parliament has refused multiple times (the last time being in September 2015 after the judgment in *Nicklinson*)[29] to relax the ban on assisted suicide. One may regard this situation as deeply unsatisfactory as neither the courts nor the legislature have been able to remedy what a majority of the judges in *Nicklinson* thought was a violation of a fundamental right. The application of the working method of institutional synergy would recommend a different outlook. Whilst both the courts and legislature have failed individuals like Mr Nicklinson who, unable to convince anyone to provide assistance to commit suicide, decided to take his own life by starving himself to death,[30] a branch of the public administration, in particular the Crown Prosecution Service (CPS), may have partially compensated for the weaknesses of courts and the legislature.

The CPS, under guidance issued by the Director of Public Prosecutions (DPP),[31] has in fact exercised its discretion and decided not to prosecute a vast majority of individuals providing assistance in suicide to legally competent adult individuals who, for reasons of disability, are unable without assistance to put into action a voluntary, clear, settled and

---

[26] Suicide Act 1961, s 2.

[27] *R (Nicklinson) v Ministry of Justice* [2015] AC 657.

[28] *Nicklinson and Lamb v UK* (2015) 61 EHRR SE7. See also the earlier *Pretty v UK* [2002] 2 FLR 45.

[29] HC Vol 599 11 September 2015, cols 656–725.

[30] *Nicklinson* (n 28) at 4.

[31] Director of Public Prosecutions, 'Policy for Prosecutors in Respect of Cases of Encouraging or Assisting Suicide' (The Crown Prosecution Service, October 2014) at www.cps.gov.uk/publications/prosecution/assisted_suicide_policy.html.

informed decision to kill themselves.[32] It was the UK Supreme Court in *Purdy v DPP*[33] that mandated the issuance by the DPP of the guidance on assisted suicide. The Supreme Court did so on the basis that interference with the Article 8 rights of disabled individuals to receive assistance in suicide could only be justifiably restricted by a measure 'required by law'. This required that the CPS's discretion to prosecute assisted suicide cases had to be sufficiently accessible and foreseeable in its application. The general guidance under the Code for Crown Prosecutors was insufficiently detailed and therefore an offence-specific guidance was needed.[34] Despite this judicial intervention, however, even prior to the publication of the judicially mandated guidance, there is solid evidence that the CPS, on its own motion, rarely prosecuted offenders under the Suicide Act.[35]

Note how the actions of the CPS/DPP conform to the idea of institutional synergy. First, the actions of the CPS/DPP were in line with the fundamental pillars of the UK's constitution culture. The DPP did not in fact decriminalise the prohibition of assisting suicide and could not constitutionally do so.[36] Second, the CPS/DPP used its own institutional strength, ie executive discretion, to ameliorate conformity, at least in outcome, with fundamental rights. In fact the CPS/DPP exercised its legitimate discretion[37] whether or not to prosecute certain crimes to provide some relief to the interference with fundamental rights caused by the criminal prohibition of assisted suicide. Finally, and importantly, the CPS/DPP's solution remedied, at least in part, the institutional weakness of the courts, ie their perceived illegitimacy to challenge the law on assisted suicide, and of the legislature, ie its unwillingness or inability to devise a legislative scheme that could protect vulnerable individuals while not interfering with the rights of individuals in Mr Nicklinson's position.

An institutional theory that gave pride of place to one institution (usually courts or legislatures) in the protection of rights could not have been able to see the silver lining in the institutional solution to the problem raised by the prohibition of assisted suicide. Such theory, depending on its preferred institution, would have simply criticised either courts or Parliament for their respective failures. The idea of institutional synergy, while still critical of these institutions, recognises the possible valid contributions of any institution, including the executive, to the advancement of rights.

To summarise, the idea of institutional synergy is born out of four interlocking ideas. First, it is a product of universal institutional scepticism and, consequently, is sceptical of theories which have a bias towards any one specific institution (usually courts or legislators). Second, it is animated by an optimistic view that institutions (even the often demonised executive branch) have specific characteristics which may compensate each other's failures. Third, it is a conservative view which, rather than seeking fundamental institutional

---

[32] Three cases only have resulted in prosecutions out of 138 cases referred from 1 April 2009 up to 31 January 2018. See Crown Prosecution Service, 'Assisted Suicide' (Crown Prosecution Service, 31 January 2018) at www.cps.gov.uk/publications/prosecution/assisted_suicide.html.

[33] *R (on the application of Purdy) v DPP* [2010] 1 AC 345.

[34] ibid at 53.

[35] The Court in *Nicklinson* (n 28) at 48 states that 'The DPP also informed the Court that it appears from Dignitas's website that, between 1998 and 2011, a total of 215 people from the UK used its services, and that nobody providing assistance in that connection has been prosecuted.'

[36] ibid at 277.

[37] The Supreme Court in Nicklinson had evidence (see n 35) that the CPS/DPP had routinely exercised his discretion to refuse to bring prosecutions in assisted suicide cases. The Supreme Court did not give any indication that this was an illegitimate use of the CPS/DPP's discretionary powers.

reforms, works within the established parameters of appropriate institutional interaction to analyse whether there are possible satisfactory solutions to rights issue. Finally, as will become more evident in the next parts of the chapter, it is not a theory which provides any substantive answer to a rights issue (whether or not in relation to the right to exemption for conscientious objectors). Rather, it is a framework through which rights issues should be considered.

III. Tackling the Allocation Problem by Analysing Five Basic Characteristics of Conscientious Exemptions

This part of the chapter tackles possible solutions to the allocation problem using the idea of institutional synergy as a lodestar. The analysis is carried out in five parts in relation to five identified general characteristics of conscientious objection claims. It is not here claimed that these five characteristics exhaust the complexity of such claims. Further characteristics could have been identified. The analysis addresses how institutions have each a role to play in relation to each of the five characteristics which it is here claimed are salient characteristics. Throughout, the employment of the idea of institutional synergy is shown to have important consequences for analytical and normative conclusions.

A. There are an Undefined Number of Forms of Conscientious Objection

We should expect that there will be an undefined number of legal obligations individuals may object to. Many are very familiar: objection to military service; to abortion; to be involved in officiating same-sex marriages; to providing emergency contraception. We should not think that these familiar forms of conscientious objection exhaust all possible claims. It may be possible that legal obligations which are thought uncontroversial might actually contravene some deeply held beliefs. For example, one might well be surprised by the Peculiar People's beliefs that parents have a religious duty not to allow their children (and themselves) to receive any medical treatment because that would otherwise contravene their interpretation of some passages in the Bible exhorting believers to pray for the sick.[38]

How could legislatures react to this feature? One way would be to bite the bullet: given that not all possible claims can be predicted and catered for in legislation in a pre-emptive fashion, new legislation should be produced as soon as practicable after new types of conscientious objection claims come to light. On this approach, members of the legislature would be reactive to lobbying from religious groups and other social groups whose beliefs, whether secular or not, are likely to give rise to conflicts between law and conscience. There is nothing wrong with this approach. It proceeds on the laudable basis that the legislature is always open to consider unforeseen conflicts between law and conscience and that the legislature

---

[38] As illustrated in *R v Senior* [1899] 1 QB 283.

should be ready to deal with those whenever they become known. There is however another approach which, inspired by the idea of institutional synergy, may be preferable. This approach recognises that the legislature may engage with particular conscientious objection cases while empowering other institutions to deal with unforeseen conscientious objection cases.

We have seen this approach above when considering the KRFRA/RFRA. In those statutes the legislature enabled the judiciary to consider a potentially unlimited number of conscientious objection cases arising from religious beliefs by reference to the compelling interest test. However, the enactment of these statutes giving the judiciary a very broad jurisdiction in conscientious objection cases did not relieve the legislature from engaging itself in dealing with some of those cases. After the enactment of the RFRA in 1993, Congress passed several conscience clauses exempting groups of individuals or institutions who could, arguably, have obtained the exemption through RFRA litigation. Congress, for example, exempted, on moral or religious grounds, organisations offering healthcare plans from being obliged to provide abortion services under the Medicaid and Medicare insurance schemes.[39]

This approach, if accepted, begs the following question: when should the legislature itself deal with legislating a conscience clause which defines the circumstances in which the exemption is to be afforded, rather than leaving the conscience issue to be determined by the judiciary? The answer here suggested is that the legislature should undertake that task itself as much as feasible and especially it should undertake that task diligently in legislation which it is reasonably expected will give rise to conscience issues. The justification for this answer lies in the view that the legislature has an important part to play in rights discourse and enjoys certain features that makes it a desirable player in the determination of rights. First, unlike most courts, legislatures usually have a direct democratic mandate and a direct responsibility to influence what the law is through legislation. It would be contrary to this democratic mandate for legislatures to routinely avoid dealing with certain controversial issues by relying on the judiciary to tackle them instead.

Secondly, whether or not a particular group of individuals should enjoy a conscientious exemption will almost always be a contestable issue. While the legislature's engagement through conferring or refusing to confer an exemption in a conscience clause does not affect the contestability of the solution adopted, its democratic pedigree is likely to confer on it a high degree of finality. This appears to be true at least in relation to the conscience clause in the UK's Abortion Act 1967 which, as stated by Lady Smith in *Doogan*, 'has given rise to very little litigation in the last 45 years, despite the fact that very many terminations of pregnancy have been carried out under its authorisations'.[40]

Finally, the legislature's direct engagement usually has the added merit of much easier predictability. We have seen that the RFRA and similar legislation grants an exemption subject to the compelling interest test. That test requires balancing the conscientious convictions of the objector with the public good protected by the obligation being objected to.

---

[39] 42 USC § 1395w-22(j)(3)(b) (2000). See also Consolidated Appropriations Resolution, 2003, Division E, Title II, Pub L No 108-7, 117 Stat 11, 163 (2003) and Consolidated Appropriations Resolution, 2003. Division J, Title VI, § 635(c), Pub L No 108-7, 117 Stat 11, 472 (2003).

[40] *Doogan and another v Greater Glasgow and Clyde Health Board* [2012] CSOH 32, at 73.

It is not easy to predict, prior to judicial announcement, whether a conscientious objector relying on the RFRA will be able to obtain the exemption sought. In *Hobby Lobby*, for example, the USSC was tasked with determining whether the RFRA could be relied on by a family of Evangelical Christians who owned a for-profit corporation, Hobby Lobby Stores Inc, to obtain an exemption for the Stores from the requirement to provide its employees with healthcare coverage, which included emergency contraception cover.[41] That complex question had to be answered by determining whether the owners of Hobby Lobby's religious freedom was being substantially burdened by a compelling governmental interest in providing contraception cover. Prior to the decision of the USSC, no one could have reliably predicted the outcome.

The USSC's decision itself was divided in a 5:4 majority. The majority judgment held that requiring Hobby Lobby to provide the coverage or to face very hefty fines would result in a substantial burden on the religious beliefs of the company's owners.[42] Furthermore, even though the reason for the imposition of the mandatory cover (providing to women cost-free access to contraception) was assumed by the court to be a compelling interest,[43] the majority found that the government could have achieved that interest in a lesser restrictive way. The government could, for example, extend the accommodation that it had already established for religious non-profit organisations to for-profit objecting employers, such as Hobby Lobby. Under that accommodation arrangement, Hobby Lobby would self-certify that it objects to providing the coverage. Upon receipt of the certification, Hobby Lobby's insurers would then be required to provide the contraceptive coverage.[44]

The minority judgment disagreed at almost every point of this analysis. First, it contended that there was no precedent supporting Hobby Lobby enjoying the protection of the RFRA given that it was not a natural person who could practice religion nor was it a non-profit organisation (eg a church) established to foster the religious interests of its members.[45] Secondly, it held that no substantial burden was placed on Hobby Lobby's religious beliefs because 'the decisions whether to claim benefits under the plans are made not by Hobby Lobby (…) but by the covered employees and dependents, in consultation with their health care providers'.[46] Thirdly, the dissent found that no precedent allowed a religious exemption to be granted when such exemption would be harmful to others. In this context harm would be caused to women who, unable to afford adequate contraceptive cover, would be subject to the health problems related to unwanted pregnancies or health problems which use of contraception could prevent.[47]

Finally, the minority pointed to the possible problems with the majority's suggestion that Hobby Lobby's insurers, on notification by the company, should be required to provide the cover. The major problem was that such accommodation arrangement, currently offered to religious non-profit organisations, might itself be incompatible with the RFRA. The week after *Hobby Lobby* was decided, in fact, the USSC granted an injunction to Wheaton College

---

[41] *Burwell v Hobby Lobby Stores, Inc* (2014) 134 SCt 2751.
[42] ibid at 31–38.
[43] ibid at 39–40.
[44] ibid at 40–45.
[45] ibid at 13–20.
[46] ibid at 23.
[47] ibid at 23–27.

from being compelled to follow the procedure under the accommodation arrangement on the basis that the College believed that by self-certifying its objection it was triggering the obligation on its insurers to provide the objected contraception. This, in the College's view, amounted to being made an accomplice to a sinful practice.[48] The USSC has explicitly avoided settling the issue of the constitutionality of this accommodation arrangement.[49]

No view is here taken as to whether the minority or majority judgment in *Hobby Lobby* were better decided. However, the diverging analysis and conclusions of the justices is indicative of the uncertainty in outcome of a judicially driven balancing exercise under a general scheme such as the RFRA. By contrast, statutory conscience clauses, albeit always subject to the courts' authority to shape their meaning through interpretation, usually have the benefit of being more straightforward. This is because the legislature, in formulating a conscience clause, has already engaged in the moral question of balancing the relevant rights and interests.

From the above, one can conclude that the legislature should undertake the task of granting exemptions as much as feasible and especially it should undertake that task diligently in legislation which it is reasonably expected will give rise to conscience issues. However, given that legislatures cannot predict all possible claims of conscientious objection, they should be supported by the judiciary which should be granted a wide power (eg a power similar to that under the RFRA) under which unpredictable claims to exemption can be considered. Depending on the existing constitutional framework, it may be that the granting of the power is not necessary as the judiciary may already be empowered to consider those claims under a constitutional protection of freedom of conscience.

The conclusion above squares well with the idea of institutional synergy. The fact that there are an undefined number of claims of conscientious objection entails that the legislature is unable by itself to consider enacting relevant conscience clauses for every imaginable claim. This shortcoming can be remedied by relying on the judiciary. In particular, if the judiciary is given a wide jurisdiction to consider claims of exemption it is then possible that those claims which the legislature could not predict and legislate for will be determined by judges. The legislature and the judiciary should then be viewed as engaging in a synergetic relationship trying to keep up with the wide variety of conscientious objection claims.

B.   Claims of Conscientious Objection may Conflict with Other Rights or with the Public Interest

The Kim Davies case was used as a useful case study of the clashes that may sometimes occur between the right to conscientious objection and other rights or the public interest. The main institutional problem this gives rise to is the legitimacy of the institution allocated to resolve those possible clashes. The legitimacy question can be put thus: given the difficult moral questions involved in such situations of conflict, can we trust the institution to provide solutions in which we ought to acquiesce? Note that the legitimacy question already presupposes that the institutions involved in the balancing exercise may sometimes get the

---

[48] *Wheaton College v Burwell* (2014) 134 SCt 2806.
[49] *Zubik v Burwell* (2016) 136 SCt 1557.

answers wrong but then requires that the authority of the institution involved be sufficient to command a large degree of acquiescence in that solution.

One may doubt that any one institution should claim the legitimacy to balance important rights, occasionally or routinely get the answer wrong, and yet still demand respect for its finding. This doubt may be accentuated if one endorses the idea of universal institutional scepticism. The preferred solution to this legitimacy problem, grounded on that scepticism, is to advocate that institutions avoid altogether engaging in the balancing exercise if that can be helped. We have seen that this is not impossible. In the Kim Davies scenario one of the solutions suggested was that the public administration uses its executive discretion to avoid apparent clashes between the right of marriage commissioners to object and that of same-sex couples to marry. An official responsible for the public service of celebrating marriages would have a list of marriage commissioners who hold a conscientious objection and would direct, without disclosing that fact, same-sex couples to commissioners who do not hold that objection. Same-sex couples' right to marry would not be interfered with and neither would the right of commissioners holding an objection. There would be no need to decide which of the two rights has to take precedence. If there is no need to balance the rights then the legitimacy question does not even arise.

It seems that such a scheme that avoids rights conflicts could be operated in any service, whether private or public, where it is practicable to have a central authority acting as a filter between the general public and the individual service provider. The central authority would filter the needs of the public with the conscientious convictions of the service provider. Note, however, that a central authority could not be put in place in various scenarios, especially in relation to private services. Take, for example, the case of *Bull v Hall*, where a same-sex couple made an online booking for overnight accommodation in a B&B ran by a Christian couple whose policy was to make available double rooms only for heterosexual married couples. The UK Supreme Court held that the refusal of the B&B's owners to provide the booked room amounted to unlawful discrimination.[50] It is not realistic to expect that B&B owners would work together to form a central authority which would deal with bookings on their behalf exclusively to avoid the possibility of conscience claims.

A scheme which relies on executive discretion to avoid rights conflicts cannot, it seems, provide a universal solution to the legitimacy question because it cannot be universally implemented. Even where it can be implemented, its workability depends on many contingent factors which might or might not be satisfied. Firstly, the scheme to be workable necessitates that not too many individuals hold a conscientious objection. If all or most service providers hold a conscientious objection so that the service to the public is affected then no measure of manoeuvring behind the scenes can avoid the conflict coming into the open and having to be decided in one way or another. In Italy the majority of medical professionals hold themselves to have a conscientious objection to abortions.[51] In this factual scenario it would be impossible to implement this scheme without the service provision to women seeking abortions being extremely delayed.

---

[50] *Bull v Hall* [2013] UKSC 73.
[51] Recent figures show that, as a matter of national average, 70% of qualified professionals are conscientious objectors. See the Italian Ministry of Health's report to the Italian Parliament in 2015, available at www.salute.gov.it/imgs/C_17_pubblicazioni_2428_ulterioriallegati_ulterioreallegato_0_alleg.pdf, table 28.

Second, this scheme, to be workable, necessitates that the legislature and judiciary be ready to allow the executive to exercise its discretion thus. As the *Canadian Marriage Commissioner* case reminds us, even though it avoids explicit conflicts, the scheme may, on full constitutional analysis, be found incompatible by the courts with the state's commitment to promoting same-sex relationships.[52] The Canadian courts still have to investigate that question: an answer in one way or another may frustrate the scheme. Equally, the scheme may be subject to legislative override. In some Canadian provinces, Prince Edward Island for example, the legislature has granted an explicit right to marriage commissioners to refuse to solemnise marriages that are not in accordance with their religious beliefs.[53] Accordingly, a marriage commissioner may openly and lawfully declare that he is opposed to celebrating same-sex marriages. The conflict between rights that could have been avoided would therefore take centre stage and its result, going on the legislative stance alone, would be that conscience would prevail against the right to marriage equality.

Finally, the scheme, even without interference from the legislature or judiciary, may not be put in place as its existence is dependent on the will by the executive to exercise its discretion in a certain way. The example given above was of *Ladele* where the City Council refused to accommodate the claimant's conscientious objection to celebrating same-sex civil partnerships.[54] The executive may lawfully exercise its discretion to take a firm stance on whether or not to support the right to conscientious objection. A decision one way or the other will bring the conflict into the open and would raise the legitimacy question once more.

It seems then that, although at times it may the avoided, an institution will need to provide an answer as to whether conscience or other conflicting rights or aspects of the public interest should prevail and, consequently, the legitimacy question will eventually need to be tackled. Much of the discussion above on the idea of institutional synergy already suggests one way to answer it: no one institution should be seen as in principle able to provide more agreeable answers to the difficult moral questions raised by balancing important rights and interests with each other. This is because all institutions are fallible and may deliver outcomes which are unworkable, badly reasoned or based on factual errors. It would then be inappropriate, on this view, to advocate that any one institution should be assigned, based on some disputable conception of institutional legitimacy, the task to undertake the balancing exercise.

Furthermore, although one can fashion various institution-specific reasons for why each branch of government might be good in balancing rights and public interests, it is not immediately apparent that any of those reasons legitimise any one institution over the other to engage in the balancing exercise. Legislatures, for example, are democratically elected and therefore can claim that their solutions to the balancing exercise, even if disputable, are legitimised by the consent of the electorate.[55] However, judges are independent legal experts who have a rule of law duty to determine the scope of rights even when they conflict.

---

[52] In the Matter of Marriage Commissioners (n 7) at 89.
[53] Marriage Act, RSPEI 1988, c.M-3, s 11.1.
[54] *Ladele* (n 16).
[55] This would be an argument which is close to that of G Webber, *The Negotiable Constitution: On the Limitation of Rights* (Cambridge, Cambridge University Press, 2009).

It is their commitment to fulfilling their rule of law duty coupled with their independent legal expertise which legitimise their solutions to the balancing exercise, even if disputable.[56] Even the executive may claim the legitimacy to be involved in the balancing exercise given that, as discussed above, its institutional strength grounded in discretion may enable explicit conflicts of rights and interests to be avoided altogether.

The approach advocated here then is that, save for well-established constitutional principles indicating otherwise, any institution of government may legitimately provide its own view of how the balancing exercise should be resolved. If that answer can be shown to be unworkable, badly reasoned or factually erroneous, it would be legitimate for another institution of government to intervene and, while residing within its constitutional powers, provide its own view of how the balancing exercise should be resolved. The difficulty of this approach will be to show that an institution has provided a solution to a balancing problem which is unworkable, badly reasoned or factually erroneous which justifies another institution intervening. That assessment will depend on a close analysis of the facts at hand and of the reasoning provided by the institution.

The idea of institutional synergy, which is at the heart of the idea that other institutions may legitimately interfere with another institution's assessment of how important rights and interest should be balanced, does not necessarily repudiate conflicted intervention. Take, for example, the highly controversial USSC decision of *Employment Division v Smith*.[57] In that case the majority of the USSC held that members of the Native American Church could not have access to unemployment benefits having lost their jobs as a result of using the criminally prohibited drug peyote which was required for their religious rites. The court ruling became particularly politically infamous for rejecting a well-settled USSC jurisprudence which had been evolving for about 30 years enshrining the compelling interest test for conscientious objections claims under the First Amendment.[58] Congress and many state legislatures sought to find an alternative basis for re-establishing the pre-*Smith* jurisprudence by enacting the RFRA and similar state-level legislation.

Rather than seeing Congress and the state legislatures' approach as an affront to the rule of law and disrespect to the highest court of the land, one should view that approach as a justified intervention to remedy an unfortunate consequence brought about by *Smith*. This unfortunate consequence was that *Smith* almost entirely eliminated the very desirable ability of courts to consider claims for conscientious exemptions. We have seen in the preceding section why such a scheme is desirable: it complements the legislature's role in dealing with predictable conscientious objection claims by empowering judges with a wide jurisdiction under which less predictable conscientious objection claims may be considered.

The intervention by Congress was not conflict-free. The USSC was not impressed by Congress' intervention and declared the RFRA unconstitutional in relation to its application to states in *City of Boerne v Flores*.[59] It held that Congress, by enacting the RFRA for states, had exceeded its power under the Fourteenth Amendment to enforce the guarantee that states must comply with constitutional rights. The RFRA was in fact a means to require states

---

[56] This would be an argument which is close to that of Allan (n 10).
[57] *Employment Division v Smith* (1990) 485 US 660.
[58] The test had been established in the 1960s in *Sherbert v Verner* (1963) 374 US 398.
[59] *City of Boerne v Flores* (1997) 521 US 507.

to comply with Congress' rather than the USSC's interpretation of the First Amendment. As such, the USSC held that 'Legislation which alters the meaning of the Free Exercise Clause cannot be said to be enforcing the Clause. Congress does not enforce a constitutional right by changing what the right is'.[60] Reacting to *Boerne*, various states enacted legislation modelled after the RFRA[61] and various state constitutional courts have explicitly refused to follow the USSC's decision in *Smith*.[62] Therefore the initial balancing of conscience and drug prohibition undertaken by the court in *Smith*, with its refusal to consider claims for conscientious exemptions under the First Amendment, gave rise not only to a heated intervention by Congress, state legislatures and courts but also to a contra-intervention by the USSC itself in *Boerne*.[63]

Institutional conflict should be expected. Institutions are likely to differ in what they view as the appropriate balance between the right to exemption and other rights and interests. They may well express their diverging views with conflictual language and may at times overstep appropriate constitutional boundaries in doing so – at least *Boerne* teaches us so in relation to Congress' attempt to make the RFRA apply to states. Conflict should not be viewed as undermining the legitimacy of institutions intervening to remedy what they view as a misguided balancing exercise by another institution. Rather, conflict should be viewed as a potentially beneficial feature of a process in which institutions are all involved in the enterprise of providing the best answer they can to the problems raised by conscientious objections. As Carolan puts it:

> mutual engagement of institutions with different perspectives has the potential to produce a decision that is superior to one that may have been achieved by any one of the participants acting alone. … The 'collaborative advantage' is the possibility of these 'synergistic gains'.[64]

The conflictual process initiated by *Smith* produced a situation which is perhaps more desirable than that which existed pre-*Smith*: there now exist at both Federal and state level various RFRA-like legislation and judicial doctrines which enable objectors to bring their claims for exemption to courts (in addition to the ability to lobby Congress and state legislatures for statutory exemptions). Following *Smith*, they may not generally claim a right to exemption under the First Amendment. However, arguably, there are now several routes under which that right may be claimed.

To summarise the view defended here, if possible, the resolution of conflicts of rights should be avoided by adopting a scheme which, relying on executive discretion, accommodates the various rights behind the scenes by avoiding public clashes. This scheme may at times be unavailable and institutions may be forced to decide how conflicts should be resolved. No institution should be seen as in principle more legitimate than another in

---

[60] ibid at 519.

[61] There are 33 states with legislation or constitutional provisions similar to the RFRA. Some of them are listed on the website of the National Conference of State Legislatures at www.ncsl.org/research/civil-and-criminal-justice/state-rfra-statutes.aspx.

[62] Ten state constitutional courts have explicitly declined to follow *Smith* in the interpretation of a state constitution. See P Linton, 'Religious Freedom Claims and Defenses under State Constitutions' 7 *University of St. Thomas Journal of Law and Public Policy* 103.

[63] Since *Gonzales v O Centro Espírita Beneficente União do Vegetal* (2005) 546 US 418, where the USSC applied the RFRA to Federal law, it is clear that the RFRA is not unconstitutional in its application to Federal law.

[64] Carolan, 'Dialogue Isn't Working' (2016) 224.

providing its own view of how the balancing act should be resolved. Rather, if another institution perceives the balancing act undertaken by another institution as lacking in some aspect, it should, acting within its constitutional powers, be seen as legitimated to intervene and provide its own view of how that balancing act should be resolved. The intervention may well produce institutional conflict. That should not be a reason for non-intervention. Institutions have different strengths and weaknesses and may approach the same problem from different perspectives. While this may create institutional conflict, it may in the end create an inter-institutional dialogue which may produce a result which satisfies all the various institutions.

C. Claims of Conscientious Objection May Raise Issues Which Require Particular Expertise to Consider

The fact that claims of conscientious exemptions may arise from unexpected sources and may conflict with varied aspects of the public good and/or other rights may give rise to a need for particular expertise either to comprehend the nature of the objection or to determine how the conflict may be resolved. Take, for example, conscientious objection in the medical context (eg to abortion or contraception) or in the military context (eg to military conscription). Clearly there are different factors at play in considering the conflicts of rights at play. Refusing a medical service to a patient raises, among others, issues of medical professionalism and public health whereas refusing to serve in the army raises issues of national security and military efficiency.

One can see then that considerations of institutional legitimacy, considered above, may directly relate with the ability of institutions to develop expertise to provide principled solutions to whether individuals should be allowed to conscientiously object to complying with legal requirements. The relationship is this: the greater the expertise of an institution in the issues which claims of conscientious objection raise the greater its chances to provide principled outcomes and, consequently, the greater is its claim that its determinations be immune from interventions by other institutions. The expertise problem, in the institutional context, is whether there are institutions which are generally more competent to deal with the issues raised by claims of conscientious objection.

Note that the expertise question is not whether there are institutions which are best suited to determine particular cases of conscientious objection claims, ie given the criteria to lawfully conscientiously object, does an individual satisfy those criteria? That is clearly a job that falls more readily within the remit of fact-finding and independent courts. The expertise question instead focuses on the expertise of any one particular institution to determine whether individuals should be given an exemption from a particular obligation on the basis of a conscientious objection and, if so, what criteria, if any, ought to be satisfied to obtain an exemption.

There seems to be no reasonable prospect to show that any one particular institution can claim superior expertise which will enable it to determine conclusively and appropriately whether or not an exemption in any scenario should be granted. One reason for this seems to be that all institutions are capable of tapping into the relevant sources of technical information, including consulting sector experts (like theologians, philosophers, doctors or marriage consultants, etc), to enable them to comprehend the issues at hand and ultimately to reach a decision one way or the other on exemptions for conscientious objectors. But the main reason for this scepticism is that the expertise problem is ultimately not one about technical expertise but about moral expertise (ie inter alia, the weight to be attached to competing considerations), and it is extremely doubtful that any one institution can claim that it is better than any other in resolving moral questions.

Some theorists have defended the view that legislatures are better moral reasoners than courts. Jeremy Waldron, for example, has argued that judicial reasoning about rights necessarily involves a mixture of pure moral reasoning (the likes of which one can observe in essays by moral philosophers) and technical legal reasoning which takes legal texts and judicial precedent as authoritative. He argues that legislatures, instead, are mostly 'in a position to reason about moral issues directly, on the merits. Members of the legislature speak directly to the issues involved, in a way that is mostly undistracted by legal doctrine or precedents.'[65] He then makes his argument for the superiority of legislative moral reasoning thus:

> We identify certain areas for decision as issues of rights because of the importance of what is actually – not textually – at stake; and it is not appropriate to have that sense of importance skewed by particular formulations, such as 'substantive due process' in the case of abortion, for example, or 'cruel and unusual' in the case of questions about capital punishment. To figure out the issues of rights that are implicated, here, we need to be open to arguments of all sorts. Just because the issues involved are arguably issues of rights, our ultimate decisions about them should not be at the mercy of theories of interpretation or the labored concoction of analogies. The issues are too important for that.[66]

It is however doubtful that the more open-ended mode of moral reasoning of legislatures can claim superiority to the more technical mode of judicial reasoning. The reason for this is that authoritative legal texts and judicial precedent also have their own moral weight and should not, without good reasons, be easily discarded in reasoning about rights. The moral merit of the more technical mode of judicial reasoning is that it takes seriously what previous authoritative texts and decisions have said in order to avoid arbitrariness of treatment: members of the community, past and present, are treated equally by the same standards in as much as those standards apply to them.[67] There might well be good reasons to depart from past standards, especially when they point to a sub-optimal moral solution, and as recent controversial judicial decisions which have departed from earlier precedent such as *Obergefell* testify,[68] the technical mode of judicial reasoning is elastic enough to allow that.

There is here no intention to defend the superiority of judicial reasoning to legislative reasoning in moral matters (or vice versa). The position here defended is that neither mode of reasoning, whatever their moral merits, can guarantee that in specific instances

---

[65] J Waldron, 'Judges as Moral Reasoners' (2009) 7 *International Journal of Constitutional Law* 2, 19.

[66] ibid 23.

[67] This is arguably the moral value exposed by the 'fit' component of Dworkin's theory of law as integrity. See A Green, 'Expanding Law's Empire: Interpretivism, Morality and the Value of Legality' (2011) 4 *European Journal of Legal Studies* 122, 134.

[68] *Obergefell* (n 11) at 23 explicitly overruled an earlier decision of the USSC (*Baker v Nelson* 93 SCt 37), which had affirmed a decision of the Louisiana Supreme Court (*Baker v Nelson* (52867) 267 So 2d 209) which had found that the Constitution does not protect a fundamental right for same-sex couples to marry.

the solutions provided by the institutions are not unworkable, badly reasoned or based on factual errors. One can find equally sub-optimal, excellent or mediocre moral reasoning and decisions about rights produced by courts and legislatures. Also, one should not forget the executive: as discussed in the context of conscientious objection to same-sex marriages, executive discretion may provide the means to avoid the clash between conscience and other rights or aspect of the public good. The quality of the moral reasoning undertaken by institutions will ultimately depend on the contingent fact of the individuals manning those institutions having the ability to engage with difficult moral problems and deal with them in a principled manner. This reinforces the conclusion reached in the discussion of institutional legitimacy: the fact that no institution can claim superior expertise in moral matters justifies institutional interventionism (if consistent with established constitutional principles) whenever an institution perceives that the balancing act undertaken by another institution is lacking in some aspect.

D. It May be Impracticable to Determine the Sincerity of a Conscientious Objector because of the Possible Idiosyncratic Nature of a Conscientious Belief

It may well be possible that a person 'makes up' his beliefs in order to fraudulently benefit from the protection given to conscientious objectors. Take the US case of *Quaintance* to see that this is a serious issue.[69] In that case, a group of related individuals who were the founding members of the Church of Cognizance were charged with being in possession of 50kg of marijuana. The alleged core belief of the members of this church is that 'marijuana is a sacrament and deity and that the consumption of marijuana is a means of worship'.[70] They maintained that the criminal prohibition of narcotics substantially burdened their religious beliefs and was in violation of the RFRA. The trial judge was faced with the challenge to determine whether their claim was sincere or whether 'the Quaintances were acting for the sake of convenience, ie because they believed the church would cloak [them] with the protection of the law'.[71] Having determined that they were drug traffickers who made use of and sold other drugs, the judge found for the latter option. There are a variety of other cases where individuals have claimed to belong to a religion which required the use of drugs. In some cases, courts have found their claims genuine and afforded them the protection of the RFRA, in others, courts have determined that such claims were fraudulent.[72]

The solution to the sincerity problem may appear straightforward: given that one of the routine businesses of courts is to assess the sincerity of individuals who appear before them, we should rely on this expertise before conferring on them the benefit of the right

---

[69] *US v Quaintance* (2010) 608 F 3d 717. The first instance judgment is *US v Quaintance* (2006) 471 F Supp 2d 1153.

[70] *Quaintance* (2006) 471 F Supp 2d 1153, 1155.

[71] ibid at 1174.

[72] Some of these cases are reviewed in J Rhodes, 'Up in Smoke: The Religious Freedom Restoration Act and Federal Marijuana Prosecutions' (2013) 38 *Oklahoma City University Law Review* 319. Successful claims have been brought under the RFRA for personal use of marijuana for religious reasons by Rastafarians. See *United States v Valrey* 2000 WL 692647.

to exemption. The Canadian Supreme Court has explicitly claimed this expertise in the context of conscientious objection when stating

> [A court] is qualified to inquire into the sincerity of a claimant's belief, where sincerity is in fact at issue. … Assessment of sincerity is a question of fact that can be based on several non-exhaustive criteria, including the credibility of a claimant's testimony …, as well as an analysis of whether the alleged belief is consistent with his or her other current religious practices.[73]

If one accepts the above claim that courts have the relevant expertise to deal with the sincerity problem, it might then follow that other solutions to it that rely on other institutions might be sub-optimal. Take, for example, certain statutory exemptions to military conscription which were specifically drafted to exempt individuals who could prove that they belonged to a group well known for its opposition to combatant military service (eg the Quakers).[74] This scheme tackles the sincerity problem in a way which makes it unnecessary to investigate whether the individual at hand actually subscribes to the moral view which gave rise to the exemption. All that the individual has to do under this scheme is to show that he belongs to a certain group, not that he actually holds the view with which the group is associated. The former is arguably an easier task than the latter (it might be sufficient to show that one has been entered into the membership register of the group). This might enable an individual to escape a legal obligation which he had no real conscientious objection to.

The example just given might strengthen the case for always requiring that an exemption should be granted to an individual only after the individual has convinced a court of the sincerity of his conscientious beliefs. However, such a case should not be endorsed without hesitation. This is because imposing such requirement might prove to be too burdensome for particular circumstances and it might be more practicable to rely on the hope that not too many individuals will abuse an exemption that does not require proving the sincerity of one's views.

Take the UK's statutory conscience clause in relation to abortion. This clause does not require a person who holds a conscientious objection to prove his beliefs before being able to enjoy an exemption. There is no evidence that this automatic right to exemption has been claimed either by individuals who do not actually hold a genuine objection or by too many individuals, creating a substantial hurdle to access to lawful abortions.[75] As explained earlier, the same cannot be said for the automatic conscience right in Italy. Furthermore, some have argued that not all conscientious objectors to abortion in Italy are genuine given the social pressure against, and possible career penalties associated with, being a non-objector.[76]

It seems then that the requirement to prove to a court the sincerity of one's views before being granted the right to be exempt should be context-dependent. It should be dependent on how likely it is that the right will be abused. One can see that there will be a high incentive to fraudulently claim the right in relation to certain areas like being able to use drugs or avoiding military service. The possibility of abuse will also depend on the social context: in a social context where there is propensity for abuse, perhaps such as the Italian one in

---

[73] *Syndicat Northcrest v Amselem* (2004) 2 SCR 551, at 51–53.
[74] An historic example in the UK is the Militia Act 1757, XXVI.
[75] See n 40.
[76] F Minerva, 'Conscientious Objection in Italy' (2015) 41 *Journal of Medical Ethics* 170, 172.

relation to abortion, then there will be a solid case to make the enjoyment of that right subject to satisfying a court of the sincerity of one's claimed conscientious beliefs. In a social context where abuse is unlikely, as in the UK in relation to abortion, this requirement may be unnecessary.

E. Conscientious Objectors May Claim Exemption from Obligations Arising from a Variety of Sources

Legal obligations which give rise to conscientious objections may arise from very different sources: primary or secondary legislation (of a federal or sub-federal nature), judicial jurisprudence (whether or not of a constitutional nature), rules of professional bodies and regulators, and even private contracts (such as employment contracts, as in *Eweida*, forbidding employees from wearing religious clothing). In considering the relevance of this issue to the allocation problem, it is obvious that certain institutions or entities will not be able to consider granting exemptions to obligations that arise from a source with superior institutional authority. Take the case of Ms Chaplin, a NHS nurse who defied her employer's dress code policy by refusing to remove her crucifix necklace while on the ward. It would be possible for a UK judge considering her claim that the dress code policy infringes her conscientious beliefs to hold that the policy violates the claimant's right to free conscience and religion under Article 9 ECHR and is therefore unlawful in its application to the claimant.[77] This outcome would not be available to a UK court considering an obligation imposed by an Act of Parliament. A UK court is in fact, given the orthodox understanding of the doctrine of Parliamentary Sovereignty, unable to strike down primary legislation and may only make a declaration of incompatibility under section 4 Human Rights Act which would not affect the legal validity of the legislation.

It might be tempting to think that this state of affairs is unsatisfactory: if the right to exemption is to be taken seriously, then it should be possible for whichever institution is capable of providing principled reasons for exemptions to be able to implement those reasons by granting the exemptions, irrespective of the sources of the obligations objected to. This temptation should be resisted. Remember that in introducing the idea of institutional synergy one of the stipulations was that in using it as a lodestar to finding solutions to the allocation problem, those solutions should have the flexibility to be adaptable to different legal traditions and constitutional arrangements. The reason for such stipulation being that it is doubtful that any one particular institutional arrangement can claim to be in principle a better arrangement for protecting rights. The stipulation is also imbued in the optimistic hope that in whatever legal tradition institutions will be configured in a way in which they can balance each other's strengths and weaknesses in upholding rights. It is in light of this view that it is argued that institutions should work within their constitutional competencies to give effect to conscientious exemptions.

One should, however, be alert to the possibility of being let down even in a legal tradition that allows various institutions, each within its competence, to contribute to upholding rights.

---

[77] *Chaplin v Royal Devon and Exeter NHS Foundation Trust* ET No 1702886/09 [2010] (unreported).

Take the example of the French statutory criminal ban of covering one's face in public[78] and its impact on the right of women in France who decide, not under coercion, to wear the burqa or niqab ('full veil') as a manifestation of their conscientious commitment to their religion.[79] The ban was adopted because the full veil was viewed as being contrary to fundamental social norms of French society. The *exposé des motifs*, which introduced the draft law into the French legislature, states that 'If the deliberate and systematic concealment of the face is a problem, it is because it is simply contrary to the fundamental requirements of "living together" in French society'.[80]

It is, however, at least very doubtful whether the aim of the law, ie to make full veil wearers more sociable members of French society, was actually furthered by the enactment of the criminal ban. The sociological studies of the Human Rights Centre of Ghent University on the implementation of the ban of face covering in Belgium conclude that 'the ban [does] not actually serve its stated purpose: the women concerned [avoid] going out, leading to their isolation and the deterioration of their social life and autonomy, and cases of aggression against them [have] increased'.[81]

Similarly, a sociological report by the Open Society Foundation on the effect of the ban on the lives of women who continue to wear the full veil in France despite the law reveals that: 'A clear majority of women substantially reduced their outdoor activities, including taking their children to school, family outings, shopping, and going to the post office. Many respondents described their perception of living 'in a jail' since the ban's enforcement'.[82]

In the French case there was ample opportunity for various institutions to intervene to influence (if not remedy) the situation whereby the law actually undermined its stated purpose to integrate full veil wearers. Given their constitutional role, not all had the authority to question an Act of the French legislature. For example, a Parliamentary Commission was set up, prior to the enactment of the law, to undertake extensive public consultation among the general public and various experts to ascertain its desirability. The Commission only heard one full veil wearer (after forcing her to remove her veil in order to testify) who actually testified that she, like other French Muslim women, had adopted the full veil freely without any pressure from her family in order to express her religious devotion.[83] Despite this, the Commission recommended the enactment of the ban of the full veil.

Similarly, the Conseil d'Etat was consulted by the French government in its advisory capacity in order to ascertain the legal options available to structure the ban. Instead of a direct ban of the full veil alone, the Conseil d'Etat suggested that a general ban on

---

[78] Law no 2010-1192 of 11 October 2010.

[79] The following discussion draws heavily on J Adenitire, 'Has the European Court of Human Rights Recognised a Legal Right to Glance at a Smile?' (2014) 131 *Law Quarterly Review* 43; Adenitire, 'SAS v France: Fidelity to Law and Conscience' [2015].

[80] Projet de loi interdisant la dissimulation du visage dans l'espace public: Exposé des Motifs, Bill No 2520, 19 May 2010, available at www.assemblee-nationale.fr/13/projets/pl2520.asp.

[81] *SAS v France* (2014) 36 BHRC 617, at 96.

[82] Open Society Justice Initiative, 'After the Ban: The Experiences of 35 Women of the Full-Face Veil in France' (Open Society, September 2013), p 9 at www.opensocietyfoundations.org/sites/default/files/after-the-ban-experience-full-face-veil-france-20140210.pdf. Further studies have been conducted affirming the earlier studies. These are reported in E Brems (ed), *The Experiences of Face Veil Wearers in Europe and the Law* (Cambridge, Cambridge University Press, 2014).

[83] Assemblée Nationale, 'Rapport d'information Au Nom de La Mission d'information Sur La Pratique Du Port Du Voile Intégral Sur Le Territoire National' (Assemblée Nationale, 26 January 2010) at www.assemblee-nationale.fr/13/pdf/rap-info/i2262.pdf.

face-covering would be less legally problematic.[84] The French government followed this advice. In contrast to the two previous institutions, the Constitutional Council had the opportunity to find that the statute violated the constitutional protection of conscience and religion and to enforce its view against the legislature's. Instead, it gave its assent to the ban on the proviso that the law did not apply in places of worship.[85] The ECtHR, another institution which is entitled to challenge the French legislature's view, also held that the legislature did not exceed the margin of appreciation that it enjoyed in complying with Article 9 of the Convention. It held that the French legislature could rely on the novel argument that the practice of full-veil-wearing impermissibly breaches, at least in the French context, 'the right of others to live in a space of socialisation which makes living together easier'.[86] The police and prosecuting authorities who, despite not being able to challenge the legislation, have some discretion in law enforcement, have enforced the law (unlike the DPP in assisted suicide cases in England and Wales). In 2015 it was reported that out of 1,623 controls by the police, fines and cautions had been issued in 1,536 cases.[87]

As the brief analysis above shows, many institutions, including supranational institutions, had the opportunity to intervene to ameliorate the conditions of full veil wearers. In particular, the Constitutional Council and the ECtHR had the legal ability to declare that the ban was inconsistent with legal standards protecting freedom of conscience. They could have done so within their appropriate constitutional role. Yet, they did not as they agreed, despite empirical evidence to the contrary, with the French legislature's assessment that the ban of the full veil furthers the value of 'living together'. This should remind us of the limits of institutional synergy: even if institutions are designed so that they may each contribute, each in its own fashion, in the discourse about rights that does not necessarily entail, in specific cases, that the final outcome will not be unworkable, badly reasoned or based on factual errors.

IV. Conclusion

The analysis undertaken above should indicate the solution here advocated for the allocation problem. No one institution is able to cater adequately for the various issues raised by claims for conscientious exemptions. Institutions may provide adequate solutions for some of those problems. For example, courts may be useful for the sincerity problem; the executive to help avoid some conflicts of rights; the legislature to provide relatively clear, although contestable, statements of who is to be exempt through conscience clauses. Yet, if a holistic solution is to be found to the various issues, the best approach is to see institutions engaged in a synergetic effort to respond to the various complex problems raised by conscientious exemptions.

---

[84] Conseil d'Etat, 'Study of Possible Legal Grounds for Banning the Full Veil' (Plenary General Assembly of the Conseil d'Etat, 25 March 2010) at www.aihja.org/images/users/1/files/fullveil.en.pdf?PHPSESSID=f83dg63dqj61v okoep4kk44ful.

[85] Constitutional Council, 7 October 2010, no 2010-613 DC, at www.conseil-constitutionnel.fr/conseil-constitutionnel/root/bank_mm/anglais/en2010_613dc.pdf, at 5.

[86] *SAS v France* (n 81) at 122.

[87] Some individuals are multiple offenders. See D Bancaud, 'Voile intégral: Quel bilan tirer de la loi cinq ans après?' (*20 Minutes*, 9 October 2015) at www.20minutes.fr/societe/1705679-20151009-voile-integral-bilan-tirer-loi-cinq-ans-apres.

12

Can Secular Non-Natural Persons be Said to Have a 'Conscience'?

FRANK CRANMER*

I. Introduction

In December 2014, I posted a note[1] on the *Law & Religion UK* blog about the First-tier Tribunal hearing in *Exmoor Coast Boat Cruises Ltd*.[2] The Tribunal upheld the refusal by HMRC to allow the company's proprietor and sole shareholder to file its VAT returns on paper instead of electronically on alleged grounds of conscience. I contrasted the judgment with the outcome of an earlier VAT case that had gone the opposite way. My major conclusion was that these kinds of cases are highly fact-sensitive and one cannot simply argue from one set of individual circumstances to another (and, in passing, the same is true of employment cases). Someone then pointed out that I had made no mention of the US Supreme Court's judgment in *Hobby Lobby*[3] – to which I replied that *Hobby Lobby* was nowhere mentioned in the judgment and that it was quite hard enough trying to keep up with developments in the three domestic jurisdictions (the UK, the European Court of Human Rights and the European Court of Justice) without worrying about foreign jurisdictions as well.

But the incident sparked off two trains of thought: first, to what extent are US cases relevant to the UK situation, given that the contextual background provided by the First Amendment is so very different from that of Article 9 ECHR? Secondly, can a non-natural person be said to have a 'conscience' in any event? I tried to address the first of these in an article in the *Ecclesiastical Law Journal*;[4] what follows is an attempt to grapple with the second.

The concept of the 'non-natural person' spans an enormously wide range of institutions – from two-person limited liability partnerships and very small companies to major corporations. I look at some of the recent cases that have considered issues of

---

* I should like to thank Russell Sandberg and John Adenitire for their helpful comments on various versions of this paper as it evolved: the final version has been improved immeasurably in consequence.
[1] F Cranmer, 'Can a Commercial Company have "Beliefs"? *Exmoor Coast Boat Cruises Ltd v Revenue & Customs*' (*Law & Religion UK*, 22 December 2014) at www.lawandreligionuk.com/2014/12/22/can-a-commercial-company-have-beliefs-exmoor-coast-boat-cruises-ltd-v-revenue-customs/.

[2] *Exmoor Coast Boat Cruises Ltd v Revenue & Customs* [2014] UKFTT 1103 (TC).

[3] *Burwell v Hobby Lobby Stores Inc* 573 US __ (2014). For a long analysis of the case, see R Ahdar, 'Companies as Religious Liberty Claimants' (2016) *Oxford Journal of Law and Religion*, 1–27.

[4] F Cranmer, 'How Relevant to the United Kingdom are the "Religion" Cases of the US Supreme Court?' (2016) 18 *Ecc LJ* 300–15.

conscience in relation to commercial activities and I suggest that the courts seem to be more willing than hitherto to give a degree of consideration to the issue of 'conscience' as a legitimate element in the operating decisions of the owners and directors of very small companies and partnerships. I conclude, however, that the arguments for its extension beyond small-to-medium enterprises are unconvincing.

The European Commission of Human Rights (not the Court)[5] had to address the issue on three occasions – and it is with those cases that we begin.

II. *Company X*

In *Company X*,[6] in a brief opinion, the Commission declared inadmissible the application of a limited liability company in the Canton of Zürich objecting to having to pay the cantonal church tax. The Commission discounted simply as a matter of principle the possibility that a limited company might have rights under Article 9 ECHR. It said:

> Even supposing that the applicant's claim may fall within the ambit of Article 9 of the Convention, the Commission is nevertheless of the opinion that a limited liability company, given the fact that it concerns a profit-making corporate body, can neither enjoy nor rely on the rights referred to in Article 9, paragraph 1 of the Convention.[7]

III. *Verein 'Kontakt-Information-Therapie'*

In *Verein 'Kontakt-Information-Therapie (KIT)'*,[8] KIT was a private not-for-profit association (*Verein*) that ran rehabilitation centres for young drug abusers; however, it was officially recognised by the Federal Minister for Health and Environmental Protection. When two of its therapists were served witness summonses in a criminal trial before the District Court, KIT's board of directors announced that neither would be released from duty nor permitted to disclose confidential information about clients. The therapists persisted and were fined.

Before the Commission, KIT and one of the therapists, Mr Hagen, alleged violations of Article 3 ECHR (inhuman or degrading treatment or punishment) and Article 3 taken with Article 13 (effective remedy), on the grounds that answering the District Court's summons would have brought them into disgrace. They also argued under Article 9 that disclosure of confidential information given by former or present clients gave rise to an untenable conflict of interest and that they could not, in good faith, have complied.[9]

On the issue of the purported Convention rights of the *Verein*, the Commission held that the right to freedom of conscience and the right not to be subjected to degrading

---

[5] The case predated the entry into force of Protocol 11 ECHR.

[6] *Company X v Switzerland* App n 7865/77 (Commission Decision, 27 February 1979).

[7] The Commission's decision is available at www.bailii.org/eu/cases/ECHR/1979/10.pdf.

[8] *Verein 'Kontakt-Information-Therapie' (KIT)* and *Siegfried Hagen v Austria* App no 11921/86 (Commission Decision, 12 October 1988).

[9] They also alleged violations of other Articles which need not concern us here.

treatment or punishment were by their very nature not susceptible of being exercised by a legal person such as a private association. It also drew a distinction between freedom of *conscience* and freedom of *religion*, because the latter could also be claimed by a church. It held the application inadmissible.

IV. *Kustannus*

The Commission considered the matter again in 1997, in *Kustannus*.[10] The case was about a claim that the church tax levied on the Freethinker Publishing Company Ltd – the purpose of which was to propagate secular, anti-religious ideas – violated its Article 9 rights because none of the company's members were members of either of the Finnish State Churches at the relevant time. The application was brought both by the freethinkers as an unincorporated association and by the limited company on the basis that the unincorporated association could potentially have rights under Article 9(1). The Commission ruled the claim inadmissible:

> The Commission has repeatedly held that a church body or an association with religious and philosophical objects is capable of possessing and exercising the right to freedom of religion, since an application by such a body is in reality lodged on behalf of its members … By contrast, the Commission has held that a limited liability company, given the fact that it concerns a profit-making corporate body, can neither enjoy nor rely on the rights referred to in Article 9 para. 1.

That said, however, the Commission went on to concede that:

> [T]he general right to freedom of religion includes, inter alia, freedom to manifest a religion or 'belief' either alone or 'in community with others' whether in public or in private. The Commission would therefore not exclude that the applicant association is in principle capable of possessing and exercising rights under Article 9 para. 1.

But, it concluded, since the complaint was 'merely' about the obligation of the applicant company to pay taxes reserved for church activities, though the company form may have been 'a deliberate choice on the part of the applicant association and its branches for the pursuance of part of the freethinkers' activities', nevertheless, for the purposes of domestic law it was a corporate body with limited liability and could not, as a company, plead Article 9.

Whether the Court would have come to that conclusion 20 years later is at least arguable. Shortly after the Commission's ruling in *Kustannus*, the Court held unanimously in *Société Colas Est*[11] – a complaint by three companies under Article 8 (Right to respect for private and family life) – that 'the time has come to hold that in certain circumstances the rights guaranteed by Article 8 of the Convention may be construed as including the right to respect for a company's registered office, branches or other business premises'.[12] Similarly, in *Bernh Larsen*,[13] by five votes to two it upheld complaints by three applicant

[10] *Kustannus Oy Vapaa & Ors v Finland* (1996) DR 85.
[11] *Société Colas Est & Ors v France* [2002] ECHR 421.
[12] ibid at 41.
[13] *Bernh Larsen Holding AS & Ors v Norway* [2013] ECHR 220.

companies that their Article 8 rights had been infringed by the actions of the Directorate of Taxation in obliging them to surrender for scrutiny backup copies of the material on their common servers.

V. *Blackburn*

The issue came up in relation to UK VAT law in 2013 in *Blackburn*,[14] which slightly predates *Hobby Lobby*. Mr and Mrs Blackburn were beekeepers trading as a partnership, Cornish Moorland Honey. The partnership had registered *voluntarily* for VAT so that the Blackburns could recover input tax on supplies made to them in course of business, such as the VAT on jars. They were also Seventh-day Adventists who shunned computers, the internet, television and mobile phones (but not fixed-line phones) as a corrupting influence.

Initially, filing VAT returns online had been made compulsory for all businesses with a turnover of over £100,000 and for any newly registered business with effect from 1 April 2010. From 1 April 2012, however, online filing was extended to all businesses. However, Regulation 25A(6)(a) of the Value Added Tax Regulations 1995/2518, as amended, exempts from the requirement to file VAT returns online a person who is 'a practising member of a religious society or order whose beliefs are incompatible with the use of electronic communications'. So the Blackburns claimed the religious exemption and were refused, HMRC arguing in a letter of 4 May 2012 that 'No connection to the beliefs of any individual religious society or order has been shown in the way contemplated by the regulation'.[15]

At their appeal against HMRC's refusal to exempt them on religious grounds, Mr Blackburn conceded that his church did not directly require adherents to avoid electronic communications – indeed, the church has its own website.[16] But the church also warns its adherents about their dangers. Radio, television and the internet

> can be great educational agencies through which we can enlarge our knowledge of world events and enjoy important discussions and the best in music. Unfortunately, however, modern mass media also can bring to their audiences almost continuous theatrical and other performances with influences that are neither wholesome nor uplifting. If we are not discriminating, they will bring sordid programs [*sic*] right into our homes.[17]

Mr Blackburn argued that their faith required them to live in accordance with the Bible and he cited several Biblical texts which he interpreted as requiring them to shun computers, television and mobile phones. He had no difficulty in dealing with people such as his suppliers who used computers; but his own choice was neither to use one himself nor to ask someone to use one on his behalf.

HMRC argued in rebuttal that the Blackburns' choice was personal rather than religious because electronic communications were not incompatible with the tenets of their church, besides which, they did not object to using non-mobile phones, so they clearly had no

---

[14] *Blackburn & Anor v Revenue & Customs* [2013] UKFTT 525 (TC).
[15] ibid at 4.
[16] www.adventist.org/en/.
[17] General Conference of Seventh-day Adventists, *Seventh-day Adventist Church Manual* (Nampa, Idaho, Pacific Press Publishing Association, 2016) 148.

principled objection to *all* electronic communications. Mr Blackburn replied that their most important belief was that only the righteous would be saved at the Second Coming and, *to be righteous, they had to act in accordance with conscience*: in short, that the requirement to file electronically would go against their conscientiously held principles, even though it was not a matter imposed on them by their religion.

Tribunal Judge Mosedale allowed the appeal. Given that the Blackburns' church did not consider its beliefs to be incompatible with the use of electronic communications, she concluded that, 'if seen purely as a question of the normal rules of construction and without reference to the effect of the Human Rights Act 1998'[18] the appellants were not entitled to the religious exemption under Regulation 25A(6)(a). However, section 3 of the Act applied and this required the tribunal to interpret the Regulations, in so far as possible, in a manner compatible with Convention rights. She also noted at paragraph 42, on a related point, that Rafferty LJ had observed in *Bull*[19] that 'unless the primary legislation dictates the contents of the Regulations …, any judge can strike down subordinate legislation: see section 4(3) of the Human Rights Act 1998'. However, that did not prove necessary because the relevant primary legislation did not constrain the construal of the Regulations, which could be read compatibly with Article 9.

TJ Mosedale accepted that using a computer or having an agent use one on their behalf was contrary to the Blackburns' religious beliefs and that they were manifesting those beliefs by shunning computers. Further, she was satisfied that their position passed the test in *Eweida & Ors*[20] that, though the act in question had to be intimately linked to the religion or belief in order to count as a 'manifestation' within the meaning of Article 9 ECHR 'there is no requirement on the applicant to establish that he or she acted in fulfilment of a duty mandated by the religion in question'.[21] She was therefore satisfied that the Blackburns were acting in fulfilment of a duty mandated by their religion *as they perceived it*.[22] Moreover, she rejected HMRC's contention that they could avoid using a computer to file online by using a terminal in a public library or employing an agent to file on their behalf.[23] She also dismissed HMRC's suggestion that they could simply avoid online filing by deregistering for VAT: recovery of input tax was a fundamental right under European Union law and it was disproportionate that they should be required to give up that right and suffer the financial consequences as the cost of abiding by their religious beliefs.[24] The requirement to file online was therefore an undue restriction of their rights under Article 9(1) and, accordingly, the Regulations had to be interpreted so as to make the exemption available to the Blackburns.[25]

She did not, however, address the issue as to whether the *partnership itself* – as opposed to the two partners individually – had a right to claim a conscientious objection since, under the terms of section 1 of the Partnership Act 1890, an unincorporated partnership does not have separate legal personality from its constituent partners.

---

[18] *Blackburn* (n 14) at 33.
[19] *Bull & Bull v Hall & Preddy* [2012] EWCA Civ 83 *obiter* at 28.
[20] *Eweida & Ors v United Kingdom* [2013] ECHR 37.
[21] ibid at 82.
[22] *Blackburn* (n 14) at 52.
[23] ibid at 54.
[24] ibid at 58.
[25] ibid at 59.

VI. *Hobby Lobby*

There were three appellants in *Hobby Lobby*: Hobby Lobby Stores, Inc, Mardel, Inc, and Conestoga Wood Specialties Corporation, all of which were closely held companies. The first two were owned and run by the Green family – conservative mainstream Christians – and the third by the Hahns, who are Mennonites. Both families held a sincere religious belief that human life begins at conception. The US Department of Health and Human Services had made a regulation under the Patient Protection and Affordable Care Act 2010 (aka 'Obamacare') that required employers to cover certain contraceptive provision for their female employees. The proprietors of the three appellant companies objected on religious and moral grounds to having to comply with the regulation. The US Court of Appeals for the Tenth Circuit had ruled in favour of Hobby Lobby and Mardel, while the US Court of Appeals for the Third Circuit had held that Conestoga did not have standing to challenge the birth control mandate.

Under the regulation, religious employers such as churches and religious non-profit organisations with religious objections were exempt; but the US government argued that the three appellants could not *themselves* claim to have religious beliefs because they were secular, for-profit corporations. Their *owners* might have religious objections; but in law the owners were separate entities from their corporations, with different rights and obligations. By a 5:4 majority, however, the Supreme Court rejected that argument and found in favour of the three companies, holding that the regulation violated the provisions of the Religious Freedom Restoration Act 1993 (RFRA)[26] because Congress had included corporations within RFRA's definition of 'persons'.

Section 2(5)(b) of RFRA states that:

The purposes of this Act are –

(1)   to restore the compelling interest test as set forth in *Sherbert v. Verner*, 374 U.S. 398 (1963) and *Wisconsin v. Yoder*, 406 U.S. 205 (1972) and to guarantee its application in all cases where free exercise of religion is substantially burdened; and

(2)   to provide a claim or defense to *persons* whose religious exercise is substantially burdened by government.[27]

Delivering the majority Opinion, Alito J rejected the argument that the owners of companies had forfeited protection under RFRA when they decided to organise their businesses as corporations rather than sole proprietorships or general partnerships: 'The plain terms of RFRA make it perfectly clear that Congress did not discriminate in this way against men and women who wish to run their businesses as for-profit corporations in the manner required by their religious beliefs'.[28] Furthermore, while

the idea that unrelated shareholders – including institutional investors with their own set of stakeholders – would agree to run a corporation under the same religious beliefs seems

---

[26] In *City of Boerne v Flores* 521 US 507 (1997) the Supreme Court had held the RFRA unconstitutional *as it applied to the states*, ruling that the Act was not a proper exercise of Congress's power under s 5 of the Fourteenth Amendment 'to enforce, by appropriate legislation, the provisions of this article': but the RFRA continues to apply to the activities of the Federal Government.

[27] Emphasis added.

[28] *Burwell v Hobby Lobby Stores*, Inc 573 US __ (2014), 2.

improbable …, The companies in the cases before us are closely held corporations, each owned and controlled by members of a single family, and no one has disputed the sincerity of their religious beliefs.[29]

The majority's reasoning, in brief, was that a corporation

is simply a form of organization used by human beings to achieve desired ends. An established body of law specifies the rights and obligations of the people (including shareholders, officers, and employees) who are associated with a corporation in one way or another. When rights, whether constitutional or statutory, are extended to corporations, the purpose is to protect the rights of these people. For example, extending Fourth Amendment protection to corporations protects the privacy interests of employees and others associated with the company … And *protecting the free-exercise rights of corporations like Hobby Lobby … protects the religious liberty of the humans who own and control those companies.*[30]

In her dissent, however, Ginsburg J accused the majority, in essence, of muddled thinking:

The First Amendment's free exercise protections … shelter churches and other nonprofit religion-based organizations. 'For many individuals, religious activity derives meaning in large measure from participation in a larger religious community,' and 'furtherance of the autonomy of religious organizations often furthers individual religious freedom as well.'[31] The Court's 'special solicitude to the rights of religious organizations,'[32] however, is just that. No such solicitude is traditional for commercial organizations. Indeed, until today, religious exemptions had never been extended to any entity operating in 'the commercial, profit-making world'.[33] The reason why is hardly obscure. Religious organizations exist to foster the interests of persons subscribing to the same religious faith. Not so of for-profit corporations. *Workers who sustain the operations of those corporations commonly are not drawn from one religious community. Indeed, by law, no religion-based criterion can restrict the work force of for-profit corporations.*[34] *The distinction between a community made up of believers in the same religion and one embracing persons of diverse beliefs, clear as it is, constantly escapes the Court's attention.*[35]

VII. *Exmoor Coast Boat Cruises*

In *Exmoor Coast*,[36] which post-dated *Hobby Lobby*, HMRC had refused the company's request for permission to file its VAT returns on paper instead of electronically. It appealed and was represented by Mr Oxenham, its sole director and shareholder. The technical VAT details of the appeal need not concern us: the interest for the present discussion is

---

[29] ibid.

[30] ibid 18 (emphasis added).

[31] *Corporation of Presiding Bishop of Church of Jesus Christ of Latter-day Saints v Amos*, 483 US 327, 342 (1987) (Brennan, J., concurring in judgment).

[32] *Hosanna-Tabor Evangelical Lutheran Church and School v EEOC* 565 US_(2012), 14.

[33] *Amos* (n 31) 337.

[34] See 42 USC §§2000e(b), 2000e–1(a), 2000e–2(a); cf *Trans World Airlines, In. v Hardison*, 432 US 63, 80–81 (1977). Title VII requires reasonable accommodation of an employee's religious exercise, but such accommodation must not come 'at the expense of other [employees]'.

[35] *Hobby Lobby* (n 28) 15 (emphasis added).

[36] *Exmoor Coast Boat Cruises Ltd v Revenue & Customs* [2014] UKFTT 1103 (TC).

that Mr Oxenham claimed exemption from the obligation to file on-line *on grounds of religious belief*, relying, like the Blackburns, on Regulation 25A(6)(a) Value Added Tax Regulations 1995/2518.

HMRC had refused the exemption because its officials were not satisfied that Mr Oxenham did not and would not use a computer and because he had not demonstrated to their satisfaction that he was a member of a religious society whose beliefs were incompatible with the use of computers. Moreover, his precise religious affiliation seemed to be in some doubt; he appeared to be claiming that he was a member of a branch of the Plymouth Brethren but TJ Mosedale was not convinced. He also appeared to be objecting to online filing because he believed that it contributed to global warming: a claim not entirely dissimilar from that in the well-known case of *Grainger v Nicholson*.[37]

Neither Mr Oxenham's appeal for exemption under Regulation 25A(6)(a) nor his appeal to Article 9 ECHR convinced Judge Mosedale. As to his claim of exemption under Regulation 25A(6)(a), she concluded that the appellant company could not benefit from it because:

(1)   The appellant does not have beliefs as it is a company.
(2)   Even if its director's beliefs were the beliefs to which the legislation referred, Mr Oxenham is not a practising member of a religious society or order whose beliefs are incompatible with the use of electronic communications.[38]

Very much in line with the majority opinion in *Hobby Lobby*, however, she did not accept that in no circumstances could a commercial company have human rights. In *Pine Valley Developments,* the ECtHR had stated that the corporate applicants in that case, Pine Valley Developments and Healy Holdings, 'were no more than vehicles through which Mr Healy [*the third applicant*] proposed to implement the development for which outline planning permission had been granted' and that 'it would be artificial to draw distinctions between the three applicants as regards their entitlement to claim to be "victims" of a violation'.[39]

On that basis, TJ Mosedale was of opinion that

a company has human rights if and to the extent it is the alter ego of a person (or, potentially, a group of people). Therefore, it must be seen as being in the shoes of that person and must possess the same human rights because any other decision would deny that person his human rights. Therefore, while it is ludicrous to suggest a company has a religion, or private life or family, nevertheless a company which is the alter ego of a person can be a victim of a breach of A9 (the right to manifest its religion) if, were it not so protected, that person's human rights would be breached.[40]

Though HMRC had accepted that Article 9 protected more than just religious beliefs and that, potentially, beliefs and a moral code about climate change could be protected under

---

[37] *Grainger plc v Nicholson* [2009] ICR 360 (EAT). In that case the claimant held the philosophical belief that 'mankind is heading towards catastrophic climate change and therefore we are all under a moral duty to lead our lives in a manner which mitigates or avoids this catastrophe for the benefit of future generations, and to persuade others to do the same'. The EAT held that this belief was a protected philosophical belief under the anti-discrimination legislation.
[38] *Exmoor Coast* (n 36) at 54 (emphasis added).
[39] *Pine Valley Developments Ltd & Ors v Ireland (Article 50)* [1991] ECHR 55, at 42.
[40] *Exmoor Coast* (n 36) at 71–72 (emphasis added).

that Article, it had *not* accepted, on the facts, that Mr Oxenham's beliefs were protected. Neither did TJ Mosedale:

> A Tribunal is very reluctant to assess the quality of a person's moral or religious beliefs. Nevertheless, it has to be the case that the law cannot protect every belief as that would be a licence to everyone to pick and choose which laws they choose to obey and those that they ignore … However, I do not need to rule on the quality of Mr Oxenham's beliefs in order to decide the case. This is because the right relied on by the appellant is the right to manifest religion and belief in practice and observance. There is no suggestion that the requirement to file online interferes with Mr Oxenham's right to freedom of thought and his right to change his religion. So does it interfere with his right to manifest his beliefs?[41]

In her view, the simple answer to that question, on the evidence, was 'no':

> Mr Oxenham has beliefs, which, while they include a strong disinclination to use the internet, nevertheless are compatible with him using the internet to advertise his business and to file (via agents acting on his or his companies' behalf) a number of other returns online. It is therefore apparent that requiring him to file another return online does not prevent him manifesting his religious or other beliefs.[42]

She dismissed the appeal;[43] and a subsequent appeal on the ground that he should be exempted from online filing under the terms of Regulation 25A(6)(c) for reason of his age was also dismissed.[44]

VIII. *Ashers Baking*

In what everyone has come to know as *Ashers Baking*,[45] the claimant, Gareth Lee, placed an order with Mrs Karen McArthur for a customised cake for a private event in May 2014 to

---

[41] ibid at 78–80.

[42] ibid at 81.

[43] *Exmoor Coast* was subsequently cited in *Harvey (T/A Sun Ice Air Conditioning) v Revenue & Customs (VAT – APPEALS: Other)* [2016] UKFTT 266 (TC), in which the claimant, Mr Harvey, was unsuccessful in his appeal against HMRC's refusal to exempt him on religious grounds from the obligation to file his VAT returns electronically. HMRC had responded with a request for further details of his religious beliefs and his answer had been that there was 'only one person who can determin (*sic*) my religious beliefs and that is me and no other. You are (or other) not qualified to make such a decision on my behalf' (at para 7) and in response to a second request had replied: 'we have provided the information required to your mandation review team, who as indicated are not qualified to judge my religious beliefs … Unfortunately, I cannot concur with your statutory regulations as these have been voted for by members of parliament, who have sworn an allegiance to the HM Queen, who is head of the Christian Church of England, which is not my choice of faith' (at para 8). Though she dismissed the appeal, Tribunal Judge Allatt pointed out, *inter alia*, that the legislation was ambiguous: it was not clear whether the 'beliefs that are incompatible' with the requirement to file electronically were those of the individual or those of the society or order to which that person claimed to belong (at para 23). And though Article 9 ECHR clearly went further than protecting only the religious beliefs of a 'religious society or order' (at para 32), she agreed with TJ Mosedale in *Exmoor Coast* that, though Tribunals were very reluctant to assess the quality of individual moral or religious beliefs, the law could not protect *every* belief, since to do so would give people *carte blanche* to pick and choose (at para 33). It should be noted, however, that *Harvey* was about a sole trader rather than a partnership or limited company.

[44] *Glen Lyn Generations Ltd & Exmoor Coast Boat Cruises Ltd v Revenue & Customs* [2018] UKFTT 394 (TC).

[45] *Lee v Ashers Baking Co Ltd & Anor* [2015] NICty 2, *Lee v McArthur & Ors* [2016] NICA 39, *Lee v Ashers Baking Company Ltd & Ors (Northern Ireland)* [2018] UKSC 49.

mark the end of Northern Ireland Anti-Homophobic Week: it was to be iced with a colour picture of 'Bert and Ernie' (the logo for QueerSpace) and the headline caption, 'Support Gay Marriage'. Ashers Baking is owned by the McArthur family, who are Reformed Presbyterians and, subsequently, Mrs McArthur telephoned Mr Lee and told him that the order could not be fulfilled as the bakery was a 'Christian business' and that she should not have accepted the order in the first place. Mr Lee won in the county court, where District Judge Brownlie cited *Kustannus* in support of her conclusion that Ashers Baking, as a limited company, could not itself invoke Article 9 rights.[46] The McArthurs appealed.

The Court of Appeal found for Mr Lee. The first and second appellants were the company's directors, Colin and Karen McArthur, but the third appellant was the company itself. The McArthurs conceded that they had cancelled the order because of their religious beliefs and opposition to the legalisation of same-sex marriage, which they regarded as sinful.

Like DJ Brownlie at first instance,[47] Morgan LCJ pointed out – almost in passing, because it did not prove necessary to explore the point further – that Ashers Baking was

> a limited company. It does not have any religious objectives in its Memorandum and Articles of Association although it is common cause that its name derives from a passage in the Bible, Genesis 49:20: "*Bread from Asher shall be rich, and he shall yield royal dainties*".[48]

Whether or not a limited company could plead conscientious objection under Article 9 ECHR was not addressed: in the county court hearing, DJ Brownlie had undertaken a painstaking analysis to establish whether the limitations placed upon the McArthurs' rights under Article 9(1) were prescribed by law, intended to achieve a legitimate objective and 'necessary in a democratic society', in accordance with Article 9(2) – and had concluded that they fulfilled the Article 9(2) criteria.[49] The Court of Appeal chose not to explore further the possibility that a non-natural person could be said to have a conscience. However, my inference from the inclusion of the reference to the company's Memorandum and Articles is that, had it been necessary to do so, the Court would have been inclined to concentrate on the conscientious objections of Mr and Mrs McArthur rather than those of Ashers Baking.

Ashers Baking and the McArthurs then appealed to the Supreme Court[50] and, in a unanimous judgment, the Supreme Court found for the appellants, concluding that there had been no associative discrimination: 'In a nutshell, the objection was to the message and not to any particular person or persons'.[51] Moreover, under the provisions of the Fair Employment and Treatment (Northern Ireland) Order 1998, 'the less favourable treatment prohibited by FETO must be on the grounds of religious belief or political opinion of

---

[46] *Lee v Ashers Baking Co Ltd & Anor* [2015] NICty 2, at 98.
[47] ibid at 12.
[48] *Lee v McArthur & Ors* (n 45) at 3.
[49] *Lee v Ashers Baking Co Ltd* (n 45) at 75.
[50] At the same time, the Attorney General for Northern Ireland referred the question of the validity of the prohibitions of discrimination in the provision of goods, facilities or services on the ground of religious belief or political opinion under the Fair Employment and Treatment (Northern Ireland) Order 1998 and the Equality Act (Sexual Orientation) Regulations (Northern Ireland) 2006, insofar as they impose civil liability for the refusal to express a political opinion or express a view on a matter of public policy contrary to the religious belief of the person refusing to express that view: *Lee v Ashers Baking Company Ltd & Ors* (Northern Ireland) (n 45) at 3.
[51] ibid at 34.

someone other than the person meting out that treatment'.[52] The objection had not been to Mr Lee because he, or anyone with whom he associated, held a political opinion supporting gay marriage: the objection had been to being required to promote the message on the cake. 'The less favourable treatment was afforded to the message not to the man' – and Ashers had been quite prepared to serve him in other ways.[53]

As to the issue of Convention rights, the Court said:

> As the courts below reached a different conclusion on this issue, they did not have to consider the position of the company separately from that of Mr and Mrs McArthur. It is the case that in *X v Switzerland* … and in *Kustannus Oy Vapaa Ajattelija Ab v Finland* … the European Commission of Human Rights held that limited companies could not rely upon article 9(1) to resist paying church taxes. In this case, however, to hold the company liable when the McArthurs are not would effectively negate their convention rights. *In holding that the company is not liable, this court is not holding that the company has rights under article 9; rather, it is upholding the rights of the McArthurs under that article.*[54]

IX. So can a Corporation be Said to Have a 'Conscience'?

In 1982, Kenneth Goodpaster and John Matthews, Jr argued in a much-quoted article in the *Harvard Business Review* that the suggestion that it was improper (or, at best, value-free) for organisations to conduct themselves in conformity with the ordinary principles of morality was not only wrong but counter-productive: 'In our opinion, this line of thought represents a tremendous barrier to the development of business ethics both as a field of inquiry and as a practical force in managerial decision making'.[55]

Jason Iuliano takes this further, contending that 'corporations possess beliefs that are truly their own. They are distinct entities with distinct intentional states'[56] and argues that not-for-profit corporations – though *not* commercial corporations – qualify for protection under the Free Exercise Clause of the First Amendment and the RFRA.

Rex Ahdar[57] suggests that 'there are some companies who pursue moral and religious objectives in tandem with profit-making. This is hardly a novel observation';[58] and goes on to quote Pope John Paul II in *Centesimus Annus*, who said:

> the purpose of a business firm is not simply to make a profit, but is to be found in its very existence as a *community of persons* who in various ways are endeavouring to satisfy their basic needs, and who form a particular group at the service of the whole of society. Profit is a regulator of the life of a business, but it is not the only one; *other human and moral factors* must also be considered which, in the long term, are at least equally important for the life of a business.[59]

---

[52] ibid at 45.
[53] ibid at 47.
[54] ibid at 57 (emphasis added).
[55] KE Goodpaster and JB Matthews, 'Can a Corporation Have a Conscience?' (1982) 60 *Harvard Business Review* 132, 133.
[56] J Iuliano, 'Do Corporations Have Religious Beliefs?' (2015) 90 *Indiana Law Journal*: 47, 49.
[57] Ahdar, 'Religious Liberty Claimants' (2016).
[58] ibid 4.
[59] *Centesimus Annus*: official English translation of the Encyclical Letter on the hundredth anniversary of *Rerum Novarum* (Vatican, 1991) available at w2.vatican.va/content/john-paul-ii/en/encyclicals/documents/hf_jp-ii_enc_01051991_centesimus-annus.html.

Maybe – but I would suggest that that statement raises almost as many questions as it presumes to answer. Is a business firm *necessarily* 'a community of persons'? And if it is, is such a community *necessarily* 'a particular group at the service of the whole of society'? (I should have thought that many businesses, even large ones, were extremely *niche* in their target clientele.) *Human* factors are undoubtedly important for the life of a business – not least, attracting customers and recruiting and retaining staff – but are *moral* factors 'at least equally important'?

In the course of preparing this paper I was helpfully directed to the judgment of the Supreme Court of Canada in *Loyola High School*.[60] In the minority judgment, McLachlin CJ noted Dickson CJ's comment in *Edwards Books*[61] at p 784 that 'a business corporation cannot possess religious beliefs'; but she then went on to point out, at paragraph 99, that 'a religious organization may in a very real sense have religious beliefs and rights'. In the majority judgment, Abella J however concluded, at paragraph 34, that it was not necessary to decide whether Loyola itself, as a corporation, had religious rights under the Charter since the Minister was 'bound in any event to exercise her discretion in a way that respects the values underlying the grant of her decision-making authority, including the Charter-protected religious freedom of the members of the Loyola community who seek to offer and wish to receive a Catholic education'. The significance of this for Canadian law is that it is not clear that religious institutions as such have a human right under the Charter of Fundamental Rights and Freedoms to freedom of religion.

In the context of English and Scots law, however, the rights of *religious*, as opposed to secular, organisations, are already given exceptional treatment under section 13 Human Rights Act 1998[62] and in matters such as employment policy[63] – which suggests that it is entirely reasonable, and settled law, to impute a moral sense to a religious corporation or trust. It may also be reasonable to impute a moral sense to the directors of a closely held company or to the partners of a small limited liability partnership where – as TJ Mosedale observed in *Exmoor Boat Cruises* – the non-natural person is 'the *alter ego* of a person (or, potentially, a group of people)'.[64] But whether a large *secular* corporation can be said to be the *alter ego* of its shareholders – many of which are, in any case, likely *themselves* to be corporations such as banks and investment funds – is very much more doubtful.

'MegaCorp plc' may well consist in part of natural *persons* – at least in terms of its directors and employees – but whether, together with their non-corporate shareholders, those persons constitute a *community* is a much more open question. Jerry Mander, for example, argues that

> a corporation is essentially a machine, a technological structure, an organization that follows its own principles and its own morality, and in which human morality is anomalous. Because of this double standard – one for human beings and another for 'fictitious persons' like

---

[60] *Loyola High School v Quebec (Attorney General)* 2015 SCC 12 (CanLII).

[61] *R v Edwards Books and Art Ltd* 1986 CanLII 12 (SCC).

[62] 'If a court's determination of any question arising under this Act might affect the exercise by a religious organisation (itself *or its members collectively*) of the Convention right to freedom of thought, conscience and religion, it must have particular regard to the importance of that right' (emphasis added).

[63] See, for example, Sch 9, paras 2–3 Equality Act 2010.

[64] *Exmoor Coast* (n 36) at 71.

corporations – we sometimes see bizarre behavior from executives who, though knowing what is right and moral, behave in a contrary fashion.[65]

– in support of which, see the various banking scandals, *passim*.[66] And Rex Ahdar himself concedes that:

> Few companies would be able to satisfy the requirement that they genuinely seek an exemption for religious and not (say) financial or competitive advantage reasons. In large public companies, the multiplicity of persons holding different worldviews and religious positions would make a coherent, sincere claim formidably difficult, if not impossible, to sustain.[67]

X. Conclusion

To return to Ginsburg J's dissent in *Hobby Lobby*, perhaps her distinction between religious organisations and for-profit corporations is now simply too blunt in a UK context – or even maybe, given the view of the majority of SCOTUS, in a US one. It seems clear from the judgments in *Blackburn* and *Exmoor Coast Boat Cruises* that UK VAT law, at any rate, may be moving towards recognising the religious rights of small businesses even though, taken together, the two judgments seem rather contradictory: same Regulations, same judge, similar claims, different results.

The reason for the difference, in my view, is that claims of this nature are highly fact-sensitive. It was clear that Mr and Mrs Blackburn had a principled objection to using computers and the internet as a matter of personal conviction even though their church did not – and I would suggest that whether their objection was, strictly speaking, on grounds of 'religion' or on grounds of 'conscience' is not of great importance, since in their case it was hardly possible to draw a distinction between the two. But, in any event, it was not necessary to consider whether or not Cornish Moorland Honey was entitled to the protection of Article 9 because the partnership did not have any separate personality from the partners. In Mr Oxenham's case, however, the company was a separate legal entity: his claim was dismissed because he was inconsistent in his refusal to use electronic communications and IT and if his objection was based on religious or philosophical principles he failed to demonstrate that fact to TJ Mosedale's satisfaction. But even as she rejected his claim, TJ Mosedale was still prepared to look beyond the corporate form of the company to Mr Oxenham's personal beliefs – however inconsistently he may have applied them.

In *Ashers Baking*, the Supreme Court was very careful to maintain a distinction between the Article 9 rights of the McArthurs and the *absence* of such rights in relation to the company – and did not appear to believe that the company, as a non-natural person, could be said to have any kind of 'conscience' at all.[68] Nevertheless, in concluding that to hold the

---

[65] J Mander, *In the Absence of the Sacred* (San Francisco, Sierra Club Books, 1991) 125.

[66] Of which, perhaps, the most flagrant was the Bank of Commerce and Credit International, whose collapse was subsequently condemned by the then Chancellor of the Exchequer, Norman Lamont, as 'a severe blow to many thousands of depositors all over the world. It was the result of a fraud unparalleled both in scale and cunning': HC Deb 22 October 1992 vol 212 c574.

[67] *Ahdar* (n 3) 3.

[68] Perhaps it is worth noting, in passing, that in the period between the oral arguments and the judgment the *Belfast Telegraph* reported that Ashers had accepted – then later rejected – an order for a cake bearing the legend

company liable would be, effectively, to negate the McArthurs' Convention rights, the Court has given fresh impetus to the issues raised in this chapter.

Peter Edge suggests that the judgment should prompt

> new discussions around the basis for corporations' possession of fundamental rights (or in the Supreme Court's terms, when they should be treated as if they had fundamental rights in order to protect the rights of natural persons), and in particular a mature discussion about *what* religious rights a corporation may be capable of possessing, and *how* legal actors are to identify the religious beliefs of a corporation.[69]

But perhaps – for the United Kingdom, at any rate – those discussions are only just beginning.

'Gay marriage rocks! Happy engagement, Andy and Joe! Lots of love xxx': A Gordon, 'Ashers Refuses to Make Gay Engagement Cake' (*Belfast Telegraph*, 1 May 2017) available at www.belfasttelegraph.co.uk/sunday-life/ashers-refuses-to-make-gay-engagement-cake-35669084.html.
[69] PW Edge, 'The Supreme Court Decision in *Lee v Ashers Baking Company* and the Religious Rights of Companies' (*Commercial Religion*, 11 October 2018) available at www.commercial-religion.blogspot.com/2018/10/the-supreme-court-decision-in-lee-v.html (author's emphasis).

PART D

Conclusion

13

Conscientious Exemptions in a Liberal State

JOHN ADENITIRE

I. Introduction

This chapter, by engaging with the various contributions in this volume, sets forth a particular approach as to how a liberal state should deal with conscientious exemptions. This approach is here called the Liberal Model of Conscientious Exemptions. The Model has the following four defining propositions:

1. The liberal state should grant a general right to conscientious exemption.
2. The liberal state should refrain from passing moral judgement on the content of the beliefs which give rise to a claim for conscientious exemption.
3. The liberal state should neither privilege nor disadvantage religious beliefs over non-religious ones when considering whether to grant a conscientious exemption.
4. The liberal state should grant conscientious exemptions to claimants who sincerely hold a conscientious objection which would not disproportionately impact the rights of others or the public interest.[1]

The Liberal Model is distinctively both liberal and interpretive. It is liberal because values which are constitutive of the liberal tradition, such as liberty, autonomy, and so on, mandate that a liberal state conforms to the Model. The Liberal Model does not claim to be acceptable to autocracies, theocracies or systems which always prioritise the general interest over individual well-being. Also, the Liberal Model is not compatible with all versions of liberalism. For example, it would reject the liberal perfectionism which is at the foundation of the approach proposed by Nehushtan and Coyle in chapter seven. As shall be explained in due course, the Liberal Model advocates for a version of liberalism – call it neutral pluralism – which requires the state not to paternalistically interfere with the moral responsibility which each person has to choose a conception of a good life. This results in the state having to endorse a state of affairs where individuals pursue plural and sometimes incompatible versions of a good life.

The Liberal Model is interpretative in the sense defended by Ronald Dworkin.[2] Its propositions need to fit with the legal doctrines which it has as its targets of inquiry.

---

[1] The Liberal Model was first defended in J Adenitire, 'The Irrelevance of Religion' (2017) 8 *Jurisprudence* 405. However, in that piece the first proposition of the Model, concerning the general right, had not yet been developed.
[2] R Dworkin, *Law's Empire* (Oxford, Hart Publishing, 1998). Although the Liberal Model is interpretive, it is not Dworkinian as Dworkin has explicitly rejected a right to conscientious exemption in R Dworkin, *Religion Without God* (Cambridge, MA, Harvard University Press, 2013) ch 3.

This chapter, for reasons of space constraints, largely leaves behind the fit aspect of the Liberal Model.[3] Instead, it focuses on showing that the propositions are morally attractive. If this is successful, the Model can lend its moral force to the legal practices which it has as its target and show them to be true propositions of law which deserve allegiance in a liberal democracy. To be sure, in line with Dworkinian interpretivism, the Liberal Model need not embrace all the aspects of the practice of conscientious exemptions. It can say that some of these practices are not sound. In this sense the Liberal Model is a critical model, however, and importantly, it is *legally* critical. The aspects of practice which it rejects as mistakes are rejected as legal mistakes: they are mistakes because they do not fit with the underlying moral principles which animate the core of the legal practice.

This chapter analyses each of the four defining propositions of the Liberal Model in turn by engaging with the various contributions in this volume. In part II it defends the proposition that a liberal state should grant a general right to conscientious exemption. Part II sets out the nature of the general right and outlines why it is morally attractive. Part III defends the proposition that a liberal state should not pass judgement on the content of beliefs which give rise to a conscientious objection. The chapter takes particular issue with the approaches proposed by Jones, and by Nehushtan and Coyle in this volume who seem to argue against this second proposition. Part IV defends the proposition that a liberal state should neither privilege nor disadvantage religious beliefs over non-religious ones when considering whether a conscientious exemption should be granted. The chapter takes issue with Corvino and with Moon who seem to argue that religious exemptions should be somewhat privileged. Issue is also taken with Nehushtan whose anti-religious stance is well known in the literature, although slightly tempered in his contribution with Coyle in this volume.[4] Part V defends the proposition that exemptions should be granted to sincere objectors whose objection will not disproportionately affect the right of others or the public interest. Part VI directly confronts the issue of objections to sexual orientation anti-discrimination laws and argues that, in general, such exemptions should not be granted given the dignitary harms they may inflict on members of sexual minorities. Particular issue is taken with Leigh, and with Chipeur and Clarke, who appear to argue in favour of exemptions from sexual orientation anti-discrimination laws.

II. The Liberal State Should Grant a General Right to Conscientious Exemption

The first proposition of the Liberal Model says that liberal states should grant a general right to conscientious exemption. The general right is here understood as a legal right to conscientiously object to whatever obligation imposed by law, whether under statute, common law or otherwise, and to obtain from a court an exemption from the duty to comply with such obligation. The general right is to be contrasted with context-specific legal

---

[3] A detailed analysis of the fit of the Liberal Model with the practice of conscientious exemptions in US, Canadian and UK law is provided in chs 2–7 of J Adenitire, 'A General Legal Right to Conscientious Exemption: Beyond Religious Privilege' (PhD thesis, University of Cambridge, 2018).

[4] Y Nehushtan, *Intolerant Religion in a Tolerant-Liberal Democracy* (Oxford, Hart Publishing, 2015).

exemptions which are usually found in statutes in relation to a particular legal obligation. Famous context-specific exemptions include exemptions from the military draft or from the duty on doctors to perform abortions. The general right is termed 'general' because it can be invoked in any legal context and does not rely on the existence of context-specific legislative exemptions. The general right defended here is not an absolute right. A court may refuse to grant an exemption if doing so would disproportionately impact the rights of others or the public interest. So the general right to exemption is a prima facie or limited legal right. The general right empowers courts to consider the moral and pragmatic issues which legislatures often do when considering to enact context-specific legislative exemptions. After considering the moral and pragmatic issues at stake, courts may accept or decline to grant an exemption to a conscientious objector.

Not much exists in the academic literature to support or argue against the existence of the general right. To be sure, Raz had tentatively argued in its favour from a liberal perspective a few decades ago when he said:

> Reflection on the nature of liberalism, it seems, may suggest that the very narrow definition of the liberal state given above should be widened to include the institution of a general legal right of conscientious objection, that is, a state is liberal only if it includes laws to the effect that no man shall be liable for breach of duty if his breach is committed because he thinks that it is morally wrong for him to obey the law on the ground that it is morally bad or wrong totally or in part.[5]

More recently, Nehushtan has also put forward theoretical arguments in favour of the recognition of this general right.[6] More will be said below as to the moral merits of the recognition of the general right. However, remember that the Liberal Model is an interpretive model which needs to fit with the practice of the jurisdictions under focus and which needs to morally justify these practices. So one needs to first mount an arguable case that the jurisdictions under analysis actually do recognise a general right to conscientious exemption before showing that such a right is morally attractive.

As indicated, this chapter will not attempt to show that the Liberal Model actually fits with the practice of conscientious exemption as that would require detailed doctrinal analysis which lack of space precludes. However, some of the contributors to this volume have already provided some evidence to suggest that the existence of a general right to conscientious exemption is actually not as implausible as it first sounds. Sure enough, no known jurisdiction has a constitutional or legislative provision clearly labelled as 'a general right to conscientious exemption'. Rather, in any given jurisdiction, several rules of law need to be conceptualised together to ground the general right.

In the US, for example, one of the grounds of the general right would be the constitutional rule recognised in *Sherbert*, abolished in *Smith* and then reinstated in statutory form in the Federal Religious Freedom Restoration Act (RFRA) and similar state-level legislation. The rule, already considered by several contributors to this volume,[7] is that government cannot substantially burden a person's free exercise of religion, unless in pursuance of a compelling state interest and unless government has taken the least restrictive means to

[5] J Raz, *The Authority of Law: Essays on Law and Morality* (Oxford, Oxford University Press, 1979) 276.
[6] Y Nehushtan, 'The Case for a General Constitutional Right to Be Granted Conscientious Exemption' (2016) 5 *Oxford Journal of Law and Religion* 230.
[7] Chapter 11 in this volume considers it in part I and part III A. Chipeur and Clarke discuss it in ch 9 in this volume, text to n 49. Corvino discusses it in ch 2 in this volume, text to n 36.

achieve that compelling interest. This rule may be grouped together with the other rule under Title VII and similar state-level legislation, considered in detail by Vickers in part II A of chapter ten, which imposes an obligation on employers to accommodate requests from employees for changes to working conditions, short of undue hardship. Under both RFRA and Title VII (and their state counterparts) individuals may seek a conscientious exemption from a wide array of legal obligations. In line with the general right defended in this chapter, the right to exemption under RFRA and Title VII is limited and courts may decline to grant an exemption if, under Title VII, an exemption would impose more than a de minimis burden on an employer or, under RFRA, government can point to a compelling state interest and can show that no less restrictive ways, short of granting an exemption, are available to achieve that interest.

Much more could be said about the legal reasons to think that a general right already exists at least under US, Canadian and UK law scattered under several legal doctrines, statutory and constitutional principles which need to be conceptualised together. That discussion is however left for another venue.[8] Nevertheless, it is hoped that the brief discussion above gives a veneer of plausibility to the claim that the first proposition of the Liberal Model actually fits the practice of several liberal democracies. If this poorly substantiated claim is accepted, then it is necessary to show that the existence of a general right is morally justified.

A. The Justification of the First Proposition[9]

None of the contributors to this volume argue against the grant of conscientious exemptions under any circumstances. Corvino, who argues against exemptions from anti-discrimination laws in the context of provision of commercial services, is happy to accept exemptions in other circumstances. Moon, who is unpersuaded about the case for exemptions for non-religious conscience, is happy to accept religious exemptions when they concern private matters. Nehushtan and Coyle, who are deeply sceptical of religious exemptions, accept that the state may grant religious exemptions based on non-unjustly intolerant views or non-morally repugnant beliefs. So it turns out that the consensus in this volume is that conscientious exemptions are sometimes warranted. On that basis, this chapter need not mount a defence against the view that exemptions should never be granted. Instead, it provides a positive case in favour of the general right to conscientious exemption. To do so, it asks what justifies granting conscientious exemptions generally and then builds on this to argue specifically in favour of the general right. A positive case is made for exemptions generally drawing on a plurality of values well established in a liberal democracy. After this a positive case is made for a general right on the basis of protecting minority moral views.

i. The Moral Case for Conscientious Exemptions Generally

One of the arguments in favour of exemptions generally derives from the liberal commitment to what will here be called the duty of neutral pluralism of the state. This duty arises

[8] See n 3.
[9] This section draws extensively on J Adenitire, 'Conscientious Exemptions: From Toleration to Neutrality; From Neutrality to Respect' (2017) 6 *Oxford Journal of Law and Religion* 268, 15–16, 20–24.

in the face of the fact of moral pluralism. Moral pluralism is not just a factual statement of the obvious truth that different people hold different views about what moral values require. Rather, it should also be understood as a positive normative statement grounded on the value of individual moral responsibility. Call this ethical pluralism. This normative position holds that there are various ways to live a good life and that, by implication, there are various legitimate conceptions of what a good life is. A person may legitimately devote his life to religious contemplation or to the study of the intricacies of astrophysics. He may choose a life centred on family values or refuse to commit to a romantic relationship so as to focus on his career as an investment banker. No doubt there will be drawbacks in any of these conceptions of a good life. A life of religious contemplation as a monk, while benefitting from high spirituality, is incompatible with the joys of family life. Studying the intricacies of astrophysics, while contributing to knowledge, is unlikely to yield the pecuniary rewards of the life of an investment banker. However, the point of moral individual responsibility is that various incompatible conceptions of a good life each exhibit something worthwhile, even while exhibiting several drawbacks, and it is up to each individual to weight for himself what is more worthwhile for him. Importantly, given that it is the individual that will benefit or suffer the consequences of a conception of a good life, the choice of which conception to follow is his and not the state's.

Note that ethical pluralism is not to be equated with moral relativism or nihilism, respectively the views that there is no universal way to establish the moral worth of different conceptions of a good life or that different conceptions cannot be better or worse than each other because morality does not exist. Rather, the main thrust of this view is that different conceptions of a good life are objectively valuable in different ways and that the individual is the best judge of what is most valuable for him. The state should stay away from dictating what conception is more valuable. Note also that this view does not lead to undermining the legitimacy of state regulation of the interaction between different conceptions of a good life. While individuals are free to choose what lives to live, they cannot impose their choices on others (they too have the right to choose what life to live). The role of the state then, as guardian of the common good, is to ensure that different conceptions of a good life are compatible. The state can therefore limit acts that would undermine the common good and that would infringe others' right to choose which conception is for them.

Ethical pluralism then, if accepted, leads to accepting the imposition on the state of a duty of neutral pluralism: ie a limited duty of non-interference by the state in the individual moral responsibility to choose one conception of a good life over another. If this duty is accepted it may partially justify a right to conscientious exemption. In fact when the state imposes a general rule, that rule may create a barrier to an individual's chosen conception (eg the prohibition of drug possession may create a barrier to living according to the Rastafarian ceremonial use of cannabis). That may of course be another of the drawbacks of being committed to that conception and the individual may need to reconsider whether that way of life is really worth it with the burden which the state has imposed. However, in imposing a particular rule which creates a barrier to the pursuit of a particular way of life, the state may be portrayed as violating its duty of neutral pluralism: the state makes certain ways of life less accessible and thereby incentivises individuals to choose other conceptions of a good life (ie the more accessible ones). If the state is to remain neutral among competing ways of life it should therefore grant an exemption to alleviate the barrier it has created. Of course, the imposition of the particular rule may be justified by reference to vital public interests or to the rights of others (eg combating drug-related criminality). So the granting of the exemption will depend on whether it would disproportionately undermine those interests and rights. This is, however, a reason to make the right to exemption non-absolute rather than rejecting the right altogether.

The argument above is essentially one that derives a non-absolute right to exemption from the state's duty of neutral pluralism. It is an argument calling for the state to respect ethical pluralism. But notice that there are other values at play here that reinforce this argument. The most obvious is perhaps the insistence that personal autonomy should be respected by the state. The idea of personal autonomy 'is that people should make their own lives. The autonomous person is a (part) author of his own life. The ideal of personal autonomy is the vision of people controlling, to some degree, their own destiny, fashioning it through successive decisions throughout their lives'.[10] It is possible to argue that committing oneself to a particular way of life (eg one committed to a particular religion) is an expression of personal autonomy. The person that is committed to a particular religion will make a variety of choices which will have a myriad of implications for his life. A portion of those implications would have been different had he committed himself to another religion or to non-religion. By being allowed to be committed to any religion or non-religion the individual is thereby being allowed to lead a more autonomous life and to shape the course of his life. The state that values and respects personal autonomy will thereby allow the freedom for individuals to pursue whichever conception of the good life they identify with. Of course, as discussed multiple times, the state cannot permit all expressions of every way of life. Some will collide with fundamental public interests and/or the rights of others. However, the state's respect for personal autonomy leads to respecting various manifestations of different ways of life, although not of all.

Respect for personal autonomy does not directly lead to justifying the assertion of a right to be exempt from various legal duties. However, respect for autonomy leads to reinforcing the case for that right: if the state grants exemptions (perhaps on the basis of the state's duty of neutral pluralism sketched above) that promotes personal autonomy and that is virtuous. In fact, as stated, an exemption from a legal duty incompatible with a way of life diminishes the costs of accessing or continuing to identify with a particular way of life; it increases options for individuals. Personal autonomy is about, among other things, access to an adequate range of options.[11] By granting an exemption the state increases the range of conceptions of a good life which an individual may identify with and live according to. It thereby promotes personal autonomy.

Respect for personal autonomy reinforces the case for granting conscientious exemptions. However, respecting autonomy also usually involves, at least in the context of conscientious objection, respect for liberty of conscience. We may understand conscience as a person's faculty 'for searching for life's ethical basis and its ultimate meaning'.[12] Consequently, we may understand liberty of conscience as the liberty to live one's life according to the normative imperatives imposed by conscience. These normative imperatives may

---

[10] J Raz, *The Morality of Freedom* (Oxford, Oxford University Press, 1988) 369.

[11] ibid 372. Raz says that 'The conditions of autonomy are complex and consist of three distinct components: appropriate mental abilities, an adequate range of options, and independence'.

[12] MC Nussbaum, 'Liberty of Conscience: The Attack on Equal Respect' (2007) 8 *Journal of Human Development* 337, 342.

originate from religious directives or from non-religious ones. Commitment to a particular way of life, whether religious or not, will normally include a judgement that that way of living is compatible and/or required by one's conscientious convictions. Otherwise the individual would find himself living in a pathological bipolar situation whereby he considers a way of life valuable but completely at odds with his convictions about what is right or wrong. No doubt such pathological cases exist. A professional killer may be committed to his way of life because of its luxurious rewards while fully appreciating its moral wrongness. However, in non-pathological cases, individuals subscribe to a particular conception of a good life, among other things, because they believe it to be right or morally required. This is usually the case for some religious believers. Individuals commit to living according to the edicts of a particular religion because they believe that living that way is required by God, the main source of their moral imperatives. It is their belief in a deity that leads them to commit to a particular way of life. In order words, it is liberty of conscience which influences the way they exercise their right to personal autonomy. It follows that when the state respects personal autonomy by granting an exemption, it normally also respects freedom of conscience.

When the state refuses to grant an exemption this may not only encroach on personal autonomy or freedom of conscience; it may occasion harm to the objector, ie undermine her well-being. Remember that when an exemption is denied the objector may be coerced to perform an act which she believes to be wrong. Being compelled to performing an act believed to be morally wrong goes against a person's conscience and that might undermine her well-being. In fact when an individual makes a claim of conscience she is normally so committed to her beliefs that acting against them 'would result in a loss of personal and moral integrity with consequences, such as profound guilt and remorse, which would have an adverse effect on the person's self-conception and self-respect'.[13] This, in turn, would affect the person's well-being. Of course the individual may refuse to yield to legal coercion and pay the consequences, eg be imprisoned for failing to perform her legal duties. However, succumbing to legal punishment rather than acting against one's conscience also undermines one's well-being. It follows that when the state grants a conscientious exemption it is usually also paying respect to an aspect of the objector's well-being.

ii. *The Moral Case for a General Right to Conscientious Exemption*

If the arguments adduced so far are correct, then a non-absolute right to conscientious exemption is justified by reference to a cluster of moral values, including the demands of the state's duty of neutral pluralism (the duty being grounded in the value of individual moral responsibility and respect for ethical pluralism), respect for personal autonomy, freedom of conscience and concern for individual well-being. No doubt other arguments could be made to show that other values are involved.[14] However, these suffice to temporarily ground the practice of granting conscientious exemptions in recognisable moral values. However, the Liberal Model cannot merely show that conscientious exemptions generally are justified

---

[13] J Adenitire, 'SAS v France: Fidelity to Law and Conscience' [2015] *European Human Rights Law Review* 78, 82.
[14] A further argument based on the state's ambition not to govern through coercion but mainly through the idea of fidelity to law was made in Adenitire, 'SAS v France' [2015].

by reference to compelling values. It also has to show that a general right to conscientious exemption is justified.

In order to provide a justification for a general right to exemption it is important to recall a feature of claims for conscientious exemptions already discussed in chapter eleven of this volume. There it was said that it should be expected that there will be an undefined number of legal obligations individuals may object to. Many are very familiar: objection to military service, to abortion, to be involved in officiating same-sex marriages, to providing emergency contraception. However, these familiar forms of conscientious objection do not exhaust all possible claims. It may be possible that legal obligations which are thought uncontroversial might actually contravene some deeply held beliefs. For example, as pointed out in that chapter, one might well be surprised by the Peculiar People's beliefs that parents have a religious duty not to allow their children (and themselves) to receive any medical treatment because that would otherwise contravene their interpretation of some passages in the Bible exhorting believers to pray for the sick.[15]

It cannot be expected of even the most diligent of legislatures to predict and cater for in specific legislative exemptions all instances in which a legal obligation may conflict with the beliefs of a conscientious objector. Of course it is open to legislatures to work in a reactive fashion whenever new instances of conscientious objections come to light. After the decision in *Smith*, for example, the Oregon legislature became aware of the need to exempt sacramental use of peyote from the prohibition of drug use and enacted a statutory exemption accordingly.[16] To the extent that the exemption was justified, the legislature ought to be applauded for its fast reaction to a genuine issue of conscience. Not all conscientious objectors, however, are as fortunate as the Oregon members of the Native American Church. Some minority groups are unlikely to be able to have sufficient social or political power to lobby for a discussion in the legislature about their conscientious beliefs to enable the legislature to deliberate properly about them. To be sure this is not always the case. Sikhs in England and Wales, while only constituting 0.8% of the population,[17] benefit from a generous statutory exemption from the obligation to wear safety headgear in the workplace and in other circumstances in favour of them wearing the turban.[18] Yet, as the example of the Peculiar People testify, unusual views that belong to a minority group are unlikely to be well known and therefore unlikely to be considered in the legislative process.

The case for a general right to conscientious exemption is therefore based on the inability of the legislature to predict all instances of conscientious objection and on the worry that minority views will be left behind in the political process when such minorities do not have enough political power to lobby the legislature for a context-specific exemption. The institution of a general right provides minority views with an alternative forum, ie a court of law, where they may be able to bring a claim and ask for exemptions from legal obligations which impinge on their consciences. To be sure, the existence of this alternative forum may not result in an exemption being granted. It may be that the exemption is not warranted because

[15] As Illustrated in *R v Senior* [1899] 1 QB 283.
[16] The current statutory exemption is s 4(a) 2015 ORS 475.752.
[17] Office for National Statistics, 'The Percentage of the Population with No Religion Has Increased in England and Wales' (4 April 2013) available at www.webarchive.nationalarchives.gov.uk/20160105160709/http://www.ons.gov.uk/ons/rel/census/2011-census/key-statistics-for-local-authorities-in-england-and-wales/sty-religion.html.
[18] Employment Act 1989, s 11.

granting it would result in a disproportionate impact on the right of others (eg granting an exemption to the Peculiar People from the criminalisation of child neglect would endanger the lives of their children). It may also be that, even if the exemption is warranted, courts may fail to reach a proper outcome through poor legal reasoning.

Independently of whether an exemption is granted in this alternative forum, the general right to conscientious exemption guarantees that minority views have a right to equal treatment under the law. Indeed, earlier it was suggested that under US law the general right may be grounded in statutory provisions which protect religious freedom (RFRA) and which prohibit discriminatory treatment on the basis of beliefs (Title VII). Majority conscientious views that are well known (eg mainstream Christian views) usually have these legal rights considered in the legislative process and statutory exemptions are sometimes granted (eg the exemption for religious institutions in the Obamacare contraceptive mandate as discussed in *Hobby Lobby*). In a liberal democracy committed to the rule of law, these legal rights are not a prerogative of only majority conscientious views. Minority views are also entitled to these legal rights and, consequently, to a forum where these rights can be adequately considered by a state authority whenever they conflict with legal obligations. A general right to conscientious exemption makes this equal consideration of legal rights possible.

Finally, the general right is also justified by reference not only to legal rights but also to moral rights. We have seen that the general practice of conscientious exemptions is justified by reference to a cluster of moral values, including the demands of the state's duty of neutral pluralism (grounded in the value of individual moral responsibility and respect for ethical pluralism), respect for personal autonomy, freedom of conscience and concern for individual well-being. There is no reason to think that these moral values are a prerogative of individuals holding well-known conscientious objections. The state ought to recognise these moral values even for less well-known conscientious views. The legal recognition of a general right to conscientious exemption enables the state to respect these values for minority and majority conscientious views alike.

III. The Liberal State Should Refrain from Passing Moral Judgement on the Content of the Beliefs Which Give Rise to a Claim for Conscientious Exemption

The second proposition of the Liberal Model says that liberal states should refrain from passing moral judgement on the content of the beliefs which give rise to a claim for conscientious exemption. The core of the idea is that the state should not judge the reasonableness, merit, truth, attractiveness, etc of the beliefs of a conscientious objector. Consistent with the fourth proposition of the Liberal Model, a liberal state may only question whether the belief is sincerely held and should grant the exemption only if doing so would not disproportionately affect the rights of others or the public interest. This part of this chapter provides a moral justification for the proposition and rejects the challenges made to it in this volume by Jones and by Nehushtan and Coyle, who all want the state to take into consideration the quality of conscientious objectors' beliefs when deciding whether an exemption is to be granted. Jones wants the state to consider whether the beliefs of the objector are well-founded in her religion. Nehushtan and Coyle want the state to consider the moral merits of the beliefs at hand.

A. The Justification for the Second Proposition of the Liberal Model

As discussed by Jones in this volume, the second proposition fits UK practice. He cites the well-established UK House of Lords decision of *Williamson*. In that case Lord Nicholls made clear that courts should not take into account whether an asserted belief that gives rise to a claim for conscientious exemption is well-founded in the claimant's religion (in that case the belief that the Bible mandated corporal punishment of children). Consistently with the second proposition, Lord Nicholls said:

> [E]mphatically, it is not for the court to embark on an inquiry into the asserted belief and judge its 'validity' by some objective standard such as the source material upon which the claimant founds his belief or the orthodox teaching of the religion in question or the extent to which the claimant's belief conforms to or differs from the views of others professing the same religion. Freedom of religion protects the subjective belief of an individual. ... Each individual is at liberty to hold his own religious beliefs, however, irrational or inconsistent they may seem to some, however surprising.[19]

Jones is not convinced that there are principled arguments to support this aspect of the practice. He does think that this approach is pragmatically justified on the basis that:

> The task could be very demanding in time and effort. It could also be difficult to execute with confidence, given that religious faiths are so internally diverse and that religious belief is not subject to ordinary rules of evidence or even logic. Due account would also have to be taken of heterodox as well as orthodox belief. Perhaps above all, it would frequently be difficult for a court to come up with decisions that escaped the sort of contention and controversy that it would not want to attract. So ... it may be reasonable that judges, or the society upon whose behalf they act, should take the view that, all things considered, the cake is not worth the candle.[20]

No issue is here taken with the pragmatic argument offered by Jones in support of the second proposition of the Liberal Model. However, this chapter rejects the view defended by Jones that 'If there is reason to abstain from screening beliefs for their well-foundedness, it is neither moral nor epistemic but pragmatic in nature'.[21] Indeed, the Liberal Model, being an interpretive model, has to show that the practice is morally justified. Therefore, the Model has to show that there are moral reasons, and not merely pragmatic ones, in favour of the second proposition. Consequently, this part scrutinises the objections to the moral arguments advanced by Jones before scrutinising the objections advanced by Nehushtan and Coyle.

B. Against Ill-Foundedness

Jones advances two arguments against viewing the second proposition as morally justified. Let us examine the first. He says that religious and secular exemptions are usually justified because they are ethically salient, in the sense that they allow the exempted individual to

---

[19] *R (on the application of Williamson) v Secretary of State for Education and Employment* [2005] UKHL 15, at 22.
[20] Chapter 3, text to n 3.
[21] Chapter 3, in part VII.

conform with an imperative which is important to his or her personal and moral integrity. He then contrasts religious belief with (non-religious) conscientious belief. The latter, he argues, is subjective in the sense that it is an individual's own conscience that is the authority of his or her moral beliefs and in the further sense that right conduct consists in compliance with the dictates of his or her own conscience. It is not so, Jones argues, for religious beliefs. First, religious beliefs are grounded in sources external to the believer such as sacred texts, religious teachings, the doctrines of an organised religion, the shared faith of a religious community, and so on. Second, Jones argues that 'by and large, religious belief and its imperatives are conceived, neither by religions themselves nor by their individual adherents, as exercises in individual self-legislation'.[22] Given this distinction between religious belief and non-religious conscientious beliefs, a principled argument cannot, in Jones' view, be grounded on freedom of conscience or freedom of religion. This is because religious beliefs are distinct from (non-religious) conscientious ones and because religion does not generally encompass subjective and self-legislated beliefs.

The problem with Jones' first argument is that it misconstrues the religious experience and, consequently, it misconstrues the scope of freedom of religion. First, the religious experience need not be sourced in an authority which is manifestly external to the person proclaiming it. Indeed, in the case of the Abrahamic religions, their alleged founders declared the new movements based on alleged private divine revelations: Moses claimed to have seen God's plan for the Israelites in a burning bush; Jesus declared himself the Son of God; Mohammed claimed that the Archangel Gabriel appeared to him dictating what would become the Quran. Jones is aware of this feature of religiosity when he claims that 'Individual inspiration can figure importantly in some faiths alongside shared external sources of belief' however he argues that 'for the most part the individuals who register legal claims with courts do so as "ordinary believers" rather than as self-professed prophets or visionaries claiming direct inspiration from God'.[23] However, this misses the point. No doubt most individuals' religiosity makes reference to external sources. Nevertheless, private revelation is a crucial element in the founding history of well-established religions and in the development of newer religions. Consider in this latter respect the origins of Mormonism in the 1820s which involved the claim that Joseph Smith was visited by angels several times and translated the Book of Mormon from golden plates revealed to him.[24] It would escape common understanding if these experiences of private revelation were not considered part of the religious experience and were therefore not covered by the scope of religious freedom. Jones' first argument therefore needs to be rejected because it leads to the idiosyncratic view that the founders of well-established religions and of newer religions were or are not engaged in religious practices and/or should not be protected by freedom of religion.

Consider now Jones' second argument. He considers whether the respect we generally owe to believers must extend routinely to enduring the costs of their error. He ponders whether it may be disrespectful to allow our assessment of an individual's belief to affect our

---

[22] Chapter 3, in part IV.
[23] ibid.
[24] Joseph Smith's own account of his private revelation is provided by the Church or Latter-Day Saints, 'The Testimony of the Prophet Joseph Smith' at www.lds.org/scriptures/bofm/js?lang=eng.

treatment of that individual. He answers negatively and provides in support an analogy with cultural practices. He says:

> Suppose I claim a practice is a constituent of my culture. Whether it is indeed a part of my culture is a matter for objective assessment. … I cannot make a practice part of my culture merely by declaring it to be so. If, having investigated the matter, a court concludes that the practice does not belong to my ethnicity and for that reason dismisses my claim … it is hard to accept that the court's judgement constitutes an intolerable act of disrespect merely because it conflicts with and overrides my own claim about my culture. But, if that is true, it is hard to see why it should not be equally true in the case of religion.[25]

The strategy of the argument does not work. It seeks to equate beliefs about cultural identity with religious beliefs. But that equation cannot be sustained. It is true that, as Jones says, individuals cannot make a practice part of their culture by declaratory fiat. This is because a culture is, as the widely quoted Edward Burnett Tylor puts it, 'that complex whole which includes knowledge, belief, art, morals, law, custom, and any other capabilities and habits acquired by man as a member of society'.[26] If this is accepted, it follows that in order to identify a cultural practice or belief, one first needs to identify a particular society to which that practice or belief belongs to. And it is implausible that a society could be made up of a single individual. It follows that cultural beliefs cannot be created by declaratory fiat.

Not so, however, with religious beliefs. As already stated, the history of religion is full of individuals who founded a religion or modified an existing religious practice by simple declaratory fiat. There is no need to make reference to Jesus or Mohammed to validate this point. Take the case of *Blackburn*[27] considered at length by Frank Cranmer in part IV of chapter twelve. The beekeepers in that case, contrary to what their church asserted and practised (the church ran a website), believed that the Bible prohibited the use of electronic communication. Mr Blackburn's explanation for his view was that:

> [H]e considered computers and television as a whole as forms of 'worldliness' which might seduce people away from 'righteousness'. … He considered that people were obsessed by them, almost regarding them as 'idols'. … He considers that modern media and in particular the 'screen' has 'blinded the minds of non-believers' and that people's time is so taken up with electronic communications that they no longer have time for religion in their lives.[28]

No doubt it is possible and indeed acceptable to tell the Blackburns that their beliefs about electronic communications are not in line with what is practised and preached by their church. But, given the theological explanation provided by Mr Blackburn, it would not be correct to argue that their beliefs are not worthy of the protection afforded to religious beliefs (including exemptions from online VAT filing) because they do not accord to what their church preaches on the subject. Doing so would be tantamount to enforcing theological orthodoxy – the very opposite of religious freedom. If there is anything that religious freedom should protect individuals from, is from being coerced to hold a particular religious belief, including the belief of a particular religious group.

---

[25] Chapter 3, in part IV.
[26] EB Tylor, *Primitive Culture: Researches into the Development of Mythology, Philosophy, Religion, Language, Art, and Custom* (London, John Murray, 1873) 1.
[27] *Blackburn & Anor v Revenue & Customs* [2013] UKFTT 525.
[28] ibid at 13.

i. Against Liberal Perfectionism

Let us now turn to the challenge to the second proposition of the Liberal Model mounted by Nehushtan and Coyle in chapter seven. Their challenge is based on the premises that liberal states should subscribe to liberal perfectionism which holds that 'some ideals of human flourishing are sound whereas others are not; that the state is justified in favouring the former; and that there is no general moral principle that forbids the state from favouring sound values, even when these values are controversial, as long as these values are indeed sound'.[29] In the context of conscientious exemptions, this entails that, contrary to the second proposition of the Liberal Model, the quality of the belief of the objector is assessed to discover whether it is in line with the state's ideals of human flourishing and, if it is not, that constitutes a reason against granting an exemption. Hence, Nehushtan and Coyle differentiate between cases where the belief of the objector is in their view morally repugnant, eg objections to anti-discrimination legislation, and where it is merely misguided or irrational, eg objections to dress code policies and to life-terminating treatment. Exemptions are never to be granted to the former, whereas exemptions may sometimes be granted to the latter.

In making their case against the granting of exemptions to anti-discrimination legislation, Nehushtan and Coyle do not rely on a normative case grounded on liberal-perfectionism. Rather they rely on the descriptive claim that

> by enacting equality laws the liberal state, through the legislature, has already expressed its view that discrimination against gay people does rely on illegitimate values. The state decided the limits of liberal tolerance by relying on content-based rather than content-neutral considerations. Equality laws set an underlying moral principle according to which less favourable treatment just because of a protected characteristic is basically indefensible.[30]

A normative argument will be advanced below against the appropriateness of a liberal perfectionist framework in the context of conscientious exemption. Here, however, it will be argued that the descriptive claim that anti-discrimination legislation is a means for the state to label as illegitimate the beliefs of those that object to anti-discriminatory legislation is false. Take in this regard the fact that the legislation to which Nehushtan and Coyle refer, ie the UK Equality Act 2010, explicitly exempts religious or belief-based organisations from the duty to comply with the prohibition of sexual orientation discrimination if the discrimination is mandated by the doctrine of the organisation or if complying with that duty would contravene the deeply held beliefs of a significant number of members of that organisation.[31] Notice then that the Equality Act, by explicitly allowing religious and non-religious organisations to discriminate on the grounds of sexual orientation on the basis of their doctrines or the beliefs of their members, cannot be held to be labelling as illegitimate those beliefs. They cannot be illegitimate if they are explicitly protected.

Nehushtan and Coyle are aware of this feature of the Equality Act but insist that although the statutory exemptions betray a form of favouritism towards religious organisations, this does not take away from their argument that equality laws express a content-based moral stance about the relative importance of the principle of equality. This is so, they argue,

---

[29] Chapter 7, text to n 3.
[30] Chapter 7, text to n 10.
[31] Equality Act 2010, Sch 23, para 2.

because 'If the state perceived the religious discriminatory conscience as morally desirable, it would not have enacted equality laws to begin with'.[32] This is, however, a logically fallacious form of reasoning as it is a form of reasoning from ignorance. There may in fact be multiple reasons for the state to enact anti-discrimination laws, none of which may have anything to do with delegitimising 'religious discriminatory conscience'. Consistently with this, it should be noted that it is well established that UK anti-discrimination law, either in the form of direct or indirect discrimination, does not concern itself with the motive of the discriminatory treatment. As reaffirmed recently by the UKSC in *Essop*, there is no need to prove a hostile or malicious motive in direct discrimination; one only needs to prove that someone has been treated less favourably because of a protected characteristic.[33] Similarly, in indirect discrimination law, there is no need to provide an explanation of the reasons why a particular provision, criterion or practice puts one group at a disadvantage when compared with others. Furthermore, the reason for the disadvantage need not be unlawful in itself or be under the control of the employer or provider.[34] Given these features of anti-discrimination legislation, it is implausible to hold that its aim is to delegitimise 'religious discriminatory conscience'. If it does not concern itself with mental states, either conscientious or not, it cannot be seeking to delegitimise them.

It seems then that the descriptive argument that anti-discrimination legislation proceeds on the basis of a liberal perfectionists account is mistaken, at least in the UK. The practice in the UK in this context therefore appears to conform to the second proposition of the Liberal Model. However, Nehushtan and Coyle, in part II of their chapter when discussing religious symbols and objections to abortions, do not rely on a descriptive claim but merely assume that liberal perfectionism is desirable. They do not provide in this volume a normative argument in favour of that assumption. However, in another venue, explicit reliance has been placed by Nehushtan on the liberal perfectionism defended by Joseph Raz.[35] This part therefore scrutinises Razian liberal perfectionism and scrutinises whether its arguments are persuasive in the context of conscientious exemptions.

Raz has forcefully argued that a liberal state should value autonomy highly and consequently should promote a range of valuable options for its citizens to pursue while discouraging the pursuit of immoral options. He argues:

> No one would deny that autonomy should be used for the good. The question is, has autonomy any value *qua* autonomy when it is abused? Is the autonomous wrongdoer a morally better person than the non-autonomous wrongdoer? Our intuitions rebel against such a view. It is surely the other way round. The wrongdoing casts a darker shadow on its perpetrator if it is autonomously done by him. … Autonomy is valuable only if exercised in pursuit of the good. The ideal of autonomy requires only the availability of morally acceptable options.[36]

Consistent with being a liberal theory, Razian perfectionism is tempered by the fact that state coercion may only be utilised against immoral acts which harm others. Nevertheless, consistent with being a perfectionist theory, the state may use non-coercive means to

[32] Chapter 7, part II E.
[33] *Essop & Ors v Home Office* [2017] UKSC 27 at 17.
[34] ibid at 24 and 26.
[35] *Nehushtan* (n 4) ch 3.
[36] Raz, *Morality of Freedom* (1988) 380–81.

dissuade individuals from subscribing to immoral views even when those views are not acted upon.[37]

If Razian liberal perfectionism is applied to the context of conscientious exemptions, it follows, as Nehushtan and Coyle argue, that the state should take into consideration the moral quality of a belief of a conscientious objector when considering whether an exemption is to be granted. If the belief is immoral, that should provide the state with a weighty reason for discouraging it and, hence, a reason not to grant the exemption. Notice that Razian perfectionism does not collapse into the view that, consistent with the fourth proposition of the Liberal Model, a liberal state should refuse to grant exemptions if doing so would disproportionately affect the rights of others or the public interest. The fourth proposition is a specific form of the harm principle and is not perfectionist. Instead Razian perfectionism urges the state not to grant an exemption on the basis that it considers that the belief of the conscientious objector is immoral. In opposition to the second proposition of the Liberal Model, Razian perfectionism requires the state to assess and discourage immoral views of conscientious objectors even when granting an exemption based on an immoral view would not disproportionately impact on the rights of others or on the public interest.

How can the Liberal Model defend itself from Razian liberal perfectionism? It may show that that version of liberal perfectionism is not morally attractive. Or it may show that Razian perfectionism misfires against the Liberal Model. The latter path will be under-taken here. Consider that in part II of this chapter the moral justification for a right to conscientious exemption was based on a multiplicity of moral values. There it was argued that a non-absolute right to conscientious exemption is justified by reference to a cluster of moral values, including the demands of the state's duty of neutral pluralism (grounded in the value of individual moral responsibility and respect for ethical pluralism), respect for personal autonomy, freedom of conscience and concern for individual well-being. The value of personal autonomy was only one part of the cluster of values invoked to justify the right. Indeed, it was argued that valuing personal autonomy does not lead to asserting a right to conscientious exemption. Rather, it was argued that respect for personal autonomy only leads to reinforcing the case for that right: if the state grants exemptions (perhaps on the basis of the state's duty of neutral pluralism) that promotes personal autonomy. By granting an exemption the state increases the range of conceptions of a good life which an individual may identify with and live according to. It thereby promotes personal autonomy.

In contrast to the cluster of values justification for the right to exemption of the Liberal Model, the Razian approach to conscientious exemptions is based entirely on the value of personal autonomy.[38] This is the reason why Razian perfectionism misfires against the Liberal Model: even if Raz is right that autonomy has no value when it is used in the pursuit of immoral options or views, the Liberal Model is able to point to other values which may be invoked when a conscientious objector holds immoral views. For example, an objector's well-being will be negatively affected when an exemption is denied, irrespective of whether the objection is motivated by immoral beliefs. A liberal state that values individual well-being will have a strong reason to promote the well-being of its subjects, irrespective of whether or not they hold morally acceptable views.

---

[37] ibid 418–19.
[38] This is consistent with the moral justification provided by Raz for a right to conscientious objection in Raz (n 5) ch 15.

The availability of other values to justify the right to conscientious exemption when the value of personal autonomy is unavailable allows the second proposition of the Liberal Model to be immune from the Razian liberal perfectionist challenge. There is however also a positive case in favour of the second proposition. This is the argument from futility.[39] This says that it is futile for the state to express a view on the merits of the content of the beliefs of the objector for two reasons. First, such moral judgement is unlikely to lead the objector to change his beliefs. Second, the moral judgement is totally unnecessary for the more important task of safeguarding the public interest or the rights of others which the acts of the objector may undermine.

The first futility argument is really about the difficulty of changing the convictions of objectors, especially, but not only, religious objectors. Judges and other state officials engaging in criticism of religious beliefs in a rational fashion are unlikely to be able to affect any meaningful change in the belief system of the objector. This is because religious beliefs, but not only, are often held as a matter of faith. As Macklem argues:

> [F]aith exists as a form of rival to reason. When we say that we believe in something as a matter of faith, or to put it the other way round, when we say that we have faith in certain beliefs, we express a commitment to that which cannot be established by reason, or to that which can be established by reason, but not for that reason ... faith treats itself as a reason to believe, and to act in accordance with belief, without submitting to the conditions of reason.[40]

When it comes to beliefs which state officials think are wrong, it is futile to engage the objector in conversations about how his beliefs are misguided unless the state official is able to speak the same faith-based language of the objector.

Even if the belief is non-faith-based and is instead reason-based, it might be equally futile to engage the objector in conversations about the merits of his beliefs. This is mainly because, in the context of a liberal democracy with free speech, the objector is likely to have already been exposed to all sorts of arguments that contradict his beliefs. Take for example the claimant in *Exmoor* who objected to filing his VAT returns online based on the belief 'that internet usage puts more CO_2 in the atmosphere than aviation'.[41] Why would a state official expressing a competitive view to his (eg that farming of non-human animals is a more serious concern for climate change because it emits more CO_2 than all transportation combined) make any difference? If the objector has gone through the trouble of litigation to secure an exemption in order to accommodate his beliefs, that alone should give an indication of how deeply held and immoveable those beliefs are. This is not to say that deeply held beliefs are not changeable. However, we may be sceptical that the lengthy process that is necessary to revise one's deeply held beliefs can be successfully affected by state disapproval.

Even if the above were wrong, the second limb of the futility argument might still be convincing. It says that the more urgent task for state officials is to determine whether granting an exemption will undermine vital public interests or the rights of others. The task of expressing negative moral judgements about the content of the objector's beliefs does not contribute to that urgent task and is therefore futile for the real task at hand.

---

[39] This was first advanced in Adenitire (n 9) 16–17.
[40] T Macklem, *Independence of Mind* (Oxford, Oxford University Press, 2008) 133–34.
[41] *Exmoor Coast Boat Cruises Ltd v Revenue & Customs* [2014] UKFTT 1103, at 27.

One may object to this second argument as Nehushtan has done. He says that express-ing a view about the content of the objector's belief may make a practical difference to the outcome. He gives the example of a prospective non-white employee who seeks employ-ment from an employer who, for religious reasons, holds that white people should not mix with non-whites and therefore refuses to employ the prospective non-white employee. Nehushtan assumes in this scenario that there is no serious problem of racism in the employment market and that the prospective employee immediately finds employment with another employer. Nehushtan argues that given that the employee will not have suffered any meaningful harm, except perhaps a slight offence having found alternative employment, it would not be possible to condemn the employer's behaviour unless the state takes into account the religiously motivated racist quality of his beliefs and denies the exemption on that basis.[42]

Nehushtan's example is not a good one against the second proposition because there is in fact a strong reason for prohibiting the act of the employer without having to judge the quality of his or her beliefs: the employer's refusal to employ the non-white prospec-tive employee for the reason of his or her race causes dignitary harm to the prospective employee. Not only does the humiliation provide reasons for offence and may occasion psychological harm, most importantly it sends the signal that the non-white employee is a lesser member of society because they are a lesser human being: in short, legal permission of this discriminatory treatment amounts to classifying the non-white employee as a social outcast.[43] This alone is a sufficient reason for not allowing such acts; it is unnecessary to have to judge the content of the employer's beliefs. More will be said about how the notion of dignitary harm should be understood in part VI below.

IV. The Liberal State Should Neither Privilege Nor Disadvantage Religious Beliefs Over Non-Religious Ones When Considering Whether to Grant a Conscientious Exemption

The third proposition of the Liberal Model says that the liberal state should neither privilege nor disadvantage religious beliefs over non-religious ones when considering whether to grant conscientious exemptions. Leigh, Chipeur and Clarke all agree in this volume with this proposition. Not much will be said about the positive case for the third proposition. This is because the clear implication of the positive argument made in part II of this chapter (the cluster of values argument) in favour of conscientious exemptions generally is that the case for exemptions is insensitive to the religious or non-religious nature of the belief of the objector. In fact, the state's duty of neutral pluralism is specifically against unequal treatment depending on the nature of the beliefs. Also, respect for autonomy, conscience and well-being are insensitive to the particular content of the beliefs of the objectors. Also, the case made in favour of the general right to conscientious exemption is insensitive to the religious or non-religious nature of the conscientious objection. It was argued that a general right to

[42] Nehushtan (n 4) 146–47.
[43] This is an argument borrowed from J Waldron, *The Harm in Hate Speech* (Cambridge, MA, Harvard University Press, 2014) ch 5.

conscientious exemption is based on providing an alternative forum, the judicial one, where minority moral views left behind in the political process may be able to bring a claim and ask for exemptions from legal obligations which impinge on their consciences. Of course, such minority moral views may or may not be religious.

Equality of treatment between religious and non-religious beliefs is also a clear implication of the second proposition of the Liberal Model. That proposition calls for the liberal state to be blind to the validity of the belief of the objector. It follows that the liberal state should also be blind to the validity of sectarian claims that religious beliefs are more or less deserving of accommodation than non-religious beliefs. The only criterion allowed, consistent with the fourth proposition, is that exemptions should not be granted if it would have a disproportionate impact on the public interest or on the rights of others. That criterion is neutral as to the religious or non-religious nature of the belief involved.

Given the clear neutralist implications of the arguments advanced so far, this part of the chapter therefore focuses on defending the third proposition from the attacks mounted by Corvino, Moon, and Nehushtan and Coyle in this volume. Corvino and Moon, especially the latter, seem sceptical of granting exemptions to non-religious objectors. Whereas, Nehushtan and Coyle would prefer granting exemptions to non-religious objectors over religious ones.

A. Against Corvino

Corvino canvasses a number of arguments which would single out religion as specially or uniquely deserving exemptions. His final answer is that exemptions are warranted as a counter-balance to unjust discrimination in the framing of laws that bind all citizens. He says that given that it is unworkable to have a rule which countenances exemptions whenever a law is unfair, it is better to identify categories that are typical sites of unjust discrimination and then require heightened scrutiny with respect to those categories. He identifies religion as one such category and hence argues that exemptions for religious objectors are warranted in the circumstances where the interests of religious minorities have been discounted. It turns out, however, that Corvino does not see religion as uniquely special after all. Indeed, he explicitly says that there are other categories that are typical sites of unjust discrimination, such as disability and sexual orientation. He is, however, sceptical that there should be in general a right to exemption for secular citizens who have deep and meaningful moral commitments that conflict with the law. In this regards he argues that while non-believers can also have their perspectives unjustly discounted, they face this problem less commonly than believers do. Furthermore, he argues that:

> [T]here are pragmatic difficulties with extending the argument of this section to secular concerns: The whole point of enumerating categories of heightened scrutiny – whether in antidiscrimination law or in constitutional interpretation – is that legislators and judges are unlikely to see their own prejudices. 'Give heightened scrutiny to laws that unjustly overlook minorities' is not a workable legal rule; 'Give heightened scrutiny to laws that implicate race, religion, sexual orientation, and so on' is.[44]

[44] Chapter 2, part V.

Corvino goes on to argue that while one ought to be sceptical of exemption claims for non-religious objectors in general, one can argue for non-religious exemptions in particular circumstances, for example in the context of the military draft.

It is however doubtful that Corvino's rationale for in effect arguing against the availability of the general right to conscientious exemption for non-religious objectors is convincing. Indeed, his argument that non-religious conscience is not a category to be given heightened scrutiny seems to be the result of a version of US parochialism. In this respect, remember the very brief discussion in part I on the general right to conscientious exemption in US law. There it was suggested that such a general right may be grounded, among others, in RFRA and in Title VII (and their state-level counterparts). Consistently with Corvino's views, these two pieces of legislation appear to confer exemptions only on the basis of a religious belief. A doctrinal argument could be advanced to show that this apparent privileging of religion in these statutes is in fact false because, consistent with the US Supreme Court ('USSC') decision in *Welsh*[45] (where a non-religious objector to military service was granted a statutory exemption on its face reserved only to religious believers), the legal definition of 'religion' in US law includes non-religious beliefs which function in the life of a conscientious objector as a religion.[46] But even if one took these statutes at their face value to the effect that a general right to conscientious exemption is reserved to religious believers alone, Corvino would not be correct to say that it is pragmatically best to reserve these exemptions to religious believers alone. This is because even under US domestic law several statutory exemptions use the category of religious and moral beliefs without much administrative difficulty. Micah Schwartzman illustrates the point:

> [F]ederal and state legislation often goes beyond the category of religion to protect non- religious ethical and moral beliefs. For a recent example, the Affordable Care Act … includes an exemption from its minimum coverage provision … for … nonprofit organization whose members 'share a common set of *ethical or religious beliefs* and share medical expenses among members in accordance with those beliefs'. Similar language is used in federal legislation prohibiting public officials from requiring health care providers to perform or assist with abortions or sterilizations when doing so would violate their 'religious beliefs or moral convictions'. The federal government is also barred from requiring employees to participate in the administration of the death penalty 'if such participation is contrary to the *moral or religious convictions* of the employee'. Numerous other federal and state statutes and regulations involving foreign aid, counseling services, vaccinations, pharmacies, organ donation, assisted suicide, and, of course, military service follow the same pattern of expressly protecting not only religious convictions but also ethical and moral beliefs, conscience, or some combination thereof.[47]

Furthermore, the use of 'conscience and religion' is a well-established category in international law and various domestic jurisdictions. Article 18(1) of the International Covenant on Civil and Political Rights (ICCPR) reads 'Everyone shall have the right to freedom of thought, conscience and religion'. The United Nations Human Rights Committee, the body that monitors compliance with the ICCPR, has interpreted the article thus: 'Article 18 protects theistic, non-theistic and atheistic beliefs, as well as the right not to profess any

[45] *Welsh v United States* (1970) 398 US 333.
[46] This argument is pursued in detail in Adenitire, 'A General Legal Right to Conscientious Exemption' (2018) ch 3.
[47] M Schwartzman, 'Religion as a Legal Proxy' (2014) 51 *San Diego Law Review* 1085, 1100–01.

religion or belief'.[48] In relation to conscientious exemptions in the military context it has stated that 'there shall be no differentiation among conscientious objectors on the basis of the nature of their particular beliefs [whether religious or non-religious]'.[49] The use of the category 'conscience and religion' is also present in Canada under section 2(a) of the Canadian Charter. As Moon recounts in part IV of chapter five, in *Maurice*, a Federal Canadian Court invoked this section to make available vegetarian meals to a prisoner who objected to eating non-vegetarian meals on the basis of non-religious beliefs.[50] The prison authorities had insisted that vegetarian meals were to be given only to religious vegetarians. The Court concluded that 'accommodating a vegetarian's conscientiously held beliefs imposes no greater burden on an institution than that already in place for the provision of religious diets'.[51]

Given these experiences that show that the category 'conscience and religion' is perfectly workable both in the US and elsewhere, Corvino's pragmatic argument that exemptions can be generally reserved for religious objectors alone should be received with high scepticism. However, Corvino is correct to say that for the most part it is religious believers that will make claims for exemptions. In Canada, leaving aside the 'seat-belt' cases discussed by Moon in part IV of his chapter, only five cases – *Roach*,[52] *Maurice*,[53] *Chainnigh*,[54] *McAteer*[55] and *Hughes*[56] – have been identified as involving a claim for exemption based on a non-religious belief relying on the Canadian Charter's protection of freedom of conscience. Of these, only *Maurice* successfully received the exemption he sought. It is however doubtful that the fact that it is religious believers that will make use more often of the general right to exemption is itself a good reason for excluding non-religious people from benefitting from the general right. The fact that injustice will be infrequent against non-religious objectors is not a good reason to eliminate the availability of a remedy against that injustice. If anything, the opposite is true. If the Canadian experience is to be believed, there will not be a huge administrative burden on courts to administer a general right to conscientious exemption for non-religious objectors. Consequently, given the little administrative cost for a gain in justice, it seems that there is a good reason to provide for a general right to exemption for non-religious objectors.

---

[48] UNCHR, 'CCPR General Comment No 22: Article 18 (Freedom of Thought, Conscience or Religion)' (1993) CCPR/C/21/Rev.1/Add.4.

[49] ibid 11. See also *Yoon and Choi v Republic of Korea* (2006) CCPR/C/88/D/1321-22/2004.

[50] *Maurice v Canada (Attorney General)* [2002] FCT 69.

[51] ibid at 13.

[52] *Roach v Canada (Minister of State for Multiculturalism and Citizenship)* (1994) 2 FCR 406. Roach, a committed republican anti-monarchist and non-Canadian citizen who was undergoing the process of naturalisation, sought to be exempted from affirming or swearing the citizenship oath which required swearing allegiance to the Queen.

[53] *Maurice* (n 50).

[54] *Giolla Chainnigh v Canada (Attorney General)* [2008] FC 69. This concerned anti-monarchists (including Roach himself) who objected to an oath of allegiance to the Queen.

[55] *McAteer v Canada (Attorney General)* [2014] CarswellOnt 10955. This also concerned anti-monarchists who objected to an oath of allegiance to the Queen.

[56] *R v Hughes* [2012] ABPC 250. The Alberta Provincial Court rejected a freedom of conscience claim against Calgary City's Responsible Pet Ownership Bylaw which prohibited the keeping of pet chickens on residential property. Hughes, being the founder of the advocacy group Canadian Liberated Urban Chicken Klub (CLUCK), testified that he kept urban hens and ate their eggs because of his philosophy regarding sustainable food choices which involved minimising the amount of consumption of non-self-grown food.

B. Against Moon

Moon is deeply sceptical about granting exemptions to non-religious conscientious objectors. This results from his rationale about when exemptions are warranted for religious objectors. His first move is to argue that freedom of religion (under s 2(a) of the Canadian Charter) should not be understood as a form of liberty right which entitles the individual to be free from state encroachment in living according to her religious beliefs unless this is necessary to protect the rights and interests of others or the general welfare. Instead, he argues that freedom of religion is best understood as a form of equality right that rests on the recognition of the deep connection between the individual and his religious or cultural group and on a concern about the standing of such groups and their members in the larger society. Religious exemptions and other forms of accommodations for religious believers therefore rest, he argues, on seeking to avoid the marginalisation of religious groups and the exclusion and alienation of their members from the larger society.

Moon continues to argue that, on this basis, non-religious objectors do not seem to deserve conscientious exemptions because non-religious beliefs are seldom linked to the equal standing of groups in wider society. He concedes that it is possible to imagine individuals organising themselves around a particular secular purpose (he gives the example of a group dedicated to the use hallucinogenic drugs to obtain valuable insights). He argues, however that:

> [A] group that is voluntarily formed around a particular issue does not play the same role in the life of the individual as a religious or cultural group that is characterised by a comprehensive world view, or form of life, that is transmitted through family and community. Such a group is not, in the same way, a source of identity or meaning for its members, and is not similarly vulnerable to discrimination and systemic exclusion. The state's rejection or regulation of the practices/beliefs of such a group is simply that – the rejection of a particular position or perspective.[57]

Accordingly, Moon argues that the few conscientious exemptions granted to non-religious objectors may be unjustified in principle and be explained by the simple fact that the beliefs and practices of the objectors (eg vegetarianism and pacifism) resemble well-known religious beliefs and practices which have traditionally benefited from exemptions.

Moon's attack against the third proposition of the Liberal Model rests on the twin view that religious freedom is best understood as a non-discrimination norm meant to protect religious groups and that non-religious groups are not systematically excluded from wider society on the basis of an unjustifiable discriminatory attitude. Both views are however unconvincing. Take the first view that religious freedom under s 2(a) of the Canadian Charter is not to be understood as a liberty norm but is better viewed as a non-discrimination norm intended to protect the standing of religious groups in society. If this was the case then we should expect the Canadian courts not to grant exemptions to individuals when their practices are not shared by their religious group. However, the Supreme Court of Canada has explicitly rejected that approach in the landmark case of *Amselem*.[58] As discussed by Jones in part II of chapter three, the case concerned whether religious freedom ought to protect the appellants' belief, not shared by their religious group, that Judaism required erecting

---

[57] Chapter 5, text to n 46.
[58] *Syndicat Northcrest v Amselem* (2004) 2 SCR 551.

a private succah on their balconies rather than use the communal succah offered by the Syndicat. The SCC, Iacobucci J delivering the majority judgment, held that the appellants' religious freedom had been unjustifiably infringed by the failure to accommodate them. The SCC explicitly rejected the contention made by the lower court in that case that, in line with the evidence from two Rabbis, Judaism does not require, contrary to the appellants' beliefs, an individual succah but permits communal succot.[59] Iacobucci J empathetically affirmed that 'claimants seeking to invoke freedom of religion should not need to prove the objective validity of their beliefs in that their beliefs are objectively recognized as valid by other members of the same religion, nor is such an inquiry appropriate for courts to make'.[60]

The view that religious freedom is applicable also when a practice is not constitutive of a religious group is tied to the notion, developed by Iacobucci J in *Amselem*, that 'religion is about freely and deeply held personal convictions or beliefs connected to an individual's spiritual faith and integrally linked to one's self-definition and spiritual fulfilment, the practices of which allow individuals to foster a connection with the divine or with the subject or object of that spiritual faith'.[61] It seems then that Moon is not right to argue that religious freedom is best understood as a non-discrimination norm intended to protect the standing of religious groups in society. This cannot be the case because the main focus of religion and religious freedom is a person's individual belief system, whether or not that belief system is shared by a larger group. Also in this regard, and crucially, as Cranmer briefly alludes to in chapter twelve, the SCC has yet to determine whether religious organisations, such as churches, schools and universities, can invoke freedom of religion. The current view is that individual members of such institutions can collectively invoke religious freedom but it remains an open question whether the institutions themselves can invoke religious freedom.[62] The current state of the law does not sit well with Moon's view: religious freedom under the Canadian Charter cannot be about the standing of religious groups in society if it is unclear whether religious freedom applies to institutions, such as churches or religious schools, whose main purpose is to lead and organise groups to follow certain religious doctrines.

The implication of rejecting Moon's view that exemptions are warranted to secure the standing of religious groups in society is that exemptions may be warranted whether or not they contribute to the standing of religious groups. Accordingly, in line with the third proposition of the Liberal Model, exemptions may be granted to religious or non-religious individuals. However, even if one accepted Moon's view that religious freedom is about the standing of groups in society, it is unclear why this rationale would not apply to non-religious groups as well. Moon argues that non-religious groups that coalesce around a particular secular purpose are not, in the same way as religious groups, a source of identity or meaning for their members, and are not similarly vulnerable to discrimination and systemic exclusion. This seems doubtful as atheist and agnostic members of secular humanist societies around the globe would attest. In the UK, for example, not only have members of the British Humanist Association (now Humanists UK) drawn meaning and identity from humanist values in social and political campaigns, they have also been vulnerable to

---

[59] ibid at 66.
[60] ibid at 43.
[61] ibid at 39.
[62] *Loyola High School v Quebec (Attorney General)* (2015) 1 SCR 613, at 33; *Law Society of British Columbia v Trinity Western University* [2018] SCC 32 (SCC), at 61.

discrimination and systemic exclusion. For example, the Northern Ireland High Court has recently accepted that the failure to recognise legally valid humanist weddings in Northern Ireland unlawfully discriminates against humanists in breach of Article 14 ECHR read in conjunction with Article 9.[63] This discriminatory state of affairs continues in England and Wales where it is still not possible to have any form of legally recognised humanist wedding.

Furthermore, certain Canadian provinces (but not all) have explicitly accepted that individuals may be targeted for discriminatory treatment on the grounds of their non-religious conscientious beliefs. For example, section 1 of the Ontario Human Rights Code,[64] an anti-discrimination statute, prohibits discrimination on the basis of creed. Prior to the non-legally binding guidance issued by the Ontario Human Rights Commission (OHRC) in 2015, it was not clear whether creed covered only religious beliefs. However, following a period of public consultation and redrafting of the guidance, the current guidance makes clear that the Code does not only protect religious beliefs when it says that 'Creed may also include non-religious belief systems that, like religion, substantially influence a person's identity, worldview and way of life'.[65] No cases have arisen under the Ontario Code to authoritatively settle in law what non-religious beliefs qualify for protection. Nevertheless, Moon's factual claim that non-religious groups are not similarly vulnerable to discrimination and systemic exclusion seems to be undermined by the recognition by an anti-discrimination body (ie the OHRC) that non-religious belief systems also need to be protected from discrimination. Of course, in the UK, this has long been recognised given that the Equality Act 2010 (and some of its predecessors) protects religious and non-religious philosophical beliefs (such as the moral responsibility to avoid climate change[66]) from discriminatory treatment.

In conclusion, Moon's attack against the third proposition of the Liberal Model needs to be rejected on the basis that religious freedom under the Canadian Charter is not best understood as an anti-discrimination norm meant to protect the standing of religious groups in society. The scope of religious freedom is better understood as encompassing a liberty right which protects the deep moral commitments of individuals to live according to their beliefs unless there are good reasons for the state to interfere. Given that individuals can also have deep moral commitments which are non-religious, it is unfair not to protect those non-religious commitments. Also, contra Moon, non-religious groups and their members can also be the target of systemic exclusion or discrimination and, consequently, they too need to be protected in order to uphold their equal standing in society.

C. Against Nehushtan and Coyle[67]

Nehushtan and Coyle, in chapter seven, state that there are good reasons for disadvantaging religious objectors over non-religious ones in the context of conscientious exemptions.

[63] *Smyth, Re Judicial Review* [2017] NIQB 55. A similar conclusion was reached by the United States Court of Appeal for the Seventh Circuit in *Center for Inquiry, Inc v Marion Circuit Court Clerk* (2014) 758 F3d.

[64] RSO 1990, Chapter H 19.

[65] Ontario Human Rights Commission, 'Policy on Preventing Discrimination Based on Creed' (2015) at www.ohrc.on.ca/sites/default/files/Policy%20on%20preventing%20discrimination%20based%20on%20creed_accessible_0.pdf.

[66] *Grainger plc v Nicholson* [2009] ICR 360.

[67] A significant portion of the following discussion relies heavily on Adenitire, 'The Irrelevance of Religion' (2017) 411–13.

The statement is grounded in their liberal perfectionism, already criticised in part III of this chapter, and in the view, not defended in this volume, that:

> While every comprehensive theory or ideology is intolerant by its nature, religion is uniquely and unjustly intolerant, and in a way that poses unique challenges to the tolerant-liberal state. If this is true ... religious symbols may not be allowed to be displayed in certain places ... even when the symbol itself does not directly convey illegitimate, unjustly intolerant values, and even if the person wearing the symbol does not intend to convey unjustly intolerant views ... This is so because religion is inherently and unjustly intolerant and because the liberal state should not support or endorse, directly or indirectly, intolerant ideologies or sets of beliefs.[68]

The authors reference Nehushtan's monograph, *Intolerant Religion in a Tolerant-Liberal Democracy*,[69] to provide support for the view that religion is inherently and unjustly intolerant. It is however doubtful that the arguments provided in Nehushtan's monograph can sustain this view. His main argument is an empirical one, though he does adduce some theoretical explanations to sustain the empirical arguments. Some of these theoretical arguments for the intolerant nature of religion are that religious groups tend to keep a distinct community and thereby exclude others; religions claim that their world-view is the absolute truth and thereby persecute heretics; the divine nature of religious commands stifles the possibility of criticism and prompts the religious person not to tolerate non-compliance.[70] No issue will be taken here against Nehushtan's theoretical arguments. He himself admits that his theoretical arguments 'might appear too sketchy. Indeed, some of the following assertions and generalisations rely on the assumption that these generalisations are, by definition, mostly true or generally accurate'.[71]

Given that these theoretical arguments cannot by themselves show that religion is inherently (or conceptually) intolerant, Nehushtan's main arrow is his empirical argument. He relies on a number of sociological/psychological studies which he interprets as proving his point. He cites various studies spanning over a considerable number of years the constant conclusions of which are best described, he says, by a review undertaken by Hunsberger and Jackson.[72] But on closer analysis this review does not in fact prove that, as a matter of conceptual necessity, religious people are unjustly intolerant. Rather, it proves that certain religious attitudes are more prone to lead to certain kinds of prejudice towards certain groups than others. Indeed, some religious attitudes actually lead to less prejudice towards certain groups, such as homosexuals and some racial groups.

Hunsberger and Jackson's review (and the studies it is based on) proceeds on the basis of four attitudes to religion, namely the intrinsic orientation, the extrinsic orientation, the quest orientation and religious fundamentalism. Hunsberger and Jackson explain these four categorisations as follows:

> An intrinsic orientation was considered to be more mature, stemming from an internalized, committed, and sincere faith. The extrinsic orientation was associated with religious immaturity, involving an externalized, consensual, utilitarian orientation to religion ... the quest orientation

---

[68] Chapter 7, text to n 35.
[69] Nehushtan (n 4).
[70] ibid 97–101; 108–12; 114–17.
[71] ibid 96.
[72] B Hunsberger and LM Jackson, 'Religion, Meaning, and Prejudice' (2005) 61 *Journal of Social Issues* 807.

involves a questioning, doubting, open, and flexible approach to religious issues ... religious fundamentalism (RF) focuses on closed-mindedness, the certainty that one's religious beliefs are correct, and the belief that one has access to absolute truth[73]

On the basis of these categorisations the review concludes that:

Our review of studies published since 1990 clearly supports the idea that the target of prejudice is important when considering prejudice-religious orientation relationships ... The Intrinsic scale was consistently *negatively* related to self-reported racial/ethnic intolerance (4 of 4 studies), but it was *positively* related to intolerance of gay men and lesbians (7/9 studies) and possibly to authoritarianism and to intolerance of Communists and religious outgroups, though there are few relevant studies. The extrinsic orientation was sometimes positively related to racial/ethnic (3/4) and gay/lesbian (4/8) intolerance. Quest showed a weak tendency to be associated with tolerance for racial groups (2/5); a much stronger effect appeared for gay/lesbian persons as targets (7/9). Finally, [religious fundamentalism] was consistently related to increased prejudice against gay/lesbian persons, women, Communists, and religious outgroups, as well as authoritarianism (39/39 findings in total), but its relationship with racial/ethnic intolerance is less clear-cut (5 positive relationships, 6 nonsignificant findings).[74]

Rather than proving Nehusthan's claim that religious beliefs necessarily lead to intolerance/prejudice, the review actually proves that certain religious attitudes may lead to certain kinds of intolerance/prejudice. The review does not however tell us how many religious people hold what religious attitudes. If the vast majority of religious individuals held the religious fundamentalism attitude then Nehusthan's claim would hold true as a quick generalisation (while still falling below the conceptual claim he makes). However, if it is shown that a vast majority of religious individuals actually hold the quest religious attitude then perfectionist liberal states, in their endeavour to combat prejudice and intolerance, would do well to promote religion. Arguably, the latter is not a conclusion which Nehushtan would be happy to reach.

Nehushtan's anti-religion approach may be more generally criticised for trying to prove a conceptual claim, one that should hold true independently of space and time, by relying on empirical evidence of limited scope. He himself admits that the empirical studies he relies on are very limited in scope. He says that 'most if not all of the reliable empirical findings and conclusions are limited not only in terms of the target group (mostly Christians) and geographic area (mostly North America) but also the relevant era (late twentieth Century)'.[75] There is a significant difference between claiming, as he does, that 'religion is inherently intolerant'[76] and claiming, as the more accurate picture might suggest, that there are meaningful links between prejudice and certain religious attitudes which exist in late twentieth Century North American Christian communities.

Furthermore, and importantly, not all claims for religious exemptions are based on prejudice. The Christian B&B owners in the case of *Bull v Hall*[77] who refused to provide a double bedroom to same-sex couples were arguably prejudiced against homosexuals and

---

[73] ibid 809.
[74] ibid 812. Nehusthan cites this passage at Nehushtan (n 4) 88.
[75] Nehushtan (n 4) 92.
[76] ibid 200.
[77] *Bull v Hall* [2013] UKSC 73.

their act of refusing a bedroom was arguably an unjustly intolerant one. However, not the same can be said about a Sikh man claiming an exemption from the legal duty to wear motorcycle helmets in order to be able to wear the Sikh turban. Nehusthan and Coyle in this volume acknowledge the fact that a claim for exemption by a religious objector may not be based on unjustly intolerant views but merely on morally misguided or irrational beliefs. While they insist that the inherently intolerant nature of religion is a good reason not to exempt individuals from legal obligations that forbid them from wearing religious symbols, they eventually concede that such exemptions may nevertheless be granted on the condition that anti-religious symbols are also allowed. They state that:

> Religious symbols may be allowed in the public sphere and the workplace after all if anti-religious symbols are accorded the same status and protection. Thus, whether one is or is not convinced by the soundness of the link between the intolerant nature of religion and the need to exclude religious symbols from the public sphere is of less importance. The more important point is that of the equal treatment that should be granted to both religious and anti-religious symbols and sentiments.[78]

It is a welcome development for Nehushtan to have softened in this volume (together with Coyle) his earlier claim that 'Religious claims … for exemptions may not be tolerated or accepted even when they do not directly rely on [unjustly] intolerant values … This is so because religion is inherently intolerant and because the liberal state should not support or endorse, directly or indirectly, intolerant ideologies or sets of beliefs.'[79] It is doubtful that the added proviso that anti-religious symbols should also be displayed along religious ones is entirely compatible with the third proposition of the Liberal Model given that that proposition calls for equal treatment of religious and non-religious beliefs; not simply religious and anti-religious beliefs. Nevertheless, given that there is no compelling evidence for the view that religion is inherently intolerant, Nehushtan and Coyle should be taken to have failed to provide even a prima facie case in favour of disadvantaging religious conscientious objectors over non-religious ones.

V. The Liberal State Should Grant Conscientious Exemptions to Claimants Who are Sincere and if the Exemptions would not Disproportionately Impact the Rights of Others or the Public Interest

The final proposition of the Liberal Model says that the liberal state should grant conscientious exemptions to claimants who are sincere and only if the exemptions would not disproportionately impact the rights of others or the public interest. Much of the analysis in this part will be reserved to providing criteria as to how the right to exemption should be balanced against countervailing considerations. Some of these considerations will then be applied in part VI in the context of cases in which the general right to conscientious

---

[78] Chapter 7, text to n 38.
[79] Nehushtan (n 4) 200.

exemption conflicts with the principle of non-discrimination on the ground of sexual orientation. It will be argued that, in general, exemptions from anti-discrimination laws should not be granted given that granting them would result in LGB people being classed as second-class citizens. It is argued that this approach does not in turn label as second-class citizens individuals who are refused exemptions given the myriad of protections granted by liberal states for individuals to make known and live out their opposition to homosexuality. Particular issue is taken with Leigh, and with Chipeur and Clarke who argue in favour of exemptions from sexual orientation anti-discrimination laws in this volume.

A. The Two Pillars of the Fourth Proposition

The fourth proposition has two pillars. The first is that only sincere conscientious objectors should benefit from the right to exemption. Much has already been said about this requirement in part III of chapter eleven of this volume. It may be recalled that it was there argued that assessing the sincerity of a person, whether or not a conscientious objector, is a job that courts are well accustomed to. To this it should be added that the sincerity test ought not, for the reasons explored in part III of this chapter, turn into a judicial enquiry into the validity, truth, reasonableness, etc of the beliefs of the objectors. Rather the focus should be on whether the belief is sincerely held.

Some have claimed that it would be more difficult for judges to assess the sincerity of secular beliefs without reference, as in religious practices, to comprehensive belief systems which have a communal dimension.[80] However, the UK and Canadian experience seem to invalidate this claim. In none of the five Canadian non-religious conscientious exemption claims was the sincerity of the claimants an issue. In the UK, two[81] cases only on non-religious conscientious exemptions have been identified, ie *Pattison*[82] and *Exmoor*. Only in *Exmoor* was sincerity an issue. That issue was resolved, as in any other case, on the basis of evidence in front of the tribunal. In that case the objector did not want to file his VAT returns online based on his belief that electronic communications greatly contributes to climate change. There was however evidence that he was not being totally sincere. He in fact did occasionally use the internet when economically expedient despite his strong disinclinations in that regard.[83] It seems then that the non-religiosity of a claim for conscientious exemption does not raise particular sincerity problems which courts cannot deal with.

[80] KA Brady, *The Distinctiveness of Religion in American Law: Rethinking Religion Clause Jurisprudence* (Cambridge, Cambridge University Press, 2015) 307.

[81] This is only in the context of the general right to conscientious exemption. Other cases on non-religious conscience exist but they concern particular statutory exemptions.

[82] *R (on the application of Pattison) v Social Security and Child Support Commissioners* [2004] EWHC 2370. The applicant objected to employment in the private sector 'on the ground that private enterprise is not democratically accountable for the way the worker feels and consequentially is under no obligation to sustain the employment of those who generate profit. Nor is it disposed to concede the employers a stake in the assets that accrue from their individual efforts' (para 2). The High Court held that the applicant's right to freedom of conscience under Art 9 ECHR was not even engaged because the Art 9 did not allow the applicant to object to obligations attached to a benefit which he was not obliged to seek. This reasoning would now be incompatible with the ECtHR's reasoning in *Eweida v United Kingdom* [2013] IRLR 231.

[83] *Exmoor* (n 41) at 81–82.

Just as in the case of religious objections, courts do not need to look at what the objector's community believes in order to determine the sincerity of the particular objector. In fact, that query is altogether unhelpful because a person, even if religious, is not required to hold the same beliefs as his or her religious or moral community. This is because that would require the court to investigate whether a person adheres to a particular religious orthodoxy. As examined in part III of this chapter, courts cannot assess the validity, including the orthodoxy, of a particular religious belief.

The second pillar of the fourth proposition is that conscientious exemptions should not be granted if doing so would disproportionately impact the rights of others or the public interest. This can be formulated in the following way:

Refusing to grant a conscientious exemption will be disproportionate unless:

(a)   the refusal pursues an objective having substantial moral weight (countervailing reason stage);
(b)   the refusal is suitable for the achievement of that legitimate objective (suitability stage);
(c)   the refusal is the most practicable way to achieve that objective (necessity stage); and
(d)   the overall reasons supporting a refusal outweigh the reasons to grant an exemption (balancing stage).[84]

In essence, the second pillar of the fourth proposition requires a proportionality analysis. The core of this analysis is balancing the reasons in favour of granting an exemption against the reasons against granting it. The proportionality analysis is nothing other than structured moral reasoning which is highly sensitive to facts and context.

B. What Factors Should Influence the Proportionality Analysis?

No robust attempt is made here to provide a full defence of the use of proportionality analysis against its most assiduous critics. Proportionality as a method of legal reasoning in human rights law generally has been criticised by various theorists for, among other things, being irrational, too formal, being incapable of providing actual guidance to adjudicators employing it, and undermining democratic legislative decisions about rights.[85] A response ought to be given to critics of proportionality/balancing reasoning within the context of conscientious exemptions, such as Kathleen Brady, who claims that it gives rise to 'manipulation, unprincipled or arbitrary decision making, and inconsistent and potentially discriminatory

---

[84] This is a way to make specific to the context of conscientious exemptions the more general proportionality test. This says that: '1. Does the legislation (or other government action) establishing the right's limitation pursue a legitimate objective of sufficient importance to warrant limiting a right? 2. Are the means in service of the objective rationally connected (suitable) to the objective? 3. Are the means in service of the objective necessary, that is, minimally impairing of the limited right, taking into account alternative means of achieving the same objective? 4. Do the beneficial effects of the limitation on the right outweigh the deleterious effects of the limitation; in short, is there a fair balance between the public interest and the private right?' See G Huscroft, BW Miller and G Webber, 'Introduction', *Proportionality and the Rule of Law* (Cambridge, Cambridge University Press, 2014) 2.

[85] The literature on this is vast. Various critiques are set out by different authors in M Klatt (ed), *Institutionalized Reason: The Jurisprudence of Robert Alexy* (Oxford, Oxford University Press, 2012). See also G Webber, *The Negotiable Constitution: On the Limitation of Rights* (Cambridge, Cambridge University Press, 2009); Huscroft, Miller and Webber, *Proportionality* (2014).

application'.[86] The response is not to say that proportionality analysis can give rise to unequivocal legal outcomes in all situations. The adequate response is that the Liberal Model can point out factors which adjudicators should weight more heavily when considering whether a particular exemption should be given under the general right to conscientious exemption. This part catalogues them while analysing each stage of the proportionality analysis.

C. The Countervailing Reasons Stage

The first stage of the proportionality analysis requires identifying reasons which may militate against granting an exemption. Those reasons will be provided by analysing the rationale for the existence of the legal duty which is being objected to. No doubts several countervailing reasons will exist in reference to one particular legal duty. In accordance with the fourth proposition, permissible countervailing reasons will be of two kinds only: guaranteeing the rights of others; or the public interest. Other kinds of reasons are not consistent with the Liberal Model. In particular, paternalistic reasons and reasons motivated by an adverse moral judgement about the way of life of the objector are not permissible.

Consider the case of *Pack* where members of the Holiness Church of God in Jesus Name sought to be exempt from the tort of public nuisance so that they could handle poisonous serpents and consume poisonous substances in accordance with their beliefs that doing so was a biblical injunction. The Tennessee Supreme Court explicitly rejected the possibility of allowing the practice between members only on the basis that 'the state has a right to protect a person from himself and to demand that he protect his own life'.[87] This is a clear case of a countervailing paternalistic reason incompatible with the Liberal Model's insistence that given that it is the individual that will benefit or suffer the consequences of a particular way of life, the choice of which life to follow is theirs and not the state's.

In *Pack*, at least two alternative permissible countervailing reasons were available. The first, and weightier reason, was to protect the right to personal safety of the children of the members of the Church who, as the court recorded, were 'roaming about unattended' during services with poisonous snake-handling.[88] The second, perhaps less weighty, reason was to safeguard the public interest in reducing or preventing the costs (if any) that would be incurred by public healthcare in dealing with cases of poisoned members or other individuals attending the services.

Consider also the case of *Lukumi Babalu Aye*.[89] The case involved the effective prohibition by the city of Hielah of the practice of animal sacrifice by individuals of the Santeria religion. The USSC found that the prohibition of Santeria ceremonial animal sacrifice was motivated by legislative animus against the religion and was therefore unconstitutional under the Free Exercise Clause. Similar religious practices of killing animals without stunning them, such as Kosher or Halal, were explicitly exempted by the city's ordinances. Furthermore, various city officials expressed similar views to the one that 'Santeria was a sin, "foolishness,"

---

[86] Brady, *The Distinctiveness of Religion in American Law* (2015) 195.
[87] *State ex rel Swann v Pack* (1975) 527 SW2d 99 at 113–14.
[88] ibid at 113.
[89] *Church of Lukumi Babalu Aye, Inc v Hialeah* (1992) 508 US 520.

"an abomination to the Lord," and the worship of "demons".[90] Such rationale, ie legislative animus against a particular religion, is incompatible with the second proposition of the Liberal Model which prohibits the state from passing moral judgement on the content of conscientious objectors' beliefs. Such rationale would therefore also be impermissible at the countervailing reasons stage of the proportionality analysis.

Lukumi is also useful to reflect on another constraint of the Liberal Model: if no valid countervailing reasons can be identified for a legal obligation which is being objected to, the optimal result is not to grant an exemption but is instead to dispense with the obligation altogether. In *Lukumi*, exempting the members of the Santeria religion from the legal obligation which was specifically enacted to target them would have made the obligation meaningless. There are no good reasons why such meaningless and discriminatory legislation should remain on the statute book. Compatibly with the Liberal Model, the USSC voided the entire legislation rather than holding that it was unconstitutional as applied to the church members.[91]

D. The Suitability and Necessity Stage

In considering the suitability stage the relevant question is whether the granting of an exemption would undermine the countervailing reasons that were identified in the first stage. The rationale here is to ensure that the countervailing reason is in fact having a role to play in the decision whether or not to grant the exemption and is not being used as a façade. Consider the countervailing reason in *Hobby Lobby* for an exemption from the contraceptive mandate. This was identified by the majority opinion as providing to women cost-free access to contraception.[92] In principle, granting the exemption would not have undermined the countervailing reason. This was because the USSC had argued that the exemption already provided to religious non-profit organisations could be extended to for-profit objecting employers such as Hobby Lobby. Under that accommodation arrangement, Hobby Lobby would self-certify that it objected to providing the coverage. Upon receipt of the certification, Hobby Lobby's insurers would then be required to provide the contraceptive coverage.[93] Accordingly, despite granting the exemption, women would still continue to have cost-free access to contraception. Admittedly, however, as already discussed in part III of chapter eleven in this volume, it was not clear that this accommodation would have been possible given that, as other religious employers have done, Hobby Lobby may also have objected to self-certifying its conscientious objection to its insurer.

Hobby Lobby is also a useful case to illustrate the necessity stage of the proportionality analysis. In the necessity stage a court asks whether the refusal of the exemption is the most practicable way to achieve the countervailing reason. In *Hobby Lobby* the USSC was able to identify a suitable and practicable alternative: extending to the for-profit the exemption

---

[90] ibid at 541.

[91] ibid at 547. This section should not be taken to mean that animal sacrifice or indeed the killing of animals for religious or non-religious purposes, including for food, is morally justifiable. The opposite is the case. However, that would require a detailed argument not relevant to the present volume.

[92] *Burwell v Hobby Lobby Stores, Inc* (2014) 134 SCt 2751, at 39–40.

[93] ibid at 40–45.

which religious non-profit already benefitted from. In essence, unless refusing the exemption is necessary to pursue the countervailing reason, the duty-bearer would have acted disproportionately. This step encourages the duty-bearer to canvass a range of options in which it may achieve its own countervailing reason while allowing the right-bearer to enjoy the exemption. It may well be that imposing an alternative obligation may be sufficient to alleviate the concerns raised by the countervailing reason. The classic example here is in the military context. A countervailing reason for refusing to exempt Quakers and pacifists from compulsory military conscription would be the unfairness to non-objectors in being required to serve their country at great cost to their lives and families. This unfairness may be significantly alleviated if exempt objectors are required, as a condition for their exemption, to perform civilian service. The necessity stage therefore requires the institution to think creatively about what other measures, short of a refusal, may alleviate the concerns raised by a countervailing reason.

E. The Balancing Stage

The balancing stage requires a decision on whether the overall reasons supporting a refusal outweigh the reasons to grant an exemption. This is a context- and fact-specific enquiry. However, a few general factors can be taken into account. First, if granting an exemption would run counter to a well-reasoned finding by a democratic institution, then that is in itself a strong but not dispositive reason for an exemption not to be granted. Consider the claim for exemption as it arose in *Williamson*.[94] In that case Christian parents objected to the statutory ban of corporal punishment of school pupils on the basis that such punishment was mandated by their religious beliefs. The UK House of Lords rejected the view that the statutory ban impermissibly breached the parents' Article 9 right. In reaching that conclusion, the Court, when undertaking the proportionality analysis, took into consideration the fact that courts owe deference to the legislature on morally and socially sensitive issues such as the permissibility of corporal punishment of minors. Lord Nicholls, delivering the Court's main opinion, stated:

> Parliament was entitled to take this course [ie enact the statutory ban] because this issue is one of broad social policy. As such it is pre-eminently well suited for decision by Parliament. The legislature is to be accorded a considerable degree of latitude in deciding which course should be selected as the best course in the interests of school children as a whole. The subject has been investigated and considered by several committees ... The issue was fully debated in Parliament. ... the proportionality of a statutory measure is to be judged objectively and not by the quality of the reasons advanced in support of the measure in the course of parliamentary debate. But it can just be noted that the desirability or otherwise of overriding parental choice was a matter mentioned in the course of debate in both Houses of Parliament.[95]

In a liberal democracy, respect for democratic institutions is part and parcel of the public interest. If granting an exemption would run counter to a well-reasoned finding by a democratic institution, then that is in itself a strong reason for an exemption not to be granted.

---

[94] *R (on the application of Williamson) v Secretary of State for Education and Employment* [2005] UKHL 15.
[95] ibid at 51.

However, it cannot be a dispositive reason. In a liberal democracy committed to individual well-being individuals have legal rights which they can enforce against wider public interests, even when those interests have been crystallised in democratic legislation. It would not conform to the liberal commitment to individual well-being if deference to the legislative process was a conclusive factor rather than a weighty factor when courts are considering whether an exemption is warranted.

Second, the nature of the person requested to grant an exemption ought to weigh heavily in the moral equation. The ability of a small family-run business to grant an exemption from the duty to work on weekends to a Sabbatarian will substantially differ from the ability of a governmental department or a publicly traded company. The more costly granting an exemption would be for the person asked to grant the exemption, the less weighty would be the case for granting an exemption.

Finally, even if it is the state itself that is being asked to grant an exemption, all things being equal, an exemption should not be granted if doing so would result in discriminatory treatment of protected groups, such as racial minorities and homosexuals. This is especially important in the contemporary flurry of litigation on whether providers of commercial goods and services, such as florists, hoteliers and bakers, can refuse their services on the ground of sexual orientation.[96] The next section is entirely dedicated to that issue.

VI. Balancing the Right to Conscientious Exemption and the Right to Non-Discrimination: Beyond Ongoing Culture Wars

A. Against Leigh: Sexual Orientation Non-Discrimination as a Human Rights Norm

Leigh (chapter six), Chipeur and Clarke (chapter nine) argue in this volume in favour of granting conscientious exemptions from sexual orientation anti-discrimination norms. The core of Leigh's argument in this respect is that freedom of conscience should take priority over non-discrimination because the former is a human right whereas the latter is not, at least under the ECHR. On the view that human rights should trump other policy considerations, a claim for exemption grounded in the human right to freedom of conscience (under Article 9 ECHR) would automatically trump the policy consideration that individuals should not be discriminated against by private service providers on ground of their sexual orientation.

It is however doubtful that Leigh's insistence on what he calls the 'reversibility test' is based on an accurate portrayal of the legal status of non-discrimination norms. Leigh claims that 'There is no general Convention right to be protected against discrimination by private

---

[96] *Elane Photography, LLC v Willock* (2013) 309 P 3d 53 (Photographer); *Bull v Hall* (n 77) (B&B hoteliers); *Masterpiece Cakeshop, Ltd v Colorado Civil Rights Com'n* (2018) 584 U S ____ 1 (USSC) (Bakery); *Lee v Ashers Baking Company Ltd & Ors* (Northern Ireland) [2018] UKSC 49 (Bakery).

persons in the provision of goods and services'.[97] There is however some scope to argue that this statement is not an accurate portrayal of ECHR law. Leigh is correct to note that the Convention, under Article 14, does not protect individuals from discrimination by private persons in the provision of goods or services. However, his dismissal of the potential applicability of Protocol 12 to the Convention is too quick. Article 1(1) of that Protocol provides:

> The enjoyment of any right set forth by law shall be secured without discrimination on any ground such as sex, race, colour, language, religion, political or other opinion, national or social origin, association with a national minority, property, birth or other status.

Leigh states that 'Protocol 12 (which the UK has not signed in any event) is wider [than Article 14] but still stops short of requiring states to prohibit discrimination by private parties'.[98] He cites as authority for this proposition paragraph 25 of the Explanatory Report to that Protocol.[99] It is true that in that paragraph the Report seems to support Leigh's assessment when it says 'On the one hand, Article 1 protects against discrimination by public authorities. The article is not intended to impose a general positive obligation on the Parties to take measures to prevent or remedy all instances of discrimination in relations between private persons'. However, the Report goes on to consider countervailing suggestions and concludes that there might be good reasons to interpret Article 1 of the Protocol to cover prohibitions of discrimination by private persons in certain circumstances. Consequently, in paragraph 25, the Report says 'On the other hand, it cannot be totally excluded that the duty to "secure" under the first paragraph of Article 1 might entail positive obligations. For example, this question could arise if there is a clear lacuna in domestic law protection from discrimination'. Crucially, the Report finds that the imposition of this positive obligation to protect individuals from discrimination would most likely arise in the context of private providers of goods and services. It says, at paragraph 28, that:

> [A]ny positive obligation in the area of relations between private persons would concern, at the most, relations in the public sphere normally regulated by law, for which the state has a certain responsibility (for example, arbitrary denial of access to work, access to restaurants, or to services which private persons may make available to the public such as medical care or utilities such as water and electricity, etc).

It seems then that the Explanatory Report to Protocol 12 undermines Leigh's assessment that there is no Convention right to be protected against discrimination by private persons in the provision of goods and services. Indeed, it seems to support the very opposite view. Importantly, this duty would prohibit discrimination on the ground of sexual orientation by private providers of goods and services. While sexual orientation is not mentioned as a prohibited ground of discrimination in Article 1 of Protocol 12, the Explanatory Report suggests that this 'was considered unnecessary from a legal point of view since the list of non-discrimination grounds is not exhaustive'.[100] There is force to this suggestion as sexual orientation is not mentioned under Article 14 either yet the ECtHR has held that sexual

[97] Chapter 6, text to n 86.
[98] ibid.
[99] *Explanatory Report to the Protocol 12 to the Convention for the Protection of Human Rights and Fundamental Freedoms* (Council of Europe, 2000), at 25.
[100] ibid at 20.

orientation 'is undoubtedly covered by Article 14 of the Convention. The Court reiterates in that connection that the list set out in that provision is illustrative and not exhaustive, as is shown by the words "any ground such as"'.[101]

Two qualifications need to be made to the view that the Convention recognises a right to be free from sexual orientation discrimination by private providers of goods and services. The first is that this view is best supported by the Explanatory Report to Protocol 12 and not by ECtHR case law. The Report does not have the status of law even though it is highly persuasive. The ECtHR has relied on the Report in a number of cases for the proposition that the meaning of 'discrimination' under Protocol 12 is identical to that under Article 14.[102] Nevertheless, the Court has yet to decide a case on the specific issue of sexual orientation discrimination by private providers of goods and services. If it does, only then will we be provided with the most authoritative confirmation that the Convention does recognise a right to be free from sexual orientation discrimination by private providers of goods and services.

The second qualification is that, as Leigh correctly notes, the UK is not a signatory to Protocol 12. This is however irrelevant for the purposes of Leigh's reversibility test. As stated, the core of Leigh's argument is that freedom of conscience should take priority over non-discrimination by private service providers on the ground of sexual orientation because the former is a human right under the Convention whereas the latter is not. However, Leigh's argument is undermined if, as argued, there is indeed a Convention right to be free from sexual orientation discrimination by private providers of goods and services under Protocol 12. Irrespective of whether or not the UK is party to the Protocol, it seems to follow that the UK legislation prohibiting providers of commercial services from discriminating on the basis of sexual orientation guarantees a Convention right. Accordingly, even under Leigh's reversibility test, there is a genuine clash of human rights norms and the right to conscientious exemption cannot automatically take precedence.

B. Against Chipeur and Clarke: Dignitary Harm and Social Standing

Chipeur and Clarke also support the notion that the right to conscientious exemption should prevail over sexual orientation non-discrimination on the basis that there appears to be only a conflict between a fundamental right (conscience and religion) and a 'vague aspiration' (sexual orientation non-discrimination).[103] Again, this unfortunately mischaracterises the legal status of the prohibition of sexual orientation discrimination as a human rights norm. In any event, Chipeur and Clarke are prepared to consider the fact that when an identifiable person is being refused a commercial service on the grounds of sexual orientation, that may constitute a dignitary harm. However, they mischaracterise the nature of dignitary harm as one involving offence to feelings. Consequently, they argue that 'we are on dangerous

---

[101] *Salgueiro Da Silva Mouta v Portugal* (2001) 31 EHRR 47, at 28.
[102] *Pilav v Bosnia and Herzegovina* [2016] ECHR 498, at 40. *Zornić v Bosnia and Herzegovina* [2014] ECHR 773, at 27. *Savez Crkava Riječ Života and Others v Croatia* (2012) 54 EHRR 36, paras 104–05 and 107 (here the ECtHR relied on the report to determine the scope of the protection from discrimination rather than on the meaning of 'discrimination'). *Sejdić and Finci v Bosnia and Herzegovina* [2009] ECHR 2122, at 55.
[103] Chapter 9, text to n 91.

territory when the State enters into the business of attempting to protect feelings.[104] There is some good reason for this mischaracterisation. Leading advocates of the notion of 'dignitary harm' in the context of conscientious exemptions refer to the hurt feelings of gay customers being denied a commercial service. Nejaime and Segal say in this respect:

> [T]he bakery owner who turns away a same-sex couple treats that particular couple as sinners. … the individualized condemnation in the bakery are actions that address third parties as sinners in ways that can stigmatize and demean. In some situations, social meaning is explicitly communicated during the religiously based refusal of service. Consider the operation of complicity-based conscience claims in the context of same-sex marriage. A bakery customer, for instance, reported being told, '[we] don't do same sex weddings because [we] are Christians and being gay is an abomination.'[105]

It is unfortunate that Nejaime and Segal interpret dignitary harm to consist only in the offence and humiliation occasioned by LGB persons being called sinners. If dignitary harm merely equated to being offended and humiliated then Chipeur and Clarke would be right to be sceptical about the state getting involved in preventing it. After all, offence and humiliation are a daily occurrence in other contexts (eg family life and friendship) and the state does not generally intervene. The notion of dignitary harm should be instead understood as the harm occasioned to members of a section of the political community when their equal social standing is undermined and when they are prevented from enjoying legal entitlements on an equal footing as members of other social groups.[106] The problem with the law allowing LGB customers being turned away from providers of commercial services is not that offence and humiliation is caused (although that is of course also problematic). It is that the law that permits such state of affairs signals that LGB people do not have the same social standing as non-LGB people and that they do not enjoy the same basic legal entitlements on an equal footing: in sum, they are labelled as social outcasts by the law itself. This legal injustice is compounded by the fact that LGB people have traditionally also been targeted by discriminatory laws (eg criminalisation of homosexuality) and, even today, continue to be the target of unjust discriminatory treatment by the law and law-makers, which signals their status as second-class citizens.

For example, the US Department of Justice has argued in *Zarda* that the prohibition of sex discrimination in employment in Title VII should not be interpreted to cover sexual orientation, with the consequence that it would not be unlawful for a gay person to be fired by their employer under that legislation on grounds of their sexual orientation alone. The Second Circuit Court of Appeal did not accept that submission and held that the prohibition of sex discrimination does include sexual orientation discrimination.[107] Similarly, in *Masterpiece*, the US Department of Justice argued that while there is a compelling state interest in combatting race discrimination, there is no compelling interest in combatting sexual orientation discrimination. The USSC did not determine that issue as it disposed

---

[104] Chapter 9, text to n 92.

[105] D NeJaime and R Siegel, 'Conscience Wars: Complicity-Based Conscience Claims in Religion and Politics' (2015) 124 *Yale Law Journal* 2516, 2576.

[106] This is an argument borrowed from Waldron, *Hate Speech* (2014) ch 5.

[107] *Zarda v Altitude Express, Inc* (2018) 883 F3d 100. The submission was the focus of the amicus brief submitted to the Court by the Department of Justice.

of the case on the basis that there had been unconstitutional animus towards the baker's religious beliefs by the judicial bodies that heard his case.[108] To this should be added that in 25 US states sexual orientation discrimination in employment is not unlawful.[109]

The argument advanced here is that the notion of dignitary harm as expressed both by Nejaime and Segal and by Chipeur and Clarke in this volume is understated. The notion is not to be equated with offence and humiliation occasioned by the expression that homosexual behaviour is sinful or immoral. Rather, it is to be construed as a form of social harm which undermines the social standing of members of a section of the political community and which takes away equal basic entitlements. Allowing the law to permit this form of social outcasting reinforces the view that LGB members of the political community are, at best, second class citizens. On the uncontroversial view that the state has a duty to promote the well-being of its subjects, it follows that the state has also a duty to protect individuals against the dignitary harms occasioned by refusing equal access to commercial services on the grounds of sexual orientation. Accordingly, exemptions from sexual-orientation anti-discrimination norms should not be granted to the service-providers.

A possible objection to this argument is that while there are dignitary harms, understood in the manner put forward above, occasioned to gay people turned away from commercial services, refusing to exempt objecting service-providers also imposes dignitary harms on them. Ryan Anderson, who accepts that there are grave social harms if exemptions from anti-discrimination laws are granted to service-providers (only in the context of race rather than sexual orientation discrimination), consequently complains:

> [A] Supreme Court ruling against Phillips [ie the baker in *Masterpiece*] would tar citizens who support the conjugal understanding of marriage with the charge of bigotry. The Court's refusal to grant First Amendment protections to Phillips would teach that his reasonable convictions and associated conduct are so gravely unjust that they cannot be tolerated in a pluralistic society.[110]

Let Anderson's charge be rephrased thus: even if we accept that the law labels LGB persons as social outcasts by permitting that they be denied basic commercial services, would the law not also label as social outcasts service-providers by forcing them to provide a service which they object to in good conscience? It is doubtful that this charge has much force to it. This is because, in a liberal society committed to defending a pluralism of beliefs, the social standing of those that oppose homosexuality is protected by liberal law in various ways: such individuals may not be denied commercial services or be fired from their jobs on the basis of their religious or moral beliefs about homosexuality (religion and belief is a standard protected characteristic in anti-discrimination legislation);[111] they may associate in secular groups and churches whose constitutive beliefs include condemning homosexuality and that

---

[108] *Masterpiece Cakeshop* (n 96). The submission was made in the amicus brief submitted to the USSC at pp 31–33.

[109] The states are: Alabama, Alaska, Arizona, Arkansas, Florida, Georgia, Idaho, Indiana, Kansas, Kentucky, Mississippi, Missouri, Montana, Nebraska, North Carolina, North Dakota, Ohio, Oklahoma, South Carolina, South Dakota, Tennessee, Texas, Utah, West Virginia and Wyoming.

[110] RT Anderson, 'Disagreement Is Not Always Discrimination: On Masterpiece Cakeshop and the Analogy to Interracial Marriage' (2018) 16 *The Georgetown Journal of Law & Public Policy* 123, 126.

[111] For application in a UK context see *Mbuyi v Newpark Childcare (Shepherds Bush) Ltd* [2015] ET 3300656/2014, unreported. The UK Employment Tribunal held that an employee was unlawfully dismissed when she responded to her colleague's queries on the issue by sharing her view that homosexuality is a sin.

exclude LGB people from their members;[112] short of incitement to violence, harassment, intimidation and disrupting public order, they may publicly condemn homosexuality.[113] In sum, liberal law, through all of these protections, guarantees their equal social standing in a liberal society. Hence, safeguarding LGB people from the dignitary harm they would suffer if the law allowed them to be turned away by providers of commercial services is a legitimate balancing of conflicting rights: this is because the social standing of both those that oppose and those that support homosexuality is protected by liberal law.

C. The No Religious Rites Principle and Conscientious Exemptions for Wedding Photographers

If the arguments advanced so far are accepted, it follows that conscientious exemptions should not be granted to commercial service-providers from sexual orientation anti-discrimination norms on the basis that doing so causes dignitary harms (a social harm rather than offence to feelings) to LGB persons. This section, however, acknowledges that there is a principle based on freedom of conscience and religion which would exonerate a limited class of service-providers, ie objecting wedding photographers such as in *Elane Photography* (who refused to photograph a commitment ceremony between lesbians),[114] from providing the requested service. The principle is the No Religious Rites Principle. It says that a person may not be compelled by the state to participate in rites which have a significant religious or moral character. The principle can be extracted from the case of *Galloway*. There city residents claimed that the town's practice of opening town board meetings with sectarian prayers violated the First Amendment's Establishment Clause. The USSC rejected the claim justifying the constitutionality of the practice on the grounds that, although it retained a religious significance, it had become a traditional practice which had survived the test of time.[115]

However, fundamental for the Court's reasoning was the fact that attendance at the prayer session was not compulsory for individuals that objected to it. Justice Kennedy, writing for the Court, said: 'It is an elemental First Amendment principle that government may not coerce its citizens to support or participate in any religion or its exercise'. He continued by stating that the outcome of the case 'would be different if town board members directed the public to participate in the prayers, singled out dissidents for opprobrium, or indicated that their decisions might be influenced by a person's acquiescence in the prayer opportunity. No such thing occurred in the town of Greece'.[116]

---

[112] The USSC held that the Boy Scouts could exclude homosexuals from its membership in *Boy Scouts of America v Dale* (2000) 530 US 640.

[113] That seems to be the view endorsed by Justice Kennedy in *Obergefell* when he said: '[I]t must be emphasized that religions, and those who adhere to religious doctrines, may continue to advocate with utmost, sincere conviction that, by divine precepts, same-sex marriage should not be condoned. The First Amendment ensures that religious organizations and persons are given proper protection as they seek to teach the principles that are so fulfilling and so central to their lives and faiths, and to their own deep aspirations to continue the family structure they have long revered'. See *Obergefell v Hodges* (2015) 135 SCt 2584 (USSC) 2607.

[114] *Elane Photography* (n 96).

[115] *Town of Greece, NY v Galloway* (2013) 134 S Ct 1811.

[116] ibid 1825–26.

Assume for the moment that the No Religious Rites Principle is valid (some objections to it are considered below). If so, it would seem to exonerate the photographer in *Elane Photography* from being compelled to provide her service to a same-sex marriage in so far as it would entail her being compelled to being physically present at the wedding ceremony to which she objects on religious or moral grounds. The principle would be inapplicable to other service-providers (such as bakers or printers) to the extent that their presence at the ceremony is not needed to fulfil their services.

The UK government has suggested that no exemptions should be granted to wedding photographers. The UK Equality Act 2010 contains a statutory exemption granted to individuals and organisations from participating in same-sex marriages. The exemption is worded thus:

> (1) A person does not contravene section 29 [ie the prohibition of sexual orientation discrimination] only because the person – …
>
> (b) is not present at, does not carry out, or does not otherwise participate in, a relevant marriage …
>
> for the reason that the marriage is the marriage of a same sex couple.[117]

The non-legally binding explanatory notes drafted by the government that proposed the legislation suggest that this applies mainly to people who would be directly involved in officiating the religious component of the ceremony (priests and organists) but would not exempt a commercial photographer. The notes state:

> A commercial photographer is asked to photograph a wedding of a same sex couple. It would be unlawful sexual orientation discrimination for her to refuse because she does not approve of marriage of same sex couples. This is because her role is not part of the religious marriage service.[118]

It is doubtful that this guidance has adequate legal backing. This is because it fails to recognise the importance for freedom of religion of the principle of freedom from religion, in particular the freedom not to be coerced to participate in a religious ceremony. The negative aspect of religious freedom has been recognised by the ECtHR which has stated that Article 9 covers the 'the freedom not to adhere to a religion and the freedom not to practice it'.[119] The practice of religion does not only consist in officiating a religious rite; in the wording of Article 9, it also consists 'in worship, teaching, practice and observance'. Physically being present at a religious ceremony can reasonably be construed as taking part in the ceremony.

One may construe the No Religious Rites Principle in either a broad or a narrow way. The narrow way would protect the photographer (or other person) from attending only those parts of the same-sex marriage ceremony which are religious in nature. This seems to be the preferred construction of the explanatory notes which agree that an organist may be exempt:

> An organist who usually plays at wedding services at a church does not wish to play at a wedding service of a same sex couple. This would be lawful because he is involved in the religious act of worship i.e. the religious ritual of the wedding service. This is the case whether he is a volunteer or employed by the church.

---

[117] Equality Act 2010, Part 6A, Sch 3.
[118] Explanatory notes to Marriage (Same Sex Couples) Act 2013, p 8.
[119] *Alexandridis v Greece*, App no 19516/06 (ECtHR, 21 February 2008), at 32.

However, this insistence on only the religious ritual of the wedding service misses a crucial aspect of the principle. Remember that the principle says that a person may not be compelled by the state to participate in rites which have a significant religious or *moral* character. Focusing on the religious parts only would disregard the moral objections of the objector in favour of the religious ones. This would entail that photographers who have a moral rather than a religious objection to same-sex marriage would not be exempt. However, this would not be compatible with the third proposition of the Liberal Model, which states that the liberal state should neither privilege nor disadvantage religious beliefs over non-religious ones when considering whether to grant a conscientious exemption. Accordingly, the No Religious Rites Principle should be interpreted in a broad way to include all religious and non-religious parts of a same-sex ceremony to the extent that the photographer would be compelled to take part in a religiously or morally significant event to which she objects.

VII. Conclusion

This chapter has defended the Liberal Model of Conscientious Exemptions as a morally attractive template for how liberal states should deal with claims for conscientious exemptions. The chapter has defended the propositions of the Liberal Model from several attacks from several of the contributors to this volume. It has argued in favour of a general right to conscientious exemption on the basis of providing an alternative forum, the judicial one, for minority moral views often overlooked in the political process. It has advocated state neutrality on the content of the beliefs of conscientious objectors. Arguments to the contrary advance by Jones and by Nehushtan and Coyle were found unpersuasive. The chapter has also advocated for equal treatment between religious and non-religious conscientious objectors. It rejected claims for preferential treatment for religious objectors advanced by Corvino and by Moon. It equally rejected claims for preferential treatment for non-religious objectors advanced by Nehushtan and Coyle. The chapter then analysed the application of proportionality analysis when the right to exemption conflicts with the rights of others or with the public interest. It was argued that in the current controversies that pitch the right to conscientious exemption of commercial service providers against sexual orientation non-discrimination norms, the latter should generally prevail. It was acknowledged, however, that objecting service-providers who would be required to physically attend an event to which they object (eg a same-sex wedding) should be exempt.

INDEX